# Agricultural Policy and U.S.-Taiwan Trade

# Agricultural Policy and U.S.-Taiwan Trade

## D. Gale Johnson and Chi-ming Hou

With Yu-kang Mao, Chaw-hsia Tu, Tracy C. Miller, and Chi-Chu Chou

The AEI Press

Publisher for the American Enterprise Institute
WASHINGTON, D.C.

1993

Distributed by arrangement with

University Press of America
4720 Boston Way
Lanham, Md. 20706

3 Henrietta Street
London WC2E 8LU England

**Library of Congress Cataloging-in-Publication Data**

Agricultural policy and U.S.-Taiwan trade / D. Gale Johnson
and Chi-Ming Hou.
  p.  cm.
  ISBN 0-8447-3827-1. — ISBN 0-8447-3826-3 (pbk.)
  1. Produce trade—Government policy—Taiwan. 2. Produce trade-
-Government policy—United States. 3. Imports—Taiwan. 4. Imports-
-United States. 5. Exports—Taiwan. 6. Exports—United States.
7. Agriculture and state—Taiwan. 8. Agriculture and state—United
States. 9. Taiwan—Foreign economic relations—United States.
10. United States—Foreign economic relations—Taiwan. I. Johnson,
D. Gale (David Gale), 1916–    . II. Hou, Chi-ming, 1924–
HD9016.T32A37  1993
382'.41'0973—dc20                                        93-19176
                                                         CIP

1  3  5  7  9  10  8  6  4  2

THE AEI PRESS
Publisher for the American Enterprise Institute
1150 17th Street, N.W., Washington, D.C. 20036

*Printed in the United States of America*

*Dedicated to the memory of*
*Chi-ming Hou, our friend and colleague*
*who is sorely missed*

# Contents

FIGURE

# Preface

This book is the result of the continuing fruitful cooperation between the Chung-Hua Institution for Economic Research and the American Enterprise Institute. The broad objective of the project culminating in this book was proposed by Dr. Chi-ming Hou. He suggested to Christopher DeMuth, president of the American Enterprise Institute, that U.S.-Taiwan trade in agricultural products was a major issue in Taiwan, in part because of a number of confrontations stemming from such trade. He believed the major problems, however, involved fundamental issues in agricultural policies in the two economies. He made it clear that conflicts arose in Taiwan because of its agricultural policies on the one hand and its interest in encouraging free or liberal trade on the other. He was kind enough not to note that similar conflicts were all too evident in the United States.

Mr. DeMuth asked me if I would participate in this project, serving as the leader for AEI. Since for more than four decades I have done research on and written about the conflicts between agricultural and trade policies in the United States and other industrial countries, I accepted the invitation and submitted an outline of the project as I visualized it. This outline was approved without change by Dr. Hou and his associates. In a meeting in Taipei in 1989, we discussed the outline in detail and our approaches as well as the general plan for carrying out the work and writing the manuscript.

Drafts of almost all the chapters were completed and presented at a major conference in Taipei in 1991. The conference was successful not only because of the number of participants but because so many individuals with important responsibilities for agricultural legislation and policies in Taiwan attended.

It is with regret that I note the circumstances surrounding Dr. Hou's participation in this project and the planning of the Taipei conference. Not long after work on the project was started in 1989, Dr. Hou became ill. He remained cheerful throughout his difficulties and continued his work on the project as well as keeping up with his other responsibilities. It was with great sadness that I learned of his death in August 1991. We are all extremely sorry that he did not see this project through to its conclusion. With the approval of those who worked on the project, we have dedicated this book to him. He is also designated, as he deserves to be, as one of the major authors of this book.

In numerous places in the book are references to the Uruguay Round of negotiations in the framework of the General Agreement on Tariffs and Trade. The references include projections of the effects on trade and international market prices assuming negotiations that significantly liberalized trade in agricultural products in the high-income market economies. We had expected that these negotiations would have been concluded so that their effects could be taken into account in our work. As this preface is being written, the negotiations are still under way. Consequently, it seems inappropriate to delay further the publication of our work. If the negotiations are concluded, the reduction in protection will be less than the full liberalization used in the various scenarios we followed in considering the adjustment and income effects. The implication is that the adjustment problems required of agriculture, which were modest in both Taiwan and the United States assuming full liberalization, will be very mild indeed. But, unfortunately, the benefits that will accrue to taxpayers and consumers will be significantly less than those with full liberalization.

It was a pleasure to work on this project with two of my former students, Tracy Miller and Chi-Chu Chou. They brought to the project very successful research on subjects crucial to the understanding of the policy problems related to the trade conflicts being studied.

I could not have been more pleased with the cooperation that I received from my associates in Taiwan. I cannot say enough about Dr. Hou, who carried on very ably when others might well have given up. Dr. Yu-kang Mao participated in the project in its entirety and was most helpful in bringing to the surface many of the subtleties that outsiders miss all too often. In addition, of course, he contributed directly to the project. We owe a great debt to Ms. Chaw-hsia Tu, who was one of the authors of the book but who also took on the task of coordinating the project in Taiwan after the death of Dr. Hou.

All of us who participated in the preparation of this book hope that it will promote understanding of the policy issues that have sparked trade tensions between Taiwan and the United States and make some small contribution to their resolution.

D. GALE JOHNSON

# Contributors

D. GALE JOHNSON, Eliakim Hastings Moore Distinguished Service Professor of Economics, Emeritus, University of Chicago. Ph.D., Iowa State College, 1945.

CHI-MING HOU, Charles A. Dana Professor of Economics, Colgate University (1968–1991) and Visiting Research Fellow, Chung-Hua Institution for Economic Research (1987–1991). Ph.D., Columbia University, 1954. He died in August 1991.

CHI-CHU CHOU, Assistant Professor of Economics, Rutgers University. Ph.D., University of Chicago, 1991.

YU-KANG MAO, Counselor, Council of Agricultural, Executive Yuan, Government of the Republic of China; Professor, Department of Agricultural Economics, National Taiwan University.

TRACY C. MILLER, Associate Professor of Economics, Dordt College. Ph.D., University of Chicago, 1986.

CHAW-HSIA TU, Associate Research Fellow, Chung-Hua Institution for Economic Research. M.A., Western Illinois University, 1978.

YU YU-HSEIN, Chairman, Council of Agriculture, Executive Yuan of the Republic of China. Ph.D., Purdue University, 1967.

# Agricultural Policy and U.S.-Taiwan Trade

# PART ONE
# Introduction

# 1
# Agricultural Policies and Trade Conflicts

*D. Gale Johnson*

The several rounds of multilateral trade negotiations that preceded the Uruguay Round in the context of the General Agreement on Tariffs and Trade were unsuccessful in stemming the increase in agricultural protection in the industrial market economies over the past three decades. Many expected that the Uruguay Round would be different, but as of the time of this writing, the outcome is uncertain.

The plan of the book is first to present information about the structures of agriculture in Taiwan and the United States and the degree to which each has changed over the past four decades. We then analyze the origins of the prevailing agricultural policies in the two economies. We do not stop at description, however, but provide our views on the effectiveness of the policies in achieving their objectives.

Part three of the book discusses the political factors behind the particular policy measures that affect the markets for agricultural products. It is the political interventions in the domestic markets that require each of the economies to intervene in the international trade in farm products. The first of the four chapters provides an overview of agricultural policy, with an emphasis on what determines the degree of protection of agricultural products. This analysis reveals systemic factors that influence the general level of protection and the varying degrees of protection in an economy. The next two chapters discuss the particular political factors influencing agricultural policies in the United States and Taiwan.

Chapter 9 addresses the general nature of the trade conflicts between the United States and Taiwan with details of some of those that have imposed the greatest strains on the relationship. The conflicts arose when the United States insisted that certain trade measures used by Taiwan adversely affected its agricultural exports.

3

In one case, the United States objected to Taiwan's paying export subsidies on rice; in another famous case, the United States objected to restrictions on poultry imports by Taiwan. The chapter introduces a new analytical approach, namely, the analysis of how outside pressure can influence governmental decisions. This subject has not previously received attention.

The book then turns to the process of liberalizing trade through multilateral negotiations. The opening chapter in this part describes the first two series of proposals made by the major participants in the Uruguay Round. Next is a presentation of selected studies of how trade liberalization affects world market prices of agricultural products and the volume of trade in those products.

The following four chapters discuss the modifications that significant trade liberalization would require in the agricultural policies and programs of Taiwan and the United States and then what adjustments trade liberalization would force on agriculture itself: with liberalized trade, domestic prices would change to accommodate international market prices. Next is a consideration of the adjustment policies to assist farmers in adapting to the circumstances brought about by trade liberalization. The book concludes with an effort to define what we believe is a new consensus on the benefits of trade liberalization—benefits that, with appropriate adjustment policies, can be realized with relatively small burdens imposed on farm people. The book closes with an afterword by Dr. Yu Yu-hsein, former chairman of the Council of Agriculture, Republic of China (ROC). The afterword is a remarkable statement, indicating a strong commitment by the ROC government to support liberalization of trade in agricultural products and to make the necessary modifications in its own policies. The authors' note at the end of the book shows the relationship between the metric and the English units of measure and the exchange rate between the new Taiwan dollar and the U.S. dollar.

It may be noted that the ROC has applied for membership in GATT. The afterword indicates that it is prepared to make the changes in its domestic policies required to fulfill its obligations of GATT membership. This is rather more than can be said about many of the existing members of GATT.

## Presentation of Detailed Information on Taiwan

The long chapter on structure and change in agriculture in Taiwan includes a great deal of statistical and descriptive information not readily available to many researchers. Since 1980, the major international organizations that publish data on the various countries of the

4

world—the United Nations, the World Bank, and the International Monetary Fund, for example—no longer include information for the Republic of China. The U.S. Department of Agriculture publishes information related to matters of interest to itself, especially with respect to trade, agricultural policies, and general characteristics of agriculture. These publications, however, have a limited circulation. While the government of the Republic of China issues the usual documents and yearbooks, they are available only to specialists with access to large libraries.

## Contrasts and Similarities

For the benefit of those with limited interest in detailed information about the agricultures of Taiwan and the United States, a summary of important comparative information may be useful. Anyone with some familiarity with the two economies knows that there are enormous differences between the two agricultures in aggregate resources, total output, and farm size as measured by average land area. But in terms of changes in the relative importance of agriculture in the national economy as measured by share of national output and labor force, the agricultures show striking similarities. The information presented in chapters 2 and 3 makes it clear that the agricultures have been highly dynamic, demonstrating a capability to adapt with remarkable speed to changing conditions.

An obvious contrast between the two agricultures is the enormous difference in the amount of cultivated land. The difference is evident regardless of the measure used—the total amount of land, land per farm, or land per farm worker. The United States currently has approximately 132 million hectares (326 million acres) of cultivated land, while Taiwan has about 890 thousand hectares (2.2 million acres). The difference in the number of farms is far smaller. In recent years, the United States has had 2,200,000 farms, while Taiwan has about 860,000 or nearly 40 percent as many as the United States. Consequently, the difference in the average size of the cultivated area per farm is very large—60 hectares in the United States and 1.0 to 1.2 hectares in Taiwan.

Farm employment in the United States is approximately three times that of Taiwan—3.2 million compared with 1.1 million in Taiwan. The number of workers per farm differs very little since the United States has approximately three times as many farms. The average farm worker in the United States has nearly fifty times as much cultivated land to work with as does the Taiwanese worker.

## Trends in Population, Farm Sizes, and Employment

There are some differences in trends in farm population and farm employment, but these are about what one would expect given the differences in per capita incomes that prevailed in the 1950s, the period for the start of the trends. In the 1950s, the per capita income of Taiwan was very low, certainly far below that of the United States, $130 compared with $2,100 in the United States. Consistent with the income differences, in 1952 farm employment accounted for 56 percent of total employment in Taiwan and 11 percent in the United States.

In Taiwan, the farm population continued to grow after 1952, increasing to 6.2 million in 1972. Its farm population declined after 1972 and by 1990 had fallen by 40 percent. In contrast, the farm population in the United States reached its maximum in 1916 and has declined continuously since. The U.S. farm population, 24.3 million in 1952, was about 5 million in 1990. From 1972 to 1990, the rates of population decline have been quite similar in the two farm economies.

The number of farms in Taiwan followed a pattern much like the population trends. Between 1952 and 1972, the number of farms increased by somewhat more than a third and then declined by a fifth by the end of the 1980s. In the United States, the number of farms declined by almost 60 percent during that period.

An important difference in agricultural adjustment over the four decades has occurred. In the United States, the decline in the number of farms and in farm employment has been similar. In Taiwan, however, the number of farms actually increased between 1952 and 1990, while the number employed fell by a third. One consequence was that in the United States the average cultivated area per farm doubled, while in Taiwan there was a small decline. Since farm employment declined in Taiwan, the average amount of cultivated land per farm worker increased by about 40 percent; in the United States, the amount of cultivated land per worker doubled.

As explained in chapter 4, a free market in land does not exist in Taiwan, which restricts the sale and rental of agricultural land. These limitations have induced farm families to retain their land while they increasingly hold nonfarm jobs.

Given the differences in the amount of land per worker, one should not be surprised that the price of a hectare of farmland is much greater in Taiwan than in the United States. In 1990 in Taiwan, the average value of land on a farm of approximately 1 hectare was $375,000, using the 1990 exchange rate of NT$26.89 per U.S.$1; the nominal price of land in Taiwan increased more than five times during the 1980s. The average price of farmland in the United States in the same year was $1,400 per hectare. The value of cultivated land in more productive regions of the United States would be in the range of $5,000 to $10,000 per hectare, the higher figure if it were irrigated.

## Types of Farm Households

In both Taiwan and the United States, the majority of the farms are part time. Farm households engaged in full-time farming in Taiwan declined from 48 percent in 1965 to 12 percent in 1990. By a rather less restrictive definition of full-time, in the United States 35 percent of the farms were full-time in 1965 and about 15 percent in 1990.

In Taiwan, a sideline farm household is defined as a farm household where the off-farm income is greater than the farm income. These households accounted for 22 percent of all households in 1965, increasing to 70 percent in 1990. In the United States, a more restrictive definition of sideline farms, namely, that less than a quarter of the family income comes from farming, reveals that 75 to 80 percent of all farms were sideline farms in 1990.

## Agriculture's Relative Importance

As we have seen, agriculture's share of total employment in Taiwan declined from 56 percent in 1952 to 13 percent in 1990, while in the United States the decline was from 11 to 3 percent. Taiwan's agriculture contributed 36 percent to gross domestic product in 1952, declining very little by 1960—to 33 precent—and then falling rapidly to just 5 percent in 1990. In the United States, agriculture's share of national output was 6 percent in 1952 and 2 percent in 1990.

## Protection of Agriculture

Given the large differences in average farm size, in amount of land per worker, and in value of farmland, most readers who have come to this point will probably have a definite view on which of the agricultures had the highest rate of protection. This view might well be reinforced by the knowledge that the United States has put pressure on Taiwan on several occasions to stop exporting products with export subsidies and to reduce restraints on imports. Surely the United States would not pressure an economy to liberalize its trade in farm products unless that economy was more protective of its agriculture than the United States.

The inference that Taiwan's agriculture has been more protected

7

than agriculture in the United States is false, however. According to estimates of protection made by researchers in the U.S. Department of Agriculture, the nominal rate of protection of agriculture in Taiwan for 1984–1987 was 31 percent, while for the United States the average level was 41 percent, or a third greater (table 13-1). (The estimate of nominal protection is defined as the excess of returns to domestic producers over world market prices adjusted to reflect the relevant border prices.)

What is perhaps even more striking is that the rate of nominal protection for rice in Taiwan was less than half the rate in the United States—54 percent compared with 114 percent. In other words, rice producers in Taiwan received a return that was 54 percent greater than the world price for rice, but the rice producer in the United States received more than double the world market price for rice of comparable quality.

It is obvious that Taiwan deviates significantly from the pattern of protection of agriculture presented in chapter 6. While it meets most of the criteria that call for a high rate of protection for agriculture—very small amount of land per capita, a net importer of farm products, a relatively high per capita income, and a low share of employment in agriculture—it has a comparatively low level of protection. If Taiwan is designated as an industrial market economy, as it properly is, it has the third lowest level of protection of such economies for which estimates are available. Only Australia and New Zealand provide less protection for agriculture than Taiwan. Unfortunately, the United States cannot claim such a distinction.

# PART TWO

# Agricultural Structure, Change, and Farm Policies

# 2
# Structure and Change in the Agriculture of Taiwan

*Yu-kang Mao*

Taiwan had 890,100 hectares of cultivated land in 1990, of which 477,000 hectares were paddy field and 413,100 hectares were dry land. Paddy field and dry land accounted for 54 percent and 46 percent of the total cultivated land, respectively (see table 2–1).

In 1945, there were 816,000 hectares of cultivated land. Cultivated land gradually increased to 917,000 hectares by 1975, an increase of 101,000 hectares in a period of thirty years, a yearly average of 3,367 hectares. The area of total cultivated land decreased at 1,800 hectares a year until 1990. From 1945 to 1975, paddy fields increased by 11,000 hectares, whereas dry land increased by 90,000 hectares; these figures indicate that the expansion of farmland in this period was due mainly to the increase of dry land. From 1975 to 1990, paddy fields decreased by 38,900 hectares, and dry land increased by 11,800 hectares. Therefore, the net decrease of cultivated land during this period resulted from the decline in paddy fields. In Taiwan, the paddy field is the farmland with constant or rotational irrigation; dry land is farmland without irrigation. Hence, paddy fields are considered better farmland than dry land. The significant decrease in paddy fields had an adverse effect on Taiwan's agricultural production. The decrease in paddy fields has resulted mainly from the conversion of farmland to nonfarm uses.

## The Agricultural Labor Force

In 1952, the agricultural labor force was 1.64 million persons, accounting for 56.1 percent of the total labor force. It increased to 1.81 million in 1964 and then began to decline rapidly. In 1990, the agricultural labor force was 1.11 million, a decrease of 700,000 laborers from its peak in 1964. The percentage share of agricultural labor in the total labor force was only 12.8 percent in 1990 (see table 2–2). This figure

TABLE 2–1

AREA OF CULTIVATED LAND IN TAIWAN, 1945–1990

(hectares and percent)

| Year | Total | Area Paddy field | Dry land |
|------|-------|-------------------|----------|
| 1945 | 816,017 | 504,709 (61.9) | 311,308 (38.1) |
| 1950 | 870,633 | 530,236 (60.9) | 340,397 (39.1) |
| 1955 | 873,002 | 532,688 (61.0) | 340,314 (39.0) |
| 1960 | 869,223 | 525,580 (60.5) | 343,643 (39.5) |
| 1965 | 889,563 | 536,772 (60.3) | 352,791 (39.7) |
| 1970 | 905,263 | 528,927 (58.4) | 376,336 (41.6) |
| 1975 | 917,111 | 515,852 (56.2) | 401,259 (43.8) |
| 1980 | 907,353 | 509,326 (56.1) | 398,027 (43.9) |
| 1981 | 900,062 | 502,822 (55.9) | 397,240 (44.1) |
| 1982 | 890,830 | 501,644 (56.3) | 389,186 (43.7) |
| 1983 | 894,326 | 500,901 (56.0) | 393,425 (44.0) |
| 1984 | 891,655 | 496,897 (55.7) | 394,758 (44.3) |
| 1985 | 887,660 | 494,535 (55.7) | 393,125 (44.3) |
| 1986 | 887,451 | 494,579 (55.7) | 392,872 (44.3) |
| 1987 | 886,281 | 487,809 (55.0) | 398,472 (45.0) |
| 1988 | 894,974 | 483,514 (54.0) | 411,460 (46.0) |
| 1989 | 894,601 | 479,954 (53.7) | 414,647 (46.3) |
| 1990 | 890,089 | 476,996 (53.6) | 413,093 (46.4) |

SOURCE: *Agricultural Year Book*, Taiwan Provincial Department of Agriculture and Forestry; various years.

showed that during 1952–1964 agriculture could still absorb a great portion of the increased rural labor force. Since 1965, the outmigration of agricultural labor has accelerated as the share of industry in GNP surpassed that of agriculture. The decrease in the agricultural labor force in the past was largely due to the migration of the young would-be laborers from the agricultural sector to the nonagricultural sectors. As a result, farm labor was aging, and rural wages surged. In turn, Taiwan's agriculture was pushed into an unfavorable position.

## Number and Size of Farms

In 1952, there were 679,750 farms in Taiwan. The number of farms peaked at 925,540 in 1972, an increase of 36.2 percent in twenty years.

From 1972 to 1980, the number of farms declined slightly to 89,120 in 1980. Since then, the number of farms has decreased rapidly; it was 723,200 in 1989, comparable to the number of farms in 1955.

In 1990, however, as a result of the implementation of the Farmers Health Insurance Program, farm households were split up into smaller units to enable the head of household to be eligible to participate in the program. Therefore, the number of farm households showed a big increase. It was 860,700 in that year (see table 2–3).

From the discussion of the agricultural labor force, we know that the number of agricultural laborers in Taiwan started to decline in 1965. The number of farms, however, still showed an increase from 1965 until 1972. This phenomenon may be explained by the change from large families to small families due to the rapid industrialization process in this period. In addition, the rigid farmland tenure system after land reform contributed to the slow change in the number of farms. Many part-time farmers leave their land to overseers to cultivate on their behalf but will not lease their land to other farmers for fear of losing social and economic security. They are afraid that the government might invoke a land reform regulation that would eventually force them to give up their ownership if land is leased to other farmers. To hold land ownership, they would rather become part-time farmers than leave their farms. Consequently, a full-time farmer in Taiwan today has extreme difficulty enlarging his farm by renting additional farmland. The system was originally designed to prevent concentration of landownership, but the same system unwittingly prevents a more productive use of land and constitutes a serious bottleneck in Taiwan's current agricultural development.

The small farm system is likely to prevail in a country with limited cultivated land and a high population density. Taiwan's average farm size was 1.29 hectares in 1952 but decreased to 0.97 hectare in 1972 because of the increase in the number of farms; it then increased gradually to 1.24 hectares in 1989 because of the decrease in the number of farms (see table 2–4). From 1952 to 1964, as the total area of farmland in Taiwan remained about constant and the agricultural labor force increased, the average cultivated land area per worker shrank from 0.57 hectare to 0.53 hectare. Since then, because of the drastic reduction in agricultural labor, the average cultivated area per worker increased to 0.95 hectare in 1989 (table 2–4). According to the agricultural census of 1990, the number of farms smaller than 1 hectare accounted for 75 percent of total farms. In the early days, small farms could be competitive because labor-intensive farming manifested no significant economies of scale. Now the situa-

## TABLE 2–2
### LABOR FORCE IN TAIWAN, 1952–1990

| Year | Total | Employed Population (1,000 persons) Agriculture | Industry | Services | Percentage Agriculture | Industry | Services |
|------|-------|-------------|----------|----------|-------------|----------|----------|
| 1952 | 2,929 | 1,642 | 495 | 792 | 56.1 | 16.9 | 27.0 |
| 1953 | 2,964 | 1,647 | 522 | 795 | 55.6 | 17.6 | 26.8 |
| 1954 | 3,026 | 1,657 | 536 | 833 | 54.8 | 17.7 | 27.5 |
| 1955 | 3,108 | 1,667 | 560 | 881 | 53.6 | 18.0 | 28.4 |
| 1956 | 3,149 | 1,675 | 577 | 897 | 53.2 | 18.3 | 28.5 |
| 1957 | 3,229 | 1,689 | 612 | 928 | 52.3 | 19.0 | 28.7 |
| 1958 | 3,340 | 1,707 | 659 | 974 | 51.1 | 19.7 | 29.2 |
| 1959 | 3,422 | 1,722 | 695 | 1,005 | 50.3 | 20.3 | 29.4 |
| 1960 | 3,473 | 1,742 | 713 | 1,018 | 50.2 | 20.5 | 29.3 |
| 1961 | 3,505 | 1,747 | 732 | 1,026 | 49.8 | 20.9 | 29.3 |
| 1962 | 3,541 | 1,760 | 745 | 1,036 | 49.7 | 21.0 | 29.3 |
| 1963 | 3,592 | 1,775 | 764 | 1,053 | 49.4 | 21.3 | 29.3 |
| 1964 | 3,658 | 1,810 | 779 | 1,070 | 49.5 | 21.3 | 29.2 |
| 1965 | 3,763 | 1,748 | 839 | 1,176 | 46.5 | 22.3 | 31.2 |
| 1966 | 3,856 | 1,735 | 870 | 1,250 | 45.0 | 22.6 | 32.4 |
| 1967 | 4,050 | 1,723 | 995 | 1,332 | 42.5 | 24.6 | 32.9 |
| 1968 | 4,225 | 1,725 | 1,072 | 1,428 | 40.8 | 25.4 | 33.8 |

| 1969 | 4,390 | 1,726 | 1,155 | 1,509 | 39.3 | 26.3 | 34.4 |
| --- | --- | --- | --- | --- | --- | --- | --- |
| 1970 | 4,576 | 1,681 | 1,278 | 1,617 | 36.7 | 27.9 | 35.4 |
| 1971 | 4,738 | 1,665 | 1,417 | 1,656 | 35.1 | 29.9 | 35.0 |
| 1972 | 4,948 | 1,632 | 1,575 | 1,741 | 33.0 | 31.8 | 35.2 |
| 1973 | 5,327 | 1,624 | 1,795 | 1,908 | 30.5 | 33.7 | 35.8 |
| 1974 | 5,486 | 1,697 | 1,882 | 1,907 | 30.9 | 34.3 | 34.8 |
| 1975 | 5,521 | 1,681 | 1,927 | 1,913 | 30.4 | 34.9 | 34.7 |
| 1976 | 5,669 | 1,641 | 2,065 | 1,964 | 29.0 | 36.4 | 34.6 |
| 1977 | 5,980 | 1,597 | 2,250 | 2,133 | 26.7 | 37.6 | 35.7 |
| 1978 | 6,228 | 1,553 | 2,447 | 2,227 | 24.9 | 39.3 | 35.8 |
| 1979 | 6,424 | 1,380 | 2,683 | 2,360 | 21.5 | 41.8 | 36.7 |
| 1980 | 6,547 | 1,277 | 2,774 | 2,497 | 19.5 | 42.4 | 38.1 |
| 1981 | 6,672 | 1,257 | 2,814 | 2,601 | 18.8 | 42.2 | 39.0 |
| 1982 | 6,811 | 1,284 | 2,808 | 2,718 | 18.9 | 41.2 | 39.9 |
| 1983 | 7,070 | 1,317 | 2,908 | 2,845 | 18.6 | 41.1 | 40.3 |
| 1984 | 7,308 | 1,286 | 3,090 | 2,932 | 17.6 | 42.3 | 40.1 |
| 1985 | 7,428 | 1,297 | 3,078 | 3,054 | 17.5 | 41.4 | 41.1 |
| 1986 | 7,733 | 1,317 | 3,207 | 3,209 | 17.0 | 41.5 | 41.5 |
| 1987 | 8,022 | 1,226 | 3,430 | 3,367 | 15.3 | 42.7 | 42.0 |
| 1988 | 8,108 | 1,112 | 3,450 | 3,546 | 13.7 | 42.6 | 43.7 |
| 1989 | 8,258 | 1,065 | 3,488 | 3,705 | 12.9 | 42.2 | 44.9 |
| 1990 | 8,283 | 1,064 | 3,385 | 3,834 | 12.8 | 40.9 | 46.3 |

SOURCE: *Monthly Bulletin of Manpower Statistics, Republic of China*, Directorate-General of Budget, Accounting, and Statistics, Executive Yuan; various years.

## TABLE 2-3
### Number of Total Households and Farm Households in Taiwan, 1952–1990

| Year | Total Households | Farm Households | Percentage of Farm Households |
|---|---|---|---|
| 1952 | 1,492,476 | 679,750 | 45.5 |
| 1953 | 1,552,922 | 702,325 | 45.2 |
| 1954 | 1,568,042 | 716,582 | 45.7 |
| 1955 | 1,629,257 | 732,555 | 45.0 |
| 1956 | 1,695,432 | 746,318 | 44.0 |
| 1957 | 1,746,020 | 759,234 | 43.5 |
| 1958 | 1,803,820 | 769,925 | 42.7 |
| 1959 | 1,868,577 | 780,402 | 41.8 |
| 1960 | 1,939,733 | 785,592 | 40.5 |
| 1961 | 2,002,493 | 800,835 | 40.0 |
| 1962 | 2,060,500 | 809,917 | 39.3 |
| 1963 | 2,118,281 | 824,560 | 38.9 |
| 1964 | 2,187,612 | 834,827 | 38.2 |
| 1965 | 2,257,031 | 847,242 | 37.5 |
| 1966 | 2,321,596 | 854,203 | 36.8 |
| 1967 | 2,388,152 | 868,731 | 36.4 |
| 1968 | 2,465,965 | 877,114 | 35.6 |
| 1969 | 2,541,867 | 887,112 | 34.9 |
| 1970 | 2,620,105 | 880,274 | 33.6 |
| 1971 | 2,702,792 | 879,005 | 32.5 |
| 1972 | 2,781,325 | 925,537 | 33.3 |
| 1973 | 2,865,801 | 917,399 | 32.0 |
| 1974 | 2,958,843 | 916,202 | 31.0 |
| 1975 | 3,066,611 | 897,739 | 29.3 |
| 1976 | 3,182,646 | 902,503 | 28.4 |
| 1977 | 3,307,224 | 900,987 | 27.2 |
| 1978 | 3,437,392 | 908,502 | 26.4 |
| 1979 | 3,593,052 | 918,152 | 25.6 |
| 1980 | 3,744,024 | 891,115 | 23.8 |
| 1981 | 3,895,196 | 847,997 | 21.8 |
| 1982 | 4,031,820 | 828,751 | 20.6 |
| 1983 | 4,144,312 | 815,830 | 19.7 |
| 1984 | 4,246,587 | 803,830 | 18.9 |
| 1985 | 4,360,647 | 779,897 | 17.9 |
| 1986 | 4,489,300 | 769,366 | 17.1 |
| 1987 | 4,644,839 | 756,745 | 16.3 |
| 1988 | 4,807,714 | 738,742 | 15.4 |
| 1989 | 4,954,075 | 721,191 | 14.6 |
| 1990 | 5,094,164 | 860,748 | 16.9 |

Notes: Since 1972, the number of farm households has included those of noncultivating farm households; the number of farm households in 1990 is excerpted from *Agricultural and Fishery Censuses of 1991*, DGBAS, Executive Yuan.
Source: *Taiwan Agricultural Yearbook*, PDAF; various years.

TABLE 2–4
AVERAGE FARM SIZE IN TAIWAN, 1952–1990
(hectares)

| Year | Average Farm Size | Average Cultivated Land per Farm Worker | Year | Average Farm Size | Average Cultivated Land per Farm Worker |
|---|---|---|---|---|---|
| 1952 | 1.29 | 0.57 | 1972 | 0.97 | 0.60 |
| 1953 | 1.24 | 0.57 | 1973 | 0.98 | 0.60 |
| 1954 | 1.22 | 0.56 | 1974 | 1.00 | 0.59 |
| 1955 | 1.19 | 0.56 | 1975 | 1.02 | 0.61 |
| 1956 | 1.17 | 0.56 | 1976 | 1.02 | 0.62 |
| 1957 | 1.15 | 0.55 | 1977 | 1.02 | 0.64 |
| 1958 | 1.15 | 0.56 | 1978 | 1.01 | 0.65 |
| 1959 | 1.12 | 0.55 | 1979 | 1.00 | 0.71 |
| 1960 | 1.11 | 0.54 | 1980 | 1.02 | 0.79 |
| 1961 | 1.09 | 0.54 | 1981 | 1.06 | 0.79 |
| 1962 | 1.08 | 0.53 | 1982 | 1.07 | 0.78 |
| 1963 | 1.06 | 0.53 | 1983 | 1.10 | 0.76 |
| 1964 | 1.06 | 0.53 | 1984 | 1.11 | 0.77 |
| 1965 | 1.05 | 0.55 | 1985 | 1.14 | 0.76 |
| 1966 | 1.05 | 0.56 | 1986 | 1.15 | 0.75 |
| 1967 | 1.04 | 0.57 | 1987 | 1.17 | 0.80 |
| 1968 | 1.03 | 0.56 | 1988 | 1.21 | 0.90 |
| 1969 | 1.03 | 0.57 | 1989 | 1.24 | 0.95 |
| 1970 | 1.03 | 0.58 | 1990 | 1.03 | 0.94 |
| 1971 | 1.03 | 0.59 | | | |

SOURCE: *Agricultural Year Book*, PDAF; various years.

tion has changed. When machines substitute for manual work to overcome the farm labor shortage, a 1-hectare farm is too small to be operated efficiently.

Describing farm size with only the average size can be misleading. A look at the distribution of farms by size may also be useful. The number and proportion of small farms in Taiwan have been on the increase because of the rigidity of the farmland tenancy system and the unwillingness of farmers to sell their land. According to table 2-5, there were 254,038 farms smaller than 0.5 hectare in 1955. This number had increased to 323,674 by 1985. Consequently, the share of farms smaller than 0.5 hectare rose from 34.4 percent in 1955 to 41.9 percent in 1985, an increase of 7.5 percentage points. The number of farms between 0.5 hectare and 1.0 hectare was 209,987 in 1955; the number rose to 237,143 in 1985, an increase of 27,156 farms during this period. The share of these farms grew from 28.4 percent in 1955 to 30.7 percent in 1985, an increase of 2.3 percentage points. In total, the number of farms smaller than 1.0 hectare increased by 96,792 or 20.9 percent from 1955 to 1985.

Conversely, farms larger than 1.0 hectare but smaller than 10.0 hectares decreased markedly from 1955 to 1985: the number was 274,338 in 1955 and 210,504 in 1985, a decrease of 63,834 farms during this period. In 1990, the number of farms increased in all size groups, especially in the size group of under 0.5 hectare, except the size group of 1–2 hectares. It is clear that the problem of farm size in Taiwan has become worse over time. The small scale of all farms has made the adoption of modern technology difficult, costly, and less efficient in Taiwan in comparison with countries with larger farms. Therefore, how to increase farm size has become a major issue for agricultural development in Taiwan.

### Type of Farm Households

Traditionally, farm households in Taiwan have been classified into three types: the full-time farm household; the type A part-time farm household; and the type B part-time farm household. According to the definitions in the agricultural census of the Republic of China on Taiwan, in full-time farm households, no member of the household engages in off-farm work or spends as many as thirty days in off-farm work. The rest of the farm households are regarded as part-time farm households. The part-time category, however, is further broken down into type A and type B part-time farm households. In type A, the income generated from the farm is greater than that generated off farm. In type B, the off-farm income is greater than the farm income.

18

TABLE 2-5

DISTRIBUTION OF FARMS BY SIZE OF LANDHOLDING, 1955, 1985, AND 1990

| Size of Landholding | 1955 (1) | 1985 (2) | 1990 (3) | (2) − (1) | (3) − (2) |
|---|---|---|---|---|---|
| | Number of Farms | | | | |
| Under 0.5 ha. | 254,038 | 323,674 | 399,274 | 69,636 | 75,600 |
| 0.5–1.0 ha. | 209,987 | 237,143 | 241,035 | 27,156 | 3,892 |
| 1.0–2.0 ha. | 188,604 | 155,111 | 152,381 | −33,493 | −2,730 |
| 2.0–3.0 ha. | 57,219 | 36,246 | 36,597 | −20,973 | 351 |
| 3.0–5.0 ha. | 23,249 | 15,206 | 16,469 | −8,043 | 1,263 |
| 5.0–10.0 ha. | 5,266 | 3,941 | 4,577 | −1,325 | 636 |
| 10.0 ha. and over | 277 | 585 | 993 | 308 | 408 |
| Total | 738,640 | 771,906 | 851,326 | 33,266 | 79,420 |
| | Percentage | | | | |
| Under 0.5 ha. | 34.39 | 41.93 | 46.90 | 7.54 | 4.97 |
| 0.5–1.0 ha. | 28.43 | 30.72 | 28.31 | 2.29 | −2.41 |
| 1.0–2.0 ha. | 25.53 | 20.09 | 17.90 | −5.44 | −2.20 |
| 2.0–3.0 ha. | 7.75 | 4.70 | 4.30 | −3.05 | −0.40 |
| 3.0–5.0 ha. | 3.15 | 1.97 | 1.93 | −1.18 | −0.04 |
| 5.0–10.0 ha. | 0.71 | 0.51 | 0.54 | −0.20 | 0.03 |
| 10.0 ha. and over | 0.04 | 0.08 | 0.12 | 0.04 | 0.04 |

NOTE: Number of farms are those with crop productions.
SOURCE: *Agricultural and Fishery Censuses*, DGBAS, Executive Yuan; various years.

TABLE 2–6

CHANGES IN FARM HOUSEHOLD TYPES IN TAIWAN, 1960–1990

| Type of Farm Household | 1960 | 1970 | 1980 | 1985 | 1990 |
|---|---|---|---|---|---|
| *Number of Farm Households* | | | | | |
| Full-time farm household | 384,501 | 276,959 | 79,757 | 115,164 | 104,494 |
| Part-time farm household | 241,060 | 371,434 | 316,584 | 168,447 | 155,874 |
| Sideline farm household | 182,039 | 267,573 | 494,774 | 496,367 | 600,380 |
| Total | 807,600 | 915,966 | 891,115 | 779,978 | 860,748 |
| *Percentage of Farm Households* | | | | | |
| Full-time farm household | 47.6 | 30.2 | 9.0 | 14.8 | 12.1 |
| Part-time farm household | 29.9 | 40.6 | 35.5 | 21.6 | 18.1 |
| Sideline farm household | 22.5 | 29.2 | 55.5 | 63.6 | 69.8 |

NOTE: The full-time farm household is one in which no member of the farm household engages in off-farm work or where the total off-farm work days are fewer than thirty. The part-time farm household is the farm household where the income generated from the farm is greater than the off-farm income. The sideline farm household is the farm household where the off-farm income is greater than the farm income.
SOURCE: *Agricultural Census*, DGBAS, Executive Yuan; various years.

For simplicity, we use the term *part-time farm household* to represent the type A part-time farm household and the term *sideline farm household* to represent the type B part-time farm household.

Data in table 2–6 show that the total number of farm households was 807,600 in 1960. It increased to 915,966 in 1970, decreased slightly to 891,115 in 1980, and then dropped significantly to 779,978 in 1985. These changes in the total number of farm households fully indicate the path of agricultural development in Taiwan during the past twenty-five years.

In 1960, the full-time farm households accounted for 47.6 percent of the total, with part-time households at 29.9 percent and the sideline households at 22.5 percent. From 1960 to 1970, the total number of farm households increased by 13.4 percent, the part-time farm households by 54.1 percent, and the sideline farm households

TABLE 2–7

RATE OF AVERAGE ANNUAL CHANGE FOR DIFFERENT TYPES OF FARM
HOUSEHOLDS IN TAIWAN, 1960–1990

| Type of Farm Household | 1960–70 | 1970–80 | 1980–85 | 1985–90 |
|---|---|---|---|---|
| Full-time farm household | −3.2 | −11.7 | 7.6 | −1.9 |
| Part-time farm household | 4.4 | −1.6 | −11.9 | −1.5 |
| Sideline farm household | 3.9 | 6.3 | 0.1 | 3.9 |

SOURCE: Computed from table 2–6.

by 47.0 percent; but the full-time farm households decreased by 28.1 percent. Therefore in 1970, the percentage share of the full-time farm households declined to 30.2 percent, whereas the percentage share of part-time and sideline farm households increased to 40.6 percent and 29.2 percent, respectively.

By 1980, the number of sideline farm households had grown drastically, and the number of full-time farm households had significantly decreased, with the part-time households decreasing moderately. The percentage share of the sideline households increased to 55.5 percent of total farm households, while the percentage of full-time households decreased to only 9.0 percent. The majority of farm households in Taiwan had clearly become either sideline or part-time by 1980.

The government was fully aware of this situation and was worried about the decline of competitiveness in Taiwan's agriculture. Therefore, several measures were enacted to promote the development of full-time farm households, such as the nucleus farms project and the creation of new farm business for rural youths. By 1985, the number of part-time farm households had dropped significantly, and the number of full-time households had increased, with the number of sideline households remaining almost unchanged. The percentage share of full-time households had increased to 14.8 percent by 1985 and the part-time farm households to 21.6 percent; the sideline farm households rose to 63.3 percent. In 1990, both full-time farms and part-time farms showed a decrease, while sideline farms continuously increased. The average annual rate of change of the different types of farm households from 1960 to 1990 is shown in table 2–7.

## Capital Requirements

Because of the high man : land ratio, land is the most scarce resource in Taiwan. To a certain degree, land is usually overvalued. Tradition-

TABLE 2–8

AVERAGE CAPITAL INVESTMENT PER FARM IN TAIWAN, 1965–1990

| Item | 1965 | 1970 | 1980 | 1990 |
|---|---|---|---|---|
| *N.T. dollars* | | | | |
| Land | 175,162 | 303,795 | 1,821,472 | 10,066,960 |
| Buildings | 25,681 | 39,396 | 308,077 | 881,056 |
| Farm machinery | 7,032 | 14,175 | 75,881 | 140,931 |
| Livestock | 9,338 | 7,869 | 27,468 | 21,956 |
| Orchards and trees | 3,420 | 5,131 | 21,995 | 80,080 |
| Total | 220,633 | 370,367 | 2,254,892 | 11,190,983 |
| *Percentage* | | | | |
| Land | 79.39 | 82.02 | 80.78 | 89.95 |
| Buildings | 11.64 | 10.64 | 13.66 | 7.87 |
| Farm machinery | 3.19 | 3.83 | 3.36 | 1.26 |
| Livestock | 4.23 | 2.12 | 1.22 | 0.20 |
| Orchards and trees | 1.55 | 1.39 | 0.98 | 0.72 |
| GNP price deflator (1986 = 100) | 24.6 | 31.1 | 80.7 | 108.8 |

NOTE: Average of northern, central, and southern rice regions.
SOURCE: *Taiwan Farm Book-Keeping Record*, PDAF; various years.

ally, land and farm buildings in Taiwan are inherited, and it is unnecessary for the current owner to pay inheritance tax. For this reason, Taiwan's farmers can better tolerate long-run low agricultural prices without bankruptcy. In addition, the excessively high prices of farmland would bring big losses to both nonfarmers and agribusinesses as participants in agricultural production, because they have to pay a high interest on land and buildings. Based on this theoretical consideration, present land policy does not allow nonfarmers and agribusinesses to buy any farmland for farming. It is believed that they are not as competitive as the present farmers.

Table 2–8 shows the average capital investment per farm of the rice regions. Data are obtained from the reports of book-keeping farms in the northern, central, and southern rice regions. In 1965, the average capital investment was NT$220,633 per farm, of which land was estimated at a value of NT$175,162 and accounted for 79.39 percent of the total capital investment; that of buildings was NT$25,681, accounting for 11.64 percent. The other capital items such as farm machinery, livestock, orchards, and trees accounted for only

8.79 percent of the total capital investment. These statistics indicate that, by far, land and buildings are the most important capital investment on the farm in Taiwan. All other items are less important. In 1990, the value of land on farms jumped to NT$10,067,000; compared with 1965, it was a 57.5 fold increase. The value of farm buildings, machinery, livestock, orchards, and trees increased at a slower rate. This resulted in a much larger percentage share of land and a smaller percentage share of others in 1990. The percentage shares of land, buildings, and other items were 89.95 percent, 7.87 percent, and 2.18 percent, respectively. It should be noted, however, that increases in the value of land and buildings are attributed mainly to an increase in the price of land and buildings, not to the expansion of their physical size. But increases in the value of other items are attributed mainly to physical expansion, because their prices are more stable in comparison with those of land and buildings. Therefore, even though the composition of capital investment in farms changed very little during the period studied, in fact, there were significant changes in farm mechanization and farm businesses.

Data on average expenditures for farm operations in selected years from 1965 to 1990 are shown in table 2–9. In 1965, the expenditure for farm operations was NT$26,673, of which expenditure on fertilizers was NT$6,662, accounting for 24.98 percent of total farm expenditures. Expenditure on feeds was NT$6,471, accounting for 24.26 percent; expenditure on hired labor was NT$3,536, accounting for 13.26 percent. These three items combined for 62.50 percent of total farm expenditures. Clearly, they were the most important items in all farm expenditures in 1965. In 1970, total expenditures increased to NT$35,905 per farm. The composition of the expenditures was about the same as in 1965. Since 1970, however, there have been some significant changes in agricultural development, such as the extension of farm mechanization, rapid expansion of livestock and poultry, reduction in fertilizer prices and farm taxes, and substitution of capital-intensive technology for labor-intensive technology. These factors greatly affected the composition of farm expenditures after 1970. In 1990, the shares of expenditure on feeds, pesticides, materials, farming tools, and hired machinery labor have increased markedly, whereas the shares of expenditure on fertilizers and hired manual labor have decreased. The decrease in the importance of fertilizers was due mainly to the reduction in fertilizer prices in recent years, not because of a decrease in their application. It is interesting to note that the tax burden on farms has been reduced since 1970 because of the special exemption on farmers' income tax and waiver of farmland tax. In 1990, a farm paid only NT$220 in tax and

## TABLE 2–9
### AVERAGE FARM PRODUCTION EXPENDITURES IN TAIWAN, 1965–1990
(N.T. dollars)

| Item | 1965 N.T.$ | 1965 % | 1970 N.T.$ | 1970 % | 1980 N.T.$ | 1980 % | 1990 N.T.$ | 1990 % |
|---|---|---|---|---|---|---|---|---|
| Seeds | 1,271 | 4.77 | 1,441 | 4.01 | 4,594 | 4.53 | 20,512 | 8.42 |
| Pesticides | 1,123 | 4.21 | 1,992 | 5.55 | 10,077 | 9.94 | 22,923 | 9.41 |
| Material | 842 | 3.16 | 1,428 | 3.98 | 5,313 | 5.24 | 16,229 | 6.67 |
| Fertilizers | 6,662 | 24.98 | 7,678 | 21.39 | 11,291 | 11.14 | 23,632 | 9.71 |
| Hired manual labor | 3,536 | 13.26 | 6,354 | 17.70 | 13,515 | 13.33 | 30,509 | 12.53 |
| Hired machinery labor | — | — | — | — | 9,861 | 9.73 | 16,801 | 6.90 |
| Hired animal labor | 229 | 0.86 | 361 | 1.01 | 432 | 0.43 | 286 | 0.12 |
| Irrigation | 1,018 | 3.82 | 1,316 | 3.66 | 2,353 | 2.32 | 775 | 0.32 |
| Depreciation; building and equipment repair | 176 | 0.66 | 394 | 1.10 | 286 | 0.28 | 9,370 | 3.85 |
| Farming tools | 341 | 1.28 | 389 | 1.08 | 4,684 | 4.62 | 15,443 | 6.34 |
| Land rent | 1,146 | 4.30 | 1,314 | 3.66 | 2,260 | 2.23 | 3,850 | 1.58 |
| Livestock and poultry | 1,794 | 6.72 | 1,968 | 5.48 | 7,795 | 7.69 | 19,067 | 7.83 |
| Feeds | 6,471 | 24.26 | 8,168 | 22.75 | 26,097 | 25.74 | 63,872 | 26.23 |
| Tax | 2,063 | 7.73 | 3,103 | 8.64 | 2,831 | 2.79 | 220 | 0.09 |
| Total | 26,673 | 100.00 | 35,905 | 100 | 101,388 | 100.00 | 243,490 | 100.00 |

SOURCE: Same as table 2–8.

TABLE 2–10

LABOR INPUT OF SELECTED CROPS AND BROILER PRODUCTION IN
TAIWAN, 1952–1990

(hours per hectare)

| Crop | 1952 | 1960 | 1970 | 1980 | 1990 |
|---|---|---|---|---|---|
| Rice | | | | | |
|   First crop | 806.40 | 864.24 | 844.40 | 394.48 | 238.55 |
|   Second crop | 765.84 | 807.84 | 829.76 | 390.48 | 233.02 |
| Corn | | | | | |
|   First crop | — | — | 624.80 | 607.10 | 297.40 |
| Soybean | | | | | |
|   Winter crop | — | — | 634.20 | 579.30 | — |
| Sweet potato | — | — | 930.10 | 862.40 | 411.80 |
| Peanut | | | | | |
|   First crop | — | — | 1,092.00 | 898.30 | 646.70 |
| Banana | — | — | 2,452.00 | 1,952.20 | 1,739.60 |
| Cauliflower | — | — | 2,327.60 | 1,679.20 | — |
| Broiler (100 head) | — | — | 44.90 | 11.98 | 4.80 |

— = no data
SOURCE: *Production Cost Survey*, PDAF; various years.

accounted for only 0.09 percent of total farm expenditures. The reduction in farm taxes is based primarily on the consideration that the income of farmers is relatively low in comparison with that of nonfarmers.

Before 1965, Taiwan had a surplus of farm labor, and therefore labor-intensive technology was applied to agricultural production. Table 2–10 shows the labor input of selected crops and broiler production in Taiwan from 1952 to 1990. The labor input was 806 hours per hectare for the first crop of rice and 766 hours per hectare for the second crop of rice in 1952. It increased to 864 hours per hectare for the first crop of rice and 808 hours per hectare for the second crop of rice in 1960. The per hectare labor input showed a slight decrease for the first crop of rice and a small increase for the second crop of rice in 1970: 844 hours per hectare and 830 hours per hectare for the first crop of rice and the second crop, respectively. Since then, labor input in rice production of both crops has significantly decreased. The labor input was only 239 hours per hectare for the first crop of rice and 233 hours per hectare for the second in 1990, a 71.7 percent and a 71.9 percent decrease in labor input for the first and the second crop of rice, respectively, in comparison with 1970. Rice production has obviously been transformed from a labor-intensive activity to a labor-

TABLE 2–11

MECHANIZATION OF RICE PRODUCTION OPERATIONS IN TAIWAN,
SELECTED YEARS, 1980–1990

(percent)

| Year | Field Preparation | | Transplanting | | Harvesting | |
|------|------|------|------|------|------|------|
| 1980 | 95.0 | (77.3) | 78.1 | (72.2) | 53.9 | (91.9) |
| 1985 | 97.0 | (70.4) | 97.1 | (71.5) | 97.0 | (82.8) |
| 1990 | 98.0 | (76.9) | 98.0 | (82.0) | 98.0 | (83.0) |

NOTE: Figures in the parentheses are percentages of mechanization accomplished by custom farming teams.
SOURCE: *Production Cost Survey*, PDAF; various years.

saving one during this period. In other words, mechanization in rice production has become more and more popular in Taiwan in recent years.

From table 2–10, we see that labor input for other crops also decreased from 1970 to 1990. The pace of that decrease in other crops, however, was rather slow from 1970 to 1980. It speeded up between 1980 and 1990. The first crop of corn required 625 hours of labor per hectare in 1970, for example. It decreased slightly to 607 hours per hectare in 1980, only a 3 percent decrease from that of 1970. In 1990, labor input in corn production was 297 hours per hectare, a significant decrease of 51 percent from that of 1980. The same trend could also be found in crops other than corn. The mechanization program in Taiwan first operated in rice production and then gradually extended to other crops.

For broiler production, the success in labor saving is remarkable. The labor requirement for a thousand birds decreased from forty-five hours in 1970 to twelve hours in 1980 and finally to less than five hours in 1990. The reduction in labor input in broiler production is due both to the expansion of farm size and to the mechanization of farm operations.

From this discussion, we know that the Taiwanese farmers have successfully adjusted themselves to labor-saving production technology to meet the challenge of the rural labor shortage during the process of economic development.

Table 2–11 shows the achievements of mechanization in rice production operations in Taiwan from 1980 to 1990. In 1980, 95 percent of field preparation, 78 percent of transplanting, and 54 percent of harvesting were accomplished by farm machinery. In 1990, however, 98 percent of all rice production operation was accomplished by farm machinery. The high degree of mechanization in rice production has been impressive. As a majority of farms in Taiwan are small, it is uneconomical for them all to own farm machinery. Therefore, the "custom-farming" teams are organized by young and able farmers who purchase machinery and work for others who do not have machinery. Figures in the parentheses of table 2–10 show percentages of mechanization accomplished by the custom-farming teams. In 1980, 77 percent of field preparation, 72 percent of transplanting, and 92 percent of harvesting were done by such teams. While the percentage of field preparation remained almost the same (77 percent) in 1990, the percentages accomplished by these teams in transplanting and harvesting have increased significantly, surpassing that of field preparation in 1990. These percentages reflect the fact that more power tillers and fewer pieces of rice transplanting and harvesting machinery are owned by farmers themselves.

### Major Productive Activities

Agriculture in Taiwan has four subsectors: crops, livestock, fisheries, and forestry. Significant differences in the growth rates of these subsectors explain the great changes in the shares of these components in gross production from 1950 to 1990. The share of crops accounted for more than 60 percent of gross agricultural production before 1969 but for less than 50 percent after 1976. The share of livestock accounted for about 20 percent of gross agricultural production in the 1950s, increasing to 30 percent during the late 1970s. The share of fisheries accounted for less than 10 percent until 1968. Since then, the share of fisheries increased rapidly to about 30 percent in the 1980s. The share of forestry varied from 4.7 percent to 7.1 percent between 1953 and 1973. In the 1980s, the share of forestry dropped to less than 2 percent because of the change of national policy toward the conservation of forest resources (table 2–12).

In 1955, the shares of crops, livestock, fisheries, and forestry were 66.2 percent, 19.6 percent, 9.4 percent, and 4.8 percent, respectively. The share of livestock and fisheries combined was about 30 percent, much lower than that of crops. Crop farming was thus the most important agricultural activity in Taiwan in the early years. In 1977, the share of crops declined to 48.3 percent of gross agricultural production. The share of livestock and fisheries increased to 30.2 percent and 19 percent, respectively, in the same year. The combined percentage of livestock and fisheries was as high as that of crops,

TABLE 2–12

PERCENTAGE SHARES OF GROSS PRODUCTION OF MAJOR AGRICULTURAL
COMPONENTS, 1953–1990

| Year | Crops | Livestock | Fishery | Forestry |
|------|-------|-----------|---------|----------|
| 1953 | 71.91 | 15.65 | 7.39 | 5.05 |
| 1954 | 64.43 | 19.32 | 9.91 | 6.34 |
| 1955 | 66.19 | 19.56 | 9.44 | 4.81 |
| 1956 | 66.07 | 19.65 | 9.24 | 5.04 |
| 1957 | 64.56 | 20.56 | 8.96 | 5.92 |
| 1958 | 63.48 | 20.42 | 9.00 | 7.10 |
| 1959 | 60.21 | 22.27 | 10.52 | 7.00 |
| 1960 | 64.05 | 20.85 | 9.59 | 5.51 |
| 1961 | 64.53 | 21.43 | 8.90 | 5.04 |
| 1962 | 63.73 | 23.40 | 8.16 | 4.71 |
| 1963 | 63.43 | 23.23 | 8.68 | 4.66 |
| 1964 | 65.95 | 21.00 | 8.27 | 4.78 |
| 1965 | 64.65 | 21.16 | 8.74 | 5.45 |
| 1966 | 63.45 | 21.38 | 9.65 | 5.52 |
| 1967 | 62.95 | 22.01 | 9.46 | 5.58 |
| 1968 | 60.15 | 22.97 | 10.62 | 6.26 |
| 1969 | 58.98 | 23.74 | 12.23 | 5.05 |
| 1970 | 57.20 | 24.11 | 13.46 | 5.23 |
| 1971 | 53.84 | 25.52 | 14.96 | 5.68 |
| 1972 | 51.66 | 26.16 | 16.69 | 5.49 |
| 1973 | 50.14 | 26.75 | 16.91 | 6.20 |
| 1974 | 55.63 | 26.31 | 13.65 | 4.41 |
| 1975 | 57.88 | 24.91 | 14.19 | 3.02 |
| 1976 | 53.04 | 27.54 | 16.14 | 3.28 |
| 1977 | 48.32 | 30.20 | 18.98 | 2.50 |
| 1978 | 46.47 | 30.60 | 20.04 | 2.89 |
| 1979 | 47.88 | 27.79 | 21.42 | 2.91 |
| 1980 | 47.15 | 28.97 | 21.59 | 2.29 |
| 1981 | 46.24 | 30.72 | 21.09 | 1.95 |
| 1982 | 47.48 | 30.06 | 20.98 | 1.48 |
| 1983 | 46.49 | 22.08 | 29.76 | 1.67 |
| 1984 | 46.59 | 22.88 | 29.26 | 1.27 |
| 1985 | 46.95 | 27.25 | 24.77 | 1.03 |
| 1986 | 41.83 | 30.81 | 26.26 | 1.11 |
| 1987 | 41.41 | 29.21 | 28.21 | 1.17 |
| 1988 | 43.12 | 27.73 | 28.11 | 1.05 |
| 1989 | 42.00 | 30.30 | 27.10 | 0.60 |
| 1990 | 44.10 | 27.00 | 28.40 | 0.50 |

SOURCE: See table 2–5.

showing that crop production in Taiwan has encountered land constraints and that agricultural development has put more emphasis on non-land-based activities. In 1990, the shares of crops, livestock, fisheries, and forestry were 44.1 percent, 27.0 percent, 28.4 percent, and 0.5 percent, respectively. The weight of crops has dropped well below that of livestock and fisheries combined. Taiwan's agriculture is thus a vital sector that can adjust itself to meet changing conditions.

We can look further into the changes in composition of crop production. Grouping crops into rice, special crops, fruits, vegetables, and other common crops enables us to observe some striking changes in composition. From 1952 to 1990, the shares of rice, special crops, and other common crops in total production declined steadily. In contrast, the shares of fruits and vegetables in total crop production increased significantly. In 1952, rice accounted for 58.7 percent of crop production; special crops, 19.7 percent; other common crops, 13.3 percent; vegetables, 4.8 percent; and fruits, only 3.5 percent.

As consumption patterns changed and the demand for vegetables and fruits increased because of higher incomes in the 1960s, farmers began to produce more vegetables and fruits. In 1970, the shares of rice, special crops, and other common crops in total crop production declined to 45.0 percent, 14.3 percent, and 12.9 percent, respectively. The share of vegetables increased to 16.0 percent, and the share of fruits increased to 11.8 percent. Compared with the 1950s, vegetables and fruits have gained greatly in their relative importance in crop production. In 1990, the share of rice fell further to 27.4 percent; special crops, to 10.5 percent; and other common crops, to 8.4 percent. The shares of fruits and vegetables increased to 29.8 percent and 21.2 percent, respectively, in the same year (table 2–13). In 1988, for the first time in Taiwan's agricultural history, the importance of fruits surpassed rice. It is likely that the shares of fruits and vegetables in total agricultural production will increase continuously in the future in response to demand.

The production of rice, the most important crop in Taiwan, increased from 1.57 million metric tons in 1952 to 2.71 million metric tons in 1976; and then it gradually fell to 1.81 million in 1990. The decrease in rice production in recent years resulted from government policy to solve the surplus problem caused by the drastic reduction in per capita consumption of rice since the late 1970s.

The production of sweet potatoes, another major crop, was 2.09 million metric tons in 1952. It increased to 3.72 million metric tons in 1967 and then decreased to 199,830 tons in 1990. Sweet potatoes made up a large part of hog farmers' self-supplied feedstock, particularly in hog production before 1965. Since then, imported feed grains have

## TABLE 2-13

### CHANGES IN THE COMPOSITION OF CROP PRODUCTION, 1952–1990

(based on current prices of respective year)

| Year | Rice | Other Common Crops | Special Crops | Fruits | Vegetables | Others | Year | Rice | Other Common Crops | Special Crops | Fruits | Vegetables | Others |
|------|------|------|------|------|------|------|------|------|------|------|------|------|------|
| 1952 | 58.7 | 13.3 | 19.7 | 3.5 | 4.8 | 0.0 | 1972 | 44.1 | 12.5 | 14.5 | 11.6 | 17.3 | 0.0 |
| 1953 | 61.3 | 10.7 | 21.9 | 2.4 | 3.7 | 0.0 | 1973 | 44.6 | 13.5 | 13.8 | 11.3 | 16.7 | 0.0 |
| 1954 | 58.1 | 14.2 | 19.3 | 3.1 | 5.3 | 0.0 | 1974 | 50.6 | 9.7 | 16.2 | 9.1 | 14.4 | 0.0 |
| 1955 | 56.4 | 14.4 | 21.0 | 3.2 | 5.0 | 0.0 | 1975 | 48.6 | 8.8 | 20.1 | 8.2 | 14.2 | 0.1 |
| 1956 | 55.6 | 15.5 | 20.8 | 3.1 | 5.0 | 0.1 | 1976 | 49.6 | 8.2 | 15.6 | 10.3 | 16.3 | 0.1 |
| 1957 | 54.7 | 14.9 | 22.0 | 3.6 | 4.8 | 0.0 | 1977 | 44.0 | 8.8 | 16.6 | 11.2 | 19.4 | 0.1 |
| 1958 | 51.7 | 16.4 | 21.3 | 4.2 | 6.4 | 0.0 | 1978 | 41.2 | 8.5 | 14.4 | 12.4 | 23.3 | 0.7 |
| 1959 | 49.7 | 16.1 | 23.1 | 4.8 | 6.3 | 0.0 | 1979 | 42.4 | 7.1 | 12.5 | 14.5 | 23.2 | 0.8 |
| 1960 | 57.0 | 15.8 | 17.4 | 4.2 | 5.7 | 0.0 | 1980 | 41.8 | 7.4 | 12.8 | 14.5 | 23.2 | 0.8 |
| 1961 | 56.1 | 15.5 | 18.9 | 4.1 | 5.4 | 0.0 | 1981 | 42.2 | 6.6 | 13.4 | 15.8 | 22.1 | 0.8 |
| 1962 | 55.0 | 15.5 | 18.3 | 5.1 | 6.1 | 0.0 | 1982 | 39.1 | 7.0 | 12.7 | 18.7 | 22.6 | 0.7 |
| 1963 | 54.4 | 12.0 | 19.5 | 5.8 | 8.3 | 0.0 | 1983 | 37.2 | 6.8 | 12.5 | 21.2 | 22.4 | 0.7 |
| 1964 | 47.6 | 14.3 | 24.0 | 7.9 | 6.2 | 0.0 | 1984 | 34.5 | 6.5 | 13.0 | 23.4 | 22.7 | 1.0 |
| 1965 | 48.9 | 13.4 | 18.2 | 11.4 | 8.0 | 0.0 | 1985 | 32.6 | 7.3 | 13.5 | 23.0 | 22.3 | 1.3 |
| 1966 | 49.1 | 14.4 | 16.0 | 11.6 | 8.9 | 0.0 | 1986 | 30.4 | 7.8 | 13.1 | 23.7 | 23.7 | 1.3 |
| 1967 | 48.1 | 15.5 | 14.9 | 12.1 | 9.4 | 0.0 | 1987 | 26.8 | 8.3 | 12.7 | 24.4 | 26.1 | 1.7 |
| 1968 | 48.0 | 13.8 | 14.5 | 12.2 | 11.5 | 0.0 | 1988 | 27.1 | 7.9 | 11.8 | 27.7 | 23.4 | 2.1 |
| 1969 | 44.7 | 15.1 | 15.0 | 12.0 | 13.2 | 0.0 | 1989 | 28.0 | 7.6 | 10.8 | 29.3 | 22.3 | 2.0 |
| 1970 | 45.0 | 12.9 | 14.3 | 11.8 | 16.0 | 0.0 | 1990 | 27.4 | 8.4 | 10.5 | 29.8 | 21.2 | 2.7 |
| 1971 | 42.9 | 13.0 | 14.9 | 12.8 | 16.3 | 0.0 | | | | | | | |

SOURCE: See table 2-5

gradually replaced sweet potatoes as feed in Taiwan. Corn has been an important feed since 1965; its production increased from 7,000 metric tons in 1952 to 339,430 in 1990. Soybean production increased from 14,600 metric tons in 1952 to 75,000 in 1967 and then declined to 65,200 metric tons in 1970. It further decreased to only 8,140 metric tons in 1990. Liberalization of corn and soybean imports, however, has put the feedstock growers in Taiwan in an increasingly difficult position competitively. High-value cash crops, such as vegetables and fruits, have shown higher growth rates than most traditional food crops, particularly in response to rapidly rising export demand and to the growing domestic consumption stimulated by higher per capita income.

Banana production in 1967 reached a peak of 654,000 metric tons. It decreased to 461,800 metric tons in 1970 and further to 201,440 in 1990, however, because of keen competition with Central and South American countries and with the Philippines in the Japanese market. Production of pineapple increased from 62,800 metric tons in 1952 to 338,200 in 1970, peaking at 358,500 metric tons in 1971 before declining gradually to 234,629 in 1990 as exports decreased. Taiwan's farmers had never engaged in the production of asparagus before 1960. In 1971, total production of asparagus in Taiwan was 127,500 metric tons, compared with the initial production of 616 metric tons in 1964. The production of asparagus declined to 17,924 metric tons in 1990 as export demand decreased. Mushrooms were also a new crop to farmers in the early 1960s. The production of mushrooms was only 2,780 metric tons in 1961 but increased to a peak of 119,460 metric tons in 1978, decreasing to 17,780 metric tons in 1990 because of shrinking foreign markets. Citrus fruits have shown a steady increase in production, with a total production of 27,800 metric tons in 1952; it rose to 209,100 metric tons in 1970 and to 528,941 in 1990. Expansion of the domestic market caused the rapid increase in citrus fruit production.

Table 2–14 shows the changes in production, area, and yield of major crops. From 1952 to 1970, production of major crops increased sharply as the harvested area of these crops increased slightly or even decreased. The increases in crop production came mainly from the increase in unit yield of crops. In a period of about two decades, the rice yield rose by 59 percent; sweet potatoes, 68 percent; sugar cane, 42 percent; and bananas and pineapples, 74 percent and 147 percent, respectively. From 1970 to 1990, the production of many crops decreased because of the sharp reduction in the harvested area. The unit yield of crops in 1990, however, was still much higher than that of 1970. During this period, the improvement of agricultural technol-

31

TABLE 2-14

CHANGES IN PRODUCTION, AREA, AND YIELD OF MAJOR CROPS, TAIWAN, 1952–1990

| Crops | Production (1,000 metric tons) | | | Harvested Area (1,000 hectares) | | | Yield (kilograms per hectare) | | |
|---|---|---|---|---|---|---|---|---|---|
| | 1952 | 1970 | 1990 | 1952 | 1970 | 1990 | 1952 | 1970 | 1990 |
| Rice | 1,570.0 | 2,463.0 | 1,806.6 | 785.7 | 776.1 | 454.2 | 1,998 | 3,173 | 3,977 |
| Sweet potatoes | 2,090.0 | 3,440.6 | 199.8 | 233.5 | 228.7 | 11.7 | 8,953 | 15,044 | 16,952 |
| Sugar cane | 4,801.0 | 5,990.7 | 5,580.9 | 98.0 | 86.2 | 65.5 | 49,003 | 69,460 | 85,270 |
| Soybeans | 14.6 | 65.2 | 8.1 | 24.3 | 42.7 | 4.2 | 602 | 1,525 | 1,945 |
| Peanuts | 60.0 | 122.2 | 65.0 | 81.0 | 87.5 | 34.4 | 741 | 1,397 | 1,892 |
| Corn | 7.0 | 57.4 | 339.4 | 5.1 | 22.6 | 81.4 | 1,365 | 2,536 | 4,172 |
| Tea | 11.6 | 27.6 | 22.3 | 38.0 | 33.3 | 22.7 | 305 | 831 | 983 |
| Citrus fruits | 27.8 | 209.1 | 528.9 | 4.6 | 22.0 | 41.5 | 6,024 | 9,514 | 12,752 |
| Asparagus | 0 | 112.3 | 17.9 | 0 | 12.6 | 3.2 | 0 | 8,924 | 5,619 |
| Bananas | 106.9 | 461.8 | 201.4 | 15.7 | 39.0 | 9.5 | 6,811 | 11,838 | 21,311 |
| Pineapple | 62.8 | 338.2 | 234.6 | 5.8 | 12.7 | 6.1 | 10,731 | 26,525 | 38,497 |
| Mushrooms | 0 | 39.0 | 19.8 | n.a. | n.a. | n.a. | n.a. | n.a. | n.a. |

n.a. = not applicable.
SOURCE: *Taiwan Agricultural Yearbook*, PDAF; various years.

ogy was the major factor contributing to higher crop production in Taiwan.

Stimulated by rising domestic and foreign demand for meat, a result of a steady increase in per capita income, Taiwan's hog production grew from 1,620,000 head in 1950 to 4,320,000 head in 1970, to 7,750,000 head in 1980, and to 12,122,000 head in 1990. The increased use of feed grains and the expansion of the scale of hog farms have helped make Taiwan's hog industry more efficient and profitable.

Fishery production, only 84,000 metric tons in 1950, reached 613,200 in 1970, 936,000 in 1980, and 1,455,500 in 1990. This increase came largely from the rapid expansion of deep-sea fishing and culture fisheries. Fishing fleets now operate in all oceans, supported by a worldwide marketing and supply system. Because of increased labor costs and moves by other countries to extend their economic waters, however, deep-sea fisheries are facing great difficulty now and will in the future.

Forestry was an important subsector of agricultural production before 1970. Since then, the conservation of soil and water has become a more important national goal than government revenue. Forestry production has decreased in recent years.

### Agricultural Development since World War II

The economy of Taiwan was primarily agricultural when it was returned to the Republic of China in 1945 in a state of ruin and disorganization. Agricultural production that year was less than half its prewar peak, with industrial output less than one-third. The situation deteriorated further in the immediate postwar years, which were marked by runaway inflation, grave shortages of food and other basic necessities, a large influx of people from the mainland, a heavy defense burden, and social and political instability. It was against this background that Taiwan's economic development got under way. The government gave the highest priority to economic stabilization and food production, while every effort was made to repair the damage sustained during the war.

In the early stage of agricultural development, the expansion of crop production resulted largely from more intensive farming, including the introduction of new and improved techniques; increased capital inputs like chemical fertilizers, pesticides, and better seeds; and substantial expansion of multicropping, intercropping, and crop rotation.

**Agricultural Growth.** Table 2–15 shows the agricultural production indexes from 1946 to 1990, compiled by the Council of Agriculture.

## TABLE 2–15
### AGRICULTURAL PRODUCTION INDEXES FOR TAIWAN, 1946–1990
(1986 = 100)

| Year | Total Production | Crop Production | Livestock Production | Fishery Production | Forestry Production |
|------|------------------|-----------------|----------------------|--------------------|---------------------|
| 1946 | 10.9 | 24.1 | 3.6 | 4.1 | 15.7 |
| 1947 | 14.4 | 30.7 | 4.3 | 4.9 | 74.0 |
| 1948 | 18.0 | 37.6 | 5.0 | 6.7 | 98.4 |
| 1949 | 20.0 | 46.3 | 5.2 | 6.4 | 58.6 |
| 1950 | 22.0 | 49.4 | 6.8 | 6.7 | 66.5 |
| 1951 | 22.5 | 47.2 | 8.6 | 8.2 | 58.8 |
| 1952 | 25.1 | 51.8 | 9.2 | 9.5 | 75.6 |
| 1953 | 28.9 | 59.4 | 11.5 | 10.4 | 74.6 |
| 1954 | 28.9 | 57.4 | 12.0 | 12.1 | 77.9 |
| 1955 | 29.7 | 57.2 | 12.4 | 14.2 | 78.8 |
| 1956 | 31.3 | 60.6 | 13.1 | 15.3 | 83.4 |
| 1957 | 33.8 | 64.3 | 14.8 | 16.6 | 91.9 |
| 1958 | 36.2 | 68.0 | 16.6 | 17.4 | 101.4 |
| 1959 | 36.8 | 68.0 | 16.5 | 18.4 | 124.2 |
| 1960 | 37.1 | 68.9 | 15.9 | 19.3 | 128.1 |
| 1961 | 39.8 | 73.4 | 17.5 | 21.8 | 149.6 |
| 1962 | 41.0 | 74.7 | 18.6 | 22.3 | 153.7 |
| 1963 | 41.7 | 74.2 | 18.7 | 23.7 | 153.6 |
| 1964 | 45.7 | 83.0 | 20.1 | 25.8 | 188.2 |
| 1965 | 48.7 | 88.5 | 21.6 | 26.3 | 192.9 |
| 1966 | 50.5 | 90.6 | 23.9 | 29.7 | 176.5 |
| 1967 | 54.1 | 95.0 | 27.0 | 32.5 | 189.4 |
| 1968 | 58.2 | 98.8 | 28.9 | 38.9 | 209.9 |
| 1969 | 57.5 | 94.6 | 31.0 | 41.6 | 177.1 |
| 1970 | 61.5 | 98.8 | 34.1 | 45.2 | 187.4 |
| 1971 | 63.2 | 99.2 | 35.0 | 48.6 | 194.6 |
| 1972 | 66.1 | 99.9 | 38.5 | 52.2 | 190.4 |
| 1973 | 70.8 | 101.2 | 44.9 | 58.8 | 183.4 |
| 1974 | 70.5 | 106.9 | 41.7 | 56.1 | 160.6 |
| 1975 | 69.5 | 103.7 | 39.4 | 61.5 | 145.9 |
| 1976 | 78.3 | 110.3 | 49.9 | 66.3 | 152.9 |
| 1977 | 82.6 | 112.6 | 56.1 | 71.6 | 119.4 |
| 1978 | 82.9 | 107.3 | 59.0 | 75.6 | 121.6 |
| 1979 | 89.4 | 111.3 | 66.7 | 83.3 | 114.7 |
| 1980 | 90.4 | 108.9 | 70.6 | 84.5 | 103.2 |
| 1981 | 89.2 | 106.3 | 71.9 | 81.3 | 107.2 |
| 1982 | 90.8 | 107.2 | 74.7 | 82.9 | 98.1 |
| 1983 | 94.4 | 104.0 | 85.6 | 85.3 | 116.0 |
| 1984 | 97.4 | 104.7 | 90.6 | 90.4 | 100.3 |

TABLE 2–15 (continued)

| Year | Total Production | Crop Production | Livestock Production | Fishery Production | Forestry Production |
|---|---|---|---|---|---|
| 1985 | 100.3 | 105.5 | 96.8 | 94.3 | 90.3 |
| 1986 | 100.0 | 100.0 | 100.0 | 100.0 | 100.0 |
| 1987 | 108.3 | 104.2 | 109.0 | 114.7 | 92.7 |
| 1988 | 109.6 | 105.6 | 110.0 | 118.2 | 60.1 |
| 1989 | 109.4 | 105.1 | 115.3 | 112.3 | 42.5 |
| 1990 | 111.8 | 100.2 | 124.0 | 119.3 | 36.3 |

SOURCE: *Agricultural Production Statistics Abstract*, Republic of China, Council of Agriculture, Executive Yuan, 1991.

From this table, the annual rates of increase in different periods are calculated (see table 2–16).

Total agricultural production increased at 19.2 percent a year between 1946 and 1950. During this period, the annual increase in crop production was 19.7 percent; livestock production, 17.2 percent; fishery production, 13.1 percent; and forestry production, 43.5 percent. The extremely high increase in forestry production was mainly due to the very low production level in 1946.

TABLE 2–16

AVERAGE ANNUAL RATE OF INCREASE IN AGRICULTURAL PRODUCTION
BY GROUPS, 1946–1990

| Period | Total Production | Crop Production | Livestock Production | Fishery Production | Forestry Production |
|---|---|---|---|---|---|
| 1946–50 | 19.2 | 19.7 | 17.2 | 13.1 | 43.5 |
| 1950–55 | 6.2 | 3.0 | 12.8 | 16.2 | 3.5 |
| 1955–60 | 4.5 | 3.8 | 5.1 | 6.9 | 10.2 |
| 1960–65 | 5.6 | 5.1 | 6.3 | 6.4 | 8.5 |
| 1965–70 | 4.8 | 2.2 | 9.7 | 11.4 | −0.9 |
| 1970–75 | 2.5 | 1.0 | 2.9 | 6.4 | −4.9 |
| 1975–80 | 5.4 | 1.0 | 12.4 | 6.6 | −6.7 |
| 1980–85 | 2.1 | −0.6 | 6.5 | 2.2 | −2.6 |
| 1985–90 | 2.2 | −1.0 | 5.1 | 4.8 | −16.7 |
| 1950–70 | 5.3 | 3.5 | 8.4 | 10.0 | 5.3 |
| 1970–90 | 3.0 | 0.1 | 6.7 | 5.0 | −7.9 |
| 1950–90 | 4.1 | 1.8 | 7.5 | 7.5 | −1.5 |

SOURCE: Computed from table 2–15.

The total cultivated land area increased from 832,000 hectares in 1946 to 874,000 in 1951, an increase of 5 percent. The total crop area increased from 975,000 to 1,502,000 hectares, an increase of 54 percent in the same period. The increase in crop area raised the multiple cropping index from 117 in 1946 to 172 in 1951. Although the annual increase in unit yield was as high as 3.6 percent, major crops still yielded less than in the prewar period. The annual increase of 14.5 percent in livestock production also made a great contribution to the rapid growth of agricultural production in this period. In the course of Taiwan's agricultural development, however, the recovery and rehabilitation in 1946–1950 were somewhat abnormal. Hence the analysis in this chapter will purposely pay less attention to the agricultural performance in this period.

After the rehabilitation period, the total agricultural production grew relatively slowly. The average annual increase rate was 4.1 percent from 1950 to 1990. The rate was 5.3 percent in 1950–1970, however, and 3.0 percent in 1970–1990. It showed a clear declining trend. The average annual increase in crop production was only 1.8 percent from 1950 to 1990. It was 3.5 percent in 1950–1970, decreasing to 0.1 percent in 1970–1990. Since 1980, crop production has gone up and down, and sometimes there has been no growth at all. The stagnation of crop production was due mainly to a declining return on crops and the government program of reducing rice production.

The growth rates of livestock and fishery production were both 7.5 percent from 1950 to 1990. The high increases in livestock and fisheries are derived from the greater demand in both domestic and foreign markets. Since the mid-1970s, pork and fishery products have become the major agricultural exports.

Forestry production averaged an annual increase of 5.3 percent in 1950–1970, decreasing to −7.9 percent in 1970–1990. The complete change in national forestry policy from felling timber for government revenue to the preservation of forestry resources is reflected in these statistics.

**The Share of Agriculture in NDP and Foreign Trade.** Through a series of economic development plans launched in 1953, Taiwan has been transformed from a predominantly agricultural economy to one in which a fairly diversified industry is now the leading sector. Table 2–17 shows that in 1952, the share of agriculture in net domestic product (NDP) was 36.0 percent, the share of industry (including mining, manufacturing, electricity, and construction) was only 18.0 percent, and that of the service sector was 46.0 percent. In 1963, for the first time the share of industry exceeded that of agriculture. Since

## TABLE 2–17

### Net Domestic Product of Taiwan by Kind of Activity, 1952–1990

(millions of N.T. dollars and percent)

| Year | Agriculture | | Industries | | Services | | Total |
|------|------------|--------|------------|--------|------------|--------|-----------|
| 1952 | 5,220 | (36.0) | 2,613 | (18.0) | 6,679 | (46.0) | 14,512 |
| 1955 | 8,009 | (32.9) | 5,134 | (21.1) | 11,192 | (46.0) | 24,335 |
| 1960 | 16,494 | (32.9) | 12,497 | (24.9) | 21,165 | (42.2) | 50,156 |
| 1965 | 24,714 | (27.4) | 25,775 | (28.6) | 39,608 | (44.0) | 90,097 |
| 1970 | 31,600 | (18.0) | 60,537 | (34.5) | 83,162 | (47.5) | 175,299 |
| 1975 | 67,851 | (14.9) | 178,028 | (39.1) | 209,047 | (46.0) | 454,926 |
| 1980 | 105,542 | (9.2) | 513,049 | (44.7) | 529,662 | (46.1) | 1,148,253 |
| 1985 | 134,076 | (6.8) | 889,924 | (45.3) | 940,515 | (47.9) | 1,964,515 |
| 1990 | 164,083 | (4.8) | 1,421,743 | (41.7) | 1,824,041 | (53.5) | 3,409,867 |

Source: *Taiwan Statistical Data Book*, Council for Economic Planning and Development, ROC, 1991.

then, the relative importance of agriculture in the national economy has declined continuously. In 1970, agriculture and industry changed their position in the economy compared with 1953. Industry accounted for 34.5 percent of NDP, and agriculture accounted for only 18.0 percent. Over this period, industry had clearly moved from a minor role to a dominant one in the economy, overshadowing the agricultural sector. In 1990, the percentage of agriculture in NDP dropped to just 4.8 percent, while that of industry increased to 41.7 percent, with services at 53.5 percent.

The process of economic transformation first began with the import-substitution policies of the 1950s and was further stimulated with the strategy of export promotion in the 1960s. Under import-substitution policies, agriculture supplied other sectors with food and industrial raw materials, earned foreign exchange for imported industrial machinery and inputs, and provided industry with low-cost labor. Most important, the agricultural sector was also a reliable market for nonfarm products, enabling the industrial sector to expand its production. Taiwan's small domestic market of consumer products that had been developed during the early 1950s was quickly saturated, however. To develop the economy further, the government changed from import substitution to export promotion in the late 1950s and early 1960s. Manufacturers in Taiwan were able to tap the surplus rural labor at a fairly low cost and exported labor-intensive goods to developed countries. In the meantime, Taiwan also exported capital- and skill-intensive goods to less-developed countries, where

TABLE 2–18
AGRICULTURAL TRADE IN TAIWAN, 1952–1990
(millions of U.S. dollars)

| Year | Agricultural Exports[a] | Agricultural Imports | Agriculture's Share of Total Exports | Agriculture's Share of Total Imports |
|------|------------|------------|------------------|------------------|
| 1952 | 114.2 | 66.5 | 95.5 | 32.1 |
| 1955 | 124.4 | 65.5 | 92.8 | 34.5 |
| 1960 | 121.0 | 75.8 | 71.0 | 30.1 |
| 1965 | 260.1 | 154.2 | 57.8 | 27.7 |
| 1970 | 310.2 | 376.5 | 21.7 | 24.6 |
| 1975 | 908.8 | 1,244.2 | 17.1 | 20.9 |
| 1980 | 1,876.5 | 3,090.0 | 9.5 | 15.7 |
| 1985 | 2,107.9 | 3,380.5 | 6.9 | 16.9 |
| 1990 | 3,488.6 | 5,778.6 | 5.2 | 10.6 |

a. Including processed agricultural products.
SOURCE: *Basic Agricultural Statistics*, ROC, Council of Agriculture, Executive Yuan, 1991.

the technical level was rather low. The industrial sector was also able to make use of its comparative advantage in various factor endowments in different export markets. In 1965, the surplus rural labor came to an end when the number of agricultural laborers began to decrease. The higher wage rates for unskilled workers stimulated the development of more capital- and skill-intensive industry in the 1970s. Thus, the dynamics of Taiwan's economic development changed in response to factor endowments and demand patterns.

The agricultural sector earned a large amount of foreign exchange in the 1950s and 1960s, helping to improve Taiwan's balance of international payments. Agriculture provided exports in exchange for the capital goods needed for industrial development. The increase in agricultural production made it possible to satisfy domestic food requirements while leaving a substantial surplus for export. Agricultural products long dominated the island's total exports, with a share ranging around 90 percent in the 1950s (table 2–18). Agriculture still financed more than half Taiwan's total imports before 1965, a crucial period in which the most serious constraint on economic development was the amount of available foreign exchange.

Even though total agricultural exports continued to increase after 1965 (see table 2–18), the share of agricultural exports in total exports decreased rapidly, because of the rapid expansion of the industrial sector. In 1970, the share of agricultural exports in total exports dropped to 21.7 percent, falling further to 17.1 percent in 1975 and to 5.2 percent in 1990. The share of agricultural imports in total imports, 32.1 percent in 1952, remained at about 30 percent until 1965. Since then, it has declined at a slower rate. By 1990, agricultural products accounted for only 10.6 percent of total imports, although this percentage was much higher than agriculture's share in total exports.

In 1952, Taiwan's major agricultural exports were sugar, rice, bananas, tea, citronella oil, and canned pineapple. Sugar and rice alone accounted for 81.4 percent of total agricultural exports that year. In 1970, the major agricultural exports were sugar, canned asparagus, canned mushrooms, bananas, timber, fishery products, other preserved vegetables, canned pineapple, tea, and preserved fruits. Together, sugar, canned asparagus, canned mushrooms, and bananas accounted for 45.8 percent of total agricultural exports. By 1990, however, the major agricultural exports had become fishery products, hogs and pork, other preserved vegetables, bananas, canned mushrooms, tea, rice, canned asparagus, sugar, and citrus fruits. Fishery products accounted for 36.1 percent of agricultural exports (see table 2–19). Nontraditional agricultural exports grew rapidly in this process. Asparagus and mushrooms, for example, were introduced to Taiwan as new crops in the early 1960s. Under the joint efforts of farmers, processors, and exporters, they became the major agricultural exports in the late 1960s. The development of aquaculture, particularly of eel and shrimp, in the 1970s also enabled these products to become among the most important exports since 1975. In addition to a steady stream of new technologies, Taiwan has actively sought out and exploited foreign market opportunities. All this agricultural diversification, however, has been due largely to successful adaptation by a well-educated, highly motivated farm population to changing demands.

Table 2–20 shows that agricultural imports of Taiwan increased very rapidly between 1960 and 1990, rising from U.S.$75.8 million to U.S.$5,788.6 million, a seventy-six-fold increase in a period of thirty years. The rate of increase in agricultural imports is obviously greater than that of agricultural exports. From 1952 to 1960, the major agricultural imports were soybeans, wheat, and cotton. Soybeans and wheat were used for human consumption, whereas cotton was used as raw material for the textile industry. By 1970, other imports such as lumber, corn, wool, dairy products, tobacco, and barley had become important. After 1970, imports of corn and fish meal increased rapidly because of the expansion of the livestock and aquaculture industries. The remarkable increase in the import of dairy

TABLE 2–19

TAIWAN'S AGRICULTURAL EXPORTS, 1952–1990

(millions of U.S. dollars)

| Item | 1952 | 1960 | 1970 | 1980 | 1990 |
|---|---|---|---|---|---|
| Total agricultural exports | 114.2 | 121.0 | 310.2 | 1,876.5 | 3,488.6 |
| Primary agricultural products | 33.7 | 21.4 | 89.1 | 695.3 | 2,192.4 |
| Rice | 23.3 | 4.3 | 0.8 | 59.9 | 13.9 |
| Vegetables | 0.8 | 2.5 | 8.8 | 36.6 | 36.7 |
| Bananas | 6.6 | 6.9 | 31.1 | 25.5 | 28.4 |
| Pineapples | 0 | 0 | 4.1 | 1.2 | 2.4 |
| Citrus fruits | 0 | 0 | 4.4 | 9.6 | 10.2 |
| Other fruits | 0.8 | 0.6 | 1.5 | 7.0 | 22.0 |
| Flax and fiber | 0.5 | 1.5 | 0.8 | 0.9 | 0 |
| Medicinal herbs | 0 | 0.2 | 0.8 | 3.3 | 0 |
| Tobacco | 0 | 0.3 | 2.1 | 7.6 | 0 |
| Hogs and pork | 0 | 2.6 | 6.5 | 63.5 | 662.1 |
| Poultry feathers | 1.6 | 1.3 | 3.5 | 34.0 | 118.5 |
| Fishery products | 0 | 0.4 | 20.6 | 396.5 | 807.3 |
| Others | 0.1 | 0.8 | 4.1 | 49.7 | 490.9 |
| Processed agricultural products | 80.5 | 99.6 | 221.2 | 1,181.2 | 1,296.2 |
| Sugar | 69.7 | 74.4 | 45.4 | 227.9 | 25.6 |
| Tea | 5.8 | 6.3 | 12.7 | 28.5 | 20.9 |
| Canned pineapple | 2.0 | 8.5 | 19.4 | 20.6 | 0.1 |
| Preserved fruits | 0.2 | 0.9 | 10.7 | 130.8 | 80.5 |
| Canned mushrooms | 0 | 0.2 | 32.0 | 108.8 | 23.5 |
| Canned asparagus | 0 | 0 | 33.6 | 134.5 | 5.0 |
| Other preserved vegetables | 0 | 0 | 20.1 | 197.8 | 292.2 |
| Citronella oil | 2.4 | 3.5 | 3.7 | 0.4 | 0 |
| Peppermint and camphor | 0.3 | 2.8 | 2.5 | 0.8 | 0 |
| Timber (excluding plywood) | 0 | 2.8 | 28.5 | 65.5 | 91.2 |
| Bamboo products | 0.1 | 0.2 | 1.2 | 11.2 | 65.4 |
| Processed fishery products | 0 | 0 | 2.1 | 164.7 | 451.4 |
| Others | 0 | 0 | 9.2 | 89.7 | 240.4 |

SOURCE: Same as table 2–18.

products and beef during the same period was in response to improved living standards in Taiwan.

In 1990, Japan was by far the most important export market for Taiwan's agricultural products, accounting for about 66 percent of the total. The United States followed with 9 percent and the European Community with 4 percent. As for agricultural imports, the United States was the main supplier, providing 41 percent of Taiwan's total

TABLE 2–20

TAIWAN'S AGRICULTURAL IMPORTS, 1952–1990

(millions of U.S. dollars)

| Item | 1952 | 1960 | 1970 | 1980 | 1990 |
|------|------|------|------|------|------|
| Corn | 0 | 0 | 41.7 | 437.6 | 702.8 |
| Wheat | 13.7 | 17.0 | 38.9 | 146.4 | 162.5 |
| Barley | 0 | 0 | 12.4 | 61.6 | 39.0 |
| Other cereals | 0 | 0 | 0.3 | 69.8 | 9.2 |
| Cotton | 13.2 | 20.3 | 66.8 | 406.7 | 408.3 |
| Wool | 2.6 | 3.1 | 22.6 | 98.5 | 142.0 |
| Soybeans | 17.4 | 17.0 | 73.6 | 292.3 | 511.3 |
| Tobacco | 0.8 | 2.1 | 12.8 | 70.7 | 191.3 |
| Dairy products | 2.0 | 2.3 | 14.0 | 110.1 | 297.6 |
| Fishery products | 4.8 | 0.5 | 2.0 | 78.5 | 219.2 |
| Hides and leather | 1.8 | 1.4 | 5.1 | 85.0 | 551.0 |
| Logs and lumber | 1.5 | 2.7 | 48.9 | 681.1 | 845.5 |
| Fruits and nuts | 0.2 | 0.1 | 3.0 | 73.8 | 251.7 |
| Vegetables | 1.5 | 0.1 | 4.0 | 22.6 | 139.1 |
| Medicinal herbs | 2.2 | 2.9 | 5.1 | 77.5 | 82.2 |
| Fish meals | 0 | 0 | 7.1 | 89.4 | 252.7 |
| Beef | 0 | 0 | 0.2 | 30.9 | 143.6 |
| Others | 4.8 | 6.3 | 18.0 | 257.5 | 839.6 |
| Total agricultural imports | 66.5 | 75.8 | 376.5 | 3,090.0 | 5,788.6 |

SOURCE: Same as table 2–18.

agricultural imports. Other sources were Malaysia, 9 percent; Australia, 8 percent; and Japan, 6 percent. An overly high concentration in both export and import markets is one of the major problems of Taiwan's agricultural trade.

## Change in the Sources of Farm Family Income

Farm family income in Taiwan consists of two major components, net agricultural income and nonagricultural income. Data on farm family income in Taiwan in the selected years from 1966 to 1990 are shown in table 2–21. In 1966, total average farm family income was NT$32,320, of which NT$21,314 was net agricultural income and NT$11,006 was nonagricultural income. The net agricultural income and the nonagricultural income accounted for 65.9 percent and 34.1 percent of the total, respectively. It clearly shows that up to 1966, the net agricultural income was much more important than off-farm income to a farm family. Since 1970, though, net agricultural income

41

TABLE 2–21

FARM FAMILY INCOME IN TAIWAN, 1966–1990

(N.T. dollars per family and percent)

| Year | Net Agricultural Income | | Nonagricultural Income | | Total |
|------|------------|--------|-------------|--------|---------|
| 1966 | 21,314 | (65.9) | 11,006 | (34.1) | 32,320 |
| 1970 | 18,480 | (45.2) | 22,378 | (54.8) | 40,858 |
| 1975 | 39,853 | (46.3) | 46,208 | (53.7) | 86,061 |
| 1980 | 58,511 | (29.6) | 139,022 | (70.4) | 197,533 |
| 1985 | 95,929 | (36.7) | 165,527 | (63.3) | 261,456 |
| 1990 | 136,841 | (35.2) | 252,014 | (64.8) | 388,855 |

SOURCE: *Basic Agricultural Statistics*, Republic of China, Council of Agriculture, Executive Yuan, 1991.

has become less important. In 1975, total average farm family income was NT$86,061, of which NT$39,853 was net agricultural income and NT$46,208 was nonagricultural income. Compared with 1966, nonagricultural income increased 319.8 percent, while net agricultural income increased only 87.0 percent. Thus, in 1975, the percentage share of net agricultural income dropped to 46.3 percent, and the percentage share of nonagricultural income increased to 53.7 percent.

From 1975 to 1980, nonagricultural income increased 200 percent, and net agricultural income grew only 46.8 percent. Therefore, the share of net agricultural income in total farm family income dropped further, to less than 30 percent in 1980. Since then, net agricultural income and nonagricultural income have expanded at more or less the same pace. In 1990, net agricultural income and nonagricultural income were 35.2 percent and 64.8 percent of total farm family income, respectively. Clearly, farm families were able to supplement their agricultural earning with other income. Since those relying on agricultural income tend to be poorer, earnings from other sources keep the income differentials between farm families and nonfarm families to a minimum and contribute to a more equitable income distribution.

Table 2–22 shows the sources of nonagricultural income of farm families from 1966 to 1990. Wages and salaries were by far the most important nonagricultural earnings. They accounted for 59.1 percent of total nonagricultural income in 1966, increased to more than 70 percent in 1970–1980, and then decreased to 59.2 percent in 1990. The rapid increase in wages and salaries of farm families from 1966 to 1980 may be attributed to the significant migration of farm family

TABLE 2–22

SOURCES OF NONAGRICULTURAL INCOME OF FARM FAMILIES IN
TAIWAN, 1966–1990

(percent)

|  | 1966 | 1970 | 1975 | 1980 | 1990 |
|---|---|---|---|---|---|
| Wages and salaries | 59.1 | 70.2 | 72.4 | 72.0 | 59.2 |
| Other professional income | 8.2 | 5.3 | 5.2 | 5.7 | 3.9 |
| Property income | 2.1 | 1.0 | 1.1 | 3.1 | 4.8 |
| Imputed house rent | 19.1 | 13.8 | 12.9 | 11.5 | 12.2 |
| Grants and subsidies | 9.1 | 7.2 | 7.3 | 7.4 | 19.7 |
| Other | 3.4 | 2.5 | 1.1 | 0.3 | 0.2 |

SOURCE: See table 2–21.

members to the industrial and service sectors during this period. Farmers' health insurance and the increase in grants and subsidies resulting from programs to shift from rice production to other crops probably explains the reduction of the share of wages and salaries in 1990. Many former rice growers received subsidies from the government after they changed from rice production to other crops or fallow.

In implementing farmers' health insurance, government shoulders 70 percent of premiums for participating farmers, an amount of about NT$198 per person per month. Through these programs, the government directly subsidizes the farmers either in production or in social welfare. In the category of grants and subsidies, however, private transfer income is also included, but the annual variation of this transfer is rather small. Hence, the big jump in the share of grants and subsidies in 1990 was caused mainly by the increase in government subsidies.

We can further analyze farm family income by type of farm household. Data are available for the years of 1980, 1985, and 1990 as shown in table 2–23. In 1980, the average total farm family income was NT$174,505 for the full-time farm, NT$194,077 for the part-time farm, and NT$231,744 for the sideline farm. The sideline farm had the highest total family income, and the full-time farm had the lowest total family income, with the part-time farm in between. This fact explains the phenomenon that more and more full-time farms have become either part-time farms or sideline farms in the past four decades. In recent years, the percentages of nonagricultural income in the part-time farm and the sideline farm decreased because of the greater increase in the net agricultural income in these farms. This

TABLE 2–23

FARM FAMILY INCOME BY TYPE OF HOUSEHOLD IN TAIWAN, 1980, 1985, AND 1990

(N.T. dollars)

| Type of Farm Household | Net Farm Income | Nonfarm Income | Total Family Income | Percent of Nonfarm to Totals |
|---|---|---|---|---|
| *1980* | | | | |
| Full-time | 118,820 | 55,685 | 174,505 | 31.91 |
| Part-time | 89,941 | 104,136 | 194,077 | 53.66 |
| Sideline | 33,234 | 198,511 | 231,745 | 85.66 |
| *1985* | | | | |
| Full-time | 136,079 | 50,501 | 186,580 | 27.07 |
| Part-time | 147,757 | 143,495 | 291,252 | 49.27 |
| Sideline | 43,646 | 281,413 | 325,059 | 86.57 |
| *1990* | | | | |
| Full-time | 171,721 | 100,283 | 272,004 | 36.87 |
| Part-time | 264,493 | 186,756 | 451,249 | 41.39 |
| Sideline | 133,165 | 403,170 | 536,335 | 75.17 |

SOURCE: *Farm Income Survey*, Taiwan Provincial Department of Budget, Accounting, and Statistics. PDBAS; various years.

change may be explained by recent, and more favorable, agricultural policies.

Table 2–24 shows farm family income by size of farm from 1980 to 1990 in Taiwan. The statistics in the table show that the net agricultural income of farm families is positively correlated with the size of the farm; in contrast, the nonagricultural income of farm families is negatively correlated with the size of farm. Hence the smaller farm has a higher percentage of nonfarm income. With only a few exceptions, total farm family income is also positively correlated with the size of farm. Total farm family income, however, is not proportionately correlated with the size of farm. Therefore, the differences in the total farm family income among different sizes of farms are not as significant as the differences in the size of farms.

## Changes in Food Consumption Patterns and the Food Self-Sufficiency Rate

During the past four decades (1952–1990), the population of Taiwan has increased at an annual rate of 2.5 percent, while agricultural

TABLE 2–24
FARM FAMILY INCOME IN TAIWAN BY SIZE OF FARM,
1980, 1985, AND 1990
(N.T. dollars)

| Farm Size | Net Farm Income | Nonfarm Income | Total Family Income | Percent of Nonfarm to Total |
|---|---|---|---|---|
| *1980* | | | | |
| < 0.25 ha. | 17,892 | 182,381 | 200,273 | 91.07 |
| 0.25–0.50 ha. | 26,905 | 173,089 | 199,994 | 86.55 |
| 0.50–0.75 ha. | 41,875 | 176,494 | 218,369 | 80.82 |
| 0.75–1.00 ha. | 58,273 | 164,884 | 223,157 | 73.89 |
| 1.00–1.50 ha. | 72,618 | 150,134 | 222,752 | 67.40 |
| 1.50–2.00 ha. | 97,059 | 135,160 | 232,219 | 58.20 |
| >2.00 ha. | 139,162 | 127,861 | 267,023 | 47.88 |
| Average | 52,898 | 164,553 | 217,451 | 75.67 |
| *1985* | | | | |
| < 0.25 ha. | 22,086 | 254,275 | 276,361 | 92.01 |
| 0.25–0.50 ha. | 38,114 | 245,803 | 283,917 | 86.58 |
| 0.50–0.75 ha. | 58,601 | 240,084 | 298,685 | 80.38 |
| 0.75–1.00 ha. | 83,517 | 223,147 | 306,664 | 72.77 |
| 1.00–1.50 ha. | 103,892 | 191,943 | 295,835 | 64.88 |
| 1.50–2.00 ha. | 134,484 | 175,874 | 310,358 | 56.67 |
| >2.00 ha. | 203,257 | 163,996 | 367,253 | 44.65 |
| Average | 74,329 | 224,325 | 298,654 | 75.11 |
| *1990* | | | | |
| < 0.25 ha. | 32,264 | 438,050 | 470,314 | 93.14 |
| 0.25–0.50 ha. | 47,535 | 421,282 | 468,817 | 89.86 |
| 0.50–0.75 ha. | 82,853 | 383,937 | 466,790 | 82.25 |
| 0.75–1.00 ha. | 93,705 | 387,706 | 481,411 | 80.54 |
| 1.00–1.50 ha. | 138,568 | 322,019 | 460,587 | 69.91 |
| 1.50–2.00 ha. | 211,278 | 308,067 | 519,345 | 59.32 |
| >2.00 ha. | 271,279 | 266,727 | 538,006 | 49.58 |
| Average | 97,109 | 380,320 | 477,429 | 79.66 |

SOURCE: *Farm Income Survey*, PDBAS; various years.

production grew at 4.0 percent. The higher growth in agricultural production indicates that agriculture has been able to provide enough food at reasonable prices to meet the rising demand of an increasing population. Daily per capita calorie intake increased from 2,078 to 3,019, and protein intake, from 49 to 90 grams from 1952 to 1990.

TABLE 2–25

PER CAPITA ANNUAL FOOD CONSUMPTION IN TAIWAN, 1952–1990

(kilograms)

| Item | 1952 | 1960 | 1970 | 1980 | 1990 |
|---|---|---|---|---|---|
| Cereals | | | | | |
| Polished rice | 126.1 | 137.7 | 134.5 | 100.8 | 68.2 |
| Wheat flour | 11.3 | 20.0 | 25.4 | 23.6 | 28.9 |
| Total | 138.1 | 159.7 | 164.1 | 138.8 | 102.4 |
| Sweet potatoes | 59.9 | 65.4 | 18.4 | 4.1 | 2.0 |
| Sugar | 9.4 | 9.4 | 15.0 | 24.0 | 25.3 |
| Pulses, nuts, and seeds | 9.9 | 11.4 | 18.3 | 18.8 | 22.4 |
| Vegetables | 61.7 | 61.1 | 84.8 | 129.6 | 105.9 |
| Fruits | 16.8 | 22.1 | 45.8 | 70.2 | 108.9 |
| Meat | 16.8 | 16.2 | 25.3 | 39.6 | 61.9 |
| Eggs | 1.6 | 1.6 | 4.1 | 8.0 | 12.4 |
| Fish | 15.1 | 21.7 | 34.2 | 38.7 | 47.4 |
| Milk | 1.2 | 3.2 | 11.0 | 27.6 | 37.2 |
| Oils and fats | 3.5 | 4.7 | 7.7 | 10.8 | 20.3 |

SOURCE: *Basic Agricultural Statistics*, R.O.C., Council of Agriculture, Executive Years, 1991.

Table 2–25 shows changes in the food consumption patterns during the period 1952 to 1990. Food consumption increased in all categories from 1952 to 1960. Since 1970, however, the per capita consumption of sweet potatoes and rice has decreased significantly, and consumption of meat, sugar, vegetables, fruits, and milk has increased markedly. The change in the pattern of food consumption came about mainly because of increased per capita income in Taiwan. The increase in meat and fish consumption has not only provided an opportunity for the development of livestock and fishery industries but also resulted in a big increase in imports of feed stuffs. Increased consumption of vegetables and fruit has also pushed farmers to change the composition of crop production toward more vegetables and fruits.

Improvements in the level and the pattern of consumption, together with slower growth in agricultural production, have in recent years caused a decline in the food self-sufficiency rate. Before 1968, when domestic food production could meet domestic requirements, the rate remained at around 100 percent (on value basis). The rate rose as high as 108 percent in 1964 but dropped to only 93 percent in 1990. Thus, about 7 percent of domestic requirements must be met

TABLE 2–26
FOOD SELF-SUFFICIENCY RATE IN TAIWAN, 1950–1990
(percent)

| Item | 1950 | 1960 | 1970 | 1980 | 1990 |
|---|---|---|---|---|---|
| Cereals | 103 | 93 | 82 | 66 | 62 |
| Rice | 110 | 102 | 104 | 113 | 110 |
| Others | 27 | 21 | 6 | 3 | 8 |
| Starchy food | 100 | 100 | 101 | 102 | 89 |
| Sugar | 826 | 739 | 280 | 200 | 94 |
| Pulses, nuts, and seeds | 60 | 66 | 31 | 16 | 12 |
| Vegetables | 100 | 100 | 160 | 147 | 111 |
| Fruits | 106 | 127 | 148 | 110 | 92 |
| Meat | 100 | 102 | 102 | 99 | 107 |
| Eggs | 100 | 100 | 101 | 101 | 100 |
| Fish | 84 | 100 | 120 | 123 | 132 |
| Milk | 4 | 13 | 11 | 11 | 27 |
| Total food | 105 | 99 | 97 | 92 | 93 |

NOTE: Rate $= \dfrac{\text{Domestic production (supply)}}{\text{Domestic consumption (demand)}} \times 100$.

SOURCE: See table 2–25.

with imports. Taiwan has had to rely heavily on imports to satisfy the domestic demand for wheat, corn, soybeans, other feed grains, and dairy products (see table 2–26).

## Stages of Agricultural Development

Postwar agricultural development in Taiwan may be divided into phases, with different characteristics.

**Recovery and Rehabilitation, 1946–1951.** In the immediate postwar years, acute pressure on food prices threatened the livelihood of the population. Because of a large influx of migrants from mainland China during 1945–1950, the population increased at an annual rate of 4.9 percent. Therefore, food prices, relative to the general price level, were favorable to farmers. With high farm prices and a steady supply of inputs, agricultural production increased rapidly. By 1951, agricultural output had surpassed the prewar peak during the Japanese colonial period.

Between 1946 and 1951, agricultural production grew 15.6 percent a year, with the growth of crops, 14.4 percent; livestock, 19.0

percent; and forestry, 30.2 percent. Three factors contributed to this agricultural recovery and rehabilitation: (1) rapid increase in labor input, expansion of crop area, and active promotion of multiple-crop diversification; (2) introduction of better production techniques, rehabilitation of irrigation facilities, and reorganization of farmers' associations; and (3) implementation of a land-rent reduction program in 1949, which induced tenant farmers to increase production.

**Sustained Growth of Agriculture, 1951–1964.** Agriculture continued to progress after its recovery. Despite limited land resources and the small size of farms, agricultural production grew 5.6 percent per year during 1951–1964, of which the growth rate of crops was 4.4 percent; livestock, 6.8 percent; fisheries, 9.2 percent; and forestry, 9.4 percent. Successful land reform (the Land-to-the-Tiller Program) was the most important factor in the agricultural progress in this period. This program, launched at the beginning of 1953, produced very desirable results. It provided an incentive for intensive use of both land and labor resources through the application of modern farming technology, such as the high-yielding varieties of crops, chemical fertilizers, pesticides, and new cropping systems and patterns.

As the economy became more sophisticated, many new and high-value products were developed, including mushrooms and asparagus. With strong foreign demand, exports of these commodities rose rapidly and helped to boost farm income. The agricultural labor force continued to increase in this phase until 1964. The multiple-cropping index also reached its peak of 189.7 in 1964. After that, both the agricultural labor force and the multiple-cropping index began to decline. Thereafter, farm machinery was introduced as a substitute for manual labor.

**Agricultural Slowdown, 1964–1973.** By the latter half of the 1960s, a considerable outflow of farm labor had resulted in a labor shortage. The situation was especially serious during planting and harvesting seasons. Consequently, farm wages rose substantially. In the meantime, significant changes in cropping systems and patterns also took place. Livestock production expanded greatly, along with per capita real income. The growth rate of crop production continued to decline, owing to the decrease in both crop area and farm labor. The multiple-cropping index fell from 189.7 in 1964 to 174.9 in 1973, indicating a less intensive use of farmland. Rice production also decreased from 2.5 million tons in 1968 to 2.2 million tons in 1973. The total area planted in winter crops (sweet potatoes, rapeseed, flax, and wheat) also showed a significant decline. The growth rate of crop production dropped to 2.2 percent in this period. The most dynamic were the livestock sector and the fishery sector, which grew at 9.3 and 9.6 percent per year, respectively. Per capita farm family income dropped from 70 percent of per capita nonfarm income in the previous period to about 60 percent. The income gap between the farm and the nonfarm sectors encouraged members of farm families to seek employment in the cities or nearby towns.

Consequently, the share of farm family earnings from sources other than farming increased considerably. Farm families became less dependent on farming for their living. Agricultural development showed signs of stagnation in this period. In the absence of government action, the disparity between the farm sector and the nonfarm sector typically becomes wider, adversely affecting economic development. When this disparity became troubling, the government started to give agriculture generous support and marked an end of this phase.

**Strong Government Support of Agriculture, 1973–1983.** During the 1960s, the annual growth of industry was much higher than that of agriculture, widening the income gap between the farm and the nonfarm sectors. In short, it was time for the government to change policy by giving the agricultural sector more support. In 1973, the Accelerated Rural Development Program was instituted. In addition to the regular budget for agricultural development, the government made a special grant of NT$2 billion to facilitate implementation of the program. In the same year, the long-awaited Agricultural Development Act was issued.

In 1974, the Rice Stabilization Fund was established to provide a guaranteed price for rice growers. The major policy measures for agricultural development since 1973 have been aimed at: (1) changing the agricultural production structure; (2) raising agricultural productivity; (3) encouraging innovation in the agricultural marketing system; (4) reducing the farmers' financial burden; (5) increasing agricultural investment; (6) maximizing the service function of farmers' organizations; and (7) enhancing rural welfare and farmers' livelihood. With strong support from the government, agriculture gathered new strength for further development. The agricultural policy also brought a significant change in farm cultivation methods and agricultural structure. During these years, farm machinery replaced a large number of farm workers in agricultural production.

The greatest influence on agriculture at this time came from measures that reduced agricultural taxation and the costs of inputs, on the one hand, and the support programs that subsidized the prices farmers received, on the other. These new price support measures brought about a supply response, with rice production reaching an all-time high of 2.71 million metric tons in 1976. When the government, in support of the rice price, purchased rice in excess of domestic demand, however, large surpluses accumulated: government stocks went from 211,000 metric tons in 1974 to 914,000 metric tons in 1977. At that time the government changed its procurement policy by limiting the purchase to 970 kilograms of paddy rice per hectare per crop. This measure had only a limited effect, as government stocks continued to grow, reaching 1.3 million metric tons in 1984. The surplus of rice had become a very serious agricultural problem. To solve it, a measure to reduce rice production was carried out in 1984, thus marking a new phase of agricultural development with policies emphasizing the structural adjustment of agriculture and facing the impact of economic liberalization.

During this period, too, the government tried to expand the operational size of the farm through encouraging group farming without affecting the existing pattern of land ownership. The government fostered many forms of group farming, particularly joint operation, entrusted farming, and joint management and promotion of specialized agricultural production areas. The most popular mode of group farming, joint operation, organizes farmers to work together on specific operations such as land preparation, transplanting, and harvesting, for example, or a combination of operations from land preparation to harvesting on adjacent farms. These groups can therefore own and use expensive machinery jointly.

Because of the individualistic nature of the farmers, highly fragmented land ownership, and the rigidity of the land tenure system, the process of enlarging the operational farm size evolved slowly and without significant achievement in this period. The growth rate of agricultural production dropped from 5.0 percent annually in the previous period to 2.9 percent in this period. The growth of crop production was only 0.3 percent, while the growth of livestock and fisheries was 6.6 percent and 4.0 percent, respectively. If there had been no strong government support, agriculture would have been in a much more unfavorable position in this phase. The turning point occurred in 1973, when the government exchanged a strategy of taxing agriculture for one of supporting it. This transition is typical of a country's graduating from "developing" to "developed."

**Structural Adjustment of Agriculture, 1983–Present.** Since the early 1980s, the government of the Republic of China has taken measures to liberalize the economy to stimulate further development. The concept of economic liberalization is very broad, embracing many meanings such as the relaxation of import controls, the reduction of price and production distortions, and the improvement of the functioning of foreign exchange rates and the monetary market. The major purpose of this policy is to enlarge both domestic and foreign markets for the expanding economy. Agriculture has to comply with the national economic policy. To some degree, import controls on agricultural products have been relaxed, a development the United States insisted on to reduce somewhat the enormous bilateral trade surplus of Taiwan. Therefore, in this phase agricultural policy is characterized by the implementation of a so-called structural adjustment.

The first action taken by the government was to carry out the second phase of the Farmland Reform Program in 1983, which was aimed to promote land use, labor productivity, and larger-scale farming. The program includes provision of loans for the purchase of land to expand farming scale; promotion of joint, entrusted, and cooperative farming; acceleration of land consolidation; extension of farm mechanization; and revision of related laws and statutes to help ensure the successful implementation of this program. Perhaps these measures can break through the bottleneck of small farm size and establish a new land tenure system that will allow the enlargement of farm operations without affecting land ownership. Following the institution of the program, the Statute of Agricultural Development and the 37.5 Percent Rent Reduction Act were amended to give entrusted farming and custom farming a stronger legal basis by clearly stating that these types of farming will be excluded from the 37.5 Percent Rent Reduction Act. This simple statement, however, does not win the confidence of farmers, and the new tenure system still faces many difficulties in the extension process.

Second, the government has been encouraging production diversification away from rice and toward higher-valued crops and products more consistent with the emerging pattern of consumer demand. A Six-Year Rice Crop Substitution Plan was implemented in 1984, which gave paid-in-kind subsidy to farmers for shifting their rice fields to other crops. To reduce the management cost of the program, the paid-in-kind subsidy was changed to a cash payment in 1988. As a result, rice production fell from 2.49 million metric tons in 1983 to 1.81 million metric tons in 1990, a decrease of 678,600 metric tons in seven years. Two other grain crops grew enormously during this same time span; that is, the production of corn and sorghum rose from 143,165 metric tons to 339,436 metric tons and from 13,699 metric tons to 101,582 metric tons, respectively.

In relative terms, rice accounted for only 12.1 percent of the value of total agricultural production in 1990, and all crops combined, for 44.1 percent, while livestock and fisheries accounted for 27.0 percent and 28.4 percent, respectively. In response to market demand, the production of fruits and vegetables showed a great increase during this period. Other common crops and special crops showed a dramatic decline. Clearly, the agricultural composition in Taiwan has undergone a significant adjustment.

Finally, a crucial development during the present phase has been the large expansion in total agricultural imports and, to a lesser extent, that of agricultural exports. In 1980, the total value of agricultural exports was U.S.$1.88 billion, and that of imports was U.S.$3.09 billion, resulting in a deficit of U.S.$1.21 billion. In 1990, the total value of agricultural exports was U.S.$3.49 billion, and the total value of agricultural imports was U.S.$5.78 billion; the trade deficit increased to U.S.$2.29 billion. Some of the import liberalization measures are likely to have contributed to the rapid expansion of imports and to the enlargement of the agricultural trade deficit. The agricultural adjustment and liberalization process is evolving rapidly at the moment. Agricultural policy in the future will probably continue to emphasize the enlargement of the operational size of farm, the training of core farmers, the encouragement of farm mechanization, some revision of protectionist policies, and the greater investment in research to identify appropriate mechanized technologies.

## References

Ho, Samuel P. S. "Agricultural Transformation under Colonialism: The Case of Taiwan." *Journal of Economic History*, 28 (September 1986).

Lee, T. H. *Intersectoral Capital Flows in the Economic Development of Taiwan, 1895–1960*. Ithaca, N.Y.: Cornell University Press, 1971.

———. *Strategies for Transferring Agricultural Surplus under Agricultural Situations in Taiwan*. JCRR Report, July 19, 1971.

Mao, Y. K. "Agricultural Development Policy and Performance in Taiwan, R.O.C." Industry of Free China, November and December 1984 and January 1985. Taipei, Taiwan.

———. "Analysis of Changes in the Type of Farm Household under Rapid Economic Growth in Taiwan, R.O.C." *Proceedings of the Conference on Direction and Strategies of Agricultural Development in the Asia-Pacific Region*. January 5–7, 1988. The Institute of Economics, Academia Sinica, ROC.

Mao, Y. K., and C. Shive. "Agricultural and Industrial Development of the Republic of China on Taiwan." Paper presented at the International Conference on Agriculture on the Road to Industrialization. September 4–7, 1990, Taiwan, ROC.

Shen, T. H., ed. "Agriculture's Place in the Strategy of Development: The Taiwan Experience." *JCRR* (Taipei), (July 1974).

Thorbecke, Erik. "Agricultural Development." In *Economic Growth and Structural Change in Taiwan*, edited by Walter Galenson. Ithaca, N.Y.: Cornell University Press, 1979.

Yager, J. A. *Transforming Agriculture in Taiwan: The Experience of the Joint Commission on Rural Reconstruction*. Ithaca, N.Y.: Cornell University Press, 1988.

# 3
# Structure and Change in the Agriculture of the United States

*D. Gale Johnson*

The United States had approximately 400 million hectares of land in farms in 1990, of which 138 million hectares was cropland from which crops could be harvested. The actual area of land on which crops were harvested was 116 million hectares. The total area in farms has gradually declined, having been 487 million hectares in 1955. Table 3–1 provides data on total land in farms, the area of land devoted to crops, the amount of cropland harvested, and the area of irrigated land.

## Cultivated Land

The amount of land devoted to crops is greater than the amount of cropland harvested for three reasons. First, some land is deliberately left fallow or unused in drier areas to accumulate moisture for the subsequent year. Second, each year some cropland is planted and abandoned because of adverse weather conditions, either too dry or too wet. Finally, under the farm programs, described in chapter 5, some land has been idled in an effort to limit the production of several crops. The idled land must generally be cultivated to control weeds and to minimize erosion. In recent years, however, several million hectares of former cropland has been placed in a conservation reserve and is no longer counted as cropland. In 1991, this reserve included 14 million hectares.

The United States does not have land comparable to paddy fields. A significant amount of land is irrigated in the United States, however. In 1987, the area of irrigated land was 18 million hectares or about a seventh of total cropland.

## TABLE 3–1

### AREA OF AGRICULTURAL LAND IN THE UNITED STATES AND AREA OF IRRIGATED LAND, 1950–1990

| Year | Total Farmland | Cropland | Harvested Land | Irrigated Land[a] |
|------|----------------|----------|----------------|-------------------|
| 1950 | 487 | 153 | 136 | 11[a] |
| 1955 | 487 | 153 | 135 | 12[a] |
| 1960 | 476 | 144 | 128 | 13[a] |
| 1965 | 461 | 136 | 118[a] | 15[a] |
| 1970 | 446 | 134 | 117[a] | 16[a] |
| 1975 | 429 | 149 | 134 | 20 |
| 1980 | 421 | 165 | 138 | 20[b] |
| 1985 | 411 | 151 | 135 | 20 |
| 1990 | 400 | 138 | 126 | 20[c] |

a. Data are for prior year.
b. 1978
c. 1987
SOURCE: U.S. Department of Agriculture, *Economic Indicators of the Farm Sector*, various issues; and *Agricultural Statistics 1991*.

## The Agricultural Labor Force and Farms

In 1952, the agricultural labor force was 6.50 million persons. The labor force has declined significantly since that time, with a particularly rapid decline between 1952 and 1970, when the farm labor force dropped 49 percent. Since that time, the decline has been modest, with employment at 3.2 million in 1990.

As a share of national employment, agricultural employment declined from 10.8 percent in 1952 to 2.7 percent in 1990 (table 3–2). The decline in farm employment was the result of migration to the cities or the cessation of farming with the family remaining in the same house. Most of the decline, however, resulted from an actual change of residence or by one or more members of a household undertaking nonfarm work.

In 1952, there were 5,198,000 farms in the United States (table 3–3), accounting for nearly the same percentage of total households as farm employment did of national employment at 11.4 percent. Farm families, however, were on the average larger than nonfarm families, and farm population accounted for 15.5 percent of total population.

The decline in the number of farms from 1952 to 1970 closely paralleled the decline in farm employment, with the number of farms declining by 56 percent, somewhat more than the decline in employ-

## TABLE 3–2
### EMPLOYED POPULATION IN THE UNITED STATES, 1952–1990

| Year | Employed Population (thousands) | | | | Percentages | | |
|---|---|---|---|---|---|---|---|
| | Total | Agriculture | Industry | Services[a] | Agriculture | Industry | Services |
| 1952 | 60,250 | 6,500 | 20,298 | 33,552 | 10.8 | 33.5 | 55.7 |
| 1955 | 63,170 | 6,450 | 20,513 | 35,207 | 10.4 | 33.0 | 56.6 |
| 1960 | 65,778 | 5,458 | 20,434 | 39,886 | 8.3 | 31.15 | 60.6 |
| 1965 | 71,088 | 4,361 | 21,926 | 44,801 | 6.1 | 30.8 | 69.7 |
| 1970 | 78,678 | 3,463 | 23,578 | 51,637 | 4.4 | 30.0 | 65.6 |
| 1975 | 85,846 | 3,408 | 22,600 | 59,838 | 4.0 | 26.3 | 69.7 |
| 1980 | 99,303 | 3,364 | 26,658 | 69,281 | 3.4 | 26.8 | 69.7 |
| 1985 | 107,150 | 3,179 | 24,859 | 79,112 | 3.0 | 23.2 | 73.8 |
| 1990 | 114,814 | 3,186 | 24,958 | 86,670 | 2.7 | 21.2 | 75.5 |

a. Including all government employment.
SOURCES: *Economic Report of the President, 1992.*

## TABLE 3–3
### FARM AND NONFARM HOUSEHOLDS AND POPULATION IN THE UNITED STATES, 1952–1990
(thousands)

| | Households | | | Population | | |
|---|---|---|---|---|---|---|
| Year | Total | Farm | Farms as % of total | Total | Farm | Farm population as % of total |
| 1952 | 45,504 | 5,198 | 11.4 | 157,022 | 24,283 | 15.46 |
| 1955 | 47,874 | 4,654 | 9.7 | 165,931 | 19,078 | 11.50 |
| 1960 | 52,799 | 3,963 | 7.5 | 180,671 | 15,635 | 8.65 |
| 1965 | 57,251 | 3,356 | 5.9 | 194,303 | 12,363 | 6.36 |
| 1970 | 63,401 | 2,949 | 4.7 | 205,052 | 9,712 | 4.74 |
| 1975 | 71,120 | 2,521 | 3.5 | 215,353 | 8,864 | 4.12 |
| 1980 | 80,776 | 2,433 | 3.0 | 227,061 | 7,241 | 3.19 |
| 1985 | 86,789 | 2,275 | 2.6 | 239,279 | 5,355 | 2.24 |
| 1990 | 93,347 | 2,143 | 2.3 | 249,975 | 4,750 | 1.90 |

SOURCES: U.S. Department of Commerce, *Statistical Abstract of the United States*, 1955, 1965, 1975, 1986, 1988 and 1990; and U.S. Department of Agriculture, *Economic Indicators of the Farm Sector*, various issues.

## TABLE 3–4

TOTAL FARMLAND, NUMBER OF FARMS AND FARM WORKERS, AND
FARMLAND PER FARM AND PER FARM WORKER IN THE UNITED STATES,
1950–1990

| Year | Cultivated Farmland[a] (millions of hectares) | Farms (thousands) | Farm Workers (thousands) | Average Cultivated Land[b] | |
|------|------|------|------|------|------|
| | | | | Farm | Farm worker[b] |
| 1950 | 153 | 5,648 | 7,160 | 27 | 21 |
| 1955 | 153 | 4,654 | 6,450 | 33 | 24 |
| 1960 | 144 | 3,963 | 5,458 | 36 | 26 |
| 1965 | 136 | 3,356 | 4,361 | 41 | 31 |
| 1970 | 134 | 2,949 | 3,463 | 45 | 39 |
| 1975 | 149 | 2,521 | 3,408 | 59 | 44 |
| 1980 | 165 | 2,440 | 3,384 | 68 | 49 |
| 1984 | 151 | 2,334 | 3,321 | 65 | 45 |
| 1985 | 151 | 2,293 | 3,179 | 66 | 47 |
| 1986 | 144 | 2,250 | 3,163 | 64 | 46 |
| 1988 | 132 | 2,197 | 3,169 | 60 | 42 |
| 1990 | 138 | 2,140 | 3,186 | 64 | 43 |

a. See table 3–1.
b. Hectares
SOURCES: U.S. Department of Agriculture, *Economic Indicators of the Farm Sector*, various issues; and *Economic Report of the President*, 1990.

ment. As in the case of the labor force, the number of farms has declined only modestly since 1970.

From 1950 to 1970, the cultivated land per farm increased at an annual rate of 2.6 percent, from 27 hectares to 45 hectares. The amount of cultivated land per farm increased much more slowly between 1970 and 1988, with an increase of 33 percent for the period and an annual growth of 1.6 percent (table 3–4). The area of cropland per farm is substantially less than the total land per farm, since only about a third of total land is devoted to crops in the United States (see table 3–1). The average cropland area per worker increased from 21 hectares in 1950 to 39 hectares in 1970, with little change by 1990.

The United States does not have an official classification of farms by whether they are full-time or part-time. The classification that comes closest is one that gives the source of income, whether farm or off-farm, by value of sales. If a farm is classified as full-time—if half or more of its income comes from farming—the available data indicate

TABLE 3–5
FULL-TIME, PART-TIME, AND SIDELINE FARMS IN THE
UNITED STATES, 1965–1988
(thousands)

| Year | Full-Time | Part-Time | Sideline | Total |
|------|-----------|-----------|----------|-------|
| 1965 | 1,178 | 254 | 1,924 | 3,356 |
| 1970 | 879 | 333 | 1,737 | 2,949 |
| 1975 | 870 | 210 | 1,441 | 2,521 |
| 1980 | 448 | 453 | 1,539 | 2,440 |
| 1985 | 486 | 171 | 1,636 | 2,293 |
| 1988 | 516 | 128 | 1,553 | 2,197 |
| *Percentage of Farm Households* | | | | |
| 1965 | 35 | 8 | 57 | 100 |
| 1970 | 30 | 11 | 59 | 100 |
| 1975 | 35 | 8 | 57 | 100 |
| 1980 | 18 | 19 | 63 | 100 |
| 1985 | 21 | 7 | 72 | 100 |
| 1988 | 23 | 6 | 71 | 100 |

NOTE: Estimates based on U.S. Department of Agriculture, *Economic Indicators of the Farm Sector: National Financial Summary,* 1979 and 1988.
SOURCE: Rough approximations estimated by D. Gale Johnson from U.S. Department of Agriculture data on farm and off-farm income by farms classified by value of sales. Part-time farms are farms where one-fourth to one-half of income was from off-farm sources.

that approximately 35 percent of the farms were full-time in 1965, declining to 30 percent in 1970, and 18 percent in 1980, and rising to 23.5 percent in 1988 (table 3–5). The increase in percentage of full-time farms, given the definition used, during the 1980s was due to the large increase in net farm incomes during the decade that resulted in some farm households receiving the majority of their income from farming rather than from off-farm sources, as was the case in 1980. This shift in income sources occurred even though the amount of income from off-farm sources increased significantly during the 1980s: income from farming increased even more. Between 1980 and 1988, net farm operator income increased by 160 percent, while off-farm income increased by 66 percent. These are national totals rather than increases per farm, which were even larger.

Many of the less than full-time farms are what could be classified as sideline farms. These farms primarily provide a place to live, with only a few incidental farming activities carried out there. On many of these farms, the estimated income from farming is negative—expenses exceed income. The farming may be carried out, at least in part, as recreation.

In 1988, there were approximately 516,000 full-time farms, which accounted for about 80 percent of all sales of farm products. The average sale per full-time farm was $280,000. The part-time farms, where agricultural activity accounted for about a fourth to a half of family incomes, were 18 percent of all farms and accounted for about 10 percent of all farm sales. The average value of sales on these farms was approximately $50,000 in 1988. The remaining or sideline farms, where farm incomes accounted for less than a fourth of total family income, were 58 percent of all farms and supplied only 10 percent of sales of farm products. These data indicate that a large percentage of total farm sales come from 520,000 out of the 2,197,000 farms in the United States and that the almost 1,700,000 part-time and sideline farms account for only a fifth of farm sales.

## Capital and Operating Expenditures per Farm

Table 3–6 provides data on the average amount of capital invested per farm in the United States for selected years. Between 1980 and 1990 the amount of capital or investment per farm increased by 2 percent in nominal terms but declined by 33 percent in real terms (adjusted for inflation). This reduction was attributable to the sharp decline in the average value of farmland. The inflation-adjusted price of land fell by about a third. The data in table 3–6, however, fail to reflect the large capital requirements of the farms that produce most of U.S. farm output. The average amount invested in the 321,000 farms that sold 79 percent of all U.S. farm products in 1990 was about $1,340,000. The average debt on these farms was $256,000, and thus the average equity was $1,084,000.

For all farms, the major capital item is land, accounting for 69 to 77 percent in recent years. Farm machinery accounts for somewhat less than a tenth. It is evident that the commercial farms that provide most farm output are highly capital intensive. Most full-time farms are family farms.

Table 3–7 breaks down the major annual operating expenditures for U.S. farms. Important expenditure categories of feed bought, of livestock bought, and of depreciation together have accounted for about 40 percent of the total expenditures. The amount of interest paid has increased markedly during the period from $2.1 billion in 1965 to 14.5 billion in 1990. The share of interest in total operating costs increased sharply, from 6 percent in 1965 to 10 percent in 1990.

TABLE 3–6

CAPITAL INVESTMENT PER FARM IN THE UNITED STATES, 1965–1990

(thousands of dollars)

| Item | 1965 | 1970 | 1980 | 1985 | 1990 |
|------|------|------|------|------|------|
| Real estate | 54 | 76 | 348 | 263 | 328 |
| Livestock | 5 | 8 | 25 | 20 | 32 |
| Crops | 2 | 3 | 14 | 10 | 10 |
| Machinery | 8 | 12 | 41 | 40 | 43 |
| Household equipment | 3 | 3 | 89 | 12 | 22 |
| Financial assets | 6 | 8 | 16 | 21 | 29 |
| Total | 78 | 110 | 452 | 367 | 463 |
| GNP price deflator[a] | 34 | 42 | 86 | 111 | 131 |
| *Percentages* | | | | | |
| Real estate | 69 | 69 | 77 | 72 | 71 |
| Livestock | 6 | 7 | 6 | 5 | 7 |
| Crops | 3 | 3 | 3 | 3 | 2 |
| Machinery | 10 | 11 | 9 | 11 | 9 |
| Household equipment | 4 | 3 | 2 | 3 | 5 |
| Financial assets | 8 | 7 | 4 | 6 | 6 |

a. 1982 = 100.
SOURCES: U.S. Department of Agriculture, *Economic Indicators of the Farm Sector: National Financial Summary, 1988* and *State Financial Summary, 1990.*

From 1982 to 1984, when there was considerable financial distress in American agriculture, interest accounted for 15.5 percent of all production expenses.

In 1990, operating expenses totaled $67,000 per farm. During that year, the net income from agriculture averaged $23,750, while off-farm income averaged $31,300 for total net income per farm operation of approximately $55,050. The average net income from farming for the 15 percent of the farms that account for 79 percent of farm sales was about $160,000 in 1990, with off-farm income of some $20,000. These farms are the primary beneficiaries of the U.S. farm price support and income programs. The average income of nonfarm families in 1990 was approximately $35,000.

The taxes in table 3–7 are property taxes; there does not exist a separate estimate of the income taxes on agricultural activity. While business enterprises generally must use an accrual basis in determining income for tax purposes, farmers can operate on a cash basis. Other than this plus the fact that nonmoney income is not taxed in the United States, however, farmers do not receive any significant

## TABLE 3-7
### OPERATING EXPENDITURES IN FARM OPERATION IN THE UNITED STATES, 1965–1990
(millions of dollars)

| Item | 1965 $ | 1965 % | 1970 $ | 1970 % | 1980 $ | 1980 % | 1990 $ | 1990 % |
|---|---|---|---|---|---|---|---|---|
| Feed bought | 5,674 | 16.9 | 8,028 | 18.1 | 20,971 | 15.8 | 20,727 | 14.4 |
| Livestock bought | 2,912 | 8.7 | 4,320 | 9.7 | 10,670 | 8.0 | 14,737 | 10.2 |
| Seed bought | 720 | 2.1 | 927 | 2.1 | 3,220 | 2.4 | 3,502 | 2.5 |
| Fertilizer and lime | 1,994 | 5.9 | 2,435 | 5.5 | 9,491 | 7.1 | 7,137 | 4.9 |
| Repair and maintenance | 2,498 | 7.4 | 2,828 | 6.4 | 7,075 | 5.3 | 7,283 | 5.0 |
| Pesticides and fuel[a] | 2,290 | 6.8 | 2,975 | 6.7 | 12,944 | 9.7 | 11,678 | 8.1 |
| Depreciation | 4,337 | 12.9 | 6,904 | 15.5 | 21,474 | 16.1 | 17,545 | 12.2 |
| Hired labor | 3,604 | 10.7 | 3,312 | 9.7 | 9,293 | 2.0 | 12,543 | 8.7 |
| Taxes on farm property | 1,874 | 5.6 | 2,596 | 5.8 | 3,891 | 2.9 | 5,623 | 3.9 |
| Interest on farm mortgage | 1,075 | 3.2 | 1,764 | 4.0 | 7,549 | 5.7 | 7,667 | 5.3 |
| Interest, other | 1,028 | 3.1 | 1,618 | 3.6 | 8,717 | 5.4 | 6,805 | 4.7 |
| Net rent[b] | 1,886 | 5.6 | 2,051 | 4.6 | 6,075 | 4.6 | 8,177 | 5.7 |
| Miscellaneous | 3,758 | 11.2 | 3,662 | 8.2 | 11,769 | 8.8 | 20,787 | 14.4 |
| Total | 33,650 | 100.0 | 44,424 | 100.0 | 133,139 | 100.0 | 144,291 | 100.0 |

a. Includes electricity.
b. To nonfarm landlords.
SOURCES: U.S. Department of Agriculture, *Economic Indicators of the Farm Sector: National Financial Summary, 1990.* ECIFS10-T. Nov. 1991.

special treatment in complying with the federal income tax. This was not always the case but has been so since 1986.

The estimate of net rents includes only the rent paid to landlords who do not operate farms. The majority of rented land is owned by other farm operators, not by wealthy nonfarmers.

## Major Productive Activities

One not altogether satisfactory measure of the relative importance of the major productive activities in U.S. agriculture is the value of sales. If production is divided into two categories—crops and livestock—we find that while there is year-to-year variation due to prices and growing conditions, the two sources have been of approximately equal importance over the past two decades. Since a significant part of feed crops are fed to livestock on the farms where the crop is produced, however, this part is not included in the value of crop sales. In addition, because livestock production depends on purchased feed, the value of the sales of livestock products exaggerates the importance of livestock in farm production.

Table 3–8 gives data on the production, harvested area, and yield per hectare of the major crops grown in the United States. Acreage devoted to certain crops shifted substantially between 1952 and 1989. The most striking shift was the large increase in the soybean harvested area, from 5.8 million hectares in 1952 to 17.1 million in 1970 and to 24.0 million hectares in 1989. The area devoted to rice increased by 38 percent. The areas devoted to wheat and cotton declined significantly.

Several of the yield increases were large, especially corn (185 percent), rice (138 percent), and potatoes (91 percent).

Between 1952 and 1990, total farm production in the United States increased by 81 percent (table 3–9), or at an annual growth rate of 1.6 percent (table 3–10). Crop production grew at an annual rate of 1.6 percent, while livestock production grew more slowly at 1.2 percent. The fastest-growing crop subsector was oil crops, with an annual growth rate of 3.7 percent. Tobacco production fell by more than a third, and cotton production varied substantially because of the functioning of the farm programs. Poultry and eggs grew at a rate of 3.2 percent, the most rapid among the livestock products.

## Agricultural Development since World War II

The American agriculture that emerged from World War II was a strong and productive one. Agriculture had had an important role

TABLE 3–8

PRODUCTION, HARVESTED AREA, AND YIELD OF MAJOR CROPS IN THE UNITED STATES, 1952, 1970, AND 1989

| | Production (million metric tons) | | | Area (million hectares) | | | Yield (kilograms/hectare) | | |
|---|---|---|---|---|---|---|---|---|---|
| | 1952 | 1970 | 1989 | 1952 | 1970 | 1989 | 1952 | 1970 | 1989 |
| Corn | 78 | 105 | 205 | 32.8 | 23.2 | 29.3 | 2,554 | 4,544 | 7,293 |
| Wheat | 36 | 37 | 55 | 28.8 | 17.6 | 25.1 | 1,237 | 2,084 | 2,206 |
| Cotton | 3.3 | 2.2 | 2.6 | 10.5 | 4.5 | 3.8 | 313 | 491 | 688 |
| Oats | 15 | 13 | 5 | 17.7 | 7.5 | 2.8 | 1,180 | 1,764 | 1,951 |
| Soybeans | 6 | 31 | 52 | 5.8 | 17.1 | 24.0 | 1,391 | 1,795 | 2,179 |
| Sorghum | 2 | 17 | 16 | 2.2 | 5.5 | 4.5 | 1,067 | 3,163 | 3,477 |
| Rice | 2.2 | 3.8 | 7.1 | 0.8 | 0.7 | 1.1 | 2,704 | 5,174 | 6,443 |
| Peanuts | 0.6 | 1.4 | 1.8 | 0.6 | 0.6 | 0.7 | 1,053 | 2,276 | 2,757 |
| Potatoes | 10 | 15 | 16 | 0.6 | 0.6 | 0.5 | 16,922 | 25,400 | 32,400 |
| Barley | 5 | 9 | 9 | 3.7 | 3.9 | 3.4 | 1,490 | 2,302 | 2,614 |

SOURCE: U.S. Department of Agriculture, *Agricultural Statistics*, various issues.

TABLE 3–9

AGRICULTURAL PRODUCTION INDEXES IN THE UNITED STATES,
1952–1990
(1986 = 100)

| | | Crops | | | | Livestock |
| Year | Total | Total | Feed grains | Food grains | Oil crops | Products |
|------|-------|-------|-------------|-------------|-----------|-----------|
| 1952 | 59 | 57 | 41 | 59 | 24 | 67 |
| 1955 | 62 | 58 | 44 | 45 | 27 | 72 |
| 1960 | 68 | 66 | 56 | 62 | 35 | 75 |
| 1965 | 74 | 70 | 57 | 63 | 48 | 81 |
| 1970 | 76 | 71 | 58 | 64 | 60 | 90 |
| 1975 | 86 | 85 | 74 | 101 | 78 | 86 |
| 1980 | 94 | 93 | 79 | 113 | 90 | 98 |
| 1981 | 106 | 107 | 98 | 135 | 104 | 99 |
| 1982 | 105 | 107 | 99 | 129 | 110 | 97 |
| 1983 | 86 | 81 | 54 | 109 | 83 | 99 |
| 1984 | 101 | 102 | 94 | 121 | 96 | 97 |
| 1985 | 106 | 108 | 109 | 113 | 106 | 100 |
| 1986 | 100 | 100 | 100 | 100 | 100 | 100 |
| 1987 | 99 | 99 | 83 | 100 | 97 | 103 |
| 1988 | 92 | 84 | 59 | 92 | 80 | 105 |
| 1989 | 103 | 98 | 87 | 100 | 95 | 105 |
| 1990 | 107 | 104 | 91 | 128 | 96 | 107 |

SOURCES: *Economic Report of the President*, February 1992.

during the war, providing food not only for the American population but also for the nation's allies. In the years immediately following the war, demand for food continued strong, as the United States shipped substantial quantities of food not only to its allies but also to its former enemies—Japan and Germany.

In 1945, farm production was 21 percent larger than in 1939. Production continued to grow through the 1940s and the early 1950s. Agricultural output in 1955 had increased a further 19 percent, in considerable part because of the incentives provided by farm income and price support legislation enacted in 1949 and subsequent years (see chapter 5). As agricultural output recovered in Europe and Japan, however, the demand for U.S. farm products increased little. Because of price supports, prices of major agricultural crops did not adjust to the imbalance in supply and demand, and the government, as the

TABLE 3–10

RATE OF AVERAGE ANNUAL INCREASE IN AGRICULTURAL PRODUCTION
BY GROUPS IN THE UNITED STATES, 1952–1990
(percent)

| Period | Total Production | Crop Production | Livestock Production |
|--------|------------------|-----------------|----------------------|
| 1952–1955 | 1.7 | 0.6 | 2.4 |
| 1955–1960 | 1.9 | 2.6 | 0.8 |
| 1960–1965 | 1.7 | 1.2 | 1.6 |
| 1965–1970 | 0.5 | 0.3 | 2.1 |
| 1970–1975 | 2.5 | 3.7 | −0.9 |
| 1975–1980 | 1.8 | 1.8 | 2.6 |
| 1980–1985 | 2.4 | 3.0 | 0.4 |
| 1985–1990 | 0.1 | −0.1 | 1.4 |
| 1952–1970 | 1.4 | 1.2 | 1.7 |
| 1970–1990 | 1.6 | 1.9 | 0.9 |
| 1952–1990 | 1.6 | 1.6 | 1.2 |

SOURCE: Computed from table 3–9.

buyer of last resort, had accumulated large quantities of cotton and grain by 1955.

Thus, during the 1950s, the United States returned to efforts to limit agricultural production and institutionalized food aid. Each continues until the present, though food aid is now a relatively unimportant component of the demand for farm products.

In spite of, as well as because of, governmental interventions in agricultural markets, productivity in agriculture increased at relatively high rates after the 1940s. This increase holds true whether productivity is measured in crop output per unit of land, total farm output per unit of labor, or output per unit of all inputs. Crop output per unit of land increased by 109 percent between 1947–1949 and 1990, labor productivity by 625 percent, and output per unit of total inputs by 136 percent. The increase in the average product of labor was due both to technological change and to the substitution of other inputs for labor. The input of labor declined by 53 percent between 1947–1949 and 1990, while purchased inputs more than doubled. Included in the purchased inputs are agricultural chemicals, which increased about ten times.

### Agricultural Growth

Tables 3–9 and 3–10 provide some details on the growth of agricultural output since World War II. The most rapid growth was in oil crops, primarily because of the great increase in soybeans (see table 3–8). Feed grains increased somewhat more than food grains, while crop production increased more than livestock production. This apparent anomaly is explained by the fact that as livestock production expanded, an increasing percentage of the total feed had to be supplied by concentrates as the total area of pasture and hay either remained constant or declined.

Growth rates varied substantially over the period. The variability in growth rates for crop production was caused primarily by two factors—weather and government programs. From 1965 to 1970, for example, cropland harvested declined by 1 percent but increased by 11 percent between 1970 and 1975, since the acreage restrictions were not binding in the last year. Growth of livestock production varied with price changes in livestock products and feeds. During the early 1970s, the strength of export demand for the grains and oilseeds increased their prices relative to the prices of livestock, and livestock output declined. The United States was the only industrial country that permitted the full impact of the changes in international market prices during the 1970s to be transmitted to the domestic market for both grains and livestock. As a result, feed grain exports from the United States increased between 1970 and 1975, even though feed grain output declined by more than a fifth from 1970 to 1974.

Tables 3–11 and 3–12 present the sectoral development of the gross national product (GNP) since 1952, both in current dollars and in percentage of the total. By 1952, agriculture was no longer a large part of the GNP, accounting for just 6.6 percent. Its share has moved along a consistent downward path except for the first part of the 1970s, when its share increased from 3 percent to 3.7 percent. In 1988, agriculture's share of GNP was only a little more than 2 percent.

A more accurate measure of the role of food and other agricultural products in the American economy, however, may be given by the importance of the entire food and fiber system, including the production of manufactured inputs for agriculture and the transportation, processing, wholesaling, and retailing of farm products. In 1987, the total value added in the food and fiber sector was $705 billion, or 15.5 percent of gross domestic product. This number was down from 20.3 percent in 1975, the earliest year for which comparable data are available (see table 3–13). The share of employment in the food and fiber sectors has been approximately the same as its share of value added—16.7 percent in 1987 and 21.5 percent in 1975.

Agriculture was not the only sector with a declining share of GNP over the four decades. The share of manufacturing declined by more than a third, as did that of transportation. Wholesale and retail

## TABLE 3–11
### U.S. Gross National Product in Billions of Dollars by Kind of Activity, 1952–1988

| Activity | 1952 | 1955 | 1960 | 1965 | 1970 | 1975 | 1980 | 1985 | 1987 | 1988 |
|---|---|---|---|---|---|---|---|---|---|---|
| Agriculture | 18.7 | 19.9 | 21.5 | 23.8 | 28.7 | 54.8 | 77.2 | 91.5 | 94.9 | 99.8 |
| Manufacturing | 89.8 | 121.0 | 143.9 | 196.3 | 250.3 | 346.0 | 581.0 | 795.8 | 853.6 | 948.6 |
| Construction | 14.5 | 18.1 | 22.7 | 32.1 | 47.4 | 66.5 | 137.7 | 182.2 | 218.5 | 232.6 |
| Electricity, gas, sanitation | 4.9 | 8.7 | 12.8 | 16.6 | 22.7 | 37.2 | 68.4 | 121.4 | 136.4 | 148.8 |
| Wholesale, retail trade | 50.9 | 66.2 | 84.6 | 112.8 | 167.3 | 272.4 | 438.9 | 652.5 | 740.4 | 780.8 |
| Transportation | 15.6 | 19.9 | 22.5 | 28.8 | 38.9 | 56.6 | 105.8 | 144.5 | 150.8 | 163.2 |
| Communications | 3.7 | 4.5 | 7.1 | 10.5 | 15.2 | 38.4 | 66.6 | 108.5 | 121.0 | 129.3 |
| Services | 26.6 | 34.0 | 49.2 | 70.7 | 113.5 | 181.8 | 374.0 | 639.4 | 793.5 | 872.5 |
| Government | 34.3 | 38.5 | 53.4 | 76.7 | 129.1 | 200.6 | 322.1 | 477.4 | 535.3 | 570.6 |
| Finance, insurance, real estate | 24.4 | 49.2 | 70.5 | 96.1 | 141.0 | 209.4 | 400.6 | 626.6 | 775.4 | 830.3 |
| Total | 283.4 | 380.0 | 488.2 | 664.4 | 954.1 | 1463.7 | 2572.3 | 3839.8 | 4419.8 | 4776.5 |

Source: U.S. Department of Commerce, *Statistical Abstract of the United States, 1955, 1976, 1977, 1987, 1989, 1991.*

## TABLE 3-12

PERCENTAGE DISTRIBUTION OF THE U.S. GROSS NATIONAL PRODUCT BY KIND OF ACTIVITY, 1952–1988

| Activity | 1952 | 1955 | 1960 | 1965 | 1970 | 1975 | 1980 | 1985 | 1987 | 1988 |
|---|---|---|---|---|---|---|---|---|---|---|
| Agriculture | 6.60 | 5.24 | 4.40 | 3.58 | 3.01 | 3.74 | 3.00 | 2.38 | 2.15 | 2.10 |
| Manufacturing | 31.69 | 31.84 | 29.48 | 29.55 | 26.23 | 23.64 | 22.59 | 20.73 | 19.31 | 19.86 |
| Construction | 5.12 | 4.76 | 4.65 | 4.83 | 4.97 | 4.54 | 5.35 | 4.75 | 4.94 | 4.87 |
| Electricity, gas, sanitation | 1.73 | 2.29 | 2.62 | 2.50 | 2.38 | 2.54 | 2.66 | 3.16 | 3.09 | 3.12 |
| Wholesale, retail trade | 17.96 | 17.42 | 17.33 | 16.98 | 17.53 | 18.61 | 17.06 | 16.99 | 16.75 | 16.35 |
| Transportation | 5.50 | 5.24 | 4.61 | 4.33 | 4.08 | 3.87 | 4.11 | 3.76 | 3.41 | 3.42 |
| Communications | 1.31 | 1.18 | 1.45 | 1.58 | 1.59 | 2.62 | 2.59 | 2.83 | 2.74 | 2.71 |
| Services | 9.39 | 8.95 | 10.08 | 10.64 | 11.90 | 12.42 | 14.54 | 16.65 | 17.95 | 18.27 |
| Government | 12.10 | 10.13 | 10.94 | 11.54 | 13.53 | 13.71 | 12.52 | 12.43 | 12.11 | 11.95 |
| Finance, insurance, real estate | 8.61 | 12.95 | 14.44 | 14.46 | 14.78 | 14.31 | 15.57 | 16.32 | 17.54 | 17.38 |

SOURCE: U.S. Department of Commerce, *Statistical Abstract of the United States, 1955, 1976, 1977, 1987, 1989.*

## TABLE 3–13
### VALUE-ADDED AND EMPLOYMENT IN THE FOOD AND FIBER SYSTEM, SELECTED YEARS, 1975–1987

| Item | 1975 | 1980 | 1982 | 1984 | 1985 | 1986 | 1987 |
|---|---|---|---|---|---|---|---|
| *Value added, billions of dollars* | | | | | | | |
| Farm sector | 43.3 | 55.1 | 75.1 | 64.5 | 71.6 | 58.8 | 55.8 |
| Nonfarm sectors | 282.4 | 444.8 | 536.2 | 595.9 | 627.8 | 635.2 | 649.2 |
| Food processing | 38.7 | 56.0 | 70.0 | 75.6 | 83.8 | 83.8 | 81.5 |
| Manufacturing | 57.0 | 83.0 | 97.5 | 1-1.5 | 102.3 | 102.7 | 100.5 |
| Transportation, trade, and retailing | 96.8 | 157.5 | 188.1 | 209.7 | 220.9 | 223.9 | 230.5 |
| Restaurants | 25.7 | 42.0 | 48.1 | 55.7 | 57.5 | 60.4 | 64.9 |
| All other | 64.2 | 106.3 | 132.5 | 153.4 | 163.3 | 164.4 | 172.0 |
| Total food and fiber[a] | 325.7 | 499.9 | 611.3 | 660.4 | 699.4 | 694.0 | 705.2 |
| Total domestic economy | 1,598 | 2,732 | 3,166 | 3,772 | 4,015 | 4,240 | 4,527 |
| *Percent of value-added* | | | | | | | |
| Farm sector | 2.7 | 2.0 | 2.4 | 1.7 | 1.8 | 1.4 | 1.2 |
| Nonfarm sectors | 17.7 | 16.3 | 16.9 | 15.8 | 15.6 | 15.0 | 14.3 |
| Total food and fiber[a] | 20.4 | 18.3 | 19.3 | 17.5 | 17.4 | 16.4 | 15.6 |

*Employment, millions of workers*

| | | | | | | |
|---|---|---|---|---|---|---|
| Farm sector | 3.0 | 2.6 | 2.6 | 2.7 | 2.3 | 2.0 | 2.0 |

| | | | | | | | |
|---|---|---|---|---|---|---|---|
| Farm sector | 3.0 | 2.6 | 2.6 | 2.7 | 2.3 | 2.0 | 2.0 |
| Nonfarm sectors | 17.2 | 18.9 | 19.2 | 18.7 | 18.7 | 18.2 | 18.1 |
| Food processing | 1.5 | 1.5 | 1.6 | 1.4 | 1.5 | 1.4 | 1.3 |
| Manufacturing | 3.2 | 3.4 | 3.3 | 3.0 | 2.9 | 2.7 | 2.7 |
| Transportation, trade, and retailing | 5.7 | 6.4 | 6.6 | 6.6 | 6.7 | 6.6 | 6.6 |
| Restaurants | 3.1 | 3.5 | 3.5 | 3.6 | 3.6 | 3.6 | 3.7 |
| All other | 3.7 | 4.0 | 4.2 | 4.1 | 4.1 | 3.9 | 3.9 |
| Total food and fiber[a] | 20.2 | 21.4 | 21.8 | 21.4 | 21.0 | 20.2 | 20.1 |
| Total domestic economy | 93.8 | 106.9 | 110.2 | 113.5 | 115.5 | 117.8 | 119.9 |
| *Percent* | | | | | | | |
| Farm sector | 2.7 | 2.0 | 2.4 | 1.7 | 1.8 | 1.4 | 1.2 |
| Nonfarm sectors | 17.7 | 16.3 | 16.9 | 15.8 | 15.6 | 15.0 | 14.3 |
| Total food and fiber[a] | 21.5 | 20.0 | 19.8 | 18.8 | 18.2 | 17.1 | 16.7 |

a. Totals may not add because of rounding.
SOURCE: U.S. Department of Agriculture, *Economic Indicators of the Farm Sector: Farm Sector Review*, 1987, p. 51.

TABLE 3–14

U.S. EXPORTS AND IMPORTS, 1952–1990

(billions of current U.S.$)

| | Exports | | | Imports | | |
|------|-------|-------------|---------|-------|-------------|---------|
| Year | Total | Agriculture | Percent | Total | Agriculture | Percent |
| 1952 | 15.2 | 4.0 | 26.3 | 10.7 | 4.7 | 43.9 |
| 1955 | 15.5 | 3.1 | 20.0 | 11.3 | 3.8 | 33.6 |
| 1960 | 19.6 | 4.5 | 23.0 | 15.0 | 4.0 | 26.7 |
| 1965 | 26.7 | 6.1 | 22.8 | 21.4 | 4.0 | 18.7 |
| 1970 | 42.7 | 7.3 | 17.1 | 40.0 | 5.6 | 14.0 |
| 1975 | 107.7 | 21.6 | 20.1 | 98.5 | 9.3 | 9.4 |
| 1980 | 225.6 | 41.2 | 18.7 | 244.0 | 17.4 | 7.1 |
| 1985 | 218.8 | 29.0 | 13.6 | 343.6 | 20.0 | 5.8 |
| 1990 | 375.3 | 39.3 | 10.5 | 491.0 | 22.8 | 4.6 |

SOURCE: U.S. Department of Agriculture, *Foreign Agricultural Trade of the Untied States: FATUS*, various annual issues.

trade had a constant share of GNP, while the financial, insurance, and real estate sector nearly doubled its share as did the services sector.

### Agriculture in Foreign Trade

U.S. agriculture was and still is a much larger contributor to exports than it is to national output or employment. In 1952, when it contributed 6.6 percent to gross national product, it accounted for 26.3 percent of the value of imports (table 3–14). While its share of exports had declined to 10.5 percent by 1990, this decline was less than the fall in agriculture's contribution to GNP.

The share of agricultural imports in total imports declined by more than did its share of exports. This reduction reflected two different changes. First, and it may surprise some, during the 1950s the United States was a net importer of agricultural products, while it became a major net exporter only during the 1970s. Second, while agriculture maintained its position as a net exporter during the 1980s, this was not true for the economy as a whole. Each of these changes contributed to the much larger decline in the relative importance of agricultural imports than in agricultural exports.

The change in the net agricultural trade balance between the 1950s and the 1960s was due in considerable part to a change in the price and income support policies and in the government's role in the marketing

TABLE 3–15

AGRICULTURAL EXPORTS AND IMPORTS OF THE UNITED STATES,
1952–1990

(millions of dollars)

| | 1952 | 1960 | 1970 | 1980 | 1990 |
|---|---|---|---|---|---|
| Exports | | | | | |
| Total agricultural | | | | | |
| exports | 3,431 | 4,832 | 7,358 | 41,233 | 39,347 |
| Rice | 157 | 130 | 314 | 1,289 | 800 |
| Vegetables | 91 | 123 | 182 | 1,189 | 2,302 |
| Fruits | 140 | 249 | 331 | 1,335 | 2,008 |
| Cotton | 874 | 988 | 378 | 1,864 | 2,783 |
| Tobacco | 246 | 379 | 4,889 | 1,334 | 1,441 |
| Meats | 50 | 125 | 188 | 891 | 2,557 |
| Eggs and dairy | 94 | 105 | 138 | 256 | 1,255 |
| Grains | 1,325 | 1,526 | 2,243 | 16,492 | 13,603 |
| Imports | | | | | |
| Total agricultural | | | | | |
| imports | 4,519 | 3,824 | 5,592 | 17,400 | 22,771 |
| Grains | 166 | 54 | 63 | 271 | 1,182 |
| Vegetables, fruits | 219 | 310 | 734 | 2,047 | 4,485 |
| Cotton | 40 | 27 | 13 | 2 | 1 |
| Tobacco | 81 | 115 | 112 | 422 | 583 |
| Meats | 178 | 393 | 1,014 | 2,346 | 2,926 |
| Eggs and dairy | 40 | 33 | 112 | 462 | 932 |
| Sugar | 473 | 555 | 725 | 1,987 | 1,171 |
| Hides and skins | 56 | 68 | 52 | 88 | 171 |
| Wool | 382 | 197 | 116 | 146 | 134 |

SOURCES: *Statistical Abstract of the United States*, 1954, 1962, 1972, 1982, 1989, 1991; *Agricultural Statistics*, 1954, 1960, 1970, 1980, 1988, 1991.

and export of farm products. During most of the 1950s, farm price supports were maintained at high levels, which discouraged exports and resulted in the accumulation of stocks by the government. Since domestic prices were higher than international prices for several farm products, the government had to be an important actor in the export business. It did not function well, and the volume of agricultural exports suffered. Starting in the late 1950s, price supports were lowered, and most of the export trade was handled by the private sector with relatively little intervention by the government except for the continuation of certain export subsidies, especially for wheat.

TABLE 3–16

SOURCES OF FARM FAMILY INCOME IN THE UNITED STATES, 1960–1990
(U.S. dollars per farm)

| Year | Total | Net Agricultural | | Nonagricultural | |
|------|-------|------------------|---------|-----------------|---------|
| | | Dollars | Percent | Dollars | Percent |
| 1960 | 4,946 | 2,806 | 57 | 2,140 | 43 |
| 1965 | 7,325 | 3,533 | 48 | 3,792 | 52 |
| 1970 | 10,843 | 4,869 | 45 | 5,974 | 55 |
| 1975 | 18,267 | 8,785 | 48 | 9,482 | 52 |
| 1980 | 23,486 | 9,223 | 39 | 14,263 | 61 |
| 1985 | 33,961 | 15,232 | 45 | 18,729 | 55 |
| 1988 | 45,972 | 22,849 | 50 | 23,132 | 50 |
| 1990 | 55,049 | 23,752 | 43 | 31,297[a] | 57 |

a. Because of a change in question asked in 1990, this figure is not comparable to earlier figures. The difference is 10 to 15 percent. The 1990 figure is probably more accurate than the earlier ones.
SOURCES: U.S. Department of Agriculture, *Economic Indicators of the Farm Sector—National Financial Summary*, 1990.

Table 3–15 provides data on the value of exports and imports of agricultural products for selected years since 1952. The most important exports are the grains, the oilseeds, and the oilseed products. Important imports are meats, fruits, and vegetables, beverages and coffee, and tea and spices.

East Asia is now the most important destination for U.S. agricultural exports, supplanting Western Europe, which held that position well into the 1960s. Japan is the most important market in East Asia, followed by South Korea and Taiwan. In 1988, Taiwan accounted for approximately 4 percent of U.S. agricultural exports.

## Change in the Sources of Farm Family Incomes

In most years since 1965, off-farm sources of income have exceeded net income from agriculture for farm households (see table 3–16). In 1980, a year of low net income from farming, off-farm sources exceeded net income from agriculture by 50 percent, though in recent years off-farm sources have averaged about 10 to 20 percent more than farm sources. During the early 1980s, the average money incomes of farm families were from 6 to 24 percent below the average for the nation. With the significant recovery of farm incomes since 1985, however, the farm operator households have had incomes significantly larger than the average for the nation, with the difference being approximately 20 percent for 1987–1990.

The most important source of off-farm income in 1984 was wages and salaries from nonfarm sources (53 percent), followed by nonfarm business and professional incomes (24 percent) and pensions, retirement income, interest, and dividends (22 percent) (U.S. Department of Agriculture 1985).

All the data given include government payments to farmers in agricultural income. For 1986–1990, government payments to farmers averaged $13.5 billion, compared with net farm income of $43.5 billion. One cannot infer, however, that government payments were the source of nearly a third of the net income. To receive the payments, farmers had to idle millions of hectares of cropland to comply with the supply management provisions. Consequently, some of the payments were required for the costs incurred in managing the idle land and for the additional inputs that were applied to the land actually cultivated as well as to compensate for the reduced output. Some of these effects were offset by somewhat higher market prices.

### Summing Up

A number of impressions are worth carrying away from this effort to describe how farming in the United States has changed since 1950. It is clear, and if it is not I have failed, that farming has undergone tremendous change. And on the whole, American agriculture has adjusted very well to changing demands that the economy and society have put upon it.

The least change has been in the area of farmland and the amount of cropland used. Some land has been removed from agricultural use, approximately 20 percent since 1950. But the amount of cropland has declined just 10 percent.

The reduction in the number of farms and the transfer of labor from farm to nonfarm employment occurred at a rapid pace from 1952 to 1970, with both declining by about half. Since then, the pace of decline has been much slower. Accompanying the decline in the farm work force has been an approximate doubling of the amount of cropland per farm worker. This change has been one of the factors that has made possible the large increase in the incomes of farm people that has occurred since 1950.

U.S. agriculture has become highly capital intensive, especially for the 15 percent of the farms that sell nearly 80 percent of all farm products. The operators of these farms have net assets of something over $1 million in 1990. The majority of the farm families depend on nonfarm sources of income for more than half of their family incomes. Less than a fourth of all farm-operator families receive half or more of their income from farming.

One of the most dynamic aspects of agriculture has been the growth of agricultural exports since 1960. As of 1960, the United States imported about the same value of agricultural products that it exported. Starting in 1970, agricultural exports started on an upward trend, reaching a peak in 1980. By 1990, the value of agricultural exports had returned to about the 1980 level. In recent years, the output of more than one out of four crop acres has been exported. This fact goes some distance in explaining the emphasis that policy makers give to the development of agricultural trade.

### Afterword

There are many obvious differences between the structures of agriculture in Taiwan and those in the United States. Differences in the average size of farms and in the amount of land per farm worker are striking. The U.S. average cropland is approximately fifty times the average farm size in Taiwan, with the difference in the amount of cultivated land per worker being approximately the same order of magnitude.

Relative to the economy as a whole, agriculture is much more important in Taiwan than in the United States. As of 1990, nearly 13 percent of total employment in Taiwan was in agriculture, compared with a little less than 3 percent in the United States. Approximately the same differences are displayed by the percentage of population living on farms.

In both countries, most farms are less than full time, and in both the percentage of farms that are full time has declined over the past three decades. A somewhat larger percentage of the U.S. farms are full time than in Taiwan—approximately 23 percent versus 15 percent during the 1980s.

While the production of crops and livestock is of about equal importance in total farm production in the United States, in Taiwan crop production is much more important than livestock production (see table 2–12 and page 63). Fisheries are included in Taiwan's agricultural output and have accounted for an increasing percentage over the years. In 1990, fisheries accounted for 28 percent of output in Taiwan, while the production or catching of fish is a very small percentage of agricultural output in the United States.

For comparable crops, yields are generally higher in the United States than in Taiwan. Rice yields in the late 1980s were 3.9 tons per hectare in Taiwan and 6.4 tons in the United States. While corn yields are significantly higher in the United States, the amount of land devoted to corn in Taiwan is so small that such a comparison has little meaning.

In growth of production, Taiwan agriculture has clearly outstripped the United States over the past four decades. While total farm production in the United States increased at an annual compound rate of 1.5 percent from 1952 to 1987, the growth rate in Taiwan for approximately the same period was 4.3 percent—nearly three times greater.

The contribution of Taiwan's agriculture to national product is about three times that of the United States—6.1 percent versus 2.2 percent for the late 1980s. As for international trade, the agriculture and food sectors have different roles. U.S. agricultural exports were 10 percent of total exports in 1990, while in Taiwan the percentage was 5. As might be expected, imports were reversed, with U.S. imports of agricultural products accounting for about 5 percent of total imports, while in Taiwan the percentage was nearly 11. It is worth noting that the relative importance of Taiwan's agricultural exports in total exports was the same as agriculture's importance in national product.

In both countries, farm families rely on off-farm or nonagricultural sources of income. The dependence on nonagricultural income in Taiwan is somewhat greater than in the United States. In 1990, approximately 65 percent of the income of farm families in Taiwan came from nonagricultural sources compared with 57 percent in the United States. The relative importance of nonagricultural sources of income has increased more in Taiwan than in the United States over the past three decades. The sources of off-farm income are quite similar, with wages and salaries being much the most important.

If there is a surprise in the comparisons, it is in the capital investment per farm. With the rapid increase in the value of farm land in Taiwan and the decline in land values in the United States during the 1980s, the difference in capital investment is quite small. Assuming an exchange rate of 26.7 New Taiwan dollars per U.S. dollar, the average investment per farm in Taiwan was $226,000 in 1988 compared with $392,000 in the United States. The closeness of the two figures reflects the much higher price of land in Taiwan—approximately $180,000 per hectare in 1988 compared with approximately $1,500 in the United States. Buildings are included with land in both countries.

These few comparisons of the agricultures of the two economies make it clear that each of the agricultures has been highly dynamic and has responded to the changing conditions generated by economic growth. Each has had significant growth in output, while reducing its labor force. An important adjustment made by farm families in both Taiwan and the United States has been through part-time farming; a minority of the farm families now depend on farming for most of their income.

But perhaps the most striking aspect of the comparison of the two agricultures is that the tiny farms, at least as measured by land area, of Taiwan have remained competitive in world markets in several commodities. As will be noted later, Taiwan's agriculture receives less protection from international competition than does American agriculture.

# 4

# Current Agricultural Problems and Policies of Taiwan

*Yu-kang Mao and Chaw-hsia Tu*

In the early stage of Taiwan's economic development, agriculture fostered industrial development. During the 1950s and the early 1960s, agriculture grew rapidly on the strength of major institutional renovations, crop diversification, maximization of crop intensities, investments in strategic infrastructure, and general advancement in agricultural research, extension, and credit systems. Since about 1965, agriculture has undergone continuous changes in the structure of farm wages, production costs, farm family income, and mode of farm management.

Significant changes have also taken place in the relative importance of crops, livestock, forestry, and fisheries and the relative importance of grain and horticultural and specialty crops. Farm mechanization has proceeded slowly in response to declining agricultural labor.

Inevitably, such radical transformation is accompanied by growing pains—maladjustments and dislocations that disturb agricultural development and impose relative hardships upon many farm families.

The purposes of this chapter are to give a brief discussion of the agricultural problems in the process of economic transformation and to highlight the agricultural policies designed to overcome these problems and to get agricultural development back on course, for the mutual benefit of the farm population and the economy as a whole. Taiwan's experiences may well serve as a good reference point for other developing nations.

## Current Agricultural Problems

By the mid-1960s, industrial production had overtaken agriculture both as a contributor to net domestic product and as a major source of exports. Agricultural development in Taiwan marked a turning point, changing from a major supporting role in development to a sustaining role. A slowdown in the growth rate of agricultural production became evident by the end of the 1960s. Moreover, the mixture of agricultural products changed in response to market opportunities and leaned toward more livestock and fishery products and high-value export crops. This change in structure presented Taiwan's agriculture with new problems, similar to those in some other industrial countries at a comparable stage of development.

With rapid expansion in industrial employment, farm operation faced rising labor costs and rising production costs as well. Consequently, on the one hand, the gap between farmers' per capita income and nonfarmers' per capita income widened, while on the other hand, the intensive use of labor in agricultural production caused the improvement in labor productivity to lag behind that in the industrial sector. The relatively low income and low labor productivity in agriculture became major issues in policy making. Such unbalanced growth between the agricultural sector and the nonagricultural sector affected production, prices, and wages in the agricultural sector and in the economy as a whole.

Contemporary agricultural development in Taiwan is also encountering various difficulties and challenges. Following are the most important ones.

**Reduction in Agricultural Resources.** During the economic development process, a great number of rural laborers moved into the industrial and service sectors. The highest record of agricultural laborers was 1.81 million in 1964. The number decreased to 1.06 million in 1989 (table 4–1), a decrease of 750,000 in a period of twenty-five years. The decrease in the total number of agricultural laborers in the past was largely attributable to the decline of the young workers enticed into the agricultural sector. As a result, aging farm labor has become a problem. The number employed as agricultural laborers is expected to decline continuously.

As for farmland, there is little frontier left on this island. At the same time, rapid industrialization and population growth, along with rising incomes, have created high demand for land. Since land for nonagricultural use is generally more productive than for farming, the conversion of farmland to nonfarm purposes is inevitable. From

TABLE 4-1

PARTICIPANTS IN THE LABOR FORCE IN TAIWAN IN AGRICULTURE,
INDUSTRY, AND SERVICES, 1952–1989

(1,000 persons and percent)

|  | Total | Agriculture | | Industry | | Services | |
|---|---|---|---|---|---|---|---|
| 1952 | 2,929 | 1,642 | (56.1) | 495 | (16.9) | 792 | (27.0) |
| 1955 | 3,108 | 1,667 | (53.6) | 560 | (18.0) | 881 | (28.4) |
| 1960 | 3,473 | 1,742 | (50.2) | 713 | (20.5) | 1,018 | (29.3) |
| 1964 | 3,658 | 1,810 | (49.5) | 779 | (21.3) | 1,070 | (29.2) |
| 1965 | 3,763 | 1,748 | (46.5) | 839 | (22.3) | 1,176 | (31.2) |
| 1970 | 4,576 | 1,681 | (36.7) | 1,278 | (27.9) | 1,617 | (35.4) |
| 1975 | 5,521 | 1,681 | (30.4) | 1,927 | (34.9) | 1,913 | (34.7) |
| 1980 | 6,547 | 1,277 | (19.5) | 2,774 | (42.4) | 2,497 | (38.1) |
| 1985 | 7,428 | 1,297 | (17.5) | 3,078 | (41.4) | 3,054 | (41.1) |
| 1989 | 8,258 | 1,065 | (12.9) | 3,488 | (42.2) | 3,705 | (44.9) |

NOTE: Discrepancies in totals are due to rounding. Percentages appear in
parenthesis.
SOURCE: Council of Agriculture, *Basic Agricultural Statistics*, ROC, 1990.

TABLE 4–2

AREA OF CULTIVATED LAND IN TAIWAN, 1945–1989

(hectares and percent)

|  | Total | Paddy Field | | Dry Land | |
|---|---|---|---|---|---|
| 1945 | 816,017 | 504,709 | (61.9) | 311,308 | (38.1) |
| 1950 | 870,633 | 530,236 | (60.9) | 340,397 | (39.1) |
| 1955 | 873,002 | 532,688 | (61.0) | 340,314 | (39.0) |
| 1960 | 869,223 | 525,580 | (60.5) | 343,643 | (39.5) |
| 1965 | 889,563 | 536,772 | (60.3) | 352,791 | (39.7) |
| 1970 | 905,263 | 528,927 | (58.4) | 376,336 | (41.6) |
| 1975 | 917,111 | 515,852 | (56.2) | 401,259 | (43.8) |
| 1980 | 907,353 | 509,326 | (56.1) | 398,027 | (43.9) |
| 1985 | 887,660 | 494,535 | (55.7) | 393,125 | (44.3) |
| 1989 | 894,601 | 479,954 | (53.6) | 414,647 | (46.4) |

NOTE: Percentages appear in parenthesis.
SOURCE: See table 4–1.

1952 to 1989, the area of paddy fields decreased by 53,700 hectares, whereas dry farmland increased by 72,200 hectares (table 4–2). The result is a net gain in farmland of 18,500 hectares, mainly through reclamation and development of slope land and wild land. In the meantime, land for buildings increased by 77,300 hectares; for roads and irrigation facilities, by 57,215 hectares; and for fishponds, by 15,670 hectares. These three categories increased by a total of 150,185 hectares, of which a large portion was converted from farmland in the fertile plains.

**Rigid Farmland Tenancy System.** After the implementation of land reform in Taiwan, the land tenure system became very rigid. Many part-time farmers left their land in the care of overseers and would not lease it to other farmers for fear that the government would invoke a regulation forcing them to relinquish ownership. Consequently, it is very difficult for a full-time farmer in Taiwan to enlarge his farm size by renting additional land. The system was originally designed to prevent the concentration of land ownership, but the same system unwittingly prevents more productive use of land and constitutes a serious bottleneck to Taiwan's current agricultural development.

Since 1960, the government has encouraged group farming to promote the efficiency of small farms. Farm mechanization has also been encouraged to realize economies of scale and to alleviate the labor shortage. Small landowners were encouraged to turn over their small pieces of farmland to full-time or large farmers for cultivation. Thus, no change in land ownership would have to be made, and owners of small farms would be free to seek full-time nonfarm jobs. Unfortunately, the legal basis for implementing this measure is still lacking, and the results are unsatisfactory. The Council of Agriculture is drafting a new law that will provide more flexibility in farmland transactions and the tenancy system. The new law is expected to prevent land speculation in rural areas and to enlarge the farm size for improving efficiency.

**Deterioration of the Rural Environment.** Rural industrialization has been popular in Taiwan. Industries in rural areas can be established either in the planned industrial zones or in the locations exempted from agricultural use. The employment opportunity created by rural industries has greatly changed the pattern of labor use in farm families and rural communities. Rural industrialization has provided rural labor with good ways to earn nonfarm income, which has contributed a great deal to the equalization of income distribution between rural and urban families. Farm families can thus not only raise their living standard but also increase their ability to invest in their farming business, a factor crucial to continuing prosperity in rural areas.

Although rural industrialization has contributed positively to the farm sector in the past, industry has become the major source of pollution in the rural areas and has affected agricultural production. The most serious problem is water pollution. All rivers and streams in western Taiwan have in various degrees been polluted by industrial wastes. Factories also took advantage of irrigation and drainage canals in rural areas to discharge untreated industrial waste water. In a few cases, industrial wastes have caused such serious soil contamination that farmland in the surrounding area had to be abandoned.

People in rural areas have become more and more cautious about the deterioration of the rural environment. They have expressed a clear unwillingness to tolerate any pollution from rural industries, a stance creating strong pressure on the government to take pollution control measures in rural areas.

In many cases, agriculture itself is responsible for the deteriorating environment in Taiwan. The overuse of fertilizers and chemicals, for example, has polluted surface water as well as ground water in rural areas. The wastes discharged from livestock farms have also caused water and air pollution. The overuse of ground water by aquacultural farms has resulted in serious land subsidence in the southern coastal area of Taiwan. To solve these problems, the government has already taken actions. Aquacultural farms, for instance, were encouraged to raise brackish-water fishes instead of freshwater ones. The livestock farms were not allowed to discharge animal wastes freely without treatment. With these measures and others, the deterioration of the rural environment is expected to come to a halt, gradually improving in the near future.

**Rapid Changes in the Structure of Food Demand.** As the per capita income in Taiwan increased rapidly, the pattern of food consumption changed significantly. Since 1970, there has been a big decrease in the per capita consumption of sweet potatoes and rice and a remarkable increase in the consumption of meat, sugar, vegetables, fruits, and milk. In 1970, for example, the annual per capita consumption of rice was 135 kilograms; it had decreased to only 70 kilograms in 1989. In the same period, the annual per capita consumption of meat increased from 40 kilograms to 60 kilograms (table 4–3). Now farmers in Taiwan are facing two big challenges, that is, to adjust the production to the changing demand and to compete with foreign agricultural

TABLE 4–3

PER CAPITA ANNUAL FOOD CONSUMPTION IN TAIWAN, 1952–1989
(kilograms)

| Item | 1952 | 1960 | 1970 | 1980 | 1989 |
|---|---|---|---|---|---|
| Cereals | | | | | |
|   Total | 138.1 | 159.7 | 164.1 | 138.8 | 105.1 |
|   Polished rice | 126.1 | 137.7 | 134.5 | 100.8 | 69.7 |
|   Wheat flour | 11.3 | 20.0 | 25.4 | 23.6 | 30.1 |
| Sweet potatoes | 59.9 | 65.4 | 18.4 | 4.1 | 1.2 |
| Sugar | 9.4 | 9.4 | 15.0 | 24.0 | 25.1 |
| Pulses, nuts, seeds | 9.9 | 11.4 | 18.3 | 18.8 | 21.9 |
| Vegetables | 61.7 | 61.1 | 84.8 | 129.6 | 122.5 |
| Fruits | 16.8 | 22.1 | 45.8 | 70.2 | 113.8 |
| Meat | 16.8 | 16.2 | 25.3 | 39.6 | 60.3 |
| Eggs | 1.6 | 1.6 | 4.1 | 8.0 | 11.9 |
| Fish | 15.1 | 21.7 | 34.2 | 38.7 | 48.4 |
| Milk | 1.2 | 3.2 | 11.0 | 27.6 | 35.4 |
| Oils and fats | 3.5 | 4.7 | 7.7 | 10.8 | 19.5 |

SOURCE: See table 4–1.

producers both in the domestic markets and in the foreign markets. The sharp increase in labor cost and the rapid switches in demand have created great pressure on Taiwan's farmers. Many of them have simply lost their interest and confidence in agriculture. It is very hard for farmers to find any product that can generate a good profit to them. As a result, farmland use has become extensive. Or in some areas farmland is idled and available for land speculation, while farmers are looking for jobs in other sectors.

**Sluggish Growth.** Taiwan's agricultural development reached its peak in the late 1960s; since then, the growth of agricultural output has followed a downward trend. The average annual growth rate of the agricultural sector registered 5 percent in the 1950s. It dropped to 4.1 percent in the 1960s and to 2.3 percent in the 1970s; it has been 1.3 percent since 1980. There are four reasons for these changes: (1) the decrease of farm resources; (2) low returns from crop production; (3) the massive influx of farm imports; and (4) changes in government policy from promoting agricultural production to adjusting the structure of agriculture.

**Small-Scale Farm Operation.** The small farm system is likely to

TABLE 4–4

AVERAGE FARM SIZE IN TAIWAN AND CULTIVATED LAND PER WORKER,
1952–1989

(hectares)

|  | Average Farm Size | Average Cultivated Land per Farm Worker |
|---|---|---|
| 1952 | 1.29 | 0.57 |
| 1955 | 1.19 | 0.55 |
| 1960 | 1.11 | 0.54 |
| 1964 | 1.06 | 0.53 |
| 1965 | 1.05 | 0.55 |
| 1970 | 1.03 | 0.58 |
| 1975 | 1.02 | 0.61 |
| 1980 | 1.02 | 0.79 |
| 1985 | 1.14 | 0.76 |
| 1989 | 1.24 | 0.95 |

SOURCE: See table 4–1.

prevail in a country with limited cultivated land and high population density. Taiwan's average farm size was 1.29 hectares in 1952, it decreased to 0.97 hectare in 1972, and it increased gradually to 1.24 hectares in 1989 because of the decrease of farm households (table 4–4). According to the agricultural census in 1985, the number of farm households with a farm size of less than 1 hectare accounted for 73 percent of total farm households (table 4–5). In the early days, small farms could be competitive because the nature of labor-intensive farming did not require significant scale economies. Now the situation has changed. When machines substitute for manual work to overcome the labor shortage, a 1-hectare farm is too small to be operated efficiently. As a result, land use has become less intensive. In 1989, the multiple cropping index dropped to 132 from its peak of 190 in 1964 (table 4–6). This decrease indicates a switch toward an extensive use of farmland and suggests that actions for a better use of the limited land resources are called for.

**Low Farming Income and Increase in Part-Time Farming.** Until the mid-1960s, agricultural work could bring fairly steady increases in real income to farm families, income commensurate with that of nonfarm families. Since then, farm income has risen slowly. In 1970, the per capita income of farm families was down to 60 percent of that of nonfarm families, or 70 percent of that of workers' families. Per

TABLE 4–5

NUMBER AND PERCENTAGE OF FARMS BY SIZE OF LANDHOLDING IN
TAIWAN, 1955 AND 1985

| Size of Landholding | 1955 | | 1985 | | Difference[a] | |
|---|---|---|---|---|---|---|
| Under 0.5 ha. | 254,038 | (34.39) | 323,674 | (41.93) | 69,636 | (7.54) |
| 0.5–1.0 ha. | 209,987 | (28.43) | 237,143 | (30.72) | 27,156 | (2.29) |
| 1.0–2.0 ha. | 188,604 | (25.53) | 155,111 | (20.09) | −33,493 | (−5.44) |
| 2.0–3.0 ha. | 57,219 | (7.75) | 36,246 | (4.70) | −20,973 | (−3.05) |
| 3.0–5.0 ha. | 23,249 | (3.15) | 15,206 | (1.97) | −8,043 | (−1.18) |
| 5.0–10.0 ha. | 5,266 | (0.71) | 3,941 | (0.51) | −1,325 | (−0.20) |
| 10.0 ha. and over | 277 | (0.04) | 585 | (0.08) | 308 | (0.04) |
| Total | 738,640 | | 771,906 | | 33,266 | |

NOTE: Number of farms are those with crop production.
a. Difference between 1985 and 1955.
SOURCE: Agricultural Census, Directorate General of Budget, Accounting, and Statistics, Executive Yuan; various years.

TABLE 4–6

THE MULTIPLE CROPPING INDEX IN TAIWAN, 1952–1989

| Year | Multiple Cropping Index |
|---|---|
| 1952 | 173.6 |
| 1955 | 172.7 |
| 1960 | 184.1 |
| 1964 | 189.7 |
| 1965 | 188.8 |
| 1970 | 183.0 |
| 1975 | 154.4 |
| 1985 | 141.6 |
| 1989 | 132.3 |

SOURCE: See table 4–1.

capita farm family income recovered steadily to 73 percent of nonfarm family income in 1989 (table 4–7) because of various supportive policies.

As the size of farms in Taiwan remained small during the past thirty years, it has become increasingly difficult for farmers to support themselves by agriculture. While economic development created

TABLE 4–7

PER CAPITA FARM FAMILY INCOME AS PERCENTAGE OF PER CAPITA
NONFARM FAMILY INCOME, 1966–1989

|  | Nonfarmers | Employees[a] | Laborers[b] |
|---|---|---|---|
| 1966 | 69.8 | 71.7 | 88.1 |
| 1970 | 60.2 | 63.9 | 70.0 |
| 1975 | 67.1 | 71.6 | 81.5 |
| 1980 | 66.4 | 72.4 | 79.9 |
| 1985 | 73.0 | 78.7 | 87.8 |
| 1989 | 72.5 | 78.4 | 87.2 |

a. Salary and wage earners.
b. Wage earners only.
SOURCE: See table 4–1.

plentiful job opportunities in industries and services, more and more
farm family members took jobs in the nonagricultural sectors. In
other words, a great many full-time farmers in Taiwan adjusted
themselves to become part-time farmers or sideline farmers in times
of rapid economic growth. In 1960, full-time farm households accounted for 47.6 percent of the total farm households, with the part-
time farm households at 29.9 percent and the sideline farm households at 22.5 percent. By 1985, full-time farm households had decreased to 14.8 percent, and the sideline farm households had markedly increased to 63.3 percent (table 4–8). These numbers indicate
that the majority of farmers in Taiwan have taken agriculture as their
sideline jobs.

**Falling Competitiveness in the World Market.** Largely because of
high wages and hence the high costs of farm production, many
Taiwanese farm products have lost the competitive edge in the world
market, and farm imports have started flooding in. Low-priced farm
imports have made domestic production of many farm products
unprofitable. Imported corn, for example, has replaced sweet potatoes as the major feed stuff and forced many farmers to give up
growing sweet potatoes. Rice and sugar are no longer profitable for
export. Once popular export items, canned mushrooms, asparagus,
and pineapple have lost their world market shares to other countries.

### Agricultural Policy in the 1970s and the 1980s

**Programs to Support Agriculture and Farmers in the 1970s.** From the
late 1960s to the early 1970s, agriculture experienced a very significant

TABLE 4–8

CHANGE IN TYPE OF FARM HOUSEHOLD IN TAIWAN, 1960–1985

(number and percentage)

| Type of Farm Household | 1960 | | 1970 | | 1980 | | 1985 | |
|---|---|---|---|---|---|---|---|---|
| Full time | 384,501 | (47.6) | 276,959 | (30.2) | 79,757 | (9.0) | 115,164 | (14.8) |
| Part time | 241,060 | (29.9) | 371,434 | (40.6) | 316,584 | (35.5) | 168,447 | (21.6) |
| Sideline | 182,039 | (22.5) | 267,573 | (29.2) | 494,774 | (55.5) | 496,367 | (63.6) |
| Total | 807,600 | | 915,966 | | 891,115 | | 779,978 | |

NOTE: The full-time farm household is one where no member of the farm household engages in off-farm work or where the total off-farm work days are less than thirty. The rest of the farm households are either the part-time farm household or the sideline farm household. The part-time farm household is the farm household where the income generated from the farm is greater than the off-farm income. The sideline farm household is the farm household where the off-farm income is greater than the farm income.
SOURCE: See table 4–5.

deceleration of output growth. The relative income position of farmers vis-à-vis nonfarmers was steadily deteriorating. These factors were behind the policy changes of the government in support of farmers. Beginning in 1973, a number of programs were carried out by the government to support agriculture and farmers. Following are the salient points of these programs.

*The accelerated rural development program, 1973–1979.* In 1972, the government announced the Accelerated Rural Development Program (ARDP) to be carried out beginning in 1973. It was aimed at increasing agricultural production, raising farm income, improving the rural environment, and accelerating agricultural modernization. Thus, a program comparable in significance to the land reform program was set in motion. The measures included in the program were as follows:

- abolition of the rice-for-fertilizer barter system
- abolition of the educational surtax on farmland tax
- easing of the terms of agricultural credit
- improvement of agricultural marketing
- strengthening of rural infrastructure
- acceleration of the extension of integrated use of improved techniques for cultivation
- establishment of specialized agricultural production areas
- strengthening of agricultural research and extension

- encouragement of the establishment of industrial plants in rural areas

The government appropriated NT$2 billion in grants in 1973–1974 to carry out the nine measures listed above. This program truly marked the change in economic development policy from "squeezing" agriculture to supporting agriculture. The program was originally scheduled to be concluded at the end of 1974. In view of the need for more concentrated efforts to lay a good foundation for modernization of the agricultural sector, however, the government decided to extend the program to 1979, with financial support for it to be made available annually. From fiscal year 1973 to fiscal year 1978, a total of NT$22.9 billion (including NT$13.6 billion of the Food Stabilization Fund) was spent on the program by the central government.

*The agricultural development statute.* To give agriculture strong legal support, the government put into effect the Agricultural Development Statute in September 1973. This was the first time in Taiwan's history that agriculture received government support and protection by law. The main features of this statute are as follows:

- For the purpose of enlarging a farm's operational scale, the contractual farming system was to be established, and it was not to be regarded as a tenancy system.
- If farmland is inherited by one inheritor for farming, the inheritance tax should be set aside and the farmland tax should also be waived for ten years. If farmland is sold to another farmer for cultivation, the land value increment tax should not apply.
- When plans are made to convert farmland to nonagricultural use, a consent from the agricultural authority is required.
- The trade authority should get consent from the agricultural authority before it approves the importation of any agricultural commodity.
- The government should increase public expenditures for strengthening rural infrastructure and for implementation of various welfare measures for farmers.
- The government should carry out agricultural insurance programs to enhance farmers' income and to maintain the rural social order.

Since the promulgation of this statute, the government has been obliged to give agriculture more favorable consideration in policy formulation.

*The guaranteed rice price.* Since the early 1970s, the emphasis of

rice policies has shifted. Most important, the barter system of fertilizer for rice was formally abolished in 1973. The government instituted a guaranteed price for rice in 1974 to ensure a reasonable
income to rice farmers and to give them an incentive to increase rice
production.

A food stabilization fund was established in 1974, with a total of
NT$3 billion to begin with. This fund is evidence of the government's
desire to participate indirectly in the rice market rather than to control
the rice supply directly. While the land tax was still collected in kind,
the rate was lowered. Finally, the farmland tax was suspended by the
government in 1987 to reduce agricultural production costs and to
increase farmers' income. Compulsory purchase of rice remains in
effect, but the purchase price is to be set at the guaranteed price,
which is much higher than the market price. Government policies are
thus moving in a direction more favorable to rice farmers.

The floor support price of rice is in principle fixed with 20 percent
profit above the production costs. Under this favorable condition, rice
production reached its highest level of 2.71 million metric tons in
1976. From 1974 to 1977, no limit was set on the quantity purchased
from rice growers. Because of heavy burdens on the public treasury,
the government has purchased a maximum of 970 kilograms per
hectare per crop from 1977 to 1989. The government also participated
in the market operations to buy rice at a price a little higher than the
market price to maintain a reasonable market price. The guaranteed
price of paddy rice was NT$10 per kilogram in 1974. It was NT$11.5
per kilogram from 1975 to 1978. Then it gradually increased from
NT$12.5 per kilogram in 1979 to NT$18.8 per kilogram in 1982. The
guaranteed price was maintained at this level until 1988. Then it
increased slightly to NT$19 per kilogram in 1989. Beginning in 1989,
the quantity of rice the government purchased at the guaranteed
price increased to 1,400 kilograms per hectare, and the quantity
purchased at the price higher than the market price was set at 1,000
kilograms per hectare. Obviously, the purpose of this policy was to
give more income to the rice growers. Through this program, the
government has incurred direct financial losses of about NT$7–10
billion annually in recent years.

**Programs to Improve the Structure of Agricultural Production and
to Enlarge Farming Scale in the 1980s.** *The programs following the ARDP.*
After the ARDP was terminated in 1979, the government launched
two subsequent programs: the Program on Enhancing Farm Income
and Strengthening Rural Reconstruction in 1979 and the Program on
Basic Infrastructure Development in 1980. These were merged into

the Program on Strengthening Basic Infrastructure and Enhancing Farm Income in 1982. This new set of programs was intended to carry out more coordinated and integrated long-term rural development projects. In 1985, the Six-Year Program on Improving Agricultural Structure and Enhancing Farm Income was launched. This program emphasized the adjustment of crop production and aimed at the reduction of rice production and the increase of high-value crops, the enlargement of the scale of farming operations, the improvement of agricultural marketing, and the strengthening of agricultural research and extension.

From FY 1979 to FY 1989, a total of NT$125.7 billion (including NT$39.8 billion on the Food Stabilization Fund) was spent on these programs. For a small island like Taiwan, a public capital investment that entails an expenditure of this magnitude to vitalize the small farm economy for a period of eleven years is impressive. This public spending on the agricultural sector is expected to grow with the expanding economy. The question is how to make the best use of public funds and resources so that new technology can be developed, the scale of farming enlarged, and the efficiency of agricultural production improved. These are the challenges for the people and the government of the Republic of China (ROC).

*The program to shift rice production to nonrice crops.* Since the mid-1970s, as per capita income increased, people have changed their pattern of food consumption significantly. The per capita consumption of rice was 140 kilograms per year in 1968. It fell drastically to 128 kilograms in 1976, to 105 kilograms in 1980, and to 70 kilograms in 1989. Because of this substantial decrease in the per capita consumption, the rice surplus became a serious problem for the government. In the late 1970s, the government carried out a program to shift rice fields to nonrice crop production through farm extension workers. Because there was no economic incentive given to the farmers in the program, however, they did not respond favorably. The rice surplus thus became a more and more serious problem.

In 1984, government decided to give a subsidy to farmers who shifted their rice fields to crops other than rice. If farmers changed their rice fields to the production of corn, sorghum, or soybeans, 1 metric ton of paddy rice per hectare per crop would be given to the farmers as a subsidy. In addition, corn, sorghum, and soybeans would be purchased by the government at the guaranteed prices. If farmers shifted from rice to the production of crops other than corn, sorghum, and soybeans, the subsidy increased to 1.5 metric tons of paddy rice per hectare per crop. Since its implementation, many farmers have participated in the program, and the production of rice has decreased significantly year after year.

In 1989, rice production was 1.86 million metric tons, a big reduction in comparison with the record production of 2.71 million metric tons in 1976. To benefit farmers and to reduce the management cost of the program, the government changed from a payment-in-kind subsidy to a cash payment in 1988. An amount of NT$16,500 and NT$24,750 per hectare was paid to farmers to replace 1 metric ton and 1.5 metric tons of paddy rice, respectively.

Taiwan's current rice policy has been criticized mainly on the grounds of contradictory purposes. Shifting from growing rice to growing other crops is to reduce rice production, at the same time that the guaranteed price for rice gives farmers an incentive to produce more rice. Although fully aware of the embarrassing situation, the government is reluctant to abolish the guaranteed rice price, largely for political reasons. The government is afraid that if the guaranteed price is abolished, farmers' interests will become a political rather than an economic issue and social instability will result. But if these policies are continued, the financial burden to the government will increase considerably, allowing the overproduction of rice to persist. A direct-payment scheme linked to farmers' income and land use is preferred to the existing policy and receives increasing attention among policy makers.

*The second phase of farmland reform.* After the completion of farmland reform programs in 1953, the land tenure system in Taiwan has become very rigid. Since 1960, group farming has been encouraged by the government to promote working efficiency in rural areas. Small landowners have been encouraged to entrust their small parcels of farmland to full-time and large owners for actual cultivation. Under this policy, the small farmers would continue to own their land but be free to seek full-time nonfarm employment. Unfortunately, because a legal basis for implementing these measures was lacking, Taiwan needed a second phase of farmland reform.

The second phase of the farmland reform program was designed to promote land use, labor productivity, and large-scale farming. This program was approved by the Executive Yuan in 1982 and was put into practice immediately. In coordination with the four-year economic plans and the program of agricultural development, the second-phase farmland reform program included: (1) loans for the purchase of farmland to expand farming scale; (2) joint, contractual, and cooperative farming; (3) land consolidation; (4) farm mechanization; and (5) supporting measures such as regional planning and the revision of related land and agricultural laws to pave the way for improving the land tenure system.

The main purpose of this program was to break through the bottleneck of small farm size and establish a new land tenure system that would allow the enlargement of farm operations without affecting land ownership. Following implementation of the program, the Statute of Agricultural Development and the 37.5 Percent Rent Reduction Act were amended to give contractual farming and custom farming[1] a stronger legal basis by clearly stating that these types of farming would not be subject to the provisions of the 37.5 Percent Rent Reduction Act. Other measures of the program mentioned above had been instrumental in promoting the expansion of farm size.

Up to now, however, because of the farmers' lack of confidence, the results of the program are considered unsatisfactory as far as the enlargement of farm size is concerned. Therefore, the Council of Agriculture is preparing a draft of a new law that would provide more flexible conditions on farmland transactions and tenancy. Under the existing land laws, only the bona fide farmers are qualified to purchase farmland. The proposed new law would allow the graduates of agricultural schools, young people with special training in farming, agribusinesses, and the agricultural production cooperatives to buy farmland for farming. The new law would also stipulate that after the promulgation of this new law, all tenancy would be liberalized except the lease contracts that were signed under the 37.5 Percent Rent Reduction Act. In addition, the law will also place more restrictive regulations on the conversion of farmland to nonagricultural uses. The new law is expected to prevent land speculation in rural areas and will give farmers a better chance to enlarge their farms to make them more efficient. It will take a long time to get the new law through all the legal procedures and to put it into action. To a certain extent, the final outcome of this new law is still uncertain.

## Agricultural Trade Policy

Before the 1960s, Taiwan adopted strict controls and highly protective policies to economize the use of foreign exchange and to nurture domestic import-substitution industries. The strict control of foreign exchange and the multiple exchange rate system were mainly ways to tax export goods, or agricultural products, because 90 percent of the exports were agricultural products. In the 1960s, owing to the

---

[1]In custom farming, work is done by a team of agricultural workers for a lump-sum payment under the instruction of the farm owner.

exhaustion of the domestic market's ability to absorb manufactured goods, an external-oriented strategy was implemented to absorb the relatively abundant labor resources. The tax rebate system and export-processing zones established to encourage exports were mainly a benefit to manufacturing industries. Agricultural products were still protected by high tariffs, though import control was lessened to some extent.

From the late 1960s through the 1970s, the threat of a foreign exchange shortage disappeared, and the trade surplus increased steadily. Government controls on imports were further decreased, but tariff protection still remained relatively high. The export-encouraging, and import-impeding, trade policies were carried out through the 1980s. In 1984, trade liberalization and economic internationalization policies were instituted by the government. The reasons were twofold. One purpose was to ease the pressure of inflation caused from the accumulation of a trade surplus. Perhaps more important, however, the bilateral trade negotiations since 1978 between the ROC and the United States also provided the impetus behind this liberalization policy. Although outside trade partners asked that both tariff and nontariff barriers be removed, trade liberalization had not been very significant. Progress lagged largely because of the export-encouraging, import-discouraging policies and the mercantilistic trade policy implanted in the minds of the policy makers.

Only in late 1986, when the trade surplus was still increasing and U.S. pressure on ROC's trade liberalization policy focused on the valuation system of the New Taiwan (N.T.) dollar, did the ROC accelerate the pace of liberalization. As of 1991, nominal tariff rates for all products were reduced to 8.89 and will be further reduced to 7 percent as scheduled by the liberalization plan. The effective rate of the tariff burden fell from 11.62 percent in 1979 to 4.95 percent in 1991. The percentage of the tariff reduction is 57.4 percent for the effective rate of tariff, or 77.28 percent for nominal tariff protection (see table 4–9).

Significantly, tariff reduction did not occur equally to the agricultural and the nonagricultural sectors. For some agricultural products, high tariff protection still remained, and the liberalization movement was not so impressive. Tariff protection on certain individual products, however, was substantially removed. The tariff on chocolate, for example, was reduced from 100 percent in 1980 to 17.5 percent in 1989; preparations of meat, from 60 percent to 20 percent; infant food, from 30 percent to 10 percent; cherries, from 50 percent to 15 percent; prunes, from 45 percent to 20 percent; and so forth. Many items, though, still have tariffs as high as 40–50 percent: fresh fruits, concentrated fruit juice, natural honey, and vegetables, for example. The average nominal tariff rate on agricultural products was 21.6 percent in 1991 and 19.8 percent in 1992. Tariffs on farm products are much higher than those on manufactured goods. The effective rate of the tariff burden on agricultural products is 11.7 percent, 59 percent higher than the 4.77 percent tariff burden on manufactured goods. It is quite obvious, then, that tariff protection on agricultural goods exceeds that on manufactured goods.

As far as nontariff barriers are concerned, although most products can be imported freely, the quantity of some items recognized as important or sensitive is restricted. Sugar and fresh milk, for example, are classified as "controlled items," the most severe restriction on imports. Another classification that also implies restrictions on imports is for "permitted items"; these limits apply to imports from specified countries and are subject to approval from the Council of Agriculture. "Specified-area restrictions" are usually the result of bilateral trade agreements and apply to very few products. "Strategic-products," which still apply to many agricultural goods, can be viewed as an import restriction, in essence whenever the Council of Agriculture recognizes that an open market might cause serious problems for domestic producers. Products in this category include rice, red beans, peanuts, edible offal, several kinds of fish, and garlic bulbs, among others. Such impediments to trade can perhaps be modified gradually in step with the unavoidable trend of liberalization.

Speedy liberalization of the ROC's trade policy has benefited the economy substantially as a major force to depress inflation since 1987. As a result mainly of the accumulation of the huge trade surplus, for example, the price level of real estate (nonimportable goods) increased by more than 200 percent in the following three years, but the consumer price index (all importable goods) increased by only 8.7 percent during the same period. The trade liberalization program, however, has also allowed increased imports of foreign agricultural products and increased competition for domestic producers. Those developments in turn have led to more complaints from farmers, which are affecting the recent policy decisions by the Council of Agriculture.

Resistance to further liberalization of agricultural trade has also arisen because of the slower pace of institutional reforms in the agricultural sector. Adjustment policies such as on-the-job training, early retirement programs, import relief systems, and a new farmland law, which would allow farmers affected by liberalization policies

TABLE 4–9

CHANGES OF IMPORT TARIFFS IN TAIWAN, SELECTED YEARS, 1955–1992

(millions of N.T. dollars and percent)

| | Customs Tax Refunds (1) | Revenue from Import Taxes (2) | Import Goods CIF Value (3) | Percentage of Tax Refund to Tax Revenue (1)/(2) | Average Tax Burden (%) (2)/(3) | Average Nominal Tax Rate (%) | | Tariff Reduction[a] (5) |
|---|---|---|---|---|---|---|---|---|
| | | | | | | Column 1 (4) | Column[b] 2 | |
| 1955 | 17 | 1,201 | 31,465 | — | 38.20 | 47.0 | | n.a. |
| 1961 | 222 | 2,039 | 12,894 | 10.8 | 15.80 | 38.8 | | n.a. |
| 1965 | 898 | 3,895 | 22,296 | 23.0 | 16.50 | 35.4 | | n.a. |
| 1971 | 5,474 | 9,059 | 64,035 | 77.3 | 14.14 | 39.1 | | n.a. |
| 1974 | 11,514 | 24,904 | 212,121 | 46.2 | 11.74 | 55.65 | | 202 |
| 1975 | 12,838 | 23,527 | 238,201 | 54.6 | 9.88 | 52.69 | | 71 |
| 1978 | 16,194 | 40,027 | 355,055 | 40.5 | 11.27 | 43.58 | | 996 |
| 1979 | 21,597 | 53,597 | 461,436 | 40.3 | 11.62 | 39.14 | | 432 |
| 1980 | 23,667 | 57,003 | 633,660 | 41.5 | 9.00 | 35.96 | 31.17 | 1,606 |
| 1984 | 18,863 | 67,622 | 875,737 | 27.9 | 7.72 | 35.95 | 30.81 | 281 |
| 1985 | 21,869 | 66,873 | 847,533 | 32.7 | 7.89 | 32.79 | 26.46 | 1,058 |
| 1986 | 15,700 | 63,838 | 832,412 | 24.6 | 7.67 | 31.77 | 22.83 | 777 |
| 1987 | 17,417 | 76,267 | 1,020,429 | 22.8 | 7.47 | n.a. | 19.37 | 1,599 |
| 1988 | 16,136 | 78,582 | 1,281,561 | 20.5 | 6.13 | n.a. | 12.57 | 3,313 |
| 1989 | 9,691 | 89,387 | 1,418,290 | 10.8 | 6.30 | n.a. | 9.73 | 4,738 |

| | | | | | | | | |
|---|---|---|---|---|---|---|---|---|
| 1990 | 5,842 | 81,879 | 1,395,244 | 7.1 | 5.86 | n.a. | 9.73 | 0 |
| 1991 | 4,425 | 79,269 | 1,599,389 | 5.6 | 4.95 | n.a. | 8.89 | 1,965 |
| 1992 | n.a. | 88,429 | 1,726,366 | n.a. | 5.12 | n.a. | (7.0) | n.a. |

n.a. = not available.

NOTE: Data are basically for the fiscal year, but the nominal tax rate and revised items are based on the calendar year. Figures in parenthesis are projected figures.

a. Number of items.

b. Under pressure to reduce tariff barriers from the United States, the ROC government applied the second column preferential tariff on imports to friendly trade partners in 1980. Since almost 90 percent of its trade partners are eligible for the second column preferential tariff by 1985, and this percentage is still increasing, the average nominal tax rate of column one has been ignored by the Ministry of Finance. Countries not eligible for the second column preferential tariff are usually the non–market-oriented economies.

SOURCE: Ministry of Finance, ROC.

more flexibility in transferring to other sectors or products, are all greatly needed now.

Domestic commodity policy, which is designed to raise farmers' incomes by purchasing farm products at guaranteed prices, may also influence agricultural trade by increasing the production of these products. Commodities supported by this program include rice, soybeans, corn, and sorghum. Since rice is the staple food in Taiwan, however, protection of rice production falls under national security concerns. Because the guaranteed price for rice is much higher than the market price, the rice surplus has become a problem. To reduce this surplus, the government promoted a rice paddy conversion program as well as a soil conservation program in 1984. These programs thus reinforce the subsidization of soybean, corn, and sorghum production by purchasing at guaranteed prices. Nevertheless, since almost 93 percent of domestic consumption of soybeans, corn, and sorghum originates from imports, the inefficiency of domestic production and the trade distortion resulting from such protection are not very significant.

## The Comprehensive Agricultural Adjustment Program, 1991–1997

The current Six-Year Program on Improving Agricultural Structure and Enhancing Farm Income was launched in 1985 and terminated in 1991. To continue agricultural development and to maintain the progress and prosperity of rural areas, the Council of Agriculture has worked out a new program for a period of six years, from July 1991 to June 1997, the Comprehensive Agricultural Adjustment Program, 1991–1997. The Executive Yuan approved it in principle in March 1991. It is worthwhile for us to highlight the key points of the program and to look into the future directions of agricultural policy of the ROC in this six-year period. The proposed policy measures of this program are as follows:

• foster core farmers and establish a licensing system for all farmers and a pension system for aged, retiring farmers
• work out regional agricultural plans; strictly enforce the law keeping farmland for agricultural uses; relax the regulations to allow nonfarmers to own farmland
• develop designated farm products; strengthen the agricultural production and marketing system; enhance the market competitiveness of farm products. Tea, fodder, orchids, ornamental plants, plant seedlings, papayas, wax apples, passion fruit, mangoes, grapes, summer vegetables, breeding animals, milk, broilers, hogs, and farm-

raised fish have been sorted out as the major agricultural products to receive priority for development for the domestic market as well as the foreign market. In due course, the list of these designated products may be changed to meet the changing conditions of the market. Rice, sugar cane, peanuts, small red beans, corn, sorghum, soybeans, sweet potatoes, and beef have been selected as farm products for some protection through price supports and production subsidies.

• set a timetable to liberalize agricultural importation and reduce the tariff rate on agricultural imports; compensate farmers for their losses caused by import liberalization

• give direct income payments to farmers; decouple the production policy and the income policy

• carry out crop insurance by area and by period, with rice as the first crop to be insured; prepare the crop insurance law to provide the legal basis; set up the crop insurance agencies

• improve the agricultural experiment and extension system; strengthen disease control and quarantine

• conserve and exploit fishery resources; restructure the fishing industry; promote international fishery cooperation

• strengthen farmers' organizations; render more and better services to farmers

• make comprehensive planning available to rural communities; replenish rural culture to enhance the quality of rural life

• make plans for conservation of natural resources and the ecosystem; control pollution in rural areas

The contents of the Comprehensive Agricultural Adjustment Program, 1991–1997, prepared by the Council of Agriculture are, in fact, the policy guidelines indicating only future policy directions. Special attention should be paid to some of the policy directions. First, it is clear from the program that future agricultural protection in Taiwan will be given only to a designated group of carefully selected products that are regarded as the most important to farmers and rural areas. Second, a timetable will be set to liberalize agricultural importation and reduce tariff rates on agricultural imports. It is worthwhile to point out that between 1979 and 1988, import tariffs on agricultural products in Taiwan were reduced significantly. The weighted "real" tariff rate decreased from 9.5 percent to 5.5 percent. It will be reduced further to roughly 3.5 percent in the next few years. A timetable for further tariff reduction on some 500 agricultural products will be worked out. So that the adjustment proceeds as smoothly as possible, it seems reasonable that tariffs should be reduced only gradually and over time. Third, the government is considering decoupling the farmers' income support policies and the agricultural price support policies, which is acceptable to the General Agreement on Tariffs and Trade. Fourth, the future agricultural development program will put more emphasis on measures to enhance farmers' welfare.

Some of the proposals in this adjustment program—such as pensions for aged, retiring farmers, licenses for farmers, liberalization of the land tenure system, crop insurance, and direct income payment to farmers—involve a great deal of public expenditure and risk. Careful and objective analysis and evaluation are needed. The cabinet (the Executive Yuan) is fully aware of this situation and has given instruction to the Council of Agriculture to make detailed feasibility studies concerning pensions for the aged, retiring farmers, crop insurance, and direct income payments to farmers. Hence these three proposals will not be carried out immediately. In the meantime, the cabinet has decided that from 1991 to 1997 at least, Taiwan's agricultural development would seek to improve production in quality rather than in quantity. Moreover, to prevent further deterioration of the rural environment, the cabinet has also decided that the hog and aquaculture industries will not be allowed to produce for export purposes before pollution can be controlled.

Finally, the Comprehensive Agricultural Adjustment Program has been incorporated into the Six-year National Construction Plan, 1991–1997, which was initiated by the Executive Yuan in 1990 and publicized in early 1991. In the construction plan, the average annual agricultural growth rate has been set at zero, of which the average growth rate of crop production will be 0.9 percent; livestock production, − 0.2 percent; fishery production, 0 percent; and forestry production, − 1.3 percent. The production targets of major selected agricultural products are shown in table 4–10.

Comparing the actual production of major agricultural products in 1990 and the targeted production in 1997, we find that production of rice, sugar cane, tea, citrus, hogs, ducks, geese, eggs, deep-sea fish, coastal fish, aquaculture, and forestry is to *decrease*, whereas the production of sweet potatoes, peanuts, soybeans, corn, sorghum, bananas, mangoes, grapes, summer vegetables, cut flowers, cattle, chickens, turkeys, milk, and in-shore fish is to *increase*. The items whose production is to be reduced in the future are those either in overproduction now such as rice, citrus, ducks, and eggs or those with high social costs such as hogs and aquaculture. The products that would be increased in production are those either with relatively high income elasticities of demand such as fruits, vegetables and

100

TABLE 4–10

PRODUCTION TARGET OF MAJOR AGRICULTURAL PRODUCTS, 1991 AND
1997, AND ACTUAL PRODUCTION, 1990

| Product | Unit | 1990 | 1991 | 1997 |
|---|---|---|---|---|
| Crops | | | | |
| Rice (brown) | 1,000 mt | 1,850 | 1,813 | 1,700 |
| Sweet potatoes | 1,000 mt | 222 | 266 | 280 |
| Peanuts | 1,000 mt | 70 | 80 | 100 |
| Soybeans | 1,000 mt | 10 | 10 | 12 |
| Maize (feed) | 1,000 mt | 288 | 294 | 300 |
| Sorghum | 1,000 mt | 105 | 132 | 150 |
| Sugar cane | 1,000 mt | 5,545 | 5,482 | 5,280 |
| Tea | 1,000 mt | 22 | 20 | 20 |
| Bananas | 1,000 mt | 133 | 183 | 200 |
| Citrus | 1,000 mt | 527 | 532 | 513 |
| Mangoes | 1,000 mt | 119 | 125 | 140 |
| Max apples | 1,000 mt | 113 | 120 | 135 |
| Grapes | 1,000 mt | 102 | 110 | 140 |
| Guavas | 1,000 mt | 106 | 110 | 120 |
| Summer vegetables | 1,000 mt | 886 | 960 | 964 |
| Cut flowers | Million dozen | 53.5 | 53.7 | 54.9 |
| Livestock | | | | |
| Hogs[a] | 1,000 head | 12,175 | 11,000 | 9,000 |
| Cattle[a] | 1,000 head | 30 | 30 | 40 |
| Chickens[b] | Million head | 227 | 212 | 238 |
| Ducks[b] | Million head | 40.4 | 40.0 | 38.0 |
| Geese[b] | Million head | 4.6 | 4.0 | 4.2 |
| Turkeys[b] | 1,000 head | 770 | 900 | 900 |
| Milk | 1,000 mt | 200 | 210 | 300 |
| Eggs | Million piece | 4,635 | 4,200 | 4,500 |
| Fisheries | | 1,358 | 1,360 | 1,370 |
| Deep-sea | 1,000 mt | 701 | 690 | 700 |
| Inshore | 1,000 mt | 296 | 318 | 340 |
| Coastal | 1,000 mt | 52 | 52 | 50 |
| Aquaculture | 1,000 mt | 309 | 300 | 280 |
| Forestry | | 224 | 221 | 207 |
| Timber | 1,000 M³ | 168 | 166 | 155 |
| Mill wood | 1,000 M³ | 56 | 55 | 52 |

Mt = metric tons. M³ = cubic meters.
a. Slaughtered.
b. Dressed.
SOURCE: Executive Yuan, *The Six-Year National Construction Plan 1991–1997*,
ROC, January 1991.

flowers or the import substitutes such as feed stuffs. These production targets seem to follow in accordance with the new agricultural policy and in response to changing market conditions.

## Summary and Conclusions

During the 1950s and the early 1960s, agriculture went through a period of rapid growth. This high growth was brought to an end by the combined effect of successful industrialization and development within agriculture itself in the late 1960s. Industrialization drew workers from agriculture, created labor shortages during times of planting and harvesting, and drove up farm wages and agricultural production costs. These developments discouraged multiple cropping and labor-intensive production methods. Within agriculture, many of the most effective measures to promote rapid growth had already been taken by the late 1960s. New measures generally produced more limited results. The small size of farms and the slowness in adopting group farming made farm mechanization proceed slowly. The income gap between farmers and nonfarmers became more and more significant. Part-time farm households increased markedly at this stage. This process contributed to the rising share of farm family income from nonagricultural sources. Therefore, the ARDP, the Agricultural Development Statute, and the guaranteed rice price were instituted in the 1970s to vitalize agriculture and the rural sector.

This development phase constitutes a crucial turning point away from a strategy to generate a surplus to help capital formation outside of agriculture and toward a strategy to protect and, increasingly, subsidize farmers' incomes. The greater government support to farmers during this phase led to fundamental changes in the level of nominal and effective protection of agricultural products in Taiwan. As rice farmers responded favorably to the support price of rice, production reached an all-time high of 2.71 million tons in 1976. The increase in rice production together with the decrease of per capita rice consumption has resulted in a serious problem of surplus rice since 1976.

In the 1980s, the government encouraged diversification away from rice toward higher-valued crops and products more consistent with the emerging pattern of consumer demand. In particular, the production of commodities facing relatively high elasticities of demand, such as pork, chicken, fruits, vegetables, and feed stuffs, was promoted. Diversification went in two directions: first, promotion of goods for the domestic market and for exports in which Taiwan enjoyed a comparative advantage, such as pork and some fruits and processed food; and second, import substitution of goods in which Taiwan had a comparative disadvantage, such as corn, sorghum, and some dairy products. The first direction was clearly desirable from an efficiency standpoint, but the second one was the next-best choice from the standpoint of domestic resources.

In addition, the government also moved toward liberalization of agriculture, liberalizing to some degree agricultural imports, reducing at least some price distortions, and improving the functioning of products and factor markets. These measures resulted in the large increase in total agricultural imports and, to a lesser extent, agricultural exports. They contributed to the emergence of an import surplus in agricultural trade on the order of U.S.$2.34 billion in 1989. Moreover, the second phase of the farmland reform was a crucial institutional development that was initiated in the 1980s and recognized contractual farming as a form of contract that protected the rights of the farm owners and opened the door to the enlargement of the operational size of farm. Because farm owners lacked confidence in contractual farming, though, the performance of the second phase of the farmland reform was not satisfactory. The size of farms remained small after the implementation of the program.

It is clear that future agricultural policy in Taiwan will emphasize qualitative improvements rather than the quantitative growth to prevent the further deterioration of the rural environment and to meet the challenge of economic liberalization. Many components of the current policy are reasonable, given the objectives under the prevailing conditions. The major effort to rationalize the structure of agricultural production through enlarging the operational size of the farm, training of core farmers, and encouraging mechanization is entirely consistent with increased efficiency. Greater investment in research to identify appropriate mechanized technologies and potential substitutes for rice and grains with high value added and less comparative disadvantage appears indicated, however. To bring domestic production more in line with the commercial demand, while avoiding extreme protection rates, the establishment of a public land reserve should also be seriously explored. Moreover, it is desirable that the government be more active in improving the efficiency of the domestic agricultural marketing system, narrowing the gaps between the prices paid by consumers and those received by farmers. Furthermore, it is equally important that the public sector should invest more heavily in the human capital of the rural population by educating and training the children of farmers to provide them the knowledge and skills required to qualify for productive employment opportunities outside of agriculture. It seems reasonable to suggest that the government should give these measures high enough priority in future agricultural policy for maintaining rural prosperity.

From the point of view of international trade and welfare maximization, however, we can hope that trade liberalization will be promoted globally. In today's markets, worldwide protection of agricultural products seriously distorts world prices. Although trade liberalization policies in a single country may cause irreversible damage to domestic production, policy makers have used recent criticism and resistance of interest groups as an excuse to maintain protective policies in perpetuity. Consequently, we still need multilateral negotiations to improve trade liberalization policies as we move toward the end of the century.

## References

Baldwin, Robert E. *The Political Economy of U.S. Trade Policy*. Cambridge, Mass.: MIT Press, 1985.

———. "Trade Policies in Developed Countries." In *Handbook of International Economics*, vol. 1, edited by Ronald W. Jones and Peter B. Kenen, 571–619. Amsterdam: North Holland Publishing Co., 1984.

Chen, H. Y., W. F. Hsu, and Y. K. Mao. *Rice Policies of Taiwan*. Food Research Institute Studies, vol. 14, no. 4. Palo Alto: Stanford University Press, 1975.

Council of Agriculture. *The Comprehensive Agricultural Adjustment Program, 1991–1997*. Taipei, ROC. 1991.

Council for Economic Planning and Development. *The Six-Year National Construction Plan, 1991–1997*. Taipei, ROC, 1991.

Hsiao, H. H. *Government Agricultural Strategies in Taiwan and South Korea*. Institute of Ethnology, Academia Sinica. ROC, 1981.

Hufbauer, Gary C., Diane T. Berliner, and Kimberly A. Elliott. *Trade Protection in the United States: 31 Case Studies*. Washington, D.C.: Institute of International Economics, 1986.

Krueger, Anne O. "Theory and Practice of Commercial Policy: 1945–1990." Working paper. Cambridge, Mass.: National Bureau of Economic Research, Inc., 1990.

Lee, T. H. *Intersectoral Capital Flows in the Economic Development of Taiwan, 1895–1960*. Ithaca, N.Y.: Cornell University Press, 1971.

Li, K. T. *The Evolution of Policy behind Taiwan's Development Success*. New Haven: Yale University Press, 1988.

Mao, Y. K. "Agricultural Development Policy and Performance in Taiwan, ROC." *Industry of Free China* (Taipei, Taiwan). (November and December 1984 and January 1985).

————. "Current Land Problems and Policies of Taiwan, the Republic of China." *Industry of Free China* (Taipei, Taiwan). (June 1987), pp. 5–24.

Mao, Y. K., and C. Shive. "Agricultural and Industrial Development of the Republic of China on Taiwan." Paper presented at the International Conference on Agriculture on the Road to Industrialization, September 4–7, 1990, Taiwan, ROC.

Shen, T. H., ed. *Agriculture's Place in the Strategy of Development: The Taiwan Experience*. Joint Commission on Rural Reconstruction, Taipei, ROC, July 1974.

Thorbecke, Erik. "Agricultural Development." In *Economic Growth and Structural Change in Taiwan*, edited by Walter Galenson. Ithaca, N.Y.: Cornell University Press, 1979.

————. "The Process of Agricultural Development in Taiwan." In *Taiwan: From Developing to Mature Economy*, edited by Gustav Ramis. Oxford: Westview Press, 1992.

Tsiang, S. C., W. L. Chen, and A. Hsien. "Development towards Trade Liberalization in Taiwan, ROC." Proceedings of conference on U.S.-Taiwan economic relations, 1985, Taipei.

Tu, C. H., and W. T. Wang. "Trade Liberalization in the ROC on Taiwan and the Economic Effects of the Tariff Reductions." In *Industrial Policies of Korea and the Republic of China: Papers and Discussions from the 1988 Joint KDI-CIER Conference*, edited by the Korea Development Institute. Seoul, Korea: Korea Development Institute, 1988, pp. 42–86.

Woo, R. J., and T. T. Fu. "Proposed Approaches to Facilitating Agricultural Trade Liberalization in Taiwan." *Industry of Free China* (Taipei, Taiwan), (November 1990), pp. 13–24.

World Bank. *World Development Report*. New York: Oxford University Press, 1986.

Yager, J. A. *Transforming Agriculture in Taiwan—The Experience of the Joint Commission on Rural Reconstruction*. Ithaca, N.Y.: Cornell University Press, 1988.

Yu, Y. H. "The Accelerated Rural Development Program in Taiwan," Agricultural Economic Research Papers, Economic Digest Series, no. 23, Joint Commission on Rural Reconstruction, October 1978.

# 5

# Agricultural Price and Income Policies in the United States

*D. Gale Johnson*

Programs to intervene directly in the markets for agricultural products to improve the income of U.S. farm families began with the establishment of the Federal Farm Board in 1929. Agriculture had not fared very well during the general economic prosperity of the last half of the 1920s, before the stock market crash in October 1929. The Federal Farm Board made loans to farm marketing cooperatives so that when prices were low, grain could be held off the market until prices strengthened. Unfortunately, the board's first efforts to stabilize wheat prices came in late 1929, as prices were plummeting. Even though it limited its activities primarily to wheat and cotton, the board soon exhausted its resources, and prices of farm products fell by 50 percent or more.

As a result of its price guarantees, the board had built up substantial stocks of commodities in late 1929 and early 1930. After accumulating nearly half a year's crop of wheat, by mid-1931 the board did not have the resources either to continue its price support operations or to hold the accumulated stocks indefinitely. Consequently, over the next two years it disposed of its stocks with depressing effects on market prices.

Some note should be taken of earlier policies designed to support the development of agriculture in the United States. The first set of policies dealt with the disposition of huge land resources. One objective of land disposal policies was to provide the basis for family farms—the cornerstone of the American farm system. This was the particular purpose of the Homestead Act of 1862, which gave land to farm families if they would promise to live on the farm for five years. The intention was to limit the size of the farm to 160 acres (65 hectares), but in many cases individuals acquired much more than

160 acres because of poor administration of the program.

Another important measure was the federal government's contribution of land to agricultural colleges in each state. These land grant colleges were to provide young people from rural areas with an education that included general studies and practical applications. The colleges were also to engage in research to solve problems confronting farmers in production and marketing. The act that established these colleges was passed in 1862. Some twenty-five years later, the federal government appropriated funds to support research in these colleges, which were state, not federal, institutions. And in 1914 the triad was completed with the establishment of the agricultural extension service, created to transfer research results to farmers in a timely and understandable manner. Federal and state governments took an active role in the development of transportation through support of roads, canals, and railroads.

Two other major policy areas are worth noting. One was a cooperative credit system, starting with the land banks established in 1916 and followed a few years later by a credit system to provide operating funds for farmers. The credit system was a response to the view universally held by farmers that interest rates are too high and that they are exploited by banks and other money lenders. Until the 1980s, the farm credit system functioned quite well. During the 1980s, however, it became overextended, was hit by hard times, and had to be rescued and substantially reformed by the federal government. The other policy area was the tariff. On the whole, farmers were adversely affected by the tariff polices that prevailed from the middle of the nineteenth century until World War II. Tariffs on industrial products were high, and exports of agricultural products were important to many farmers before the middle of that century. Southern farmers, especially, saw high tariffs as inimical to their interests. These farmers were good economists, since it is now known that tariffs on imports are taxes on exports (Clements and Sjaastad, 1984).

### The Great Depression of the 1930s

The framework of the farm price and income policies of the 1980s was established in the legislation designed to assist farmers during the Great Depression of the 1930s. That legislation was based, to some degree, on the lessons learned from the failure of the Federal Farm Board.

The board had no control over the supply of the commodity when it attempted to support the price: it could only transfer some of the total supply to stocks. There is a limit to how large the stocks can be, and eventually they must be disposed of. It was agreed that a stock policy, even though it could theoretically even out the highs and lows in prices, could not influence the average price level. To influence the average price level, which had fallen disastrously low in 1932, the legislation enacted measures to control the total supply produced.

The economic situation of farmers was considered so serious that drastic steps were taken to reduce production nearer a level that, given the demand, would return significantly higher prices to farmers. By the time the legislation was passed in May 1933, most crops had been planted. The legislation provided for payments to farmers to plow up crops already planted, principally cotton and tobacco, as a means of reducing supply. To reduce the supply of hogs, whose price had fallen by almost two-thirds between 1929 and 1932, farmers were offered premium prices to sell young pigs and pregnant sows. The slaughter of young pigs and pregnant sows was so unpopular that it occurred only in 1933 and early 1934.

For the major crops, output was to be restricted by paying farmers to reduce the acreage of a crop. The 1934 program for corn, for example, called for farmers to reduce the acreage of corn by 20 percent compared with the average of 1932 and 1933, and for doing so they would receive a payment of $.30 per bushel for the expected yield from the acreage not planted. Participation in the program was voluntary. As an incentive to participate in addition to the payment for not planting, only participants were eligible for a minimum price in the form of a price support loan. Programs for other crops had similar features. In summary, for the crops with price and income programs, there were four common features. The programs were voluntary, participation required a reduction in acreage planted, payments were made related to the amount and productivity of the acreage diverted, and participating farmers were eligible for price support loans. These same features are included in the farm legislation passed in 1985.

This is not the place to evaluate the farm programs of the 1930s, except to note that the economic circumstances confronting farmers were extremely dire, and some form of governmental intervention was inevitable. Net farm incomes had fallen on average by almost two-thirds between 1929 and 1932, and in the American Midwest, where much of the corn and wheat was produced, by even more. Many farmers were threatened with the loss of their land because they could not pay the interest on their loans, and many rural banks were failing because of the farm crisis. Measures relating to farm credit and many others were adopted in an effort to mitigate the adverse situation in rural areas, thus preserving the structure of American agriculture. This structure was capable of a large growth of output during World War II, making the United States the major source of food supplies for the Allies during the war and for much of the world after the war. In this important sense, the farm programs were successful. As for increasing farm incomes, however, accidents of nature (severe droughts in 1934 and 1936, for example) and monetary expansion were probably more important than the farm programs.

### Policy Debates—1945 to 1980

Political factors were obviously important in shaping the farm policy debates both within Congress and between Congress and the executive branch.[1] These factors were at work in the debate during World War II over how the country should prepare for peace and what the role of government in agriculture was to be.

During World War II and immediately thereafter, there was a lively exchange over the future course of agricultural policy generally and of farm price policy particularly. Many professionals, academics, and policy makers favored full production and moderate price supports. By "moderate," they meant price supports that would be effective only occasionally, in response to a bumper crop or a sharp fall off in demand. The alternative was price supports that could be maintained only by limiting output and by surplus disposal operations, such as food aid and export subsidies.

While the Agricultural Act of 1948 embodied these views, the effective application of the legislation was not scheduled to take effect until 1950. The 1948 legislation became a major issue in the presidential election in 1948. When the act was passed, Congress was controlled by the Republicans. President Truman, a Democrat, campaigned throughout the Midwest by claiming this legislation proved that the Republicans were out to harm farmers by reducing price supports to such low levels. He made effective use of caricature showing that the Congress "had stabbed the farmer." Truman was reelected, to the surprise of most politicians, by winning farm states that normally supported the Republicans.

Thus, it was not too surprising that the 1948 legislation was replaced soon after the election. The new act, passed in 1949, represented a victory for the proponents of high price supports. In both acts, price supports were to fall within a range depending on supply

---

[1]This section draws heavily on Johnson (1985).

relative to normal use. Roughly speaking, the 1949 act set price supports at 25 percent higher than the levels in the 1948 act, a sharp increase. In spite of efforts to reduce output and of large-scale foreign aid disposal, the government quickly accumulated large quantities of most crops with price supports.

The election of a Republican as president in 1952 changed nothing because Congress remained under Democratic control. The inability of a divided government to agree on price policy during the next several years allowed price supports to remain high for most of the 1950s. Without agreement on the need to limit agricultural output, given the high price supports, the efforts that were made were ineffective. The primary policy responses to the rapid accumulation of stocks by the Commodity Credit Corporation (CCC) in the early 1950s were the Agricultural Trade and Development Act of 1954 and the payment of substantial export subsidies on several farm products. The 1954 act provided for large-scale food aid—what was later called Food for Peace—as a means of finding an outlet for the excess stocks.

The critical farm problem of the early 1950s was that the productive capacity of U.S. agriculture was greater than markets could absorb at politically acceptable prices. In other words, excess resources were engaged in agriculture. The high price supports did nothing to encourage the withdrawal of resources from agriculture; on the contrary, the price supports were responsible for holding resources—labor and capital—in agriculture and encouraging increased use of current purchased inputs.

There was fairly general agreement that the conflicts over agricultural policy during the Eisenhower administration created a legacy of high-cost programs that were ineffective in improving the income of farmers and that were responsible for the accumulation of enormous quantities of farm crops by the CCC. The executive branch pushed for lower price supports to discourage production and expand utilization. Significant reductions in the real or inflation-adjusted price supports were achieved for wheat and corn by the end of the 1950s—the wheat price support declining by 30 percent between 1951 and 1959, while the corn price support fell by 40 percent. Congress was clearly disappointed that reduced price supports did not at once significantly reduce output and sharply increase domestic use and exports.

The conflicts, trials, and errors of the 1950s might have ended when both a Democratic Congress and a Democratic president were elected in 1960. But the dissension continued. President Kennedy believed that the large and growing costs of the farm programs were not sustainable; he proposed increasing the government's role through strict and mandatory supply management, covering most farm commodities, thus reducing direct payments to farmers and largely eliminating the costs of holding surplus farm commodities in storage. But Congress refused to support the president. During the 1950s, Congress had persisted with efforts to achieve a balance between supply and demand at unrealistically high prices through surplus disposal abroad and by voluntary efforts to remove land from cultivation. Because the price supports were high, the payments to obtain voluntary participation in land retirement also had to be high. Despite the failures of the voluntary programs during the 1950s, Congress maintained its adherence to voluntarism.

Although President Kennedy wanted mandatory controls to lower the budgetary costs of the program, he was apparently unconcerned that costs to consumers would increase. Congress was unwilling, however, to give up the credit for distributing substantial payments to farmers and, at the same time, accept the onus for approving mandatory controls that would displease the overwhelming majority of their farmer constituents. In the end, the conflict was resolved by a series of costly voluntary programs to limit crop production and a gradual reduction of almost all price supports for crop products to or below world market levels. With most crop prices at world market levels—a transition largely completed by 1964—farm incomes were maintained at politically acceptable levels by direct payments and by a gradual reduction in the quantity of excess resources in agriculture.

The structure of farm programs remained relatively unchanged through the 1960s and 1970s. Price supports were kept at or below world market levels, farm incomes were supported primarily through direct payments, and voluntary means of supply management were used when deemed necessary. One innovation was made in the 1973 farm legislation: the introduction of a so-called target price. The target price was not a "real" price or a market price but a given figure that was used to determine the amount of certain payments that farmers were to receive. The payments, which were called deficiency payments, were related to the difference between the target price and the actual market price; if this difference was large, the payments were large. If the market price went above the target price, there would be no payment of this type. To receive the deficiency payment, farmers participated in the supply management program. They might receive additional payments for idling land in excess of a certain area. Before 1973, there had been payments similar to the deficiency payments, but the method of determining the amount of the payments varied from commodity to commodity. The target price was

111

designed to create uniform procedures for setting the payment levels. The improvement was more in appearance than in substance, however, since there was no consistency in the relationship between the target price and the expected market prices for the various commodities. The target prices were set in the legislation, without any obvious economic criteria. Political criteria, in effect, determined the absolute and relative target prices for the different crops.

Dairy products are the only animal products that have had price supports and significant governmental intervention in markets. (The intervention in the markets for hogs had lasted only a year or so.) Dairy price supports, though, have prevailed continuously over this period. The price objectives have been achieved by tight control over imports and by government purchases of dairy products whenever market prices go to or below the price support levels. The price supports have not been for the fluid or drinking milk but for products manufactured from milk: butter, cheese, and dry skim milk. The excess products acquired by the CCC have been used in domestic welfare programs and exported as food aid, usually with heavy export subsidies.

## The 1980s

Major farm bills were enacted in 1981 and in 1985. Unfortunately, the 1981 act reflected the impression that the long-run agricultural problem throughout the world was to meet the rapidly growing demand for food just when output was slowing down. William Lesher, assistant secretary of agriculture when the 1981 legislation was passed, wrote the following:

> At the time the 1981 Farm Bill was formulated, the main concern was that world food needs would outpace production. Many believed—inside and outside of government—that *the* agricultural issue of the 1980s was going to be how to produce enough for a starving world rather than surpluses. Many believed that the United States was the only country that possessed the potential to expand food production enough to meet world needs.

Given these erroneous impressions about the underlying world supply-and-demand relationships for food, the target and support prices were set high. That is, prices generated a larger supply than could be absorbed at market prices near the price support levels. As will be noted in the section on evaluation, the 1981 farm bill had disastrously adverse effects on agriculture. Instead of demand grow-

112

ing more rapidly than supply, more was produced than could be sold, and stocks held by the government increased from $2.8 billion on December 31, 1980, to $10.6 billion by the end of 1983. Because of the high price supports and the rise in the foreign exchange value of the dollar, the United States rapidly lost its share in world export markets. In spite of a severe drought in 1983 and the diversion of a substantial amount of cropland in all years, stocks held by the government were at high levels, and the export position was continuing to deteriorate at the end of 1985—the last year included in the 1981 legislation. The government costs of the farm price and income program were large, and farm incomes in real terms were low. The costly farm programs had not protected the incomes of farmers because macroeconomic variables, especially interest rates and the foreign exchange value of the dollar, were much more important than the programs in determining the net income from farming.

The 1985 farm bill had features designed to recover export share and to reduce the large stocks held by the government. The measures to recover export markets included the substantial lowering of price supports—in nominal terms by approximately a third—and the reintroduction of export subsidies. The export subsidies were not general subsidies affecting all exports of a commodity but were targeted to particular markets where there was competition with the European Community. The support prices were lowered, and the concept of a marketing loan was introduced for rice and cotton. The marketing loan was a loan at the established price support level for the cotton or the rice; the amount of the loan depended on the quantity involved, given the price. But when farmers sold their rice or cotton, they repaid not the amount received but an amount equal to the "world" or export price times the quantity involved. For some months in early 1986, rice producers received as much as 70 percent of their total returns from government payments and only 30 percent from the market. The consequences for other rice exporters, especially Thailand, were especially bad.

Two features of the 1985 legislation are worthy of note. First, for two years starting in 1988, the target prices were to be reduced by 2 or 3 percent annually in nominal terms. With an inflation rate of about 4 percent, by the last year covered by the legislation the real or inflation-adjusted target prices would have been reduced by about 20 percent. Second, the deficiency payments, based on the difference between the target and the market prices, were "decoupled." The amount of the deficiency payment has never been based on actual production but rather on some notion of the normal yield for the amount of land devoted to the crop. Under earlier legislation, the normal yield was a three-to-five-year moving average of past yields. Thus, by increasing the current yield, a farmer could increase the amount of future payments.

The objective of the supply management program had been to reduce production, but this method of calculating payments induced farmers to produce more than they would on the basis of current prices and returns. Under the 1985 legislation, the yields were frozen at the existing level, and a high yield one year no longer increased payments in future years. A somewhat less significant change was to remove the requirement that a farmer had to plant essentially all the land permitted him under the supply management programs to receive the maximum amount of subsidies. Producing less by leaving more land idle resulted in a loss of government subsidies. Presumably, society wanted farmers "to work" for their subsidies. In the 1985 legislation, farmers could plant as little as 50 percent of their allowable acres to a crop and receive 92 percent of their maximum payments. Subsequently, this provision was changed so that none of the allowable acres had to be planted, and the farmer could still receive 92 percent of the payments.

The 1990 farm legislation made few changes from the 1985 farm bill. The target prices for crops remained at their 1990 level. The minimum price support for milk was set at $10.10 per hundredweight ($22.25 per 100 liters). Price support levels for wheat and feed grains, which may directly affect market prices, reflect the view of Congress that the direction of markets can be anticipated as much as five years in advance. Under the 1985 legislation, the secretary of agriculture had the authority to reduce the so-called basic or statutory loan rates by 20 percent; in the 1990 legislation, the statutory loan rate may be reduced by up to 10 percent, according to a formula relating the ending stocks-to-use ratio plus authority for an additional 10 percent discretionary reduction. While the change is modest, it indicates the willingness of Congress to limit the discretionary authority of the secretary of agriculture, often with disastrous consequences—as was the case with the 1981 farm legislation.

Congress did not continue the gradual reduction in the nominal target prices that was introduced in the 1985 farm bill and became effective in 1988. Soon after the 1990 farm bill was passed, reductions in government expenditures were to be legislated as part of the effort to reduce the budget deficit. The managers of the farm bill did not want to subject their constituents to "double jeopardy"—first by reducing target prices in the legislation and then by further reducing the costs of the farm programs. The budget legislation that was passed required a reduction in the $54 billion, five-year farm bill by approximately $13 billion, or almost a fourth. Expenditures were to be reduced mainly by a 15 percent reduction in the acreage on which deficiency payments were paid. If the deficiency payment were 40 percent of the target price, the reduction in payment acreage would have the same effect as a 6 percent reduction in the nominal target prices. If the rate of inflation were 4 percent annually from 1991 to 1995, the reduction in the real target price would be a further 22 percent. The two effects, taken together, imply a reduction in the real target prices of more than a quarter during the life of the legislation.

The 1990 legislation continued the acreage reduction programs, including required acreage reductions for receipt of deficiency payments, and it permitted paying farmers for additional land diversion. The yields used to calculate payments were frozen at the levels authorized under the 1985 legislation. Under certain conditions, farmers could leave all or part of their base acreages idle and receive up to 92 percent of the deficiency payments to which they would otherwise have been entitled. The 15 percent of the base acreage for which no deficiency payments were to be made, called flex acres, could be planted to certain crops other than program crops as permitted by the secretary of agriculture. Unfortunately, neither the 1985 nor the 1990 legislation provided for freezing the acreage bases. By staying out of the programs, farmers could increase their base acreages, since such acreages are established as the "average of acres planted and considered planted during the previous five years" for wheat and feed grains. But for cotton and rice, the previous three-year average would be used. Although aggregate base acreages did not increase over several years, it might have been better to freeze base acres as well as base yields, if decoupling is to be taken seriously.

These provisions continued the decoupling effort started in the 1985 farm legislation. Decoupling is designed to minimize the effects of the deficiency payments on the current production decisions made by farmers. The objective is for farmers to determine the use of inputs that affect yields of grains and cotton on the basis of market prices only. By freezing yields used in calculating payments, the government hopes that inputs such as fertilizer will not be used to increase current yields as a basis for future deficiency payments. This hope will be fulfilled only if farmers trust the government to disallow increases in the yields used to determine these payments. As fixed yields lag further behind actual yields, which increase through productivity improvements, the temptation to permit increases in the base yields will grow. Only time will tell whether the political process can withstand the temptation to make such yields "more realistic" and in the process undo much of what had been accomplished by freezing the yields and reducing the incentives the payments had in increasing production.

How does the mixture of policy measures affect production of wheat, rice, feed grains, and cotton? In addition to the requirement that participants in the programs must idle part of their cropland, farmers have been paid to place land subject to erosion in the Conservation Reserve Program. As of mid-1991, approximately 14 million hectares (34.5 million acres) of land had been put in the reserve. This land cannot be used for cultivated crops. Grass grows on most of it, though trees are increasingly being planted. The program requires a commitment of ten years. At the end of that time, some part of the land will return to cultivated cropping, but meanwhile the reserve effectively reduces crop production. But there is no definitive answer to the question that opened this paragraph. Yet, an answer is important to the position the United States takes in the GATT negotiations and to how other countries will respond to it.

There are price and income support programs for farm products other than the major crops discussed earlier. Two other crops—peanuts and sugar—have price support programs. The peanut program is a two-price program, with a price for peanuts used as peanuts or in peanut butter much above world market levels and a price for peanuts crushed for the oil and oilmeal much lower. The higher price is only for products consumed in the United States. An import quota for peanuts normally prohibits imports.

Although at one time the sugar program tried to limit the production of sugar in the United States, this has not been the case for the past decade. A high price support for sugar, however, has encouraged some increase in domestic production. The increase in production of cane and beet sugar along with the incentive provided by sugar price supports for the production of high-fructose sugar from corn have substantially reduced sugar imports. In the late 1970s, sugar imports were 4 million tons annually; during the 1980s, imports were reduced to 1 million tons at considerable expense to low cost sugar exporters. Until recently, the U.S. sugar market had been protected by a quantitative import quota on sugar that was adjusted at least annually to equate supply and demand in the U.S. market at a specified price.

Australia, which is a low-cost sugar producer, filed a complaint with GATT in 1989 that the quantitative import quota used by the United States since 1982 violated GATT rules. Article XI of GATT does permit quantitative import restrictions, but such restrictions must be no more restrictive of imports than of domestic production. Since the United States had no control over sugar production, there was no restraint on domestic production. Consequently, the sugar quota was found to violate GATT rules. But in the short run, there was no significant change in the sugar program. The quantitative restriction was replaced by a tariff quota equal to the former quantitative restriction; the tariff quota is allocated to exporters as before. All imports in excess of the tariff quota are subject to a duty of 16 cents per pound, raw basis. Unless world sugar prices fall to very low levels, no sugar will be imported in excess of the tariff rate quota amounts. The 16 cents per pound duty, however, can now serve as a basis for negotiations in GATT.

### Programs for Livestock Products

The only price support programs for livestock products are for dairy and wool; there are no price support programs for beef, sheep, pork, or poultry. Legislation does permit limiting imports of beef and veal when imports exceed a certain level. During the 1980s, the limitation on beef and veal imports achieved by so-called voluntary export restraints was effective in four years; in the remaining years imports were below the level that would have required restraints. Of the total value of marketings of livestock products of $89 billion in 1990, only 23 percent went to dairy products and wool.

There has never been a significant effort to offset the incentive effects of the dairy price supports on production. Several futile attempts, such as a program to buy out dairy cows that had a modest short-run output effect, had no long-run effect on dairy production.

### Evaluation

This evaluation of the effectiveness of the farm programs will emphasize the recent legislation, especially in the 1980s. First I shall discuss the effectiveness of the farm programs in increasing the absolute and relative incomes of the farm population in the 1950s and 1960s.

While farm programs in the United States have had a number of objectives, such as conservation of land, price stability, and maintenance of the family farm, the primary emphasis has been farm income, especially the net incomes of farm families from all sources, including agriculture. This concern has focused on both the absolute incomes of farm families and the relative incomes of farm families compared with those of all families or nonfarm families.

Between 1950 and 1954, the per capita disposable income of the farm population from all sources averaged 57 percent of that of all families; between 1955 and 1959, the average declined to 47 percent.

117

But in the following decade, farm family incomes improved significantly relative to all families, increasing to 70 percent of all family incomes between 1965 and 1969. On the basis of the increased relative income of farm families, farm price and income support programs would appear to have been successful during the 1950s and 1960s. A closer look at the source of the increased real incomes of farm families, however, refutes the conclusion that the farm programs improved either their relative or their absolute incomes.

In 1967 prices, the per capita incomes of the farm population increased from $1,242 in 1950–1954 to $2,143 in 1965–1969, or by 72 percent. Only a small fraction of the substantial increase in real incomes, however, came from farm income. In real terms, per capita incomes from farming increased by only 24 percent, while incomes from nonfarm sources increased by 176 percent. Thus, it was the success of general economic policies that increased the real incomes of the entire population and improved the integration of farm families into the rest of the economy: that success was primarily responsible for improving the incomes of farm families.

In fact, the government price support programs, in spite of their large costs to taxpayers and consumers, could not prevent a sharp decline in the total real income that farm people derived from farming. Total income of the farm population from farming, in 1967 prices, declined from an average of $18.2 billion in 1950–1954 to $11.9 billion in 1965–1969, or by 35 percent. Per capita income from farm sources increased primarily because the farm population declined at a faster rate than real farm income. Between 1950 and 1969, that population declined from 23.0 million to 10.3 million, or by 55 percent, a decline made possible by the significant increase in nonfarm employment opportunities. The rate of migration from agriculture increased the relative income position of farm families. Thus, the migration was not a response to the "immiseration" of farm people, since both the relative and the absolute income positions of farm families improved during those two decades. But the improvement in incomes, in fact, was primarily in response to general economic policies and not to specific agricultural policies.

The supply management did not prevent the substantial decline in real farm prices between 1950 and 1970 and the more than doubling of the real cost to the government for the farm income and price support programs. The deflated or real prices received by farmers for all products declined by a third between 1950 and 1970. Direct payments to producers in 1970 equaled 7 percent of cash receipts, thus somewhat tempering the price decline. Net income, however, did not fully reflect the direct payments, since farmers had to idle part of their land to receive them. Increased productivity and the reduction of the farm labor force made possible the rise in net income from farming per capita, while real farm prices fell by a third. This was quite a remarkable achievement. But again it may be noted that the outcome was not due to the farm price supports and supply management.

During the early 1970s, market prices were above target and support prices. The higher market prices, however, were short-lived, and by 1975 real farm prices had returned to the 1970 level. Farm incomes declined sharply between 1973 and 1976. One response was to increase price support and target price levels in 1976 and 1977. As a result, agricultural output in 1977 was substantially larger than the market would absorb at the support prices. Consequently, supply management programs were put in place in 1978 and 1979; substantial amounts of land were withdrawn from crop production just five years after conventional wisdom had predicted that world food shortages were inevitable.

Even though crop production increased in both 1978 and 1979, farm prices increased significantly in nominal terms—and modestly in real terms—from the 1977 level. Net farm income increased by more than a third. The rapid growth of farm exports associated with world inflationary trends (growing out of higher oil prices and the recycling of the petrodollars) improved farm prices. Developing-country debts rapidly increased, and some part of that increase paid for increased agricultural imports. The value of U.S. agricultural exports increased from $23.6 billion in 1977 to $34.7 billion in 1979.

A new farm bill was considered in 1980 and passed in 1981. Several factors influenced the outcome, which was a substantial increase in all target prices and price supports. Among the most important factors were adverse weather conditions in the American Midwest, where most of the feed grains are produced; the continued growth of exports, which reached record levels of $41 billion in 1980 and $43 billion in 1981; and a sharp decline in net farm income in 1980. The decrease in net farm income was caused to a considerable degree by the sharp increase in interest expenses—expenses that doubled between 1977 and 1980, mostly because of higher interest rates. Other expenses, however, also increased, and net farm income fell from $24 billion in 1979 to $16 billion in 1980.

As noted earlier, when the 1981 farm bill was written, both Congress and the administration believed that agriculture had an optimistic future.

The 1981 farm bill established target prices and price supports at high and rigid levels for four years, ending in 1985. Not only did the legislators assume that demand would outrun supply, but they also assumed that inflation would continue at the relatively high rates of 10–13 percent. As a consequence of a shift in monetary policy in the late 1970s, however, inflation declined rapidly to less than 4 percent in 1982. Simultaneously, the foreign exchange value of the dollar increased.

As a consequence of high price supports, declining inflation, and the sharp increase in the value of the dollar, by mid-1982 farm output exceeded the demand for farm crops at the support prices mandated by the 1981 farm bill. As a result, the number of hectares of cropland withdrawn from production in 1983—31 million hectares—was the largest on record. Even with a severe drought that reduced the production of feed grains by 114 million tons from the previous year's level to 136 million tons in 1983, the beginning stocks were so large that exports increased and domestic use fell by only 10 percent. Within just two years, the stocks of feed grain increased significantly and exceeded the high level at the beginning of the 1983 crop. The effects of the adverse weather were short-lived.

The government costs of the farm programs rose from $3.2 billion in 1980 to $14.7 billion by 1982 (the first year under the new legislation) and reached $21.5 billion in 1985 (the last year of the bill). In 1985, the government costs of the farm programs equaled 66.6 percent of net farm income, compared with 13.1 percent in 1979 and 19.9 percent in 1980. In inflation-adjusted dollars, net farm operator income in 1985 was about a sixth less than the average for 1978 and 1979 and was essentially the same as in 1981. Thus, the enormous increase in government costs was not enough to return income to the 1978 and 1979 levels or to increase farm incomes over the life of the legislation.

The 1981–1985 experience indicates that unfavorable national economic policies and changes in macroeconomic variables were far more important influences on farm income than the income and price support programs. In fact, in some respects the farm policies worsened the effects of macroeconomic factors, particularly the changes in the exchange rate. The high and rigid support prices increasingly priced U.S. farm exports out of the world markets as the foreign exchange value of the dollar rose during the 1980s through 1985.

A major negative influence on net farm income was the increase in interest paid by farmers, primarily as a result of the sharp rise in market interest rates that followed the shift from an inflationary to a deflationary policy that started with a reduction in the growth of the money supply in 1978. The effects, of course, were not realized all at once. Total interest paid, however, increased from $8.2 billion in 1977 to $12.5 billion in 1979 and to $21.1 billion in 1984. As interest rates subsequently declined and as farm debt was reduced, in part by foreclosure or renegotiation, interest payments declined to $15.2 billion in 1988.

The positive developments not directly related to the farm programs were the decline in the number of families and persons dependent on farming and the near stability, in real terms, of the deflated value of off-farm earnings. In 1979, off-farm income was 23 percent higher than net income from farming; by 1985, the difference had increased to 31 percent.

As noted earlier, the 1985 farm legislation was changed to overcome some of the major defects of the 1981 bill. Some of the changes, such as the lowering of price supports and the increases in both export and domestic subsidies, had large short-run effects on world market prices—especially for rice and cotton—and adversely affected developing countries that exported these products. The support prices were lowered to achieve two related objectives: to regain the U.S. export market share lost during the first half of the 1980s and to reduce stocks of farm commodities held by the government. Generally, both objectives have been met. For the grains, though, the effects of adverse weather in 1988 contributed more to the reduction of stocks than did the policy changes up to that time.

In contrast to the 1981 legislation, the 1985 farm bill has contributed to the adjustments that agriculture must make, that is, to reduce its labor and capital resources. The combination of economic conditions and the overly optimistic price assumptions of farm legislation from 1976 to 1983 slowed the transfer of labor out of agriculture and thus delayed necessary adjustments. Reduced price support assisted this adjustment only by indicating to farmers that market prices were declining and were substantially below target prices. Starting in 1988, the 1985 farm bill called for the reduction of nominal target prices by 3–4 percent a year. With inflation at an annual rate of about 4 percent, the real target prices will be reduced by nearly 30 percent over the five-year life of the bill, a significant contribution toward a liberal trade regime.

The 1985 legislation was reasonably successful on several scores. The target price changes signaled lower prices and declining deficiency payments. Therefore, farmers increasingly depended on returns from the marketplace. The 1990 farm bill maintained the general features of the 1985 legislation.

Another measure of success has been that government costs of the farm program have declined significantly. Based on fiscal year data (the earlier estimates of costs were for a calendar year to be consistent with the farm income data), government costs declined from $25.8 billion in 1986 to $11.3 billion in 1989. Most of the expenditures in fiscal year 1986 were for the programs under the 1981 act. The decline in expenditures did not come at the expense of farm incomes. Net farm incomes increased from $42.6 billion in 1985 to $53 billion in 1989. Not only did farm incomes increase but also the net value of farm assets increased by more than a fifth from the end of 1985 to the end of 1989, after falling almost 35 percent in the previous five years.

Since 1950, the ratio of prices received to prices paid by farmers has declined continuously, except for a brief period in the first half of the 1970s. With 1977 equal to 100, the ratio of prices received to prices paid for production items in 1950–1954 was 132; in 1984–1988 the ratio was 87. Thus, over this period farm prices (adjusted for changes in prices paid) declined by 29 percent.[2] Over the same time, however, the per capita disposable income of farm families increased from 54 percent of the average for nonfarm families to approximate equality for 1984–1988. The improvement in the absolute and relative incomes of farm families stemmed from two primary causes: the substantial increase in off-farm employment opportunities for farm families and the major increase in productivity in U.S. agriculture. Between 1950–1954 and 1984–1988, the change in farm output per unit of input increased by 101 percent. Since relative prices declined by only 29 percent, the real return to farm resources increased markedly over this time.

The increase in productivity of agriculture did not result from farm price and income support policies but from the investment in research, both in the public and in the private sectors. It would have been impossible to have maintained relative farm prices at their 1950–1954 level except at a cost to the government and consumers several times what the actual costs were in 1984–1988. Even the government costs alone in the mid-1980s were two-fifths of net farm income; if the costs to consumers are included, the total costs would have been nearly three-fifths of net farm income.

### Adverse Effects on Trade Liberalization

The combination of farm sector and national economic policies of the mid-1970s to the mid-1980s moved the United States from a position

---

[2]The prices-received index for 1984–1988 was increased to reflect the total returns due to direct government payments. Since farmers incurred costs to receive the payments, the method used gives an upper limit to price equivalency of the payments.

of relatively low protection in agriculture to a position of relatively high protection—a significant negative consequence. According to OECD calculations, the United States had an average level of nominal protection of 19 percent in 1979–1981.[3]

The PSE includes a wide variety of transfers to farmers—such as agricultural research and extension, as well as costs of operating the government farm programs—that farmers never see as a part of their net income.

Based on the same measure, the nominal protection increased in the United States to 75 percent in 1986 (a PSE of 43 percent) (OECD 1989, 70). By 1988, the rate of nominal protection had declined to 51 percent and declined further in 1989–1992. But U.S. agriculture clearly faces a further significant decline in the returns for its products if there is free or low protection. As will be indicated in chapter 11, however, with liberalization of world trade in farm products will come increased market prices for most farm products, decreasing the adjustment required of U.S. farmers.

As a political response to the relatively high price supports during the first half of the 1980s and the rise in the foreign exchange value of the dollar, the United States reinstituted export subsidies. It had abandoned almost all such subsidies in the early 1970s. But in the effort to reduce government-held stocks and to offset some of the advantages that the European Community had gained because of

---

[3]The OECD uses the producer subsidy equivalent—the PSE—as a measure of protection. I believe this measure gives a mistaken impression of the degree of protection, especially for the majority of individuals who are not familiar with the concept. The PSE is a measure of the ratio of the value of all policy transfers to the total income from farm production, including the policy transfers. If nominal protection is defined as the ratio of the value of the policy transfers to what the value of production would be in the absence of the policy transfers, such a measure is equal to the difference between domestic and border prices when the only measure of protection is a border measure, such as a tariff or an import quota.

We should agree on how we are to measure protection and what we call the concept. The term *nominal protection* may be misleading, since it is normally used to measure the difference between domestic and border prices and to ignore various subsidies. The Australians have used the term "price adjustment gap," while in the GATT negotiations the term aggregate measure of support (AMS) has gained some degree of acceptance. I believe that we should use a measure that reflects the difference between the actual returns received by farmers and what they would receive under free trade as the measure of protection. But obviously this is a matter for agreement among us (OECD 1987, 117).

high U.S. price supports, stock accumulations, and the increased value of the dollar, selective export subsidies were included in the 1985 farm legislation. These subsidies clearly violate the spirit of GATT and justify similar disregard of GATT obligations by other nations—and quite reasonably so. If the United States will not abide by a framework it was largely responsible for, there is little reason to expect others to do so.

## References

Clements, Kenneth W., and Larry A. Sjaastad. *How Protection Taxes Exporters*. London: Trade Policy Research Centre, 1984.

Johnson, D. Gale. "The Performance of Past Policies: A Critique." In Gordon C. Rausser and Kenneth R. Farrell, eds. *Alternative Agricultural and Food Policies*. Berkeley: Giannini Foundation of Agricultural Economics, University of California, 1985.

OECD. *Agricultural Policies, Markets and Trade: Monitoring and Outlook 1987*. Paris: OECD, 1987.

———. *Agricultural Policies, Markets and Trade: Monitoring and Outlook 1989*. Paris: OECD, 1989.

# PART THREE

# The Political Economy of Agricultural Policies

# 6
# A World View

*Tracy C. Miller*

Throughout the world, government policy toward agriculture, though quite variable, has some common characteristics. This chapter looks at some of the generalized facts about agricultural protection of different commodities and attempts to identify some characteristics that affect policy-induced transfers between farm groups and the rest of the population. A simple model of competition among pressure groups through the political process is used to explain the basis for policy in a variety of countries, not just Taiwan and the United States.

## Systematic Factors Affecting Protection

Data from a number of different studies are consistent with the following propositions explaining the direction and level of income transfers affecting farmers:

- High-income countries subsidize their farmers, while low-income countries often tax farmers and subsidize urban consumers.
- Large farmers are more likely to be benefited and generally receive greater benefits from policy than small farmers.
- Protection is higher or taxation lower for imported commodities than for exported commodities.

The most obvious pattern is that high-income countries tend to subsidize their farmers, while low-income countries tax theirs (table 6–1). Although there are exceptions to this pattern in that some farmers are subsidized in low-income countries, it is virtually impossible to find an example of a commodity taxed by policy in high-income countries for any length of time. Numerous studies document the prevalence of agricultural protection in the European Community (EC) and other West European countries, Japan, Canada, the United States, and Australia (OECD 1987; USDA 1988). Even the high-income oil-exporting countries have protected agriculture, with Saudi Arabia supporting wheat prices more than any other country (Byerlee 1986).

TABLE 6–1

RELATION BETWEEN PROTECTION AND REAL GROSS DOMESTIC
PRODUCT PER CAPITA FOR SELECTED COUNTRIES, 1985

| Country | Real GDP per Capita | Average Producer Subsidy Equivalent |
| --- | --- | --- |
| United States | 12,532 | 23.9 |
| Canada | 12,196 | 34.8 |
| Japan | 9,447 | 70.1 |
| Australia | 8,850 | 10.8 |
| European Community | 8,500[a] | 38.3 |
| Mexico | 3,985 | 41.8 |
| South Africa | 3,885 | 28.6[b] |
| Taiwan | 3,581 | 22.3 |
| Argentina | 3,486 | −9.8 |
| Brazil | 3,282 | 12.0 |
| South Korea | 3,056 | 58.2 |
| India | 750 | −21.9 |
| Nigeria | 581 | −40.1 |

a. European Community GDP is a rough approximation of average GDP in member countries.
b. PSE data for South Africa were an average for the period 1982–86. The 1985 figure was an outlier, while 1985 PSE's were close to the average in other countries.
SOURCE: Data on real GDP per capita are estimated in 1980 dollars and were calculated by Summers and Heston. Data on average producer subsidy equivalents were computed by taking weighted averages of select commodities as calculated by USDA 1988.

In a practice less prevalent than protection in high-income countries, many low-income countries discriminate against the producers of agricultural commodities. (For data on agricultural commodity prices and protection in low income countries see USDA 1988; Byerlee 1986; Binswanger and Scandizzo 1983; Krueger, Schiff, and Valdez 1988.) Such policies are common in Latin America and Africa and in low-income countries in Asia.

Not only is the positive relationship between protection and income clear from cross-country data, but also it appears in time series, as the recent history of policy in Japan, Taiwan, and Korea (table 6–2) shows. Similar trends are seen in other high-income countries. Before the twentieth century, U.S. land policy and trade policy discriminated against farmers. Protection of agriculture was introduced following industrial development in Germany, France,

TABLE 6–2

WEIGHTED AVERAGE NOMINAL RATES OF PROTECTION IN
EAST ASIA, 1955–1982

(percent)

| | 1955–59 | 1960–64 | 1965–69 | 1970–74 | 1975–79 | 1980–82 |
|---|---|---|---|---|---|---|
| Japan | 44 | 68 | 87 | 110 | 147 | 151 |
| Korea | −15 | −5 | 9 | 55 | 129 | 166 |
| Taiwan | −21 | 2 | 2 | 17 | 36 | 55 |

NOTE: Rate of protection is defined as the percentage by which the domestic price exceeds the border price.
SOURCE: Anderson, Hayami, and Honma 1986.

and Italy in the late nineteenth century and in the early twentieth century in Japan (Hayami 1986).

Some evidence indicates that large farmers are more likely to benefit from agricultural policy than small farmers. Discrimination by size occurs in various forms, including higher protection for commodities grown primarily on large farms; projects that favor larger, more innovative farmers; and subsidies provided first to those with the right connections. Since many transfers to producers occur through policies that raise the output price or lower input prices, larger farmers receive greater benefits than small farmers. According to the OECD, "Larger farmers benefit more from a rise in support prices (about in proportion to each farmer's sales) than their smaller counterparts" (OECD 1983, 43–44). This tendency of larger farmers to gain more from policy than small farmers is evident in the European Community as shown in table 6–3. Similar data showing a positive correlation between farm size and the share of government payments for the United States are discussed in chapter 8.

The likelihood that commodities grown on large farms will receive higher average rates of protection than those grown on small farms can be seen in Kenya, where large farms are important, in comparison with Ghana, where small farms dominate (Bates 1987). Watts and Bassett (1986) discuss the high protection of sugar, which is grown on large estates, compared with cocoa and coffee in the Ivory Coast.

Bates presents some very convincing evidence from African countries that projects and input subsidies usually favor large farmers whose political support is needed by government officials. Barker (1985) suggests a similar propensity in Senegal. Zazueta (1989) notes

TABLE 6–3

EFFECTS OF 5 PERCENT DECLINE IN REAL FARM PRICES ON INCOME
FROM FARMING PER PERSON EMPLOYED IN AGRICULTURE, 1980

| Farm Size Group[a] | West Germany | France | United Kingdom | EC-9 |
|---|---|---|---|---|
| Less than 2 | 146 | 98 | 160 | 110 |
| 2–8 | 689 | 285 | 494 | 334 |
| More than 8 | 1,253 | 828 | 1,127 | 988 |

NOTE: Full-time equivalent in U.S. dollars per work unit.
a. European size units; ESU equal to a standardized gross margin of 1,000 ECUs.
SOURCE: K. J. Thomson and D. R. Harvey, "The Efficiency of Common Agricultural Policy," *European Review of Agricultural Economics*, vol. 8 (1981): 74

a bias toward large farmers in Mexico during the 1940s and 1950s. Braverman and Gausch (1986) discuss the tendency for subsidized credit to be provided primarily to large farmers, citing the example of Brazil, where all agricultural output is taxed to subsidize credit for those farmers wealthy enough to qualify. In the high-income countries, owners of farmland, many of whom are relatively wealthy, receive a disproportionate share of the benefits compared with farm workers and those who rent the land they farm, since most of the benefits of production subsidies are capitalized into land rent (Johnson 1991).

Another tendency, seen in both cross-section and time series data, is that countries protect import commodities and tax export commodities. Krueger, Schiff, and Valdes (1988) demonstrate that direct protection is positive for most imported food products and negative for most exports in a sample of developing countries. Binswanger and Scandizzo (1983) found a similar relationship using an ordinary least-squares model, but their results were marginally significant. Using Binswanger and Scandizzo's protection data, Miller (1986) presents evidence from a cross-section probit model showing a negative relationship between exports and the likelihood of positive protection. (Probit analysis uses maximum likelihood techniques to estimate the probability of a one value for a dichotomous dependent variable, assuming a cumulative normal distribution relating probability to a vector of explanatory variables [Kennedy 1985, 190].) The most important export commodities are also usually taxed the most. Commodities grown primarily for export, including coffee, tea, cocoa, and cottonseed, are the most heavily taxed in a number of low-income countries (Binswanger and Scandizzo 1983; Paukert 1988). Among the high- and middle-income countries, Japan, Korea, and Taiwan, which have the highest producer subsidy equivalents (PSEs), are primarily net importers of agricultural commodities. The United States, Canada, Australia, and New Zealand have lower PSEs for most commodities (USDA 1988). Most of the commodities with higher PSEs in each country are imported or would have been imported in a world of free trade, while most of those with lower PSEs are exported (USDA 1987).

## Types of Policy

A variety of different types of policies are used to subsidize or tax agricultural commodity production. Policy can be distinguished by how it affects producers, consumers, taxpayers, input suppliers, and middlemen, among others. The type of policy used will determine which groups benefit and how the benefits and costs are distributed among the different groups.

Many low- and middle-income countries subsidize food consumption. Compulsory procurement, export taxes, and import subsidies, reduce the consumer price, while transferring part of the cost of the subsidy to producers. Compulsory procurement has been used in Bangladesh, Burma, Egypt, India, Indonesia, and Sri Lanka (Davis 1977). Governments of many countries cover part of the cost of food subsidies with budgetary outlays. Expenditures to subsidize consumers are substantial in several countries. Wheat prices below free market prices are financed primarily by government subsidies in most developing countries. India and Pakistan are exceptions, with producers paying most of consumer subsidies for wheat (Byerlee 1986). Government monopsony power maintains low prices in some countries, such as Mali and Zambia, while export taxes maintain low prices in Argentina, India, Zaire, Pakistan, Nepal, Brazil, and Thailand (USDA 1988; Davis 1977; Jaeger and Humphreys 1988; Braverman and Gausch 1986).

Some governments subsidize both domestic production and consumption, raising the producer price while lowering the consumer price. Byerlee (1987) observes that both production and consumption of wheat were subsidized in 11 of the 56 countries in his sample of developing countries. Discrimination against producers frequently occurs in the absence of explicit taxes, and sometimes in spite of subsidies, because of the overvalued exchange rates common in many African countries and in some Asian and Latin American countries (Jaeger and Humphreys 1988; Byerlee 1986).

131

Government procurement at low prices has a very limited effect on many producers, because many continue to sell most of their output in informal markets or consume it at home. Reusse suggests that government agencies rarely purchase more than 20 percent of marketed output destined for domestic markets in low-income countries. Export taxes are frequently evaded through smuggling commodities across unprotected borders.

In high-income countries, farm prices are supported by tariffs or quotas on imported commodities, export subsidies, supply restrictions, and direct purchase of surplus commodities (OECD 1987). In addition to the price-stabilizing effects of direct purchase and stock holding by governments, prices are held above average world prices by production subsidies, export subsidies, and import tariffs. Supply restrictions are sometimes used along with government purchases and subsidies, primarily to reduce the cost of agricultural policy to the treasury in exporting countries. Production is also subsidized through government research and extension services, as well as through credit and input subsidies, although consumers gain substantially from the resulting lower commodity prices.

The budgetary costs of export and production subsidies have grown quite large in recent years in the United States, the EC countries, and Japan. In the EC countries, import tariffs generate some government revenue, but high prices have led to growing exports and declining imports of agricultural commodities in recent years, raising budgetary costs. Japan has spent a considerable amount subsidizing farmers to divert land from rice production to other uses (Otsuka and Hayami 1986).

There is substantial evidence that agricultural policy stabilizes prices in both high- and low-income countries. In high-income countries, the stabilizing effects of target prices and intervention prices are evident (Miller 1987, 95–100; Bullock 1989; Honma and Hayami 1986). Domestic prices for commodities in developing countries often vary less than world prices, with larger consumer subsidies during years of high world prices, as shown in Davis, among others.

## A Model to Explain Policy

The purpose of this chapter is not to evaluate or criticize the policies of various governments, but to explain why policies are used. Any explanation requires an understanding of the goals of the government officials involved in policy making and the incentives they face. Policy can be explained using a model of political competition among interest groups in pursuit of income transfers. The implications of an interest group model are developed below. The interest group model will be compared with alternative models for explaining the existing mixture of policies in different countries.

The model of competition among interest groups, formalized by Becker, implies that policy can be explained as the result of attempts of farmers, consumers, taxpayers, and others to influence politicians and government officials to enforce policies that benefit one group at the expense of other groups in the economy. Those interested in agricultural policy can be divided into groups based on whether they are benefited or harmed by each type of policy. Producers benefit from policy that increases agricultural commodity prices, while consumers benefit from policy that lowers prices. Taxpayers benefit from policy that lowers the producer price while raising the consumer price, or from import tariffs or export taxes. Government bureaucrats benefit from policies that require greater discretion and more administrative input, such as research and infrastructure development projects. Input suppliers want policy that maximizes demand for the inputs they supply, which means policy that stimulates demand for output, subsidizes the use of the input and its complements, or discourages the use of substitute inputs. Distributors and processors want policy that raises retail demand, while lowering the purchase price to them of commodities. Foreign consumers benefit from policy that increases exports, while foreign producers benefit from policy that reduces exports or increases the demand for imports.

It is assumed that the goal of political action by an interest group is to maximize the welfare of group members. The most important measure of group welfare is likely to be real income, but other goals such as altruism or envy toward others outside the group may also play a role, as suggested by Bullock (1989).

Interest groups influence policy by spending time and money lobbying elected officials and bureaucrats or persuading voters to support a candidate or proposal, and through the use of violent or nonviolent demonstrations. Government officials supply policy to maximize their length of tenure in office, enhance their power or prestige, and to increase their income. The supply of policy-induced transfers will be directly related to political expenditures in support of existing programs and inversely related to expenditures in opposition to the current government programs.

**Determinants of Political Involvement.** The incentive of individuals to organize to influence policy will depend on the potential gains from a policy change, the costs of organizing a group, the ease of communicating with government officials, and the responsiveness of the government to group political pressure. Groups are more likely to organize and will spend more to influence policy where the costs of organizing and enforcing participation by group members are low relative to the potential benefits from changing policy. Group size and the distribution of benefits among group members strongly affect whether a group organizes to participate in the political process (Olson 1965).

Farmers' costs of organizing are likely to be small relative to potential benefits when most of the output of a commodity is produced on large farms. The fewer the number of farms given the total value of output, the lower the costs of organizing and enforcing political participation. Greater specialization by farmers may increase the farmers' incentive to be politically involved by lowering the transactions costs of influencing policy and reducing the number concerned with the price of each commodity.

Similarly, consumers and taxpayers will be more likely to organize to influence agricultural policy for commodities that consume a large share of household expenditures or a large share of national income. If taxes are paid by a relatively small proportion of the population, taxpayers will be more likely to resist agricultural policy that involves a significant budgetary cost or seek policy that generates revenue for the government. If nonagricultural firms are concentrated and labor intensive, the desire to keep wages low may lead them to seek to influence agricultural policy. Similar considerations are likely to determine whether input suppliers, wholesale distributors, and foreign interests will organize to influence agricultural policy.

Besides potential gains from agricultural policy, the ability of a group to obtain income transfers through the political process will depend on how easily the group can communicate its demands to government officials. Farmers' ability to communicate effectively may depend on how modern the country is, how dense the population is, and how geographically concentrated and stable agricultural production is. The type of political system is also important. A representative democracy may allow geographically dispersed groups more opportunity to participate in the political process, while a dictatorial government may respond to mass demonstrations, which are likely to be staged by geographically concentrated groups.

Information plays an important role in the determination of agricultural policy. One reason why programs to help farmers are tied to output in high-income countries could be to disguise the redistributive effects of those policies. Interest groups have an incentive to subsidize information that makes policies appear to be in the public interest and to suppress information about the losses borne by the majority as a result of policy. Part of the reason why attempts to decouple income support from production have often been unsuccessful in high-income countries is that the redistributive effects of such policies would be more obvious to the public.

The complexity of current programs is partly to blame for the relatively high transactions costs of policy change, especially in representative democracies. Because of these high costs, agricultural policy is unlikely to change very rapidly as the distribution of political power and the costs and benefits of policy change.

The high transactions cost of policy combined with the high fixed costs of organizing an interest group makes political involvement more like an investment decision (Gardner 1981). Variations in economic conditions may lead to policy changes with the lowest transactions costs, such as small or moderate adjustments of budgetary costs, greater or lesser average transfers, and minor alterations in eligibility for program benefits. Differences in methods for redistributing income, significant rearrangements in the distribution of benefits and costs within each group, and changes in the identity of groups involved in the policy process are likely to occur more slowly and less frequently.

Variations in the amounts transferred to and from different groups in response to fluctuations in world prices are built into some types of policies, such as U.S. target prices and EC threshold and intervention prices. Other types of policies such as export taxes and ad valorem tariffs can be designed to maintain relatively constant budgetary effects and transfers in the face of changing world market conditions.

**Determinants of Policy Size.** Each group participating in the political process will spend additional resources only where the expected marginal benefits exceed the marginal costs. The expected marginal benefits of additional political expenditures by one interest group will be a function of the expected response of competing interest groups. If competing groups increase their political expenditures in an attempt to prevent additional transfers from occurring, marginal benefits may be small at best. The size and likelihood of an increase in political expenditures by competing groups will depend on the marginal cost to them of additional transfers.

The marginal benefits to the gainers and the marginal costs to the losers are likely to depend on the elasticity of market supply and demand, the type of policy used, and any other efficiency gains or losses associated with the policy. If subsidies or taxes are used, with no restrictions on output or consumption, producers will have a

135

smaller incentive to seek a production subsidy requiring an outlay of a given size and a greater incentive to resist a production tax, the more elastic the supply of the commodity; consumers and related interest groups will have a smaller incentive to seek a consumption subsidy and a greater incentive to resist a consumption tax, the more elastic the demand for the commodity.

As Gardner (1981) suggests, the type of policy used may depend on the elasticity of supply and demand. Output-reducing policies may be more efficient for transferring income to producers when world excess demand is inelastic and domestic supply is elastic. Output-reducing policies are often tied to a specific input such as land, which facilitates transfers to landowners, who are often the most politically powerful group. Such policies lead to inefficient use of related inputs, raising the marginal cost of a transfer of a given size.

An important factor affecting the marginal cost and benefits of income redistribution is the ability of farmers to sell their commodities through informal marketing channels. Production taxes are relatively easy to evade for commodities sold in domestic markets, especially if little processing is required. Export taxes can be evaded easily in countries that share a border with neighbors with higher prices. The opportunity to evade government-controlled prices may reduce the incentive of producers to seek changes through the political process, but it is also likely to reduce the potential benefits to consumers, the government, or taxpayers of policies that tax production.

The type of policy chosen and the rate of protection or taxation of farmers will depend on the distribution of benefits and costs. A specific policy will often benefit a coalition of several politically powerful groups. The distribution of costs and benefits of subsidies and taxes will depend on whether the commodity is exported or imported and on the mixture of domestic production, domestic consumption, and imports or exports. Government costs and tax evasion can be limited only if imports or exports are taxed or subsidized. Import subsidies and export restrictions have a tendency to lower both the price to domestic consumers and the price to producers, with lower costs to taxpayers than consumption subsidies. The budgetary cost of price supports can be reduced or eliminated with export subsidies or import quotas. Restrictions on the export or import of commodities can also generate rents for distributors involved in the export or import business, giving them an incentive to provide political support.

If policies are paid for out of the government budget or if

agricultural policy generates revenue for the government, the excess burden of taxes, as well as the cost of collection and compliance, will be important. For policies that involve a relatively small percentage of the budget, as in some high-income countries, the marginal cost associated with increasing or reducing taxes provides a good approximation of the marginal cost or benefit of policy to the government.

Where agricultural policy raises revenue, as with export taxes, import taxes, or commodity taxes, other taxes can be reduced or government spending increased. It follows that everything else being the same, policies that raise revenue for the government are likely to receive greater support and meet less resistance than policies that must be paid for out of the government budget. Thus, prices should be higher and protection more common for imported commodities, since tariffs can be used, while exported commodities are more likely to have negative protection as the result of export taxes.

There should be a greater tendency to tax than to subsidize agricultural products the higher the marginal cost of alternative taxes. The marginal cost of an additional dollar of tax revenue is likely to be higher the bigger the government, everything else being the same. It may be difficult to isolate this relationship since the size of government could be negatively correlated with the cost of collecting taxes.

The previous discussion implies a positive relationship between farm size and the magnitude of policy-induced transfers to farmers and a positive relationship between the importance of the commodity in household budgets and the magnitude of transfers to consumers. This does not necessarily imply higher rates of protection of farmers where farms are large or higher consumer subsidy rates where the commodity is important in household budgets, because larger farms, or households that consume greater quantities, will receive a larger transfer for a given rate of protection or subsidization than smaller farms or households that consume smaller amounts. If the amount transferred by policy is a function of the amount spent to influence government officials, and if there are diminishing returns to political expenditures, larger average-sized farms could be associated with lower rates of producer protection (but with slightly larger gains per farm) and greater consumption per household could be associated with lower consumer subsidy rates.

Another important factor affecting policy is likely to be the competitiveness of the political system. The more competitive the political system, the more quickly government officials should respond to political pressure using the most efficient methods of redistribution. Where political systems are less competitive, politicians and government officials may earn substantial rents from policy, as appears to be the case in several African countries, according to Bates (1987).

Popular attitudes and values associated with the culture of each country should play a role in the determination of policy. Bauer makes a strong case for the importance of basic cultural values and attitudes in determining economic performance. For similar reasons, the culture is likely to have an important impact on the government and its choice of economic policy. Where the "work ethic" is important, government policy is more likely to reward productivity than merely to provide subsidies in response to political support. Cultural factors may also determine the importance of altruism or envy in the policy process.

## Empirical Evidence

Few empirical studies of agricultural policy have tested the hypotheses suggested by the theory of competition among pressure groups. The few studies that have been done provide some support for the theory and do not contradict the model, as discussed above. Alternative explanations of protection as the result of attempts to further goals related to the public interest fail to account for the types of policies pursued by most countries.

If policy were designed to further the public interest, then it might be expected to accomplish some of the stated objectives of government officials, such as food security, improved income distribution, faster economic development, and overcoming market failures. Although the government might make occasional policy mistakes, these mistakes should be corrected over time, as more information became available.

There are numerous examples where governments pursue policies that do not enhance the public interest, however, even as defined by the governments themselves. Food security is a frequently stated goal in many countries. The willingness of governments of high-income countries to destroy surplus stocks of some commodities is certainly not consistent with food security. As Johnson (1991) points out, self-sufficiency is not equivalent to food security, especially in Japan and the EC countries, where farmers rely on large quantities of imported inputs, particularly fuel and chemical fertilizers manufactured with petroleum.

During the 1950s and 1960s, a frequent justification for the policies of low-income countries was the necessity of taxing farm products to promote economic development. The persistence of low farm prices relative to the prices of manufactured goods in many developing countries, as evidence mounts for the negative effect of distortions on economic development, raises questions about the veracity of the economic development justification for policy. (See Agarwala [1983] for some evidence on the relationship between price distortions and growth in developing countries.)

The income distributional effects of agricultural policy are often at odds with most popular views of what constitutes an equitable income distribution. Agricultural policy rarely assists the poorest groups in the population and often favors the relatively wealthy. Although poor urban consumers may benefit from policy to reduce food prices, small farmers and farm workers, the poorest groups in many developing countries, are often harmed. In the long run, most of the benefits of high farm prices, input subsidies, credit subsidies, or development projects go to large landowners, most of whom are not low-income farmers. Similarly, the owners of land and capital in the cities are likely to reap most of the benefits of food subsidies in poor countries.

The argument that the goal of policy in high-income countries is to raise incomes of farmers hides the fact that only the producers of certain commodities are benefited. If raising farm incomes were the goal of policy, then the most efficient method would be used to achieve it. Numerous examples exist, however, where less efficient methods of redistribution are used, thereby increasing the benefits or reducing the costs to other politically powerful groups at the expense of groups lacking political power. This explains why consumers bear most of the cost of farm policy in many countries, while part of the benefits go to groups other than farmers. Anderson (1986) notes that beef import quotas in Japan provided excess profits to selected distributors of imported beef, which gave them an incentive to form a coalition with producers to support quotas, as opposed to import tariffs, which would be more efficient if raising producer prices were the only goal.

Evidence concerning the primary participants in the policy process as well as the results of the policy process does not contradict some type of theory of interest group competition. Benson and Faminow note that public debate about recent agricultural policy changes in Canada contained no major input from consumers and agribusiness interests. Agribusiness interests have become more involved in recent U.S. farm policy but have sought to form a coalition with farmers; as a result, government has increased expenditures to subsidize production and exports (Babcock, Carter, and Schmitz 1990).

The observed relationship between income and protection can

easily be explained as the result of competition between interest groups, though other explanations are possible (such as the theory that taxation of agriculture is necessary to provide surplus for industrialization). Balisacan and Roumasset (1987) suggest that as incomes increase, food declines as a share of household expenditures and industrial wages, while wages decline as a share of manufacturing costs, reducing the incentives of consumers and owners of nonagricultural firms to seek low food prices. At the same time, the incentive of farmers to seek protection increases as specialization and output per farm increase, while farm numbers decline, lowering the costs of organizing to influence policy. Improvements in transportation and communication also reduce the costs of organizing rural interest groups in comparison with urban interests.

The anecdotal evidence cited above concerning the relationship between the size distribution of farms and protection seems to be consistent with the theory, with large farmers more likely to be subsidized by policy than small farmers. The theory is less clear on the relationship between the number of farms and protection. Although it may be more difficult to organize a group with many members because of free-rider effects, large groups have more voting power in democratic societies. Miller (1991) found a significant negative relationship between the number of farms and protection, but only for commodities with negative protection. Gardner (1987) found that commodities with the greatest number of farms had the lowest rates of protection in the United States; but his data suggest that the highest protection is achieved by intermediate-sized producer groups. The evidence on the relationship between the number of farms and protection in countries with positive protection is inconclusive, suggesting that voting power may at least partially offset the free-rider effect when there are a large number of producers.

High rates of protection for commodities where farm size remains small and farm numbers large, as in Japan, can be partly explained by the growth of agricultural cooperatives since 1947, serving the economic, financial, production, welfare, social, and cultural needs of farmers (George and Saxon 1986). Though organized at the local level, they are federated into a large national organization with great political power.

Another characteristic that might be expected to reduce the political power of producers is greater variability in the commodities they produce. Where policy decisions are made on a commodity-by-commodity basis, costs of organizing a group and communicating preferences through the political process will be higher the greater the percentage of producers who change the mixture of their produce. Gardner (1987) finds an index of geographical movement in production to be negatively associated with protection in the United States.

### Efficient Redistribution

If policy can best be explained as the result of competition between pressure groups, then governments should generally seek to use the most efficient methods of redistribution, given the relative weight they attach to the welfare of each interest group. Some have suggested that lump-sum transfers would be the most efficient method of redistributing income, eliminating dead-weight costs, and maximizing aggregate income. Lump-sum transfers may not be the most efficient method, however, if the purpose is to target policy to politically powerful groups. The administrative costs of distributing lump-sum transfers according to farm size may exceed the dead-weight losses of price distortions. Policies tied to production provide a method of limiting transfers based on output, reducing the costs of determining eligibility, and lessening the potential for abuse.

Transfers will be larger where income can be transferred more efficiently, with a smaller ratio of costs per unit of benefit received. Whether a policy is an efficient method of redistributing income will depend partly on the political power of the groups involved. A given policy can be considered an efficient method of redistribution if the costs weighted by the political power of those who bear the costs are minimized relative to the weighted benefits received, not if the aggregate sum of costs are minimized relative to benefits. If a group such as foreign consumers, for example, is not involved in the political process, then policy will maximize the weighted sum of net gains to involved groups irrespective of the losses to foreign consumers.

There is some evidence that existing methods of redistribution are efficient, in the sense of minimizing the dead-weight losses of income transfers, weighted by the political power of each group. Export taxes, frequently used on tropical beverages, are an efficient method of raising tax revenue partly at the expense of foreign consumers when a country produces a large share of world output. Recent reductions in export taxes, which have occurred in some countries, may reflect declining market shares over time. Decline in market share may increase the burden of export taxes on domestic producers while reducing government revenues.

Evidence on the relationship between comparative advantage and protection also seems consistent with the hypothesis of efficient

141

redistribution. In addition to the evidence cited on the relationship between net exports and protection, Honma and Hayami (1986), in a study of high-income countries, provide additional evidence that higher average rates of protection are found in countries with no comparative advantage in agriculture.

High protection in importing countries is maintained through import quotas or tariffs. Quotas and tariffs reduce the quantity imported, increasing demand for domestically produced products. Quotas enable selected importers to earn rents, while tariffs generate revenue for the government. Import restrictions are relatively easy to enforce if there are only a few major ports through which international trade occurs. Where taxpayers have enough political power, tariffs are likely to be popular because they substitute for other taxes. With dead-weight losses and collection costs of taxes saved, the marginal benefits to taxpayers and producers are likely to be high relative to the loss to consumers.

The use of export subsidies is harder to reconcile with notions of efficient redistribution. As Gardner (1981) shows, output restrictions and production subsidies are likely to be less costly methods of increasing producer incomes, particularly in major exporting countries. One possible advantage of export subsidies over production subsidies is that part of the cost is borne by consumers. Where consumers have less political power than taxpayers, export subsidies may be preferred over production subsidies. In some countries, export subsidies are really a form of price discrimination, with lower prices to the more elastic foreign markets financed by a levy on domestic producers. This is the approach used to partially finance export subsidies for dairy products in Austria (OECD 1987).

In the United States and Japan, export subsidies have been primarily used as temporary measures to dispose of accumulated stocks resulting from price support policies (Gardner 1981; Otsuka and Hayami 1986). Such policies may persist, even as more efficient alternatives become possible, because of the transactions costs associated with changing policy. Export subsidies and import restrictions are more important in the European countries and Japan than they are in the United States, Canada, Australia, or New Zealand. The EC countries and Japan import many commodities, while their exports are small enough to have little effect on world prices, with a few exceptions. High-income exporting countries rely more heavily on policies financed by taxpayers, keeping consumer prices relatively low, while putting less downward pressure on world prices (OECD 1987, 131–32).

The hypothesis that economic incentives influence the size of income transfers is consistent with results from Miller (1991), showing that higher government consumption is associated with greater taxation of farmers in low-income countries. High government consumption may be associated with high marginal costs of additional tax revenue, increasing the likelihood that taxes on farm commodities will be used instead of other taxes. Alternatively, political preferences for greater redistribution of income may explain both the size of government and the amount of redistribution resulting from agricultural policy.

## Other Factors Affecting Policy

It has not been possible to determine whether the type of government affects the size or direction of policy-induced transfers, partly because of the difficulty of classifying governments and partly because the type of government correlates with per capita income, with higher-income countries tending to have more democratic governments. According to Benson and Faminow (1986), parliamentary systems may result in policy outcomes different from those in other forms of democratic government. Evidence from low-income countries suggests that countries with a variety of political systems pursue similar policies.

Cultural and historical factors probably play a role in such policy differences. Authoritarian governments, with little opposition, may have more stable policies that reflect beliefs held by the elite and are less influenced by pressure from farmers and other interest groups. Nevertheless, even authoritarian governments must choose policies that do not provoke great opposition from farmers or other interest groups.

The policies of Japan, Korea, and Taiwan, where farm size remains small in spite of increasing scale economies, illustrate the role of cultural factors. Government land policy may partly reflect unique cultural factors. Differences in policy among European countries in the nineteenth century may also reflect cultural differences. Britain may have pursued market-oriented policies because of a more individualistic culture, while class and family solidarity led to protection of agriculture in Germany and France (Kindleberger 1951).

Considerable evidence suggests that income maximization is not the only goal of interest groups. The tendency of policy to stabilize domestic prices relative to world prices is not easy to explain based on differences in marginal benefits and costs of redistribution. It is difficult to find a reason why marginal benefits of most types of agricultural protection should be lower or marginal costs higher when

143

the world price is high relative to long-term trends. Bullock (1989) suggests that the price-stabilizing tendency of policy in the United States results from the concern of nonfarm interest groups in the well-being of farmers, an attitude that diminishes resistance to income-support policies for farmers when market conditions bring about low prices for farm products.

The willingness of consumer and business interests to accept high food prices in Japan may reflect concern for the relative well-being of farmers in a period of rapid economic growth. People might be less inclined to express their dissatisfaction with policies of existing government officials if they are experiencing rising standards of living, even though the policies may reduce the rate of increase somewhat. Thus, as Hayami (1986) suggests, in rapidly growing countries such as Japan, Korea, and Taiwan, farmers seek protection in response to high costs of structural adjustment, while members of nonfarm groups are willing to supply protection because the cost is a small share of their rising standards of living.

## Predicting Future Policy

The theory of competition among interest groups as applied to agriculture is not sufficiently well developed to be useful for detailed predictions of future policy. The assertion that as the number of farmers continues to shrink in high-income countries, so will the political power of farmers, however, is doubtful. Such a decline in farmers' political power in high-income countries is more likely to accompany reduced productivity and income in the nonfarm sector, a possibility that few consider in this era of economic growth.

The theory and empirical evidence suggest that taxation of agriculture in low-income countries will decline and disappear as income increases. Improvements in transportation and communication will tend to increase the political power of farmers, even as food prices become less important to urban consumers. Declining comparative advantage of agriculture as countries develop mining or manufacturing sectors can also be an important impetus toward reduced taxation or increased protection of agriculture (Anderson 1986).

Some look to global trade policy forums, such as the GATT, to promote a reduction in agricultural protection, but little has been accomplished so far. Bilateral trade negotiations have had some effect in reducing barriers to agricultural trade between some high-income countries, but often at the expense of other countries not included in the negotiations (Anderson and Hayami 1986). The costs of protection of agricultural products or the cost of trade retaliation by the exporters of agricultural products will have to rise considerably before significant liberalization of agricultural trade occurs.

## Summary

Any proposal for the reform of agricultural policy needs to account for the dominant role of interest groups in the political process. Changes in agricultural policy are likely to be driven primarily by changes in the political power of interest groups and the economic environment rather than by evidence that current policy fails to maximize aggregate income or welfare. In light of this reality, economic analysis may lead to improved policy in three ways: (1) suggest oppportunities for mutually beneficial improvements in the international trading environment; (2) assist in discovering more efficient methods of transferring income; and (3) suggest ways to alter the balance of political power between interest groups.

## References

Agarwala, Ramgopal. "Price Distortions and Growth in Developing Countries." World Bank Staff Working paper no. 575. Washington, D.C.: World Bank, 1983.

Anderson, Kym. "Economic Growth, Structural Change and the Political Economy of Protection." In *The Political Economy of Agricultural Protection: East Asia in International Perspective*, edited by Kym Anderson and Yujiro Hayami. Sydney: Allen and Unwin, 1986.

———. "The Peculiar Rationality of Beef Import Quotas in Japan and Korea." In *The Political Economy of Agricultural Protection: East Asia in International Perspective*, edited by Kym Anderson and Yujiro Hayami. Sydney: Allen and Unwin, 1986.

Anderson, Kym, and Yujiro Hayami. "Lessons and Implications." In *The Political Economy of Agricultural Protection: East Asia in International Perspective*, edited by Kym Anderson and Yujiro Hayami. Sydney: Allen and Unwin, 1986.

Anderson, Kym, Yujiro Hayami, and Masayoshi Honma. "The Growth of Agricultural Protection." In *The Political Economy of Agricultural Protection: East Asia in International Perspective*, edited by Kym Anderson and Yujiro Hayami. Sydney: Allen and Unwin, 1986.

Babcock, B. A., Colin A. Carter, and A. Schmitz. "The Political Economy of U.S. Wheat Legislation." *Economic Inquiry* 28 (April 1990): 335–53.

Balisacan, Arsenio, and James Roumasset. "Public Choice of Eco-

145

nomic Policy: The Growth of Agricultural Protection." *Weltwirtschaftiches Archiv*, 123 (1987): 232–48.

Barker, Jonathan. "Gaps in the Debates about Agriculture in Senegal, Tanzania, and Mozambique." *World Development* 13 (January 1985): 59–76.

Bates, Robert H. *Essays on the Political Economy of Rural Africa*. Berkeley: University of California Press, 1987.

Bauer, P. T. *Equality, the Third World and Economic Delusion*. Cambridge: Harvard University Press, 1981.

Becker, Gary S. "Competition among Pressure Groups for Political Influence." *Quarterly Journal of Economics* 98 (August 1983): 371–400.

Benson, Bruce, and M. D. Faminow. "Regulatory Transfers in Canadian/American Agriculture: The Case of Supply Management." *Cato Journal* 6 (Spring/Summer 1986): 271–94.

Binswanger, Hans P., and Pasquale L. Scandizzo. "Patterns of Agricultural Protection." Report ARU 15. Washington, D.C.: World Bank, 1983.

Braverman, Avishay, and J. Luis Gausch. "Rural Credit Markets and Institutions in Developing Countries: Lessons for Policy Analysis from Practice and Modern Theory." *World Development* 14 (1986): 1253–67.

Browne, William P. *Private Interests, Public Policy, and American Agriculture*. Lawrence, Kans.: University Press of Kansas, 1988.

Bullock, David. "The Volatility of Government Transfers to U.S. Agriculture: A Political Pressure Group Approach." Ph.D. diss., University of Chicago, 1989.

Byerlee, Derek. "The Political Economy of Third World Food Imports: The Case of Wheat." *Economic Development and Cultural Change* 35 (January 1987): 307–28.

Byerlee, Derek, and Gustavo Sain. "Food Pricing Policy in Developing Countries: Bias against Agriculture or for Urban Consumers?" *American Journal of Agricultural Economics* 68 (November 1986): 961–69.

Davis, Jeffrey M. "The Fiscal Role of Food Subsidy Programs." *IMF Staff Papers*. March 1977: 100–27.

Gallagher, Paul W. "The Grain Sector of the European Community: Policy Formation, Price Determination, and Implications for Trade." *American Journal of Agricultural Economics* (November 1988): 767–78.

Gardner, Bruce. "Causes of Farm Commodity Price Supports in the U.S." *Journal of Political Economy* 95 (April 1987): 290–309.

———. "Efficient Redistribution in Agricultural Commodity Markets." Chicago: Center for the Study of the Economy and the State, working paper no. 20, 1981.

George, Aurelia, and Eric Saxon. "The Politics of Agricultural Protection in Japan." In *The Political Economy of Agricultural Protection: East Asia in International Perspective*, edited by Kym Anderson and Yujiro Hayami. Sydney: Allen and Unwin, 1986.

Griffin, Keith. *The Political Economy of Agrarian Change.* Second edition. London: Macmillan Press, 1979.

Hayami, Yujiro. "The Roots of Agricultural Protectionism." In *The Political Economy of Agricultural Protection: East Asia in International Perspective*, edited by Kym Anderson and Yujiro Hayami. Sydney: Allen and Unwin, 1986.

Honma, Masayoshi, and Yujiro Hayami. "The Determinants of Agricultural Protection Levels: An Econometric Analysis." In *The Political Economy of Agricultural Protection: East Asia in International Perspective*, edited by Kym Anderson and Yujiro Hayami. Sydney: Allen and Unwin, 1986.

Jaeger, William, and Charles Humphreys. "The Effect of Policy Reforms on Agricultural Incentives in Sub-Saharan Africa." *American Journal of Agricultural Economics* 70 (December 1988): 1036–43.

Johnson, D. Gale. "Constraints to Price Adjustments: Structural, Institutional, and Financial Rigidities." Office of Agricultural Economics Paper no. 87:7. University of Chicago. February 1988.

———. *World Agriculture in Disarray.* London: McMillan, 1991.

Kennedy, Peter. A Guide to Econometrics. Second Edition. Cambridge: MIT Press, 1985.

Kindleberger, C. P. "Group Behavior and International Trade." *Journal of Political Economy* 59 (1951): 30–46.

Krueger, Anne O., Maurice Schiff, and Alberto Valdes. "Agricultural Incentives in Developing Countries: Measuring the Effect of Sectoral and Economywide Policies." *World Bank Economic Review* 2 (1988): 255–71.

Miller, Geoff. *The Political Economy of International Agricultural Policy Reform.* Canberra: Australian Government Publishing Service, 1987.

Miller, Tracy C. "Explaining Agricultural Price Policy across Countries and across Commodities Using a Model of Competition between Interest Groups." Ph.D. diss. University of Chicago, 1986.

———. "Agricultural Price Policies and Political Interest Group Competition." *Journal of Policy Modeling* 13 (1991): 489–513.

Olson, Mancur. *The Logic of Collective Action.* Cambridge: Harvard University Press, 1965.

Organization for Economic Cooperation and Development. *The Implications of Different Means of Agricultural Income Support.* Paris: OECD, 1983.

———. *National Policies and Agricultural Trade.* Paris: OECD, 1987.

Otsuka, Keijiro, and Yujiro Hayami. "Revealed Preference in Japan's

Rice Policy." In *The Political Economy of Agricultural Protection: East Asia in International Perspective*, edited by Kym Anderson and Yujiro Hayami. Sydney: Allen and Unwin, 1986.

Paukert, Felix. "Price Policies as a Form of Incomes Policy in Developing Countries." *International Labour Review* 127 (1988): 293–316.

Peltzman, Sam. "The Growth of Government." *Journal of Law and Economics* 23 (October 1980): 209–87.

Reithmuller, Paul, and Terry Roe. "Government Intervention in Commodity Markets: The Case of Japanese Rice and Wheat Policy." *Journal of Policy Modeling* 8 (1986): 327–49.

Reusse, E. "Liberalization and Agricultural Marketing: Recent Causes and Effects in Third World Economies." *Food Policy* (November 1987): 299–317.

Summers, Robert, and Alan Heston. "A New Set of International Comparisons of Real Product and Prices for 130 countries, 1950–85." *Review of Income and Wealth* 34 (March 1988): 1–25.

Thomson, K. J. and D. R. Haney. "The Efficiency of Common Agricultural Policy." *European Review of Agricultural Economics* 8 (1981): 74.

USDA ERS. "Estimates of Producer and Consumer Subsidy Equivalents: Government Intervention in Agriculture, 1982–86." Agriculture and Trade Analysis Division, April 1988.

———. "Government Intervention in Agriculture." *Foreign Agricultural Economic Report* 229, April 1987.

Watts, Michael J., and Thomas J. Bassett. "Politics, the State and Agrarian Development: A Comparative Study of Nigeria and the Ivory Coast." *Political Geography Quarterly* 5 (April 1986): 103–25.

Zazueta, Aaron E. "Agricultural Policy in Mexico: The Limits of a Growth Model." In *State, Capital, and Rural Society*, edited by Benjamin S. Orlove, Michael W. Foley, and Thomas S. Love. Boulder, Colo.: Westview, 1989.

# 7
# The Political Economy of
# Taiwan's Agricultural Policies

*Chi-ming Hou and Chaw-hsia Tu*

During the past four decades, economic development in Taiwan has been characterized by a successful structural transformation from a predominantly agricultural economy to a newly industrialized one. The fast growth of the industrial sector rapidly increased labor cost and deteriorated the economic conditions and environment for agricultural development. Farm productivity and farm income both increased relatively slowly when compared with the growth of the nonagricultural sector. The role of agriculture in the economy changed from an export surplus sector to a net import sector in 1970. Public sector policies have been dominated principally by the government because of its unencumbered powers (in common with most developing countries); therefore, strategy was easily switched from taxing agriculture to increasingly supporting it since 1972.

In addition to domestic policies to subsidize and support agriculture and farmers, tariff and nontariff barriers protected domestic products from foreign competition. The high protection offered by the trade barriers in the 1950s and 1960s was mainly the result of facing the problem of extreme shortage of foreign exchange in the early 1950s. So government used both strict control and import tariffs to protect the domestic market. The concept of mercantilism became well embedded in this period. Therefore, in the 1970s, when exports surpassed imports and the threat of foreign exchange shortages diminished, government controls on imports were lessened to some extent, but tariff barriers still remained relatively high.

In the 1980s, trade liberalization policies were adopted more aggressively to relieve the pressure of the price inflation that resulted from the continuous accumulation of huge trade surpluses. Whereas most import barriers were substantially removed, both the width and the depth of import liberalization of agricultural products were less than those of manufactured goods, perhaps because of the relative inability of agriculture to adjust and keep pace with such fast liberalization. Nevertheless, the protection of agricultural products that have lost their comparative advantage in the market may incur huge costs from the inefficient use of inputs and redistribution of income within the economy. In addition, the policy-making system was also changing, and farmers, who were playing an increasingly important role as determinants of agricultural policy, were asking for more protection from the goverment.

This chapter highlights changes in agricultural policy and their effects on the incomes of various groups in Taiwan since 1949. This chapter will also look at the trade liberalization policies recently implemented by the government of the Republic of China (ROC) and their influence on agricultural policy, the cost-benefit analysis of agricultural policy on various groups under current protective policies, and political and economic policy changes.

## Domestic Agricultural Policy and the Income Redistribution Effect

The objectives of agricultural policy in Taiwan fall into two stages. In the first stage, before 1972, government policies for agricultural products were mainly tax measures and programs established for promoting agricultural production. After 1974, in the second stage, government policy shifted to a subsidy and protection program for farmers.

Table 7-1 highlights the key policies adopted in the past four decades. The land reform policy from 1949 to 1953 gave farmers a great incentive to work harder and make the land more productive through more capital investment and the application of more fertilizer. Thus, the foundation of sustained growth in agriculture was laid in the 1950s and 1960s. Since the rent or purchasing price of the land that the farmer paid to the landlord or to the government was relatively low, this policy also had a wealth redistribution effect and contributed to a more equitable distribution of income. Aside from this, to achieve greater rice production and greater control over rice marketing for maintaining a stable rice price, the land tax in kind and bartering rice at a favorable price for fertilizer freed farmers from price instability in the early 1950s and also had a positive effect on farm production and therefore affected farm income positively as well. This positive effect, however, turned out to be a negative one later on, when production of fertilizer increased and its relative price in terms of rice dropped significantly. All these devices for controlling the rice market, together with the compulsory purchases of rice in

## TABLE 7-1
### Main Agricultural Policies and Income Redistribution Effect in Taiwan since 1949

| Policy Implementation | Time | Policy Means | Income Redistribution Effect on | | | | Indirect Economic Effect on | |
|---|---|---|---|---|---|---|---|---|
| | | | Farmer | Land-owner | Tax-payer | Con-sumer | Pro-duction | Price stability |
| 37.5 rent reduction | April 1949–July 1949 | Maximum rent not to exceed 37.5% of the total annual yield | + | − | | | + | + |
| Sale of public farmland | 1951 | Public farmland to be sold to tenant cultivators at the price equivalent to 2.5 times of the total annual yield | + | − | | | + | + |
| Land to the tiller | July 1953–Dec. 1953 | Compulsorily sold land, from landlord who held more than 3 chia of paddy fields or 6 chia of dry land to the government for resale to tenant farmers | + | − | | | + | + |
| Maintaining control of rice market-ing | 1947–1987 | Paddy land taxes in kind | + | | | | | |

*(Table continues)*

151

TABLE 7–1 (continued)

| Policy Implementation | Time | Policy Means | Income Redistribution Effect on | | | | Indirect Economic Effect on | |
|---|---|---|---|---|---|---|---|---|
| | | | Farmer | Land-owner | Tax-payer | Con-sumer | Pro-duction | Price stability |
| | 1947–1973 | Compulsory purchases of paddy from paddy landowners | − | − | + | + | + | + |
| | 1952–1993 | Rent or sale on government-owned farmland in kind | | | | | | |
| | 1948–1973 | Barter of fertilizers for rice | | | | | | |
| Purchasing rice at a guaranteed price[a] | 1974–1993 | Guaranteed price fixed in principle with the 20% profit above the production cost | + | | − | | + | + |
| | | Rice stabilization fund established in 1974 to subsidize rice production | | | | | | |
| Rice crop substitution plan | 1984–1987 | Pay-in-kind subsidy of 1 or 1.5 metric tons of paddy rice per hectare to rice field owner for shifting to small grains or other crops; Small | + | | − | | − | |

| | Years | Description | | | | | | |
|---|---|---|---|---|---|---|---|---|
| | | grains purchased by the government at the guaranteed prices | | | | | | |
| | 1988–1993 | Cash payment (N.T.$16,500 or 24,750 per hectare to farmers) instead of pay-in-kind | | | | | | |
| Accelerating rural development and basic-level construction in the agricultural sector | 1973–1993 | Encouraging innovation in agricultural marketing systems; reducing the farmers' financial burden; increasing agricultural investment; enhancing rural welfare and farmers' livelihood | + | | − | | + | |
| Second phase of farmland reform | 1982–1987 | Loan for expansion of farm size and enlargement of farm operation | + | + | − | | | |
| Purchasing small grain at guaranteed prices | 1971– July 1988 | Small Grain Fund: financial resources from compulsory donation small grain imports (a kind of surtax) | + | | | − | + | |
| Stabilizing the market prices of milk | 1975– July 1989 | Fresh milk, dairy farmers contract with milk factories at guaranteed prices, Milk Development Fund: compul- | + | | | − | + | + |

*(Table continues)*

153

TABLE 7–1 (continued)

| Policy Imple-mentation | Time | Policy Means | Income Redistribution Effect on | | | | Indirect Economic Effect on | |
| --- | --- | --- | --- | --- | --- | --- | --- | --- |
| | | | Farmer | Land-owner | Tax-payer | Con-sumer | Pro-duction | Price stability |
| Stabilizing the market price of sugar | 1966–1993 | sory donation from importer to dairy farmers Sugar farmers contract with Taiwan Sugar Corporation before planting begins, to ensure purchasing price of sugar. Sugar Stabilization Fund: domestic price for sugar decided by government | + | | | − | + | + |

a. The quantity of rice purchased under guaranteed price is unlimited between 1974 and 1976; then it decreased and was limited to 970 kg. per hectare per crop between 1977 and 1988; in 1989 this limitation increased to 1,400 kg. per hectare per crop.

SOURCE: Chen, Hsu, and Mao 1974; Kuo 1975; Shen 1974 and Chen 1990.

kind at an unfavorable price to the farmer, constituted a hidden tax on the farmer (Kuo 1975).

From 1966 to 1969, agricultural production, mainly in farm crops, grew slowly in comparison with the preceding years. Industrial output, however, grew continuously at a very fast pace. Farm family per capita incomes therefore deteriorated to a level less than two-thirds of nonfarmers' per capita incomes. After 1972, the government adopted several policies marking the turning point of government policy toward agriculture: policy changed from an agricultural development strategy geared to generating a surplus to help capital formation outside of agriculture toward a strategy of protecting and increasingly subsidizing farmers' incomes (Chen, Hsu, and Mao 1974).

In 1973, the fertilizer-rice barter system was abolished and the guaranteed price was implemented to improve farmers' incomes. Since the guaranteed price was fixed with a 20 percent profit above the production cost, the rice price for farmers was isolated from market demand. Farmers' incomes increased by 9.85 percent yearly over the following few years, and rice production reached its highest level in 1976. As per capita incomes of nonagricultural sectors increased as well, however, patterns of food consumption became more diversified, and per capita consumption of rice decreased significantly. The increase in rice production and the decrease in rice consumption resulted in a rice surplus that induced the government to adopt other policies to alleviate this problem.

The rice stabilization fund, established in 1974, operated as the financial support unit for subsidizing the difference between the purchasing price and the domestic market price of rice. Since the domestic market price was separated from the world market price by the licensing of imports, this subsidy eventually became a burden on both the consumers and the public treasury, and the rice surplus became a serious problem for the government. In 1984, the government initiated a rice crop substitution plan to encourage rice farmers to grow other crops. If farmers changed their rice fields to the production of corn, sorghum, or soybeans, one metric ton of paddy rice per hectare would be given to the farmers as a subsidy. In addition, corn, sorghum, or soybeans would be purchased by the government at the guaranteed prices. If farmers shifted to other crops or left the land idle, the subsidy increased to 1.5 metric tons of paddy rice per hectare. In 1987, to restrict the production of vegetables and flowers, the subsidy of paddy rice decreased to 1.0 metric ton of paddy rice per hectare for other types of crops. Since guaranteed prices of corn, sorghum, and soybeans were much higher than market prices, raising farmers' incomes and distorting domestic prices once again resulted from policy implementation. The original purpose of the rice crop substitution plan—to reduce the rice surplus—was partially accomplished. But part of the government's financial burden of purchasing rice at guaranteed prices was transferred to the consumer, since the deficiency payment of purchasing corn, sorghum, and soybeans came from surtaxes on those commodities when imported.

Other than raising farmers' incomes, stabilization of the price of agricultural products was regarded as the main target of government policy. The purchase at guaranteed prices for several export products provided reassurance to farmers before planting. Such products covered in this program included pineapples, mushrooms, asparagus, bamboo shoots, tomatoes, onions, bananas, seedless watermelons, silkworm cocoons, eels, and others. The guaranteed prices, however, were basically contracted between farmers and factories, where government did not subsidize or interfere by financial means. The government's interventions gave encouragement and help to both farmers and factories to fulfill the terms of the contract.

Stabilization funds for sugar and hog production were established in 1967 and 1976, respectively. Instead of coming from government expenditures, though, as in the case of rice, the funds for the stabilization of sugar and for the production and marketing of hogs derived mainly from extra profits from sales of sugar and hogs. Whenever selling prices were high enough to reach certain levels, for example, a fixed proportion of the revenue was drawn and put into the fund. Therefore, the government subsidized only at the initiation of these funds, and the amount was relatively small. Considering that the domestic price of sugar is also decided by government and that sugar cannot be imported freely, however, domestic consumers bear the cost of protection whenever the domestic price is higher than the world price.

As for certain grains, because domestic production of corn, soybeans, sorghum, and wheat cannot compete with foreign suppliers and the relatively high prices of feed grains may impede the competitiveness of domestic downstream poultry and animal industries, import controls on these items were dropped in 1966. Domestic production consequently diminished to an almost insignificant level. To prevent the dry lands from becoming eroded, however, the government set guaranteed prices for corn, soybeans, sorghum, and wheat in 1971. The small grain fund, which subsidized farmers, came from the compulsory contribution (a kind of surtax) from importers of small grains. This arrangement, in effect, raised the domestic selling price, so that consumers carried the burden of protection.

For dairy products, the dairy development fund, established in 1975, operated much like the mechanism of the small grain fund to subsidize dairy farmers and to encourage domestic production of fresh milk. Since the surtax on imports of small grains and dairy products was regulated by administrative order only, however, the dairy fund did not have a legal basis for forcible execution. Importers questioned the appropriateness of such subsidization when democratic reform progressed in the 1980s. Consequently, these funds were abolished in 1988 and 1989, respectively.

In short, although price supports are the key elements of the domestic agricultural program, other methods of subsidies such as subsidized imports, marketing assistance, research, and tax benefits also exist. But they are minimal in quantity. Therefore, the domestic agricultural program in Taiwan is characterized by : (1) maintaining stable and self-sufficient production of rice; (2) stablizing the prices of agricultural products by setting up guaranteed prices for farmers before planting begins; (3) relying on price policies as the major instrument to stabilize the supply of agricultural production; (4) using price supports to raise farmers' incomes rather than other transfer payment programs; and (5) raising stabilization funds mainly from importers of the relevant goods (except for rice) and making government and taxpayers share a relatively small portion of the cost of the protective policy in comparison with other developed countries. Consumers, however, bear most of the cost of the price support system.

Now we will look at some of the trade policies affecting agricultural products, which were inherited mostly from the high tariffs and severe import controls of the past. This combination of import restriction and maintenance of higher domestic prices constitutes a major part of protection on some commodities.

## The Evolution of Trade Policy

In general, agricultural trade policy in Taiwan is part of, and generally in accordance with, its macroeconomic development strategy. In the early 1950s, like most developing countries, Taiwan adopted highly protectionist trade strategies to overcome foreign exchange shortages and to nurture import substitution industries. These so-called highly protectionist strategies included an overvalued New Taiwan (N.T.) dollar to lower import costs and restrictions on imports through stringent import quotas and exchange control systems. Since 90 percent of total exports were agricultural or processed agricultural products, the strong governmental intervention policy was effected mainly through a system of taxes on export goods or taxes on agricultural products.

In the 1960s, owing to the exhaustion of the domestic market's ability to absorb manufactured goods, unemployment rose, and the economic growth rate fell. An external-oriented strategy was implemented to absorb the relatively abundant labor resources. Thus, the currency was devalued to a more natural level, and foreign exchange, interest rates, and import barriers were revised in ways that decreased government control and strengthened market forces. Since import protection was still recognized as a measure to encourage domestic industries and tariffs were an important source of government revenue, however, the loosening of controls on imports resulted mainly in lessening import quotas. Consequently, tariff protection still remained very high, and market forces were strengthened primarily in the export sector. A mercantilistic trade policy was most evident in the established tariff rebates and export processing zones, which encouraged exports in tandem with high tariffs on imports. Since foreign buyers do not bear a tariff burden, high tariff protection on imports has never been an impediment to exports. Agricultural products, however, did not benefit from such a tariff rebate system and were still encumbered with high tariffs.

In the late 1960s, as the economy progressed through the external-orientation policy, the set of social and economic problems changed. The foreign exchange shortage was replaced first by a balance in international payments, followed in the 1970s with an export surplus. Now, Taiwan has a shortage of skilled labor and increasing real wages, which is radically different from the early unemployment problem. Thus, lifting tariff protection or putting equal emphasis on imports and exports would have been desirable for unrestrained domestic consumption at that earlier time. This was not the case, however, and policy makers do not think that a trade surplus and foreign exchange accumulation should be corrected by government policy, though some economists have suggested this approach. Therefore, import barriers still remained very high. In addition, to develop capital goods and intermediary goods industries, the so-called second phase of import substitution strategy was promoted in the 1970s, and tariff protection on some products was raised even higher. The trade surplus increased steadily, and foreign exchange reserves accumulated year after year through the 1980s.

In the 1980s, the huge trade surplus induced a strong increase in the money supply, generating inflationary pressure. In 1984, trade liberalization and economic internationalization policies were issued by the Executive Yuan to ease pressure from foreign trading partners.

The United States has requested the removal of both tariff and nontariff barriers, since the beginning of bilateral trade negotiations between the ROC and the United States in 1978. In addition to the tariff concessions requested by the United States, U.S. negotiators also wanted to discuss opening markets for domestic services and financial industries, protection of intellectual property rights, and simplifying import and export licensing and customs duty evaluation systems. It is apparent that the U.S. government wanted to push Taiwan to bear most of the obligations prescribed by the GATT and the rules established in the Tokyo Round.

As an economy that has not been a contract party of the GATT since 1950, however, Taiwan has not always designed policy to meet the open market requirements stipulated by the GATT. It was very hard for both the policy makers and the public to accept such a big liberalization step. In large part, this hesitancy was due to mercantilism lingering from preceding years and to the view that an open market meant gains only for the foreign trade partners, not for the local enterprises and consumers. Of course, this is significantly different from what trade theory proposes, in which any given country gains when it has free trade. Nonetheless, to respond to U.S. pressure to open markets and reduce the trade surplus, the Executive Yuan of the ROC announced that trade liberalization and economic internationalization would be the focus of policy after 1984.

Policy to liberalize trade was formulated under outside pressure, but progress was minimal in its first year, 1984. In 1986, when the trade surplus was still increasing—reaching a record high of U.S.$15 billion—Taiwan implemented substantial liberalization, reducing nominal tariff rates even further after a significant slash in 1985. In late 1986, after U.S. pressure focused on the valuation system of Taiwan's currency, the N.T. dollar appreciated by 35 percent over the next two years. The ROC government realized that liberalization policies must be implemented quickly and more seriously. From that time both tariff and nontariff barriers were removed in a sweeping program.

In 1989, to quell the antagonism of the U.S. Congress toward protective policies in foreign markets and to convince the Congress that the ROC government would pursue liberalization policies, Taiwan initiated a four-year liberalization plan. According to that plan, average nominal tariff rates will be reduced to 7 percent, and the effective rate of tariff burden will be reduced to 3.5 percent. Meanwhile, the tariff rebate system has been simplified and is to be abolished at the end of the Uruguay Round. In 1991, the nominal tariff rate was reduced to 8.89 percent, and the effective rate of the tax burden on imports was then 4.95 percent. The significant 77.28 percent tariff reduction in the 1980s—from 39.14 percent in 1979 to 8.89 percent in 1991 (table 7–2)—has made Taiwan a country with relatively low tariff protection.

Slashing tariffs is one of the major steps the ROC has taken to open its markets to foreign competition. Other measures such as loosening import controls and opening the services market, removing nontariff barriers, and relaxing controls on foreign exchange have also been initiated. Thus, inflationary pressures have been effectively relieved in recent years. This relief was necessary, as the price level in areas such as real estate increased by two- to threefold between 1987 and 1990. It is apparent that the economy has benefited from freer trade, and there is now little opposition to such policies. Most of the industries influenced by the liberalization policies have moved through a gradual transition period.

The import liberalization movement, however, has not been so smooth in the agricultural sector. Many people are very sympathetic to the agricultural industry because of the relative rigidity of adjusting production at the present time. Clearly, liberalization policies in the agricultural sector have resulted in lower benefits than in the industrial sector.

## Trade Barriers to Agricultural Products

As already mentioned, the ROC's protection of agricultural products can be distinguished as tariff and nontariff protection, price support systems, and income subsidy policies. Income subsidy instruments include preferential interest rates on agricultural production loans, reduction of agricultural taxation, and subsidies for agricultural irrigation, electricity, and insurance.

Price support systems were designed by fixing the purchase price on rice, sugar, and major grains and guaranteeing those prices by the government. Because guaranteed prices are usually much higher than average world market prices, domestic production increases, and imports decrease. Nevertheless, the quantity of major grains produced is rather small, and almost 93 percent of domestic consumption is from imports; thus the trade distortion effect is quite limited. The distortion, however, is more serious for rice and sugar, where domestic commodity programs give support through import controls.

Rice is a staple food of Taiwan, and sugar has been recognized as highly important for many years. Neither of these items can be imported freely. Table 7–3 summarizes both the border measures and the domestic commodity program for eleven agricultural products in Taiwan in 1990. Among these, rice is classified as a permitted item; that is, it can be imported. A rice importer, however, must have his import license approved by the relevant administrative unit, a requirement that usually limits the importation of the item. Since foreign competition in rice has been separated from the domestic market, consumers are paying a high price relative to the world price. The ratios of consumer prices of rice and sugar to world prices were 1.88 and 1.84, respectively, in 1988. Therefore, consumers bear most of the cost of protection of sugar. As for rice, because the government purchases rice at a guaranteed price (which is higher than the domestic free market price) and the rice stabilization fund is financed by budgetary expenditure, both taxpayers and consumers bear the cost of protection. Other products still subject to government control include peanuts, red beans, edible offal, several kinds of fish, garlic bulbs, and fresh milk. These products were recognized as sensitive items where open market policies might cause serious problems for domestic producers.

As far as tariff protection is concerned, high tariffs are usually put on high-value agricultural products such as fresh fruit, concentrated juices, processed foods, and vegetables. The average nominal tariff on agricultural products is 23.4 percent, and the effective rate of the tariff burden is 12.25 percent (as shown in table 7–2) in 1992. Notably, the tariff protection on agricultural goods is much higher than the 4.78 percent tariff burden on nonagricultural goods.

A timetable of liberalization policy was established by the ROC government in 1988, which states that the nominal tariff rate on agricultural products will be 19.8 percent at the completion of the Uruguay Round. Other nontariff trade barriers can also be expected to be removed gradually. There is no doubt that the administrative department wants to fulfill its promises of further liberalizing trade policies. Reductions on nontariff barriers are being continuously announced by Board of Foreign Trade of the Ministry of Economics. But for tariff reductions, the degree of progress falls behind a little bit in comparison with the promised timetable. The reason is that the tariff reduction proposal has to be reviewed and approved by the Legislative Yuan, while the approval of the bill by the Legislative Yuan has been delayed because of other political issues. Besides, resistance to further liberalization by interest groups also influenced the approval of such proposals in the Legislative Yuan. Therefore, the tariff reduction proposal raised by the Ministry of Finance in 1990 did

## TABLE 7-2
### ITEMIZED ANALYSIS OF TAIWAN'S TARIFFS, SELECTED YEARS, 1955–1992
(percent)

| Year | Average Nominal Tax Rate | | Average Tariff Burden of All Imports | Average Tariff Burden of Agricultural Products | Average Tariff Burden of Nonagricultural Products |
|---|---|---|---|---|---|
| | Column 1 | Column 2 | | | |
| 1955 | 47.0 | | 38.20 | n.a. | n.a. |
| 1961 | 38.8 | | 15.80 | n.a. | n.a. |
| 1965 | 35.4 | | 16.50 | n.a. | n.a. |
| 1971 | 39.1 | | 14.14 | n.a. | n.a. |
| 1974 | 55.65 | | 11.74 | n.a. | n.a. |
| 1975 | 52.69 | | 9.88 | 16.84 | 10.67 |
| 1978 | 43.58 | | 11.27 | 13.13 | 8.82 |
| 1979 | 39.14 | | 11.62 | 20.42 | 10.38 |
| 1980 | 35.96 | 31.17 | 9.00 | 19.19 | 8.27 |
| 1984 | 35.95 | 30.81 | 7.72 | 12.40 | 8.26 |
| 1985 | 32.79 | 26.46 | 7.89 | 13.71 | 8.69 |

| 1986 | 31.77 | 22.83 | 7.67 | 14.71 | 7.11 |
| 1987 | n.a. | 19.37 | 7.47 | 13.40 | 7.14 |
| 1988 | n.a. | 12.57 | 6.1 | 11.10 | 5.80 |
| 1989 | n.a. | 9.73 | 6.3 | 11.76 | 6.50 |
| 1990 | n.a. | 9.73 | 5.4 | 11.64 | 5.37 |
| 1991 | n.a. | 8.89 | 4.95 | 11.02 | 4.70 |
| 1992 | n.a. | (7.0) | 5.12 | 12.25 | 4.78 |

n.a. = not available

NOTE: Data are basically for the fiscal year. Figures in parenthesis are projected figures.

a. See footnote on table 4–9.

SOURCE: Ministry of Finance, Republic of China.

163

## TABLE 7-3

### NOMINAL IMPORT TARIFF RATES, IMPORT REGULATIONS, AND PROGRAMS FOR AGRICULTURAL COMMODITIES IN TAIWAN, 1990

| Commodity | Nominal Tariff Rate (%) | Import Regulations | Commodity Program |
|---|---|---|---|
| Rice | 0 | Permitted/L; subject to approval of administrative department | Price support; plan conversion; soil conservation |
| Corn | 2.0 | Permitted/L | Price support; deficiency payment |
| Soybeans | 1.5 | Permitted/L | Price support; deficiency payment |
| Sorghum | 3.0 | Permitted/L | Price support; deficiency payment |
| Wheat | 6.5 | Permitted/L | Price support (contracted) |
| Beef | N.T. $23.5/kg (prime or choice) N.T. $30.0/kg (medium) | Permitted/RA | Price support |

| | | Permitted/F (prime); permitted/ L (medium) | |
|---|---|---|---|
| Pork | 15.0 | | — |
| Chicken | 40.0 | Permitted/L | — |
| Milk, fresh | 40.0 | Controlled | Price support (contracted) |
| Milk, powdered | 20.0 | Permitted/F | — |
| Sugar | | | Price support (contracted) |
| Cane and raw cane | 25 | Controlled | |
| Rock | 35 | Controlled | |
| Cube | 35 | Controlled | |
| Maple | 40 | Permitted/F | |
| Fruits | 15–50[a] | Controlled; permitted/F; permitted/RA; subject to approval of administrative department | Price support; marketing order (selected products) |

Empty cell = no commodity program.
Permitted/F = free to import.
Permitted/RA = import permitted only from restricted areas or countries.
Permitted/L = import permitted with licenses issued by the Board of Foreign Trade.
a. Grapefruit and citrus have seasonal import tariffs.
SOURCE: Woo and Fu 1990.

not get approved until 1991, which then delayed the proposals for tariff reductions for 1992.

Protection levels of agricultural products, usually measured by the producer subsidy equivalents (PSEs), indicate the excess return to producers above the world market prices. This amount includes direct assistance to farmers via border measures that keep the domestic producer price above the import price and government assistance financed through the budget, such as input subsidies.

Often cited studies by the U.S. Department of Agriculture (USDA) of PSEs in Taiwan state that the average level of PSEs in Taiwan between 1982 and 1986 was 19 percent. This is lower than in most industrialized countries. This average figure, however, may not be sufficient to represent the level of protection in recent years, since the N.T. dollar has appreciated substantially (by 35 percent since 1987). This rise may have led to higher protection than most people think. To have a clearer picture of Taiwan's protection of agricultural products and the resulting benefits and costs to farmers, consumers, and taxpayers, we calculated the PSE in Taiwan for 1986 and 1988. The net social losses resulting from such policies are discussed in the next section.

The estimated figures are given in table 7-4, which shows findings very similar to those of the USDA. Our figures, however, are generally larger than the USDA's, but the differences are very small. In addition, several interesting points can be raised. First, the data reveal that most of the products with a relatively high PSE are also products with a small market share in comparison with domestic production. The production of pork accounted for almost one-third of total agricultural production, and the PSE of pork is only 1.15 percent. Therefore, the average level of PSE for the total products group is held to 29.43 percent. Next to pork, fruit and rice are the second and third most important agricultural products in Taiwan, of which the PSE is 34.5 percent and 47.6 percent, respectively. For fruit, the 34.5 percent PSE clearly resulted mainly from the high border protection measures. Protection of the fruit market will be lower when GATT negotiations are completed. For rice, however, the 47.6 percent PSE seems different from widely held perceptions that the protection of rice in all East Asian countries is very high. In view of the inevitable economic effects on domestic production from the trade liberalization of rice, it is often believed that a 47.6 PSE is an underestimated figure. After all, the guaranteed purchasing price of rice (around NT$18.0 per kg in 1988) is about 150 percent higher than the world market price (around NT$7.2 per kg of Thailand first-class

TABLE 7–4

PRODUCERS' SUBSIDY EQUIVALENT FOR SELECTED AGRICULTURAL
COMMODITIES IN TAIWAN, 1986 AND 1988

| Commodity | PSE (%) | | Value of Production (millions of N.T. $) | |
|---|---|---|---|---|
| | 1986 | 1988 | 1986 | 1988 |
| Rice | 43.37 | 47.65 | 36,424.08 | 36,517.71 |
| Corn | 77.40 | 83.60 | 3,108.14 | 3,909.78 |
| Soybeans | 66.50 | 74.65 | 305.24 | 336.72 |
| Sorghum | 79.40 | 82.79 | 1,357.72 | 1,648.64 |
| Wheat | 72.35 | 80.24 | 72.01 | 58.54 |
| Beef | 32.28 | 28.45 | 869.13 | 975.84 |
| Sugar | 64.13 | 46.40 | 11,751.58 | 11,383.51 |
| Milk | 53.45 | 59.89 | 1,832.37 | 2,902.83 |
| Fruits | n.a. | 34.50 | n.a. | 37,482.14 |
| Chickens | n.a. | 31.48 | n.a. | 16,215.67 |
| Pork | 1.39 | 1.15 | 52,820.63 | 52,498.96 |
| Total value of production or weighted average PSE | 26.76 | 29.43 | 108,540.90 | 163,930.3 |

n.a. = not available.
SOURCE: USDA, *Agriculture in the Uruguay Round: Analyses of Government Support* (Washington, D.C.: 1988).

rice in 1988). The explanation behind this PSE figure for rice is as follows.

It is true that the guaranteed purchasing price of rice by the government is about 150 percent higher than the world market price. Considering the quality differences in rice, however, we prefer to use the import price of rice in Hong Kong as the world market price. The difference between the guaranteed price and the Hong Kong price was 110 percent in 1988. In addition, since the guaranteed purchase price was fixed to a certain quantity of rice, the benefits to farmers of such a system were restricted. In 1988, rice sold at the fixed price accounted for less than 50 percent of each rice farmer's production. Half the remaining 50 percent was purchased by the government at a price a little higher than the domestic market price, and the other half flowed to the domestic market freely. The benefits that each farmer can receive, beyond the world market price, are thus reduced to 84 percent, and the PSE of rice is consequently reduced to 47.6

167

percent. Since the quantity of government-purchased rice increased somewhat in 1989, however, the PSE of rice may rise in the future.

Second, in a comparison of the 1986 and the 1988 figures, it is evident that (except for sugar and beef) almost all protection levels were higher in 1988 than in 1986. Even though trade liberalization has been promoted consistently since 1986 and tariff protection has been lowered (with government budgetary expenditure remaining about the same), the higher PSEs show that the appreciation of the N.T. dollar has let the protection level of agricultural products in Taiwan increase significantly. Therefore, the increased protection was not due to government intervention.

## Distribution of Gains and Losses from Agricultural Policies

Income redistribution and reduction are the main results of the protection policy. Producers gain, consumers lose, and taxpayers, in effect, bear the costs of government subsidies to farmers. From the point of view of the whole economy, however, though producers gain through agricultural protection, social losses occur through inefficient production of food: artificially high food prices mislead producers into using too many resources for producing food and induce consumers to purchase less.

A method for estimating costs and benefits of agricultural policy has been developed. In the appendix to this chapter, we give a detailed description of this process. Table 7–5 gives the results. It shows that agricultural policies helped farmers gain about U.S.$1.477 billion in 1988, whereas consumers lost about U.S.$1.726 billion and taxpayers lost about U.S.$0.297 billion. The total costs to the whole economy were U.S.$0.556 billion, at about 0.45 percent of gross domestic product (GDP). The transfer ratio is 1.37; that is, for every $1 (any unit of exchange) of farmers' gain, the economy has to pay $1.37. It shows the inefficiency and waste of resources from the inappropriate redistribution of income and protective agricultural policies.

As for individual commodities, the transfer ratio for beef is the highest one, followed by chicken. But the total cost of protection of chicken is much greater than that of beef, because the domestic self-sufficiency ratio of chicken is almost 100 percent, whereas the self-sufficiency ratio of beef is only 12.3 percent.

As far as the gains to producers are concerned, support of rice prices increased farmers' incomes by the greatest amount, followed by the high tariff protection on fruit. But the cost to consumers of protecting fruit is heavier than that of protecting rice, since part of the support comes from government subsidies and taxpayers bear the cost. Government subsidies for rice amounted to NT$10 billion in 1988 and have been the main source of government expenditures on agriculture.

## The Politics of Agricultural Policy

Unlike most other developed countries, where farm policy originates in the legislative branch of the government and is administered by the executive branch, in Taiwan, the executive branch has dominated policy formulation. The executive branch sometimes opposed agricultural legislation when it was thought that the protective policy was costly to the public. Even in the period of reductions and subsidization of production, the administrative branch dominated agricultural policy. It was not until the late 1980s, when democratic reform had progressed substantially, that the government domination of policy making became weaker.

Before 1972, agriculture was mainly a supporting sector for industrial development. The objectives of the agricultural program emphasized greater production of rice and other crops to displace imports and to generate adequate capital for industrial development and foreign exchange to buy industrial capital goods. The Economic Stabilization Board (ESB), created in 1953, was the highest administrative organ involved in agricultural policy at the national level and coordinated with other sectors such as the Ministry of Economics and the Ministry of Finance. The Joint Commission on Rural Reconstruction (JCRR) assisted the board with policy formulation and provided technical services and financial assistance for policy implementation. In 1973, when the organization for economic planning in the central government changed, the JCRR assumed the functions and duties of the ESB in agricultural planning. After two reorganizations, the JCRR was renamed the Council of Agriculture in 1974. The council is now the most important organization for agricultural policy in Taiwan.

Since 1973, government policy switched from a strategy of taxing agriculture to one of increasingly supporting it. The protection of agricultural products increased gradually when the difference in growth between the agricultural and the manufacturing sectors became larger. Both Honma and Hayami (1986) and Thorbecke (1992) believed that the very rapid development of the manufacturing sector could sustain the social cost of agricultural protectionism. Otherwise, social instability might be another problem. It is indeed true that the inequality of income between these two groups might be worse

TABLE 7–5

BENEFITS AND COSTS FROM TAIWAN'S FARM POLICY, 1988

(millions of N.T. dollars)

| Commodity | Welfare Gain of Producers[a] (1) | Welfare Loss of Consumers[b] (2) | Taxpayer Cost[c] (3) | Net Social Cost (2) + (3) − (1) | Transfer Ratio (2) + (3) / (1) |
|---|---|---|---|---|---|
| Rice | 17,408.24 (18,958.42 − 1,550.177) | 10,411.99 (9,595.0 + 816.99) | 10,069.2 (3,151.89 + 5,172.6 + 1,038.93 + 705.78) | 3,072.95 | 1.17 |
| Corn | 2,186.26 (3,256.48 − 1,070.22) | 3,647.996 (3,415.802 + 232.194) | 83.69 (293.14 + 259.92 − 469.37) | 1,545.426 | 1.70 |
| Soybeans[d] | 185.15 (247.24 − 62.23) | 5,008.24 (4,731.25 + 277.09) | −511.95 (20.47 + 19.42 − 551.84) | 4,311.24 | NA |
| Sorghum | 586.72 (1,388.25 − 801.53) | 297.14 (267.281 + 29.86) | 440.25 (118.8 + 75.09 + 225.816 − 9.456) | 150.676 | 1.25 |
| Wheat[d] | 27.48 (44.08 − 16.6) | 522.849 (296.64 + 226.2 + 0) | −249.669 (44.08 + 2.9 − 296.649) | 245.7 | NA |

| | | | | | |
|---|---|---|---|---|---|
| Beef | 215.181 (217.12 − 1.939) | 1,975.09 (1,769.60 + 205.49) | −764.98 (60.55 − 825.53) | 994.93 | 5.62 |
| Sugar | 4,450.7 (5,149.97 − 699.27) | 6,093.19 (5,149.97 + 943.22) | 135.95 | 1,778.44 | 1.39 |
| Milk | 1,371.92 (1,610.62 − 238.70) | 2,925.79 (2,613.54 + 312.25) | −811.4 (106.5 − 917.92) | 742.47 | 1.54 |
| Fruits | 12,706.58 (12,953.83 − 247.25) | 13,488.18 (13,189.73 + 298.45) | −275.13 (1.92 − 1,419.44 + 1,142.39) | 506.47 | 1.03 |
| Chickens | 3,097.3 (4,418.43 − 1,321.13) | 4,978.31 (4,418.43 + 559.88) | 686.906 | 2,567.91 | 1.82 |
| Total (millions of US $) | 42,330.50 (1,477.15) | 49,348.87 (1,726.14) | 8,496.767 (297.20) | 15,916.19 (556.72) | 1.37 |

NA = not applicable.
a. Total subsidies minus net social loss in production.
b. Cost to consumer plus net social loss in consumption.
c. Direct plus indirect government subsidies minus import tariff.
d. Domestic production of soybeans and wheat is very limited; it accounts for less than 2 percent and 1 percent of domestic consumption for each of them, respectively. Since the number of farmers who benefited from domestic price supports is quite limited, the transfer ratio will be meaningless by calculating the data given above.
SOURCE: See text of chapter.

without protection of agriculture. Government, therefore, adopted policies protective of the agricultural sector at a cost to consumers, without causing strong opposition from the public. It was not until the second half of the 1980s that the authoritarian policy-making system became weaker and the public became more vocal.

The authoritarian rule in Taiwan was relatively strong in the very early stages of its economic development. Taiwan then faced the problems of resource shortages and the immaturity of the democratic policy-making system. Most policy formulations were dictated by government. This system, combined with the infant-industry argument for government intervention and protection, effectively accelerated economic development.[1] Since the late 1960s, the growth of agricultural production has slowed, and agriculture has become a declining sector. The fast pace of economic restructuring forced policy makers to adopt protective policies for agriculture.

Theoretically, political leadership attempts to introduce distortionary policies up to the point where the benefits to the groups supporting these policies equal the political cost to the government of displeasing opponents of these policies. In most countries, the political cost to the government comes from taxpayers and consumers, who bear the cost of protection. But it was a very special situation in Taiwan that the government had to face: the political threat from mainland China. Consumers' and taxpayers' interests thus did not attract the same attention as in other countries.

In addition, the experience of hyperinflation on the mainland and extreme shortages of foreign exchange in the early stages of economic development contributed to the adoption of severe controls and export-oriented but import-impeding policies on trade. Pragmatically, national security, economic stability, prosperity (not efficiency), and income equality all became the aims of policy. Besides, protection of agricultural products increased steadily as the agricultural sector declined.

The weight of political considerations, however, diminished as the economy became stronger and as international opposition between East-West became weaker in the 1980s. To improve relations with its trading partners and to strengthen its economy, Taiwan has focused on economic internationalization since 1984. Nevertheless, since government interventions do not usually shrink naturally as the

---

[1] The infant-industry argument is the only generally accepted reason why temporary protection might improve global economic welfare in a world in which all other markets function competitively and prices appropriately reflect marginal rates of transformation and substitution.

economy grows and as industry leaves its infancy stages, trade liberalization did not occur as smoothly as policy formulations. Besides, from a rent-seeking point of view, once any measure establishing government intervention is undertaken, groups with vested interests arise in support of the perpetuation, if not the strengthening, of the intervention. Both tariff and nontariff barriers were removed under the pressure of inflation resulting from the huge trade surplus and requests from Taiwan's major trading partner, the United States.

Withdrawal of protective policies requires external forces. This condition has been necessary in developed countries as well, especially when protectionist measures extended into international trade, as in the 1930s. Therefore, a more liberal trade regime must be promoted by international organizations that provide reciprocal mechanisms, such as the GATT. Taiwan was not a contracting party of the GATT in the 1970s, so most protectionist trade policies were not removed because external demands and forces were absent. Nevertheless, Taiwan still benefited from more liberal trade regimes under the GATT, essentially from its main trading partners, the United States and Japan. Since 1978, consecutive bilateral negotiations with the United States have worked as an external force pressing for the removal of Taiwan's trade barriers.

Uncertainty has developed, though, mainly because of disillusionment with the democratic reforms of the 1980s. The public is demanding more authority in policy formation.[2] The government's domination of policy making became weaker as the legislative arm, authorized by the public, began to supervise the administrative departments more effectively. Therefore, the original authoritarian process quickly changed as the legislative body became more and more important. Such a system in most developed countries, however, has revealed a new source of protectionism: as the international competitiveness of some industries declines, they may gain power through the domestic political process and demand protection that does not correspond to the maximization of any social welfare function nor result in an optimal outcome.

Clearly, current institutional arrangements lag far behind liberal trade policies. Especially in the agricultural sector, progress in trade liberalization has slowed.

---

[2] There were forty-one demonstrations held by farmers from December 1987 to January 1989. Their protests concerned many areas, but the basic problems were that income earnings of farmers were relatively low for a long time and that agricultural production was influenced by liberalization policies.

Assuming that the multilateral trade negotiations promoted by the GATT will be developed continuously in the future and that the ROC will be part of this organization, however, further liberalization of the ROC's trade policy will be needed. To remove the resistance of protected groups that have lost their comparative advantage, though, Taiwan will need to create adjustment programs and to implement institutional reforms.

## Technical Appendix

In this appendix, which is adapted from Bale and Lutz (1981), we quantify the costs and benefits of government agricultural policies in 1988. The calculations are derived using standard partial equilibrium comparative static analysis in the Marshallian economic surplus framework. Price distortions are generally defined as the differences between domestic prices and border prices. Domestic prices are defined as the prices at the farm for producers and wholesale prices for consumers. Border prices are the import or export prices at the same time in the same place.

In some special cases of imports—for example, rice—however, the import price might be distorted by nontariff barriers. In this case, we use the import price of rice in Hong Kong instead.

The basic analytic structure of the model is represented by equations (1) through (5):

(1) net social loss in consumption
$$NSL_c = -\tfrac{1}{2}(C_w - C)\,(P_c - P_w)$$
$$= -\tfrac{1}{2}t_c^2 n_d W$$

(2) net social loss in production
$$NSL_p = \tfrac{1}{2}(Q_w - Q)\,(P_w - P_p)$$
$$= \tfrac{1}{2}t_p^2 n_s V$$

(3) welfare loss of consumers
$$G_c = C(P_c - P_w) + NSL_c$$

(4) welfare gain of producers
$$G_p = Q(P_p - P_w) - NSL_p$$

(5) change in government revenue
$$dG = (NSL_p - NSL_c) - G_p + G_c = -(G_p - NSL_p - G_c + NSL_c)$$

where $C_w$ is consumption at world prices; $C$, consumption at domestic prices; $P_c$, price faced by domestic consumers; $P_w$, border prices; $Q_w$, production at world prices; $Q$, production at domestic prices; $P_p$, price faced by domestic producers; $t_c$ and $t_p$, proportion of tariff in domestic price at the consumer ($t_c$) or the producer ($t_p$) level; $n_d$, elasticity of domestic demand; $n_s$, elasticity of domestic supply; $W$, value of consumption at $P_c$; and $V$, value of production at $P_p$.

**Data Sources.** The *Taiwan Agricultural Yearbook,* 1989 edition, was used as a source for production levels and producers' prices for most of the products. But the relevant data for sugar was taken from *Taiwan Sugar Statistics,* 1990 edition. Imports and exports were obtained from the *Agricultural Trade Statistics of the ROC,* 1989. Consumption and government subsidies or expenditures were obtained from the statistics given by the Council of Agriculture. Import prices and tariffs were derived from the magnetic tape of *Import and Export Statistics of the ROC Customs.* Consumer prices were obtained from *Monthly Small Grains and Animal Products, Taiwan Sugar Statistics,* and *Commodity-Price Monthly in the Taiwan Area of the ROC* for each relevant product.

For calculating net social loss in production and net social loss in consumption, the price elasticities of supply and demand for different products were taken from other studies as follows.

### Appendix 7A:
### Price Elasticities of Supply and Demand for Selected Agricultural Products in Taiwan, 1989

| Product | Supply Elasticities | Demand Elasticities |
|---------|--------------------|--------------------|
| Rice | 0.32 | −0.24 |
| Corn | 0.95 | −0.74 |
| Beef | 0.12 | −1.56 |
| Soybeans | 0.81 | −0.46 |
| Wheat | 0.11 | −1.45 |
| Sorghum | 1.64 | −1.06 |
| Sugar | 0.60 | −0.80 |
| Milk | 0.53 | −0.91 |
| Fruit | 0.24 | −0.20 |
| Chicken | 2.19 | −0.93 |

SOURCE: For rice, Kuo 1989; for corn and beef, see Liu 1989; for soybeans and wheat, see Chang 1979; for sorghum, sugar, and milk, see Council of Agriculture 1986; for fruit, see Wu 1989; and for chicken, see Lee 1989.

### References

Anderson, Kym, and Yujiro Hayami, eds. *The Political Economy of Agricultural Protection: East Asia in International Perspective,* Boston: Allen & Unwin, 1986.

Bale, Malcolm D., and B. L. Greenshields. "Japanese Agricultural Distortions and Their Welfare Value." *American Journal of Agricul-*

*tural Economics,* vol. 60 (1978), 59–64.

Bale, Malcolm D., and Ernst Lutz. "Price Distortions in Agriculture and Their Effects: An International Comparison." *American Journal of Agricultural Economics,* vol. 63 (1981), 8–22.

Chang, Chih-I. "Econometric Study of Supply and Demand of Staple Food in Taiwan." *Bank of Taiwan Quarterly,* vol. 30 (December 1979), 140–73.

Chen, Chia-lin. "Agricultural Policy and Benefits for Farmers in the Republic of China on Taiwan." *Industry of Free China,* vol. 73, no. 5. Council for Economic Planning and Development, Executive Yuan, ROC, May 1990.

Chen, H. Y., Wen-fu Hsu, and Yu-kang Mao. "Rice Policies of Taiwan." Paper presented at the Workshop on the Political Economy of Rice, sponsored by the Food Research Institute, Stanford University, Los Banos, Philippines, July 1974.

Chine, William R., Noboru Kawanabe, T. O. M. Kronsjo, and Thomas Williams. *Trade Negotiations in the Tokyo Round: A Quantitative Assessment.* Washington, D.C.: Brookings Institution, 1978.

Council of Agriculture. *Agricultural Trade Statistics of the Republic of China,* Executive Yuan, Taipei, 1989b.

———. *Study of the Econometric Model of the Agricultural Sector in Taiwan,* Executive Yuan, Taipei, 1987.

———. *Taiwan Agricultural Yearbook,* Executive Yuan, Taipei, 1989a.

Directorate-General of Budget, Accounting & Statistics. *Commodity-Price Monthly in the Taiwan Area of the ROC,* Executive Yuan, Taipei, various issues.

Honma, M., and Y. Hayami. "The Determinants of Agricultural Protection Level: An Econometric Analysis." In *The Political Economy of Agricultural Protection: East Asia in International Perspective,* edited by Kym Anderson and Yujiro Hayami. Boston: Allen & Unwin, 1986.

Josling, Tim. *Agricultural Protection and Stabilization Policies: A Framework of Measurement in the Context of Agricultural Adjustment.* Food and Agriculture Organization of the United Nations, 1975.

Kuo, I-chung. "Impacts on Rice Production of Economic Liberalization." Paper presented at the conference Impacts on the Agricultural Sector of Economic Liberalization, in Taipei, National Taiwan University, 1989.

Kuo, Shirley W. Y. "Effects of Land Reform, Agricultural Pricing Policy and Economic Growth on Multiple-Crop Diversification in Taiwan." *Philippine Economic Journal* (1975). 149–74.

Lee, Chun-cheng. "Adjustment of Economic Liberalization and Agricultural Trade Policy." Paper presented at the conference Impacts on the Agricultural Sector of Economic Liberalization, in Taipei,

National Taiwan University, 1989.

Li, K. T. *The Evolution of Policy behind Taiwan's Development Success.* New Haven: Yale University Press, 1988.

Liu, Hsiang-hsi. "Influence on Feed Grains Production of Economic Liberalization." Paper presented at the conference Impacts on the Agricultural Sector of Economic Liberalization, in Taipei, National Taiwan University, 1989.

Shen, T. H., ed. *Agriculture's Place in the Strategy of Development: The Taiwan Experience.* Joint Commission on Rural Reconstruction, Taipei, ROC, 1974.

Taiwan Grains & Feeds Development Foundation. *Monthly Small Grains and Animal Products,* Taipei, various issues.

Taiwan Sugar Corporation. *Taiwan Sugar Statistics,* Taipei, 1990.

Thorbecke, Erik. "The Process of Agricultural Development in Taiwan." In *Taiwan: From Developing to Mature Economy,* edited by Gustav Ranis. Oxford: Westview Press, 1992.

Tsiang, S. C., W. L. Chen, and A. Hsien. "Development Towards Trade Liberalization in Taiwan, ROC." Paper presented at the conference, U.S.-Taiwan Economic Relations, in Taipei, 1985.

Woo, R. J., and T. T. Fu. "Proposed Approaches to Facilitating Agriculture Trade Liberalization in Taiwan." *Industry of Free China,* Taipei, Nov. 1990, 13–24.

World Bank. *World Development Report.* New York: Oxford University Press, 1986.

Wu, Min-ming. "Adjustment of Economic Liberalization and Farm Product Marketing." Paper presented at the conference Impacts on the Agricultural Sector of Economic Liberalization, in Taipei, National Taiwan University, 1989.

# 8

# The Political Economy of U.S. Agricultural Policies

*Tracy C. Miller*

Farmers have played an important role in the U.S. political system ever since its inception. During the nineteenth century, although farmers were sometimes a vocal part of the political debate, government trade and tax policy favored manufacturing interests at their expense. Government revenue was raised primarily through tariffs on imported manufactured commodities, raising their prices and reducing the level of imports, the foreign demand for exported agricultural commodities, and real farm incomes. Producers of import-competing commodities like sugar were the exception, receiving positive protection through tariffs (Lopez 1989).

Farmers' political power increased somewhat in the latter part of the nineteenth century and the early twentieth century, as tariff rates on manufactured commodities fell. It was not until the Great Depression of the 1930s, however, when farm policy measures were passed as part of the New Deal, that U.S. farmers began to receive significant net transfers from the rest of the population. Since that time, farm policy has raised farm prices and income. This chapter presents an explanation of some of the political and economic forces responsible for U.S. agricultural policy, as well as the costs and benefits of farm programs to various groups in recent years.

## The Policy Process

Though similar to that of other high-income countries, U.S. farm policy has a number of distinctive features. Some of these may result from the fact that among the high-income countries, the United States is a low-cost producer of most agricultural commodities. Other features may be influenced by the structure and functioning of the U.S. political system.

Like other government programs, farm policy originates in the

178

legislative branch of government and is administered by the executive branch. In the past, the ability of farmers to gain favorable legislation was apparently influenced by the number of representatives from agricultural districts, as well as the number of senators from agricultural states. A state that is predominantly agricultural has a much smaller population, but the same number of votes in the Senate as has an urban state. For example, North Dakota and Montana, two agricultural states with less than half of 1 percent of the U.S. population, have 4 percent of the votes in the Senate—a higher percentage than that of farmers in the entire U.S. population. The senators from these and other states with significant farm populations may be able to constitute a majority in the Senate.

As the number of farmers has declined, they have maintained their political power by voting as a bloc, providing campaign contributions, and forming coalitions with other groups. Representatives and senators from districts and states with politically active farm groups form coalitions with those from urban districts, combining food stamps, nutrition programs, and policy for a number of different commodities into one legislative package. The majority of the population has inadequate incentives to become informed about the costs of agricultural policy and therefore will have little impact on agricultural policy legislation.

The committee structure of the Senate and the House of Representatives works to the advantage of farmers. Farm legislation is designed by the House and Senate Agriculture Committees. These committees are composed almost entirely of legislators who are disposed to favor the interests of farmers (Truman 1971, 373).

Both the implementation and the design of agricultural policy are affected by the executive branch of government. Presidents, representing the general interest of taxpayers and consumers against narrower special-interest groups, have sometimes opposed agricultural legislation that they thought excessively costly to the public.[1] The U.S. Department of Agriculture (USDA) provides input into the legislative process and is responsible for administering farm programs. USDA policy proposals often reflect the position of the president.

---

[1]During the 1920s, Calvin Coolidge vetoed the McNary-Haugen bill, an early attempt at price supports, claiming that the bill would employ the coercive powers of government against the many for the benefits of the few (Luttrell, 6). Republican administrations have attempted to reduce or eliminate agricultural price support programs (Navarro 1984, 110; Cigler and Hansen 1983).

Program implementation and administration are the responsibility of the USDA. Although Congress makes the rules concerning program eligibility and benefits, detailed implementation, explanation, and enforcement are the responsibility of regional, state, and county offices of the Agricultural Stabilization and Conservation Service (ASCS). Local farmers elect committeemen to serve in county offices of the ASCS (Gardner 1981, 31–32). This provides farmers with additional political power in determining eligibility for program benefits at the local level. As might be expected, political pressure sometimes leads local officials to make judgments contrary to the rules or intent of program legislation.[2]

Farm groups are heavily involved in the policy debate, with most of the input provided by groups concerned with such individual commodities as wheat, sugar, peanuts, and cotton. Dairy farmers, perhaps the most politically active farm group, contributed more than a million dollars through their political action committees in several recent election campaigns (Knutson et al. 1983; Navarro 1984).

Three major groups—USDA administrators, legislative committee members, and industry lobbyists—have a central role in agricultural policy making (Gardner 1987b, 350). Nonagricultural interests receive little representation, except through agencies like the Congressional Budget Office and the Office of Management and Budget. There is very little lobbying by groups opposed to farm bills, with only a few exceptions. During the 1980s, the farm-supply industry, the livestock industry, and food processors lobbied against farm bill provisions that would raise prices of certain commodities (Gardner 1987b, 350; Navarro 1984, 121). Some consumer groups, however, expressed support for farm income support programs in the 1970s (Guither 1980, 90–94).

The political effectiveness of commodity groups has been enhanced by the willingness of senators and representatives to form coalitions and trade votes across commodities (Abler 1989). This has resulted in the passage of legislation to benefit producers of commodities such as tobacco and peanuts. These producers are represented by a small proportion of legislators. In recent years, those who

---

[2]Gardner (1981, 32) provides an example of how local officials advised farmers in a manner inconsistent with the eligibility rules of federal regulations. More recently, the Wall Street Journal (May 8, 1990) reported an example of a farmer who collected subsidies far in excess of the $250 thousand annual payment limitation. In this and similar cases, local USDA officials approved arrangements that enabled farmers to violate the law.

oppose farm policies have attempted to form coalitions to resist agricultural policy, while attempting to create division among the coalition of farm groups that dates back to the New Deal. Concern over budget pressures led to conflict among commodity groups for shares of program benefits in 1981. This conflict made it difficult to pass omnibus farm legislation that year (*Farm Policy* 1984, 80–81). Farm groups bounced back from this and demonstrated their ability to unite in support of "payment-in-kind" and other farm programs during the 1980s. The 1985 farm bill, by lowering market prices while maintaining target prices, pleased farmers and agribusiness firms, both of whom were major participants in the debate surrounding that bill (Babcock, Carter, and Schmitz 1990).

## Types of Policies

The magnitude and distribution of benefits and costs of farm programs depend on the method of government intervention. Most U.S. agricultural policy operates to affect the demand or supply of farm commodities, although some attempts have been made to increase farm incomes without affecting supply or demand. Discussion of U.S. agricultural policy usually focuses on programs concerned with output prices, but a number of other programs have an important effect on farm incomes. These include tax and subsidy policies that affect the cost of various inputs, disaster payments that compensate for prevented plantings or low yields, government-financed research and extension, information, and various kinds of marketing assistance (USDA, ASCS 1988).

Three types of policy are used to raise or stabilize market prices: (1) direct government purchase at a price above the market clearing price; (2) policy to restrict supply; and (3) subsidies, called deficiency payments, equal to the difference between a target price and the market clearing price (Gardner 1981, 21–22). The major differences between these approaches have to do with the share of cost borne by consumers, as compared with taxpayers; with the extent that producers' choices are restricted; and with the effect of policy on output. Often, different approaches are combined to raise the price of a given commodity.

The first attempts of the U.S. government to raise farm prices involved the use of government purchase and storage of surplus commodities (Knutson, et al. 1983, 213–14). As government stocks accumulated, the cost of storage and the threat of a price decline associated with release of government stocks motivated policy makers to implement production control programs. More recently, target prices have been used, with the government paying deficiency payments to those who comply with voluntary acreage restrictions.

In recent years, supply reduction for major commodities has been accomplished by paying farmers to idle certain acres or by tying eligibility for deficiency payments to percentage set-aside requirements. Both tobacco and peanut programs continue to use mandatory acreage allotments to limit production, and rice allotments were used until 1981 (Knutson et al. 1983, 233).

Maintaining high farm prices has necessitated policy to restrict imports of dairy products, sugar, and various other products for which the United States is a high-cost producer. For export commodities such as wheat, rice, and feed grains, export subsidies have been used in years of low world prices. Each year, food aid under Public Law 480 and subsidized credit reduce prices for a portion of output sold outside the United States.

Most transfers to agriculture have been through price support or direct payments related to past or current output, but in recent years almost one-third of transfers have come in the form of subsidized inputs, marketing assistance, research and extension, and tax benefits (USDA, ASCS 1988). Among the more important of these are credit subsidies, irrigation subsidies, and government-funded research.

## Distribution of Program Benefits

Although the public has often been led to believe that the purpose of agricultural subsidies is to protect the incomes of farmers who are struggling financially, most farm program benefits go to larger farms, and in many cases they enhance the incomes that already exceed those of most nonfarm people. As shown in table 8–1, the largest 10 percent of farms receive about 45 percent of government payments. The share of program benefits going to the largest farms is slightly larger (U.S. Senate 1984). Government payments make up a larger proportion of the income of medium-sized farms—those with sales between $40,000 and $100,000—than of larger farms (Gardner 1987b, 146). Some evidence suggests that, on balance, farm programs increase income inequality (Gardner 1987b, 147).

The distribution of benefits across factors of production from agricultural policies depends on the elasticity of factor supply. Those factors whose supply is most elastic, such as fertilizer, insecticide, and seed, gain little from agricultural programs. Policy that increases commodity prices leads to an increase in demand for production factors with a corresponding increase in quantity supplied and little

TABLE 8–1

DISTRIBUTION OF FARMS, FARM SALES, LAND IN FARMS, CROPLAND,
AND FEDERAL PAYMENTS BY FARM SIZE IN THE UNITED STATES, 1987
(percent)

| Farm Acreage Class | Of All Farms | Of Farm Sales | Of Land in Farms | Of Cropland | Of Payments |
|---|---|---|---|---|---|
| 0–99 acres | 43.4 | 15.9 | 3.5 | 4.8 | 2.1 |
| 100–179 acres | 16.0 | 8.2 | 4.7 | 6.6 | 4.2 |
| 180–259 acres | 9.2 | 7.1 | 4.3 | 6.2 | 5.0 |
| 260–499 acres | 13.7 | 16.9 | 10.7 | 16.4 | 17.3 |
| 500–999 acres | 9.6 | 19.8 | 14.4 | 23.0 | 28.2 |
| 1,000–1,999 acres | 4.9 | 15.0 | 14.4 | 20.9 | 24.4 |
| 2,000 or more acres | 3.2 | 17.1 | 48.0 | 22.1 | 18.7 |

SOURCE: 1987 Census of Agriculture.

change in price for most purchased inputs. Labor may be somewhat more inelastic in the short run, but the elasticity of labor supply has increased in recent years, as farmers have been able to commute to nonfarm jobs while retaining their residence on the farm. Land is the most inelastic input used in agriculture, especially in rural areas. It follows that the largest share of program benefits go to land.

Using elasticities that are consistent with other empirical work, Gardner (1987b, 99) suggests that the price of land would rise by about 66 percent more than the price of nonland inputs under a target price for corn, while acreage restrictions would result in twenty times greater an increase in the price of land than nonland inputs, if the government were to compensate farmers for the rental value of the diverted acres. With a target price, the long-run share of benefits going to land will probably exceed the short-run benefits, since the supply of labor and purchased inputs are considerably more elastic in the long run.

In the short run, an acreage control or target price program will yield gains to firms that sell inputs that are strong substitutes for land, such as fertilizer. Sellers of inputs that are complementary to land, such as machinery, may lose from an acreage restriction program. One contributing factor to U.S. farm equipment manufacturers' financial problems in the 1980s may have been the payment-in-kind program, which idled so many acres of cropland. Farm equipment purchases were excessive during the preceding years because of high support prices and implicit subsidies provided by inflation, tax laws, and credit policy.

To the extent that farm policies lead to increases in output and sales of domestically produced commodities, processors may gain a share of program benefits. Domestic sugar processors may have received a significant share of benefits from sugar programs. Policies that lead to a reduced output of domestically produced commodities will lead to a reduction in revenue for those involved in processing and marketing farm products. Some policies, most notably sugar import quotas, may lead to a substitution of processed imports that are not subject to trade restrictions. Hence U.S. producers of prepared foods may experience reduced incomes because of high government-supported prices of agricultural commodities.

Policy has tended to give disproportionate benefits for the production of certain commodities. Dairy and sugar have received some of the highest rates of protection. Wheat and rice have traditionally received more protection than feedgrains, while oats, soybeans, and livestock products have received little protection (Johnson 1981; USDA 1988). Policies that increase corn and feedgrain prices may actually reduce returns to livestock.

### Factors Influencing the Choice of Farm Programs

Much of U.S. agricultural policy can be explained as the result of the ability of farmers to organize and persuade politicians to support legislation in their interest. As noted in chapter 6, competition among interest groups leads to policies favoring groups that organize to influence policy at small cost relative to the potential gains. Policy also favors groups that have relatively easy access to decision makers in government.

The representative structure of the U.S. Congress, as well as the modern transportation and communications systems in the United States, provides farmers with easy access to the political process. Many agricultural commodities are grown by a relatively small number of farmers who share common interests. As a result, the cost of organizing for political activity is low. The large average size of U.S. farms makes the potential benefits per farm of price policy quite high in the United States as compared with the per capita cost to consumers.

As Gardner (1987a) has shown, differences in the level of support received by different commodities can be explained by factors related to political power and the marginal cost per dollar of benefits received. Political power should be a function of the number of farmers, average farm size, and variables such as geographical concentration and movement, which may affect the cost of group political organization. Cattle and other commodities grown by a large number of farmers have less protection than others. Geographical concentration may explain high protection of such commodities as tobacco and peanuts, while geographical movement of production appears to reduce political power and protection, as may have been the case with cotton in the 1950s and corn in the 1970s. Commodities grown primarily on large farms receive somewhat more protection than commodities grown on small farms. This may explain high protection for cotton and rice and rising protection for some commodities over time.

The government should be more willing to protect commodities the lower the marginal cost to taxpayers or consumers per dollar of benefits received. It is less costly to protect imported commodities, since tariffs and quotas can be used, while subsidies may be necessary for exported commodities. This may explain the high rates of protection for sugar and dairy products. It is more costly to protect commodities with a high elasticity of supply or demand, because gains will be offset by higher input costs or larger government purchases of surplus output. Gardner (1987a) found higher elasticity to be associated with lower protection. Thus soybeans, with a high elasticity of supply, receive less protection than cotton, which is more inelastic.

Studies of congressional voting on agricultural policy show a significant relationship between the importance of agriculture in a state or district and the proportion of votes in favor of price support programs (Navarro 1984). Abler (1989) found that the number of farms that grew a particular commodity correlated with the probability that the representative of that district would support policy benefiting the producers of that commodity. He also found a significant relationship between support for each commodity program and money from political action committees associated with that commodity.

Vote trading is also an important part of the political process. Congressmen from districts with large numbers of dairy, tobacco, rice, cotton, sugar, or peanut farms opposed programs that reduced benefits to the producers of other commodities, school lunch subsidies, or food stamp benefits during the 1985–1986 session of Congress (Abler 1989). Tobacco, sugar, peanut, and dairy farmers, along with poor groups, appear involved in vote trading during this period. With limited representation in Congress, some of these groups may need to form coalitions to gain majority support for their programs.

Farm policy debates and legislation often mention goals of price stability, saving family farms, and conservation. If these were the primary goals of farm policy, we would expect to see results consistent with these goals or else changes in policy if the goals were not achieved. Our reliance on the same policy instruments for decades, despite their failure to achieve stable prices or to prevent a decline in the number and importance of family farms, suggests that other goals, such as income support, are more important. Better methods are available for preserving the family farm or conserving resources, if those are the primary goals. Actual policy choices have not been consistent with the goal of price stability. Few attempts have been made to use stocks to reduce prices when they were abnormally high, and such attempts have met with strong political opposition (Gardner, 1987b, 346).

A national survey of political preferences (Variyam, Jordan, and Epperson 1990) further supports an explanation of U.S. agricultural policy as the result of political pressure from farmers rather than as the expression of the political preferences of a majority. Although a small majority favors government policy to ensure the survival of family farms, most people are not willing to pay higher food prices in the process. More than half of those surveyed believe farms should be treated like other businesses.

## Efficient Redistribution

Although they are inefficient in the sense that aggregate income is reduced, some evidence suggests that existing U.S. agricultural policies may use an efficient method of redistribution consistent with political preferences. A method of redistribution is efficient if a transfer to one group is accomplished at least cost to other groups, weighted by the political power of each group. A cost to a group that has little or no political power, such as foreign consumers, will not matter in the choice of policy. The efficiency of U.S. agricultural policy can be analyzed by considering types of policies that are used and recent trends in the choice of policy.

In the early 1980s, there was a growing reliance on supply control policies, which may have reflected pressures to limit the budgetary costs of policy as well as unanticipated growth in government stocks caused by declining exports. Policies that reduce the acreage of certain crops may efficiently redistribute income from domestic consumers to domestic producers if the elasticity of export demand is not too great, since some of the cost would be borne by foreign consumers. In the short and medium runs, domestic policies that restrict imports or exports in other countries may reduce the elasticity of excess demand for U.S. commodities. In the case of wheat, a rising

U.S. share of world wheat exports in the early 1980s may have increased the potential gains to producers from acreage restrictions. Sharples (1982) suggests that export demand for wheat is inelastic in the short run, partly because countries choose to maintain stable trading relationships for political reasons.

As a result of the 1985 farm bill, the government costs of policy increased as high target prices were maintained while price support levels were reduced, lowering the consumers' share of policy costs. One explanation for this change is political pressure by agribusiness firms in response to declining exports (Babcock, Carter, and Schmitz 1990). The lower loan rates would lead to a substantial increase in both domestic and export demand. The increased cost to taxpayers was small enough on a per capita basis not to elicit significant opposition. Target prices have become increasingly important since the 1970s, reflecting the increased political power of consumers and agribusiness firms, as well as growing export demand. This seems consistent with observed trends in political activity and incentives. The 1970s were the decade of consumerism, with the rise of public interest lobbies. Public interest organizations concerned with consumer prices, nutrition, and the environment have been more involved in food and agricultural lobbying since 1970 (Knutson et al. 1983, 79). The high inflation of the 1970s may have increased consumers' sense of being harmed by government policies.

The difference in support among commodities may partly reflect differences in costs of protection. It costs less to provide a given level of protection for imported commodities such as sugar and dairy products. Import quotas involve considerably less cost than subsidies and direct government purchase, which are required to maintain prices of export commodities. Costs associated with resource allocation are reduced if commodities with high cross elasticities of supply or demand, such as wheat and corn, have similar rates of protection.

If a major purpose of agricultural policy is to benefit landowners, it follows that land-intensive crops should receive the greatest protection. This seems consistent with the observed pattern of protection. Commodities with the least protection, such as poultry, pork, and grain-fed beef, do not require a great deal of land, while protected commodities do. The growing availability of disaster payments can be explained as a method of increasing land values in risky production areas (Gardner 1981).

The political power of foreign producers should not be neglected. It may provide the best explanation for the use of quotas rather than tariffs in the sugar program. During the 1950s, the Cuban government and the Dominican Republic spent millions of dollars on lobbying campaigns in the United States (Navarro 1984, 46). Similarly, the political power of foreign consumers may have had some effect on the amount of food aid given to countries such as Egypt.

Part of the choice of policy may depend on how easily the true costs of policy can be concealed from taxpayers or consumers. This may explain why subsidies in kind rather than cash subsidies have been used in recent years.

The reliance on policies that do little to help farmers in the long run can be explained by a number of factors—incorrect forecasting of supply and demand, for example, changing market conditions, or high transaction costs. This may explain why the United States continues to use acreage reduction programs in spite of evidence of an elastic long-run demand. Some policies may be efficient as a means of adjusting to past policy mistakes. Thus, for example, export subsidies may be used to reduce the size of accumulated stocks that resulted from past forecasting errors.

Another explanation of policy is that it serves the interest of the bureaucracy. To the extent that bureaucrats and some politicians are protected from competition, they can be expected to earn rents from policy. Government officials may enhance their income and job security by implementing policies that provide short-term benefits but not long-term solutions to problems, particularly where the causes and solutions to the problem are complex and not easily understood by the public. If the so-called farm problem were ever solved, many government employees would no longer be needed.

Besides economic interests, plenty of evidence suggests that ideology plays a major role in decisions about agricultural policy. Navarro, in a study of voting on grain and dairy policy during debate on the 1981 Agriculture and Food Act (1984), found ideology to be the most important explanatory variable. Abler (1989) also found political conservatism to be important. The importance of ideology in congressional voting is consistent with an interest-group model, since interest groups can still gain beneficial programs by supporting candidates whose ideology predisposes them to support those programs.[3]

## Farm Commodity Program Costs and Benefits

The correct measure of the costs and benefits of U.S. farm commodity programs depends on what is used as the free-market price. If we

---

[3]Peltzman (1984) demonstrates that there is a strong relationship between ideology (ADA ratings) and the interests and characteristics of a senator's supporters and constituency.

consider U.S. policy as separate from the rest of the world's, then world prices in the absence of U.S. policy should serve as the reference point. If, in contrast, other countries can be persuaded to reduce distortions along with the United States through multilateral negotiations, then we have to compare U.S. prices with world prices as they would be if distortions were reduced or eliminated in all countries.

U.S. farm commodity programs involve substantial costs to the government and to consumers, with most of the benefits going to the owners of farmland. Government costs include deficiency payments, direct purchase and stockholding costs, payments for land diversion, various subsidies, and administrative costs. Producer gains include the difference between the product price with policy and the price in the absence of policy, as well as any input price reductions and direct payments received. Consumers lose because of the higher price they must pay as the result of government intervention. A listing of the components of benefits to producers and costs to consumers and the government is given in table 8–2.

Government costs are ultimately paid by taxpayers (including savers who must pay inflation taxes). Besides direct outlays, taxpayer costs include the enforcement costs, compliance costs, and dead-weight costs associated with the required tax increases. Dead-weight costs result when people change their behavior in response to a tax or subsidy: for example, working less in response to an income tax. No corresponding tax revenue is associated with the loss in surplus caused by reduction of the taxed activity.

Dead-weight losses also reduce producer gains and increase the costs to consumers of policy. Gains to producers are reduced by the forgone rents on diverted acres, the higher marginal opportunity costs associated with additional inputs used, and the compliance costs. In addition to losing on the higher prices that benefit producers, consumers lose consumer surplus on the difference between the quantity at market equilibrium prices and the quantity consumed at the policy price.

It is difficult to determine how much policy raises or lowers prices. Commodities affected by import quotas, tariffs, or export subsidies have domestic prices that exceed the world price. The difference between existing domestic and world market prices does not give an accurate estimate of U.S. price distortions for most commodities, because the United States produces a large enough share of world output to have some influence on the world price. Where target prices and acreage restrictions are used, the world price and the domestic price will be equivalent, but different from free-

TABLE 8–2

COMPONENTS OF BENEFITS AND COSTS OF U.S. AGRICULTURAL POLICY, 1984–1985

| Producer Gain | Taxpayer Cost | Consumer Cost |
|---|---|---|
| Deficiency payments | Commodity purchases | Higher prices of farm products $(P_m - P_e) \times Q_d$ |
| Difference between current price $(P_m)$ and equilibrium price without policy $(P_e)$ $(P_m - P_e) \times Q_s$ | Direct payments to producers (money + in-kind payments) | Loss to consumers, due to reduced consumption in response to policy price $1/2 (P_m - P_e) \times (Q_d - Q_e)$ |
| − Increase in marginal cost of output resulting from incentive price $(P_i)$ being greater than equilibrium price[a] $1/2(P_i - P_e) \times (Q_s - Q_e)$ | Input subsidies Administrative costs Dead-weight loss caused by taxes | |
| + Payments for voluntary acreage diversion | − Tariff revenue | |
| − Forgone income from set aside acres | − Unanticipated gain in value of government stocks | |
| Reduction in costs due to input subsidies | Cost of export subsidies | |

a. Prior to the 1985 farm bill, the incentive price was a function of the target price. The 1985 farm bill decouples present and future deficiency payments from current yields and allows farmers to receive most of the deficiency payment even on eligible acres kept idle. This reduces the incentive price for planting and input utilization decisions to slightly above the greater of the market price or the support price. In recent years, this incentive price has not been far above the prevailing world price, and it may have been below what the world price would have been without U.S. policy.
SOURCE: Author.

TABLE 8–3

Comparison of Current Market Price with Price in the Absence of U.S. Policy, 1984–1985 Crop Year

| Commodity | Market Price[a] (dollars) | Equilibrium Price (dollars) | Distortion (percent) |
|---|---|---|---|
| Wheat (per bushel) | 3.38 | 2.47–3.01 | 12–37 |
| Corn | 2.60 | 2.09–2.39 | 9–24 |
| Soybeans | 5.84 | 5.42–5.56 | 5–8 |
| Rice (per hundredweight) | 8.04 | 5.69–7.14 | 13–41 |
| Barley | 2.29 | 1.98–2.17 | 5–16 |
| Sorghum | 2.32 | 2.21–2.34 | −1–5 |
| Oats | 1.67 | 1.54–1.63 | 2.5–8 |
| Cotton (per lb.) | 0.59 | 0.49–0.56 | 5–20 |
| Sugar (per ton) | 276 | 100–110 | 150–176 |
| Beef (per ton)[b] | 2,140 | 2,035 | 5 |
| Dairy (per ton)[c] | 283 | 189–196 | 44–50 |

a. Average price received by farmers.
b. Data on beef prices, output, and trade were for 1984 from Sullivan et al. (1989).
c. Data on dairy were for 1985. The equilibrium price of dairy is calculated using estimates of the effects of unilateral liberalization from Tyers and Anderson (1989) and Roningen and Dixit (1989).
Source: Calculated using output, price, and cost data from the USDA Economic Indicators of the Farm Sector, USDA Agricultural Outlook, USDA ASCS Commodity Fact Sheet on the 1987–1988 Dairy Price Support Program, and USDA Estimates of Consumer and Producer Subsidy Equivalents. Data on subsidized exports were obtained from Dvoskin (1988). Elasticity data were taken from Hertel et al. (1989) and Sullivan et al. (1989).

market prices. To the extent that programs are output-restricting, the result will be higher domestic and world prices. To the extent that high target prices and government purchase and storage of surplus commodities lead to an increase in domestic production or a reduction in domestic consumption, U.S. policy will lower the world market price. In the early 1980s, U.S. policy had the effect of increasing the world price of most food grains and feedgrains. Since the 1985–1986 crop year, sales of accumulated stocks, combined with lower support prices and export subsidies for some commodities, have contributed to lower world prices.

Table 8–3 provides estimates of the percentage increase in the market price of U.S. commodities caused by policy in the 1984–1985

191

crop year, holding the policies of all other countries constant. World prices in the absence of U.S. policy are calculated by estimating what total production and use of U.S. commodities would have been in the absence of acreage controls and export subsidies, and solving for equilibrium, given elasticities of supply and demand.[4] Two cases were considered, one with low elasticities and the other with higher elasticities associated with an adjustment period of three to five years.[5] Major U.S. commodities sold for prices from 5 to 50 percent greater than free trade equilibrium prices in 1984–1985. Sugar had by far the greatest protection, with U.S. policy increasing the price by at least 150 percent over what it would have been otherwise. The price of soybeans, a commodity with little direct intervention, was raised significantly because of substitutions on both the supply and the demand side in response to high feedgrain prices. Sorghum was the only major commodity that may have had its market price lowered slightly by a combination of high target prices and a low set-aside percentage.

Using the information from table 8–3, as well as data on production, consumption, and government outlays, I have calculated short-run benefits and costs of U.S. agricultural policy to each group (table 8–4). The no-policy case assumes complete elimination of all U.S. policy, while other countries continue to intervene in agricultural markets. Long-run benefits to producers are likely to be smaller, because alternative earning opportunities for farm household labor and for capital would offset much of the gain from farm policy. Gains to producers from input subsidies are measured as the amount of the subsidies. This overstates gains to the extent that subsidies lead to greater utilization of inputs and higher costs. Taxpayer costs include an estimate of government expenditures plus an allowance for other costs associated with taxes. These include the dead-weight losses, administrative costs, and compliance costs. I assume that costs exceed the amount of revenue raised by 20 percent, based on estimates provided by Musgrave and Musgrave (1989).

For major export commodities, including feedgrains, food grains, cotton, and soybeans, foreign consumers paid a significant share of

[4]Gardner (1987, 56–72) performs similar calculations for major commodities for the 1985–1986 crop year.

[5]Demand elasticity estimates were taken from Hertel et al. (1989), while supply elasticity estimates were obtained from Sullivan et al. (1989). Estimates from these studies were compared with elasticities used by Johnson et al. (1985), Lichtenburg and Zilberman (1986), and Gardner (1987b) to identify a reasonable range for each commodity.

TABLE 8-4

BENEFITS AND COSTS OF U.S. FARM POLICY, 1984–1985

(millions of dollars per year)

| Commodity | Gain to Producers | Cost to U.S. Consumers | Taxpayer Cost[a] | Net Gain or Loss (domestic economy) |
|---|---|---|---|---|
| Sugar | 700–750 | 1,300–1,400 | 250 | (800–850) |
| Dairy | 5,800–6,300 | 5,700–6,100 | 2,000[b] | (1,700–1,750) |
| Wheat | 3,600–4,900 | 450–1,100 | 4,000 | (250–900) |
| Feedgrains | 5,800–8,300 | 1,200–3,000 | 7,528 | (300–900) |
| Rice | 550–750 | 50–150 | 1,000 | (400–500) |
| Cotton[c] | 1,000–1,500 | 100–300 | 1,500 | (350–600) |
| Soybeans | 1,200–1,500 | 335–511 | 1,080 | 25–200 |
| Totals[d] | 18,000–23,500 | 9,000–12,500 | 14,500 | (3,500–5,500) |

a. Taxpayer costs were calculated by multiplying government costs by 1.2 to account for the dead-weight loss, administrative costs, and compliance costs associated with taxes.

b. Estimated value of CCC stocks, most of which are donated for an assumed value of $5 per hundredweight, is subtracted from government costs ($575 million). Gardner (1987b) suggests a $5 per hundredweight value for donated milk products.

c. No figures were available for input subsidies, marketing assistance, research, and other programs to benefit cotton producers. These other types of programs account for as much as ⅓ of the producer gains for some commodities.

d. Inclusion of social costs for the peanut and tobacco programs would increase social costs by about $500 million (Economic Report of the President, 159). Other programs are much smaller and should have a negligible effect on the total.

SOURCE: United States Department of Agriculture, Estimates of Producer and Consumer Subsidy Equivalents, and U.S. Department of Agriculture 1985 Farm Sector Review.

the costs of U.S. commodity policy in the 1984–1985 crop year. In subsequent years, as exports declined and U.S. market prices fell, U.S. policy for food grains and feedgrains may have benefited foreign consumers.

A considerable part of the costs of U.S. agricultural policy can be attributed to low world prices caused by excess supply in other high-income countries. If other countries completely eliminated price-support policies, U.S. farmers would lose considerably less from an end to U.S. farm programs. The effect on prices of liberalization by all major producing countries is shown in table 8–5 for each commod-

TABLE 8-5

ESTIMATED EFFECT OF TRADE LIBERALIZATION BY ALL MAJOR
PRODUCING COUNTRIES FOR SELECTED COMMODITIES, 1984–1985

| Commodity | Increase in World Price (percent) | Gains to U.S. Farmers vs. 1984–85 Market Price (millions of dollars) | Gains to U.S. Farmers vs. Unilateral Liberalization (dollars) |
|---|---|---|---|
| Wheat | 10–15 | 900–1,370 | 1,835–3,635 |
| Maize | 4–11 | 790–2,220 | 2,370–6,000 |
| Barley | 3–14 | 40–195 | 105–375 |
| Oats | 17–20 | 135–160 | 155–210 |
| Soybeans | −3–2 | −325–215 | 175–975 |
| Rice | 1–14 | 10–160 | 120–460 |
| Beef and veal[a] | 4–18 | 850–2,200 | 295–3,350 |
| Dairy | 40–60 | 4,250–2,400 | 1,500–3,040 |
| Sugar | 25–50 | −720−−650 | 30–85 |

a. Calculated using 1984 prices, output, and trade.
SOURCE: Various studies of world trade liberalization cited in Valdes (1987); Anderson and Tyers (1984); Krissoff and Ballenger (1987); Tyers and Anderson (1988); Roningen and Dixit (1989).

ity. Producers of most U.S. commodities would receive higher prices, though not as high as target prices. The major exceptions to this are dairy and sugar, where the U.S. price is currently substantially above the world price. If other countries eliminated their intervention in agriculture, the U.S. government could eliminate the purchase and storage of most commodities while reducing deficiency payments considerably, and it could still maintain producer incomes at current levels. The gains to U.S. producers from complete liberalization as compared with 1984–1985 prices are shown in table 8–5.

### Trends in U.S. Farm Policy

Government costs of farm income stabilization programs were $12.0 billion in 1990 (OMB 1991). U.S. government expenditures for farm income stabilization reached a peak of nearly $30 billion in 1986. Excessive program costs combined with rising farm incomes have resulted in a willingness of farmers to accept a reduction in the level of target prices and support prices for most commodities in recent years. Decoupling of deficiency payments from current yield and acreage planted should result in a decline or a smaller increase in output of commodities with high target prices. So far, reductions in acreage planted of program crops have been limited by rules which restrict the planting of substitute crops on the idle land. I know of no systematic evidence showing that decoupling that occurred since 1985 succeeded in reducing yields of program crops compared with what they would have been. Farmers may not yet be convinced that current yields will not have some effect on future program yields on which payments will be made.

Although USDA officials and others have sought a continuation of downward trends in government support, political pressure from farm groups will probably limit the rate of decline, particularly if several years of bumper crops and low world prices occur to offset the effects of recent droughts. Recently, the freezing of program yields and the triple base option, which allows for greater flexibility in planting, have partially decoupled farm program benefits from production decisions. Complete decoupling is unlikely because it eliminates an important test for eligibility that is related to political power. Farmers are unlikely to be willing to share program benefits with those who left farming ten or twenty years ago, and they may be unwilling to share them with farmers who switched crops five years ago.

## Appendix: Calculating Free Market Prices

Free market prices in the 1984–1985 crop year for each commodity were calculated by estimating what output would have been at the current supply price and what utilization would have been at the current market price. In 1984–1985, the supply price exceeded the current market price for commodities where deficiency payments were made. To receive deficiency payments farmers had to set aside an area of 10 to 30 percent of base acreage, leaving the land idle for the year. Base acreage was a function of acreage planted in previous years and deficiency payments were paid on program yield, a weighted average of prior year yields. Although a substantial per-centage of the producers of some commodities did not choose to participate in set-asides and were ineligible for deficiency payments, they might still base their land use and input use decisions on the target price. To the extent that future base acreage and program yields were expected to be a function of current acreage and yields, farmers who expected to participate in the future would base their current decisions on expected future target prices, which were likely to be related to current target prices.

The supply price was calculated by taking the weighted average of the target price and the net return on set-aside acres. Market output at the current supply price was calculated by adding potential output from set-aside acres to actual output. The additional output if there were no set-asides was calculated by multiplying the number of set-aside acres by .6 times the average yield per harvested acre. This accounts for lower yield potential and the possibility that farmers may not have planted every eligible acre in the absence of set-asides.

Demand at the current market price was calculated by taking utilization and subtracting a portion of exports that were made available as food aid under PL480 or sold with a subsidy. An estimate of the percentage of subsidized exports that would not have been sold at current prices was available for wheat in the U.S. Department of Agriculture Outlook. For other commodities, I subtracted half of exports under PL480 from demand to get an estimate of market demand.

For commodities with effective price-support programs, I assumed that a net increase in stocks was associated with excess supply and a net decrease with excess supply. All CCC dairy purchases were assumed to be excess supply. If there were no set-asides, there would have been excess supply of almost all commodities except oats in 1984–1985.

Equilibrium prices were calculated by solving a system of equations with groups of three related commodities. This allowed for cross effects, such as the reduction in demand and increase in supply of soybeans that would result when wheat and corn prices were lowered to their equilibrium levels. To calculate the equilibrium prices of wheat, corn, and soybeans, the six equations were:

| | |
|---|---|
| supply of wheat | $Q_{s1} = K_{s1}P_{s1}^{.6}P_{s2}^{-.25}P_{s3}^{.05}$ |
| supply of corn | $Q_{s2} = K_{s2}P_{s1}^{-.09}P_{s2}^{.48}P_{s3}^{-.07}$ |
| supply of soybeans | $Q_{s3} = K_{s3}P_{s1}^{.03}P_{s2}^{-.12}P_{s3}^{.6}$ |
| demand for wheat | $Q_{d1} = K_{d1}P_{d1}^{-.95}P_{d2}^{.5}P_{d3}^{.09}$ |
| demand for corn | $Q_{d2} = K_{d2}P_{d1}^{.11}P_{d2}^{-1.02}P_{d3}^{.11}$ |
| demand for soybeans | $Q_{d3} = K_{d3}P_{d1}^{.04}P_{d2}^{.23}P_{d3}^{.79}$ |

Lower elasticities were also used to provide a range of equilibrium price estimates. Constants for each supply equation were estimated by substituting the supply price and the market supply for each commodity into the supply equations, while constants for each demand equation were estimated by substituting the market price and demand for each commodity into the demand equations. It was then possible to solve the system of equations for the set of prices where supply would equal demand for each commodity. Table A8–1 shows the data and calculations for wheat, corn, and soybeans.

**Appendix 8A:**
## Calculation of Equilibrium Price in the Absence of Policy, 1984–1985

| Crop | Wheat | Corn | Soybeans |
|---|---|---|---|
| Output, million bushels | 2,595 | 7,656 | 1,861 |
| Total use, million bushels | 2,578 | 7,036 | 1,861 |
| Noncommercial exports[a] | 160 | 46 | 50 |
| Demand[b] | 2,418 | 6,990 | 1,811 |
| Supply price[c], $ per bushel | 4.11 | 2.91 | 5.84 |
| Market price | 3.38 | 2.60 | 5.84 |
| Set-aside acres, in millions | 18.6 | 3.9 | 0 |
| Excess capacity[d] | 433 | 249 | 0 |
| Market supply[e] | 3,028 | 7,923 | 1,861 |
| Equilibrium price | 2.97 | 2.39 | 5.57 |
| Equilibrium output | 2,610 | 7,457 | 1,835 |

a. Exports under PL480 and GSM credit that would not have been exported without subsidies. Estimate for wheat is taken from United States Department of Agriculture Outlook Report. Estimates for corn, soybeans, and other commodities are approximately 50 percent of concessional exports. Data for commodities other than wheat are from Dvoskin (1988).
b. Calculated by subtracting noncommercial exports from total use.
c. Calculated by subtracting from the target price the set-aside percentage divided by 1, minus the set-aside percentage times the forgone net return per bushel on set-aside acres, times a yield reduction factor of 0.8, and adding the payment rate times the percentage of acres, where diversion payments were provided. A similar approach was used by Gardner (1987b).
d. Calculated by multiplying average yield times set-aside acres times 0.6. This is roughly consistent with estimates of the relation between harvested and set-aside acres and between yields on harvested and set-aside acres found by Dvoskin (1988).
e. Calculated by adding output and excess capacity.
SOURCE: Author.

## References

Abler, David G. "Vote Trading on Farm Legislation in the U.S. House." AJAE 71 (August 1989):583–91.

Anderson, Kym, and Rodney Tyers. "European Community Grain and Meat Policies: Effects on International Prices, Trade, and Welfare." *European Review of Agricultural Economics* 11 (1984):367–94.

Babcock, B. A., C. A. Carter, and A. Schmitz. "The Political Economy of U.S. Wheat Legislation." *Economic Inquiry* 28 (April 1990):335–53.

Cigler, Allan J., and John M. Hansen. "Group Formation through

Protest: The American Agriculture Movement." In *Interest Group Politics*. Ed. Allan J. Cigler and Burdett A. Loomis. Washington: Congressional Quarterly Press, 1983, pp. 84–109.

Dvoskin, Dan. "Excess Capacity in U.S. Agriculture: An Economic Approach to Measurement." USDA ERS. Agricultural Economic Report # 580, 1988.

*Economic Report of the President*. Washington, D.C.: GPO, 1987.

Edwin, Ed. *Feast or Famine: Food, Farming, and Farm Politics in America*. New York: Charterhouse, 1974.

*Farm Policy: The Politics of Soil, Surpluses, and Subsidies*. Washington, D.C.: Congressional Quarterly, Inc., 1984.

Gardner, Bruce. "Causes of U.S. Farm Commodity Programs." *Journal of Political Economy* 95(1987): 290–310.

———. *The Economics of Agriculture*. New York: Macmillan, 1987.

———. "Farm Commodity Programs as Income Transfers." *Cato Journal* 6 (Spring/Summer 1986):251–61.

———. *The Governing of Agriculture*. Lawrence, Kans.: Regents Press of Kansas, 1981.

Guither, Harold D. *The Food Lobbyists*. Lexington, Mass.: D. C. Heath, 1980.

Hertel, Thomas W., V. Eldon Ball, Kuo S. Huang, and Marinos E. Tsigas. *Computing Farm Level General Equilibrium Demand Elasticities for Agricultural Commodities*. Agricultural Experiment Station Research Bulletin # 988, Purdue University, 1989.

Johnson, D. Gale. "Agricultural Policy Alternatives for the 1980s." In *Food and Agricultural Policy for the 1980s*. Washington, D.C.: American Enterprise Institute Press, 1981.

———. *World Agriculture in Disarray*. London: Macmillan, 1990.

Johnson, Stanley R., Abner W. Womack, William H. Myers, Robert E. Young, and Jon Brandt. "Options for the 1985 Farm Bill: Analysis and Evaluation." In *U.S. Agricultural Policy*. Ed. Bruce Gardner. Washington, D.C.: American Enterprise Institute Press, 1985.

Knutson, Ronald D., J. B. Penn, and William T. Boehm. *Agricultural and Food Policy*. Englewood Cliffs, N.J.: Prentice-Hall, 1983.

Krissoff, Barry, and Nicole Ballenger. "Trade Liberalization with Endogenous Exchange Rates." Paper presented at the American Agricultural Economics Association Annual Meeting, 1987.

Lichtenberg, Erik, and David Zilberman. "The Welfare Economics of Price Supports in U.S. Agriculture." *American Economic Review* 76 (December 1986): 1135–41.

Lopez, Rigoberto. "Political Economy of the United States Sugar Policies." *American Journal of Agricultural Economics* 71 (February 1989): 20–31.

Luttrell, Clifton B. *The High Cost of Farm Welfare*. Washington, D.C.: Cato Institute, 1989.

Musgrave, Richard A., and Peggy B. Musgrave. *Public Finance in Theory and Practice*, 5th ed. New York: McGraw-Hill, 1989.

Navarro, Peter. *The Policy Game*. New York: Wiley, 1984.

Peltzman, Sam. "Constituent Interest and Congressional Voting." *Journal of Law and Economics* 27 (April 1984): 181–210.

Sharples, Jerry A. "The Short-Run Elasticity of Demand for U.S. Wheat Exports." USDA ERS Staff Report. no. AGES 89–36, April 1982.

Sullivan, John, John Wainio, and Vernon O. Roningen. "A Database for Trade Liberalization Studies." U.S. Department of Agriculture ERS Staff Report no. AGES 89–36, March 1989.

Roningen, Vernon O., and Praveen M. Dixit. *Economic Implications of Agricultural Policy Reforms in Industrial Market Economies*. Economic Research Service, U.S. Department of Agriculture Staff Report no. AGES 89–36, August 1989.

Truman, David B. *The Governmental Process* 2nd ed. New York: Knopf, 1971.

Tyers, Rod, and Kym Anderson. "Liberalizing OECD Agricultural Policies in the Uruguay Round: Effects on Trade and Welfare." *Journal of Agricultural Economics* 39 (May 1988):197–216.

———. "Price Elasticities in International Food Trade: Synthetic Estimates from a Global Model." *Journal of Policy Modeling* 11 (Fall 1989): 315–44.

U.S. Congress, House Committee on Agriculture. *Milk Price Support Program and Other Policies Affecting the U.S. Dairy Industry*. Washington, D.C.: U.S. Government Printing Office, 1988.

U.S. Department of Agriculture, Agricultural Stabilization and Conservation Service (USDA, ASCS). *ASCS Commodity Fact Sheet: 1987 Dairy Price Support Program*, April 1988.

U.S. Department of Agriculture, Economic Research Service (USDA, ERS). *Agricultural Outlook*.

———. *Economic Indicators of the Farm Sector: Farm Sector Review*. Agricultural and Rural Economy Division.

———. "Estimates of Producer and Consumer Subsidy Equivalents: Government Intervention in Agriculture, 1982–1986." ERS Staff Report no. AGES 880127.

U.S. Senate, Committee on the Budget. *The Distribution of Benefits from the 1982 Federal Crop Programs*. Washington, D.C.: U.S. Government Printing Office, 1984.

Valdes, Alberto. "Agriculture in the Uruguay Round: Interests of Developing Countries." *World Bank Economic Review* 1 (September 1987): 571–93.

199

Variyam, J. N., J. L. Jordan, and J. E. Epperson. "Preferences of Citizens for Agricultural Policies: Evidence from a National Survey." *American Journal of Agricultural Economics* 72 (May 1990): 257–67.

# 9
# Trade Conflicts between the United States and Taiwan

*Chi-Chu Chou*

The trade conflict between Taiwan and the United States is a typical expression of the inherently political nature of international economic relations. International trade had long been jointly determined by economic and political considerations. Many, if not most, countries intervene in their imports and exports through various policy measures such as protective tariffs, quotas, export subsidies, export taxes, and other trade barriers. Since the mid-1980s, the United States has increasingly pressured Taiwan to open its protected markets. Bilateral trade negotiations between Taiwan and the United States have been in process on such items as citrus fruits, beef, liquor, and tobacco, as well as on the services industries. Because agriculture is one of the most highly protected industries in both countries, agricultural products have constituted particularly difficult negotiations. This chapter provides a brief description of the trade conflicts between Taiwan and the United States with respect to agricultural products and assesses the effects of the U.S. pressure on trade and domestic production in Taiwan.

## Causes of Agricultural Trade Conflicts

Agricultural trade conflicts result from structural changes in the economies of trading partners. One of the most important such changes is the movement of resources from the agricultural sector to the nonagricultural sector. Along with increased per capita income in the economy, more resources or production factors move from agricultural to nonagricultural uses. Labor migration is a key indicator in this long-term, dynamic transition. It is all too common, however, for governments to intervene in price adjustments in agriculture. According to many cross-country studies, government policy often switches from taxing agriculture to protecting agriculture as the country's

201

economy grows (see Johnson 1973; Schultz 1978; Anderson and Hayami 1986; and Miller 1986). To carry out the protection of domestic agriculture, governments also have to intervene in the international trade of agricultural products. The supply of lower-cost products from abroad must be banned partly or completely by tariff or nontariff measures. As a result, trade conflicts arise between trading partners.

Taiwan has been following the same agricultural policy as the Western European countries and other East Asian countries. In the late 1960s and early 1970s, as Taiwan's economy grew, governmental policy changed from taxing or negatively protecting agriculture to protecting agriculture. The extent of protection in agriculture increased rapidly in the 1970s. Greater agricultural protection in Taiwan caused trade tensions between Taiwan and the United States, a major exporter of agricultural products.

In addition, during the 1980s the United States became increasingly alarmed by its large trade deficits. These deficits have become not only targets of political critics but also indicators to which financial markets respond sensitively. Taiwan, like Korea and Japan, has accumulated a large trade surplus from exports to the United States and is therefore subject to enhanced pressures from the United States to remove its trade barriers. Since Korea and Japan have also adopted the same adjustment pattern in the transformation of their agricultural policy, all three East Asian countries are facing the same demands from the United States. Section 301 of the new trade bill, the Omnibus Trade and Competitiveness Act of 1988, was aimed mainly at these three countries.[1] This chapter next examines the U.S. treatment of the three East Asian countries as a single target for pressure to open up markets for U.S. farm products.

## Increased U.S. Pressures on East Asia in the 1980s

Three sources of information provide appropriate signals of U.S. pressures: presidential announcements, negotiations with East Asian countries conducted by the U.S. trade representative (USTR), and actions of the U.S. Congress. Other countries study these sources carefully for information about U.S. trade policies. The words from

---

[1]The amendments to section 301 in the Omnibus Trade and Competitiveness Act of 1988 (H.R. 4848), signed by President Reagan on August 23, 1988, require that the trade representative, subject to any specific direction of the president, take action under section 301 in response to a violation of a trade agreement or an "unjustifiable" practice that hurts or restricts U.S. commerce.

the president's announcements, from officials of the USTR, and from congressional members are scrutinized by governments and related pressure groups in East Asian countries for clues about how the U.S. administration intends to deal with U.S.–East Asian trade-related conflicts. The data obtained from the USTR are incomplete, and some classified documents cannot be used. Since the president of the United States has traditionally been more free-trade-minded and less interventionist than Congress, presidential announcements on trade issues are generally a passive response to pressure from Congress. Sometimes, however, presidential remarks represent resistance to a bill under discussion in the House or Senate, such as when the president threatens to veto a protectionist bill. As a result, the presidential announcements on trade issues provide rather passive and sometimes confusing signals of U.S. pressures. Thus, it is not easy to rely on the signals sent by the president.

The pressures from Congress can be traced through the detailed and complete congressional records and make a convenient measure of those pressures. Therefore, I use congressional pressure as a proxy of the cross-country pressure. In an effort to measure the degree of this approximated cross-country pressure, I list in the appendix all the important events that occurred in the Congress in the 1970s and 1980s concerning U.S. trade relations with East Asian countries. The indicators of U.S. congressional pressures are shown in figure 9–1.

The data presented in the appendix show that U.S. pressures on East Asian countries increased sharply in the 1980s, an increase reflecting the changing political and economic structure in both the United States and East Asia. The equilibrium conditions for the international politico-economic markets shifted in the 1980s. On the one hand, agricultural groups in East Asia have been gaining protection from their governments. On the other hand, in the early 1980s American farmers suffered a serious export slump and declining land values, which have contributed to an increase of U.S. pressure on the East Asian markets. Meanwhile, other macroeconomic factors relevant to shifts in American trade policies changed in the 1980s. Among others are U.S. trade deficits and the federal government's budget deficits (table 9–1). The sharply increased U.S. trade deficits in the 1980s have given many political groups good reasons to ask governments to intervene more in trade policies. The critics of trade deficits have heightened the domestic pressures from export-oriented and import-competing producers, who accuse foreign countries of conducting unfair trade practices. Japan, Korea, and Taiwan have been among these most often mentioned as unfair trade partners. The U.S. trade deficit with these three countries increased sharply in the 1980s

FIGURE 9–1

U.S. CONGRESSIONAL PRESSURES ON EAST ASIAN COUNTRIES TO OPEN
THEIR MARKETS TO U.S. AGRICULTURAL PRODUCTS, 1970–1989

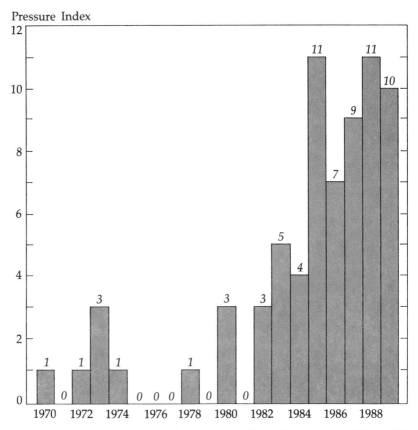

Pressure Index

Note: Instances of congressional pressure are listed in the appendix to this
chapter.
SOURCE: Congressional Quarterly Almanac, various issues, Washington,
D.C.: Congressional Quarterly Inc.

(table 9–2), leading the United States to adopt aggressive bilateral
trade negotiations with them. The exchange rates, particularly the
undervalued Japanese yen, Korean won, and New Taiwan (N.T.)
dollar, have been the important item in these negotiations. The U.S.–
Taiwan exchange rate discussions caused a 30 percent appreciation of
the N.T. dollar between 1985 and 1988. In addition to exchange rate
negotiations, the United States has focused on opening markets for

TABLE 9–1

THE U.S. BUDGET DEFICIT AND TRADE DEFICIT, 1970–1990

(billions of dollars)

| | Federal Budget Deficit | Merchandise Trade Balance | Balance on Goods, Services, and Income | Balance on Current Account |
|---|---|---|---|---|
| 1970 | −2.8 | 2.6 | 8.5 | 2.3 |
| 1971 | −23.0 | −2.3 | 6.0 | −1.4 |
| 1972 | −23.4 | −6.4 | 2.7 | −5.8 |
| 1973 | −14.9 | 0.9 | 14.1 | 7.1 |
| 1974 | −6.1 | −5.5 | 11.2 | 2.0 |
| 1975 | −53.2 | 8.9 | 25.2 | 18.1 |
| 1976 | −73.7 | −9.5 | 9.9 | 4.2 |
| 1977 | −53.6 | −31.1 | −9.3 | −14.5 |
| 1978 | −59.2 | −33.9 | −9.6 | −15.4 |
| 1979 | −40.2 | −27.5 | 5.6 | −1.0 |
| 1980 | −73.8 | −25.5 | 9.5 | 1.1 |
| 1981 | −78.9 | −28.0 | 15.2 | 6.9 |
| 1982 | −127.9 | −36.4 | 3.9 | −5.9 |
| 1983 | −207.8 | −67.1 | −30.2 | −40.1 |
| 1984 | −185.3 | −112.5 | −86.4 | −99.0 |
| 1985 | −212.3 | −122.1 | −106.9 | −122.3 |
| 1986 | −221.2 | −145.1 | −129.4 | −145.4 |
| 1987 | −149.7 | −159.5 | −147.7 | −162.3 |
| 1988 | −155.1 | −127.0 | −113.9 | −128.9 |
| 1989 | −152.0 | −114.9 | −95.3 | −110.0 |
| 1990 | −123.8 | −108.7 | −78.2 | −99.3 |

SOURCE: U.S. Department of Commerce, Bureau of the Census, *Statistical Abstract of the United States*, 1991.

U.S. exports in this area. Therefore, the heavily protected agricultural products of East Asia are at the top of the hit list in trade negotiations.

Figure 9–1 portrays the profound changes in trade relations between the United States and the East Asian countries. In the 1970s, congressional pressures showed no pattern at all, while in the 1980s mounting pressures became a trend. The peak of the pressure was in 1985. The pattern coincides with the situation of the U.S. trade deficit. In 1984, the trade deficit jumped from $67.1 billion to $112.5 billion and increased sequentially in 1985 and 1986 (table 9–1). Accordingly, congressional pressure on the administration to reduce imports and increase exports intensified. As noted in the appendix, Congress took

TABLE 9–2

THE U.S. MERCHANDISE TRADE BALANCE WITH JAPAN, KOREA,
AND TAIWAN, 1975–1990

(millions of dollars)

|  | Japan | South Korea | Taiwan |
|---|---|---|---|
| 1975 | − 1,862 | + 320 | − 287 |
| 1980 | − 9,924 | + 538 | − 2,517 |
| 1984 | − 33,560 | − 3,370 | − 9,765 |
| 1985 | − 46,152 | − 4,057 | − 11,696 |
| 1986 | − 55,029 | − 6,374 | − 14,267 |
| 1987 | − 56,326 | − 8,888 | − 17,209 |
| 1988 | − 52,070 | − 8,899 | − 12,674 |
| 1989 | − 49,002 | − 6,264 | − 13,003 |
| 1990 | − 41,071 | − 4,095 | − 11,184 |

SOURCE: U.S. Department of Commerce, Bureau of the Census, *Statistical Abstract of the United States*, 1990 and 1991.

strong measures to deal with the country's trade imbalance. In 1985, the Democratic leaders in Congress even put forward a bill to impose a 25 percent surcharge on products from Japan, Taiwan, South Korea, and Brazil (see table 9–2). In the same year, members of Congress proposed an omnibus trade bill that would have changed basic U.S. trade policies and procedures. Among others, the proposals would have:

- increased government support for exporters
- mandated quicker and stronger action against the trading practices of other countries
- set goals for U.S. negotiations in a new round of global trade talks
- authorized talks with Japan aimed at securing trade concessions in exchange for access to petroleum and natural gas from Alaska

In addition to the omnibus trade bill proposals, both the Senate and the House passed nonbinding resolutions calling on the president to retaliate against Japan if it refused to remove barriers to U.S. exports. The Senate passed the resolution (S Con Res 15) by 92 votes to 0, and the House passed a similar resolution (H Con Res 107) by 394 to 19.

The majority of Congress believed that U.S. exports were not getting fair treatment abroad and were prepared to support a tough stance against foreign protectionism. Congressional pressure points (events) increased from four points in 1984 to eleven points in 1985 (see figure 9–1).

## The U.S.–Taiwan Turkey-Trade Conflicts

Turkey meat was not an important item on the U.S.–Taiwan trade agenda before the mid-1980s, because the trade volume and value were negligible. U.S. export of turkey meat to Taiwan increased sharply, however, in 1987. Compared with 1986, the export quantity increased more than 168 times in one year, from 15.9 metric tons in 1986 to 2,685 metric tons in 1987 (table 9–3). Poultry prices, especially for chicken, declined in Taiwan. The Taiwan government then banned turkey imports in response to the great lobbying efforts of domestic chicken producers. Although the "liberalization and internationalization" of the Taiwan economy had been a major policy goal, the government could not resist the immediate political pressure from the chicken producers. Thus began a year-long trade confrontation between the United States and Taiwan. The causes and consequences of the turkey-trade conflicts will now be explored from the viewpoint of cross-country pressure group theory.

**Background of the Turkey-Trade Conflicts.** Before 1987, Taiwan had no restrictions on the importation of turkey meat. Turkey importation had never constituted an issue on the U.S.–Taiwan trade agenda. Since sometime in 1987, however, imports of U.S. turkey parts increased sharply, primarily turkey wings used in Taiwan's growing fast food industry. Imports of turkey meat in 1986 were 15.9 metric tons, leaping to 2,685 metric tons in 1987. In January 1988, turkey meat licenses were issued for 4,010 metric tons (see table 9–3). As a result of the surging imports, poultry prices in Taiwan declined. The average price of imported turkey meat dropped from $2.87 per kg in 1986 to $0.70 in 1987 (see table 9–3). Chicken producers were the main group affected. There are 12,000 full-time poultry farm families and 180,000 part-time poultry farm families in Taiwan (Board of Foreign Trade 1989). Chicken producers and other poultry farmers had lobbied vigorously to ban the turkey imports. Facing the sharply increased pressure from the chicken lobby in 1988, the Taiwan government's Board of Foreign Trade announced that the Council of Agriculture would have to approve all requests for import licenses for turkey. No licenses were issued for imports of turkey parts for more than a year. The government of Taiwan effectively banned all imports of turkey meat by refusing to issue import licenses.

The restriction of turkey imports in Taiwan hurt the turkey

TABLE 9–3

Taiwan Imports of U.S. Turkey Meat, January 1986–January 1988
(kg/U.S.$)

|  | Quantity (kg) | Value ($) | Average Price ($/kg) | Licensed Quantity |
|---|---|---|---|---|
| 1986 Jan. | 0 | 0 | | |
| Feb. | 0 | 0 | | 900 |
| March | 0 | 0 | | |
| April | 0 | 0 | | 400 |
| May | 0 | 0 | | |
| June | 0 | 0 | | |
| July | 0 | 0 | | |
| Aug. | 0 | 0 | | |
| Sept. | 54 | 325 | 6.02 | 4,500 |
| Oct. | 0 | 0 | | 1,400 |
| Nov. | 14,485 | 40,783 | 2.82 | 10,400 |
| Dec. | 1,325 | 4,415 | 3.33 | 7,700 |
| 1986 total | 15,864 | 45,523 | 2.87 | 25,300 |
| 1987 Jan. | 6,804 | 3,630 | 0.53 | 183,400 |
| Feb. | 964 | 6,328 | 6.56 | 3,200 |
| March | 9,641 | 7,729 | 0.80 | 0 |
| April | 0 | 0 | | 1,000,600 |
| May | 25,925 | 19,489 | 0.75 | 240,400 |
| June | 42,826 | 34,202 | 0.80 | 134,300 |
| July | 96,430 | 69,611 | 0.72 | 91,500 |
| Aug. | 98,777 | 103,719 | 1.05 | 416,800 |
| Sept. | 177,081 | 129,728 | 0.73 | 977,700 |
| Oct. | 348,051 | 277,103 | 0.65 | 1,414,900 |
| Nov. | 860,930 | 564,742 | 0.66 | 3,219,100 |
| Dec. | 1,017,077 | 710,820 | 0.70 | 35,495,200 |
| 1987 total | 2,684,506 | 1,877,101 | 0.70 | 42,904,100 |
| 1988 Jan. | | | | 4,940,600 |

Source: "Reasons for Controlling the Imports of Turkey Meats to the R.O.C.," memo., August 1988, CCNAA, Documents provided by the Council of Agriculture, Executive Yuan, ROC.

producers and turkey exporters in the United States. They expressed indignation at Taiwan's new restrictive practices and called on the office of the USTR for help. Congressional representatives were also quite concerned about Taiwan's ban on turkey imports. The pressure did not come from turkey producers alone; several groups of fruit growers, including growers of apples, oranges, grapefruits, and table grapes, also expressed anxiety about the turkey case, because the Taiwan government had been requesting the United States to agree to voluntary export restraints on those fruit items. According to a USTR document, an important consideration at every stage of the U.S. negotiations on turkey parts was that an accommodating U.S. position on turkey parts would lead to intensified pressure in Taiwan for restrictions on fruit.[2]

In responding to pressure from turkey producers as well as other concerned groups, the U.S. government immediately initiated a series of meetings with Taiwan authorities to reach agreement on a schedule for lifting the restrictions on imports of turkey parts. The United States also requested compensation for export losses of $10 million per year incurred as a result of the restrictions.

During the negotiations, three rounds of meetings were held— the first in February 1988 in Taipei, the second in August 1988 in Hawaii, and the third in January 1989 in Washington, D.C. An agreement between the United States and Taiwan was reached in the third meeting. The Sino-American Trade Ad Hoc Committee of the Executive Yuan decided to meet with U.S. representatives to resolve the turkey trade conflicts based on the following considerations:

• The Trade Policy Review Group, under section 301 of the 1988 Omnibus Trade Bill, had decided to recommend retaliation against Taiwan's exports.

• The new trade bill required the Office of the USTR to select by April 1989 a list of countries that the United States considered the most unfair traders. The USTR would have to begin negotiations that could lead to trade retaliations against those unfair trade partners.

• The turkey-trade conflicts threatened a good U.S.–Taiwan relationship. After a year of negotiations, the United States and Taiwan reached a mutually acceptable agreement. The United States also agreed to stop the proposed retaliation against Taiwan.

## Theoretical Viewpoint of the Turkey-Trade Conflicts

The year-long trade dispute between the United States and Taiwan highlights the essence of international politico-economic relations.

---

[2]The delegation of the Coordination Council for North American Affairs at the August 1988 consultations had proposed cutbacks on fruit to the 1984–1986 level, which would have cut back U.S. exports to Taiwan of apples by 12 percent; of oranges by 77 percent; of grapefruits by 78 percent; and of grapes by 47 percent.

Pressure groups in both countries competed for political support that hurt groups in the other country, leading to bargains made by the governments of the two countries. Any change in the politico-economic equilibrium in one country inevitably calls for adjustments in its trading partners. Both the U.S. and the Taiwan governments tried their best to influence the other side's policy decisions to maximize its domestic political gains or minimize its domestic political losses. The final results depend on the relative cross-country pressures, which in turn are a function of the domestic pressures of various groups and of other political and economic factors.

The politico-economic equilibrium in Taiwan was broken by sharply increased turkey imports from America. Yielding to increasing pressures from the chicken producers, the Taiwan government implemented the restrictive trade measures that authorized the Council of Agriculture not to issue the turkey import licenses. The measures actually banned all turkey imports from the United States. The domestic political equilibrium among various groups was restored through the new protection measure that taxed consumers while subsidizing chicken producers. The turkey farmers in the United States, however, were hurt by this measure. According to one estimation, the losses to U.S. turkey raisers were $10 million per year. Inevitably, the induced political adjustment would occur in the United States. The U.S. government began pressuring the Taiwan government, demanding removal of the restrictive measures.

The relative cross-country pressure, or the relative strength of Taiwan's resistance to exports from the United States and demands from the United States for Taiwan to reopen its turkey market, determined the final resolution of the issue. The relative cross-country pressure is a function of domestic pressures from various groups in both countries and of other factors, such as the relative dependency of the other U.S.–Taiwan traded goods and other political and economic relations between the two countries. In trade relations between the United States and Taiwan, particularly in times of trade conflict, Taiwan has been on the defensive because of its huge trade surplus with the United States as well as other political factors. The "buy American" policy has been viewed as a way to gain American political support. Given this situation, U.S. turkey producers effectively transformed the pressure on their government into cross-country pressure, pressing the Taiwan government to remove the newly established trade barriers and to compensate their losses.

The extent and form of Taiwan's response to the pressure from the United States depended on how and to what degree the Taiwan government effectively transmitted this cross-country pressure to the active domestic pressure groups. The final result of the U.S.–Taiwan trade negotiation confirms a proposition of the cross-country pressure group theory (Chou 1990).[3] The net effect of increased expenditures by the turkey producers in the United States lowered the taxes of consumers and subsidies of the chicken producers in Taiwan.

The theory developed by the author views all the domestic readjustment in one country as a response to foreign governmental pressures. One proposition of the author's theory states that the foreign pressure decreases both taxes and subsidies in the pressure-recipient country. The case involving the U.S.–Taiwan turkey trade also supports this proposition. The Taiwan government's strategy to appease the domestic lobby was to offer substitute subsidies to the chicken producers, including direct cash support to establish chicken farmers' cooperatives and to build automatic slaughterhouses on behalf of chicken producers, in addition to loans at subsidized interest rates. Therefore, the protectionist subsidies to the chicken raisers and the potential consumer losses in terms of higher prices were replaced by substitute subsidies. In the long run, the once-and-for-all substitute subsidies will be much lower than subsidies involving trade restrictions.

During the negotiations between the United States and Taiwan, U.S. demands for Taiwan to reopen the turkey market caused the affected groups, mainly chicken producers of Taiwan, to increase their political expenditures dramatically. It is hard to estimate their direct monetary expenditures. Nevertheless, from the frequency of their protest rallies and other public appeals, it is evident that the chicken producers had invested substantial amounts to influence government policies, political expenditures including money, time, and other resources devoted to gain political favor from the government. There is little evidence to indicate whether consumers changed their political expenditures or if they are an active pressure group at all. Although consumers of chicken and turkey meat in Taiwan benefited from imported U.S. turkey meat, the net effect of the political influences among various pressure groups on this issue was overwhelmingly dominated by the chicken producers. Therefore, according to the high-profile activities performed by the chicken raisers, part of another proposition from the author's theory can be confirmed: the political expenditures of members of a subsidized

---

[3]A theory of trade conflicts has been developed by Chou (1990). The theory states that the net effect of an increase in expenditures of pressure groups in any one of the two countries lowers taxes of the taxed group and subsidies of the subsidized group in the other country.

group will rise as the pressure from abroad increases.

The restrictions on turkey trade were removed completely on September 1, 1990.[4] In addition, Taiwan also offered to lower the tariff on processed turkey products from the current 40 percent to 20 percent. The equilibrium protection level of turkey meat and poultry products will be substantially lower, which confirms another proposition of the author's theory: the increase of foreign pressure in any country lowers the "equilibrium" protection level in the pressure-recipient country.

## Transformation of Protection Policy in Taiwan

In the 1980s, the trade-related conflicts between the United States and East Asian countries moved up to the top of the national agenda in Taiwan in the face of increasing U.S. pressures. The situation became particularly urgent for these countries when the U.S. Congress passed the Omnibus Trade and Competitiveness Act in 1988. The amendments to Section 301 in the trade bill require the Office of the USTR to compile a list of unfair traders and to begin negotiation with these countries on removing the trade barriers that hurt U.S. exports. The negotiation process could lead to trade sanctions unless those countries agree unilaterally to implement the trade reforms sought by the United States. Taiwan was aware that it was a good candidate for the top of the list. Although Japan was the only country in East Asia that was on the list when the USTR announced the unfair traders in May 1989, Korea and Taiwan were removed from the list only at the last minute. Both Korea and Taiwan had negotiated with the USTR and achieved some agreement on trade reform, thus exempting these two countries from the USTR's hit list. In this section, I discuss the policy adjustment in Taiwan in response to the new pressure under Section 301 of the 1988 trade bill.

In view of the pressure from the United States on Taiwan throughout the 1980s to open up its markets to American goods and services, Taiwan has developed a long-term economic development strategy to liberalize and internationalize its economy and trade. In an effort to deal with more urgent pressure from the United States, especially the possibility of being listed among unfair traders, authorities in Taiwan put forward a comprehensive plan to the United States

---

[4]According to the Agreed Minutes reached on January 6, 1989, imports of turkey parts without quantitative limitation was to be resumed on September 1, 1990. Source: "Report of the Case of Sino-American Turkey Parts Negotiations" (1989).

TABLE 9–4

EXPECTED TARIFF REDUCTION SCHEDULES IN TAIWAN, 1988–1992

(average import duty percent)

|  | 1988[a] | 1989 | 1990 | 1991 | 1992 |
|---|---|---|---|---|---|
| All products | 12.57 | 10.25 | 9.17 | 8.08 | 7.00 |
| Agricultural products | 25.99 | 24.21 | 23.25 | 21.32 | 19.82 |
| Industrial products | 10.20 | 8.03 | 7.03 | 6.02 | 5.02 |
| Average effective rate of import duty | 5.66 | 4.70 | 4.30 | 3.90 | 3.50 |

a. The average effective rate of import duty for 1988 equals total tariff revenues divided by total imports (excluding gold imported by the Central Bank of China).
SOURCE: "Detailed Action Plan for Strengthening Economic and Trade Ties with the United States," Council for Economic Planning and Development, Executive Yuan, ROC, March 1989.

in March 1989, which included a "detailed action plan" to reduce the trade surplus with the United States and to reduce both tariff and nontariff trade barriers to U.S. exports (CEPD, 1989).

The plan promised to take effective measures to expand domestic demand and increase imports so that the trade surplus with the United States is reduced. Taiwan set a goal of reducing its trade surplus with the United States by 10 percent annually. As for agricultural products, the plan states, "We will continue to review the proposal that we liberalize the importation into our country of agricultural products." The plan also includes a timetable for tariff reduction. By 1992, the average effective rate of import duty will be reduced to 3.50 percent from the rate of 5.66 percent, which had prevailed in 1988. The average nominal rate of import duty was scheduled to fall from 12.60 percent to 7.00 percent, while tariffs on agricultural products were scheduled to fall from 25.99 percent to 19.82 percent (table 9–4).

Although the major agricultural products still receive considerable protection from the Taiwan government, liberalizing the agricultural markets for foreign competitors has become the government's established policy. U.S. pressure on Taiwan to open up its protected markets has been successfully pushing Taiwan to transform its protection policies. This transformation of agricultural policies reduces the dead-weight costs of protection policies in Taiwan and therefore raises the economic efficiency of the Taiwan economy. The case of U.S. exports of turkey meat to Taiwan confirms a proposition of the

213

theory of trade conflicts: the increase of foreign pressure in any country lowers the equilibrium protection level in the pressure-recipient country. The cross-country pressure from abroad is an external constraint on the level of domestic protection. The increasing pressure from the United States serves as a counteractive force against the increasing protection level in Taiwan and further decreases that level. Without this counteractive effect, the Taiwan government would not be able to transform its current agricultural policies even if it intended to do so. In the international political and economic markets, the trade of pressure, in addition to the trade of goods and services, can be seen as an important factor in achieving an international division of labor.

## References

Anderson, Kym, and Yujiro Hayami. *The Political Economy of Agricultural Protection—East Asia in International Perspective.* Sydney: Allen & Unwin, 1986.

Becker, Gary S. "Public Policies, Pressure Groups, and Dead Weight Costs." *Journal of Public Economics* 28 (1985): 329–47.

———. "A Theory of Competition among Pressure Groups for Political Influence." *Quarterly Journal of Economics* 98 (1983): 371–400.

Bhagwati, J. N. "Directly-unproductive Profit-seeking (DUP) Activities." *Journal of Political Economy* 90 (1982): 988–1002.

Bhagwati, J. N., and T. N. Srinivasan. "Revenue Seeking: A Generalization of the Theory of Tariffs." *Journal of Political Economy* 88 (1980): 1069–87.

Board of Foreign Trade. *Records on 1987 Foreign Trade Negotiation.* Memo. Board of Foreign Trade, Ministry of Economic Affairs, Taipei, ROC, April 1988.

———. "Report on the Case of Sino-American Turkey Parts Negotiations." Memo. Board of Foreign Trade, Ministry of Economic Affairs, Taipei, ROC, January 5, 1989.

Bureau of the Census. *Statistical Abstract of the United States.* U.S. Department of Commerce, Bureau of the Census, 1990 and 1991.

CCNAA. "Reasons for Controlling the Imports of Turkey Meats to the R.O.C." Memo. CCNAA, Documents provided by the Council of Agriculture, Executive Yuan, ROC, August 1988.

CEPD. "Detailed Action Plan for Strengthening Economic and Trade Ties with the United States." Council for Economic Planning and Development, Executive Yuan, ROC, March, 1989.

Chou, Chi-Chu. *The Political Economy of the East Asia-U.S. Agricultural Trade Relations.* Ph.D. diss. University of Chicago, 1990.

Congressional Quarterly. *Congressional Quarterly Almanac.* Various issues, Washington, D.C.: Congressional Quarterly Inc.

Johnson, D. Gale. *World Agriculture in Disarray.* London: Macmillan, 1973.

Kuo, Shirley W. Y. *The Taiwan Economy in Transition.* Boulder, Colo: Westview Press, 1983.

Miller, Tracy C. *Explaining Agricultural Price Policy across Countries and across Commodities Using Political Interest Group Theory.* Ph.D. diss. University of Chicago, 1986.

Schultz, T. W. *Distortion of Agricultural Incentives.* Bloomington: Indiana University Press, 1978.

Stigler, George J., ed. *Chicago Studies in Political Economy.* Chicago: University of Chicago Press, 1988.

Tolley, G. S., V. Thomas, and C. M. Wong. *Agricultural Price Policy and the Developing Countries.* Baltimore: Johns Hopkins University Press, 1982.

### Appendix 9A: Indicators of U.S. Congressional Pressures, 1970–1989

| Events | State of Pressure |
|---|---|
| *1970* | |
| The House passed a strong protectionist bill (HR 18970); the Senate passed one too (HR 17550) on Dec. 29. Insufficient time to resolve differences between the Senate and House versions. | Increasing pressure |
| U.S. employment fell in the textile and footwear industries—by 100,000 during 1970 alone in textiles. | |
| Congress tried to pass a foreign trade bill (HR 18970) that would have curbed imports, broadened the president's powers to resist the unfair trade practices of other countries, and increased assistance to U.S. industries and workers harmed by imports. Legislation not enacted. | |
| President Nixon proposed parts of the trade bill and "reluctantly" supported its textile import quota provision. He opposed the footwear quota provision and threatened to veto it if it contained quotas on imports other than textiles. | Ambiguous pressure |
| *1971* | |
| The 1948 Sugar Act was extended through 1974, adjusting production quotas for foreign and domestic producers. | Ambiguous pressure |
| Domestic producers were granted a quota reflect- | |

ing the amount they were able to produce (62% of total U.S. consumption), according to HR 8866. The remainder was allocated to various foreign countries depending on whether they were friendly to the U.S., reliable sources of sugar, reciprocal in their trade policies, dependent on sugar markets for their economic survival, or just in their treatment of sugar farmers.

### 1972

The U.S. reached agreements with Japan and the EEC on immediate steps to liberalize trade and to conduct more comprehensive trade negotiations in 1973.

Increasing pressure

### 1973

The House passed major trade reform legislation (HR 10710) by a 272–140 recorded vote, but the Senate deferred action on the bill until 1974.

Increasing pressure

After a two-month delay requested by President Nixon in considering HR 10710, the House approved broad presidential powers to negotiate trade expansion agreements with major foreign industrial nations, particularly the European countries and Japan.

In 1971, the U.S. had a trade deficit of $2.7 billion, its first deficit since 1888. In 1972, the deficit jumped to $6.8 billion. Reacting to a large trade deficit, President Nixon asked Congress to grant broad new negotiating powers to U.S. representatives at international trade talks in Tokyo.

Japan and the EEC were the key targets of U.S. negotiators. In 1972, the U.S. had a trade deficit of $4.1 billion with Japan, nearly two-thirds of the entire deficit. Although the U.S. and Japan had successfully negotiated the removal of some restrictions, quotas and other barriers to U.S. exports and investments still existed.

Increasing pressure

Nontariff barriers had become of increasing concern to the U.S. The three-year Kennedy Round of tariff-cutting negotiations, held under the auspices of the GATT, resulted in a 1967 agreement reducing duties an average of 35 percent on some 60,000 items and affecting more than $40 billion annually in world trade. With tariffs on a downward trend in recent years, nontariff barriers had been growing. The secretariat of GATT had reported 27 types of nontariff barriers, such as export subsidies, preferential government procurement practices, antidumping duties, customs valuation practices, quotas, discriminatory bilateral agreements, variable levies, discriminatory taxes, and product standards that protect domestic producers.

Trade reforms were proposed to permit the president to retaliate against any country that maintained unjustifiable or unreasonable tariffs or other restrictions or had discriminatory policies, such as nontariff barriers, that burdened or restricted U.S. trade.

*Increasing pressure*

### 1974

In June the Senate passed a bill (S 1486) to authorize the secretary of commerce to carry on activities to expand U.S. exports. With only 4 percent of U.S. firms in the export business and an uncertain U.S. balance of payments situation, there was agreement that new programs were needed to encourage more firms to get into export trading.

*Increasing pressure*

The bill authorized the secretary of commerce to make grants and loans, give technical assistance to local governments for export projects, and conduct training programs for firms to encourage them to enter the export trade. The House took no action on the bill.

The administration opposed the bill as unnecessary and administratively burdensome.

### 1975

No events

*Unchanged pressure*

### 1976

No events

*Unchanged pressure*

### 1977

No events

*Unchanged pressure*

### 1978

Congress gave final approval on Oct. 14 to the Agricultural Trade Bill, designed to boost U.S. agricultural exports by liberalizing credit terms for some export sales and increasing marketing and promotion efforts abroad.

*Increasing pressure*

The measure (S 3447-PL 95-501) allowed the Commodity Credit Corporation to extend short-term credit (up to three years) to the People's Republic of China. China had been ineligible under provisions of the 1974 Trade Act.

Farm exports were one of the biggest positive

contributions to the heavily negative ($31.2 billion in 1977) U.S. balance of trade.

### 1979

No events

Unchanged pressure

### 1980

The Senate unanimously passed an export trading company bill (S 2718), a companion measure reported by the House Foreign Affairs Committee (HR 7230), but the bill failed to reach the House floor before adjournment. Therefore, the 96th Congress did not complete action on legislation designed to encourage the formation of export trading companies to help U.S. firms market their goods abroad.

Increasing pressure

Support for the legislation (S 2718):
• The Senate passed its version of the bill on Sept. 3 by a 77–0 vote.
• "U.S. exporters do not receive the government support and subsidies of their foreign competitors," said Sen. Adlai E. Stevenson. Supporters of the legislation said that export trading companies, widely used in other countries, would stimulate exports by acting as middlemen to help small- and medium-sized companies with marketing, financing and transportation services.

Increasing pressure

• Agricultural products, machinery, and high-technology manufactured goods were the chief U.S. exports, but since 1970 Germany had succeeded the U.S. as the world's leading exporter of manufactured goods. USTR Reubin O'D. Askew told the Foreign Affairs Committee, "Today, Japan threatens to drop the United States into third place."

Increasing pressure

### 1981

No events

Unchanged pressure

### 1982

Legislation designed to increase U.S. exports was cleared by Congress on Oct. 1. The bill (S 734-PL 97-290) aimed to encourage the formation of export trading companies to help small- and medium-sized firms sell their goods abroad.

Increasing pressure

Senate bill (S 734) eased antitrust barriers that had inhibited joint export activities and permitted banking institutions to be active partners in the ventures. It directed the secretary of commerce to establish an office to promote the formation of export trading companies.

Bills seeking "reciprocity" in trade relations were reported by congressional committees but did not reach the Senate or House floor in 1982. — Increasing pressure

 The controversial concept of reciprocity would require retaliatory action against nations that did not provide American firms with access to markets equal to that afforded to foreign firms by the U.S.

The pressure for reciprocity legislation reflected increasing congressional frustration over the nation's mounting trade deficit, especially with Japan, and with foreign practices and politics that had caused difficulties for U.S. businesses. — Increasing pressure

### 1983

A bill to establish a new Department of International Trade and Industry was reported by the Senate Government Affairs Committee on Oct. 18, after committee Democrats tacked on a watered-down "industrial policy" proposal. The full Senate did not act on the bill before adjournment. — Ambiguous pressure

 The bill would combine the trade representative's office and the Commerce Department in a single department, whose secretary would be the president's principal adviser on international trade policy.

The Senate on April 21 passed "reciprocity" trade legislation (S 144) that would expand the president's authority to retaliate against unfair trading practices by other countries and require the administration to seek new international agreements on trade in services and high technology. — Increasing pressure

The trade provisions of the bill (S 144) would require annual estimates on significant barriers to the export of U.S. goods and services and on curbs on U.S. foreign investment. — Increasing pressure

The bill also directed the president to seek new international agreements removing barriers to trade in services and high-technology products, as well as restrictions on foreign direct investment by U.S. companies. — Increasing pressure

In addition, the bill allowed the USTR to begin investigations of potential unfair trading practices under Section 301 of the Trade Act of 1974 on his own initiative. — Increasing pressure

The bill would create a "fast track" legislative process for requests from the president for new authority to retaliate against unfair trading practices.

*Increasing pressure*

### 1984

On Oct. 9 Congress cleared an omnibus bill (HR 3398-PL 98-573), an amalgam of more than 100 measures. The Senate on Sept. 20 unanimously approved the bill (HR 3398) after its managers fended off protectionist amendments aimed at aiding import-sensitive domestic industries. The vote on passage was 96–0.

*Increasing pressure*

The push for more extensive laws against unfair trade practices came on the heels of a record-high U.S. trade deficit in 1983 of $70 billion.

*Increasing pressure*

The measure extended the president's authority to retaliate against unfair trade practices and to expand trade in services and broadened the definitions of unfair trade subsidies.

*Increasing pressure*

The bill also approved a limited version of powers, long desired by the Office of the USTR, to negotiate free-trade area agreements with other countries.

*Increasing pressure*

### 1985

Pushed by deepening U.S. difficulties in international trade, Congress displayed an enthusiasm for trade legislation not seen on Capitol Hill for decades.

*Increasing pressure*

Partisan political maneuvering was another factor behind the explosion of interest in trade legislation. Many Democrats, eager to gain political advantage for the 1986 elections, seized on a tough stance on trade as a way to allow them to appear strong on national security. Republicans, in contrast, worried about the political costs of being associated with Reagan's free-trade stance.

Leading Democrats proposed strong retaliation against some of the nation's toughest trading partners. Led by House Ways and Means Committee Chairman Dan Rostenkowski, leaders put forth a bill to impose a 25 percent surcharge on products from Japan, Taiwan, South Korea, and Brazil.

*Increasing pressure*

Congressional members continued to propose a variety of trade packages in hopes of influencing a future "generic" trade bill that would change basic U.S. trade policies and procedures instead of offering help for

*Increasing pressure*

specific industries. The first such bill to come out was a House Republican plan, released on Oct. 8.

The trade packages of the plan included proposals to step up government support for exporters, to provide quicker, stronger action against unfair trading practices of other countries, and to set goals for U.S. negotiators in a new round of global trade talks.

*Increasing pressure*

The proposal authorizes talks with Japan aimed at securing trade concessions in exchange for access to petroleum and natural gas from Alaska.

*Increasing pressure*

The Textile-Import bill cleared Congress on Dec. 3 (HR 1562).

*Increasing pressure*

The textile bill was vetoed by President Reagan on Dec. 17.

*Decreasing pressure*

An earlier version of the bill would have forced cutbacks of about 30 percent in textile imports from Taiwan, South Korea, and Hong Kong.

*Increasing pressure*

As cleared by Congress, the bill would set the strictest import limits on Hong Kong, Taiwan, and South Korea, each of which provided more than 10 percent of total U.S. textile and apparel imports in 1984.

*Increasing pressure*

Frustrated by slow progress in trade negotiations with Japan, members of Congress pushed for retaliation against Japan's continuing barriers to U.S. goods.

*Increasing pressure*

Members of Congress pointed to a variety of studies showing that Japan blocked imports through "nontariff" barriers, such as elaborate testing requirements and lengthy inspections of foreign-made goods.

*Nonbinding resolutions:*
The first move in the Senate was a nonbinding resolution. By a 92–0 vote, the Senate on March 28 approved a resolution (S Con Res 15) calling on the president to retaliate against Japan if it refused to increase its purchases of U.S. exports. The resolution urged the president to use duties, quotas, or other barriers against Japanese imports unless Japan bought enough U.S. goods to offset its increases in auto shipments.

*Increasing pressure*

The House passed a related nonbinding resolution (H Con Res 107) by a 394–19 vote on April 2. The House resolution urged the president to take "all appropriate action" to make Japan end unfair trade practices. It asked the President to "develop a concrete plan for

*Increasing pressure*

reducing the deficit by attacking its causes, including the high dollar." Unlike the Senate resolution, however, the House measure did not suggest that the United States offset the expected jump in auto imports with curbs on other Japanese goods.

### 1986

On Aug. 6 the House sustained President Reagan's veto of legislation (HR 1562) to restrict textile imports into the U.S. The vote was 276–149, eight shy of the two-thirds needed to override the veto.

Decreasing pressure

USTR Clayton Yeutter called the House vote a "very gratifying victory" for the administration, which had lobbied vigorously to kill the bill.

The omnibus House trade bill (HR 4800) was passed by a 295–115 vote on May 22.

Increasing pressure

The primary focus was on stiffer responses to countries accused of keeping out American goods at a time when imports had helped to push the U.S. trade deficit to record levels, $148.5 billion in 1985.

Increasing pressure

In many areas, the bill would have forced the president to retaliate against countries that discriminated against U.S. exports, unless taking action would harm American economic interests.

Increasing pressure

The House Ways and Means Committee approved (April 30) 24–11 an amendment by Richard Gephardt, that would single out countries maintaining large trade surpluses with the U.S. and other nations.

Increasing pressure

Under Gephardt's proposal, the president would have to negotiate swift trade agreements with such countries, aiming for annual 10 percent reductions in their trade surplus with the U.S. Failure to achieve the reductions would force the president to take actions, such as higher tariffs, to bring down the offending countries' surpluses.

Increasing pressure

Countries affected by Gephardt's plan would be Japan, Taiwan, and West Germany. In 1985, Japan posted a $51.5 billion trade surplus with the U.S. The figures for Taiwan and West Germany were $13.4 billion and $12.6 billion, respectively.

Increasing pressure

During the May 20–22 floor debate, one amendment, by Philip Crane, would have eliminated portions of the bill (HR 4800) outlining U.S. responses against unfair foreign trading practices under Section 301 of the trade

Increasing pressure

laws. The amendment, rejected by 137–276, would have struck the export targeting section, the mandatory reductions in other countries' trade surpluses.

### 1987

| | |
|---|---|
| "The first imperative in the 100th Congress will be to come to grips with the steady decline in American competitiveness and the corollary increase in the trade deficit," House Speaker Jim Wright of Texas told a symposium of congressional leaders and representatives from business, labor, and academia. | Increasing pressure |
| The House and Senate passed separate versions of an omnibus trade bill (HR 3) by overwhelming margins: the House by a 290–137 vote on April 30, the Senate by 71–27 on July 21, but conferees made minimal progress in reconciling House-Senate differences. | Increasing pressure |
| The bill (HR 3) is the most sweeping set of proposed changes in U.S. trade laws since the 1974 Trade Act. | Ambiguous pressure |
| The chief impetus for the trade legislation was the nation's record $166.3 billion merchandise trade deficit in 1986 and the likelihood that it would be even worse in 1987. | Increasing pressure |
| Both the Gephardt amendment and the House Ways and Means provision were aimed narrowly at a few countries, notably Japan, South Korea, and Taiwan, whose exports to the U.S. exceeded imports by 75 percent. | Increasing pressure |
| Support for the Gephardt plan stemmed in part from a widely held Democratic belief, shared by some Republicans, that moves in Congress to push for a tough, even "protectionist" trade bill had strengthened the administration's negotiating stances with U.S. trading partners. | Increasing pressure |
| The bill established specific authority for the USTR to modify or terminate retaliation for unfair trade practices if the retaliation violated the GATT, failed to achieve the desired results, was harmful to U.S. economic interests, or had succeeded in its objective. | Increasing pressure |
| The bill required the USTR to impose quotas or tariffs or to revoke trade concessions to yield 10 percent annual reductions in a country's bilateral trade surplus if that country did not eliminate its unfair practices in the year following a determination that its surplus was unwarranted. | Increasing pressure |

The House on Sept. 16 passed a bill (HR 1154) that imposed stiff quotas on textile, garment, and shoe imports, but the 263–156 victory margin was insufficient to override an anticipated presidential veto. The Reagan administration strongly opposed the bill.

The bill (HR 1154) was the second textile-import bill to pass the House in three years. A similar bill cleared Congress in 1985 but was vetoed by President Reagan. An override attempt, delayed until August 1986, failed in the House by a narrow margin following an intensive eleventh-hour lobbying campaign by the White House.

Increasing pressure

Sponsors of HR 1154 made two significant changes from the 1985 bill in hopes of increasing their support. First, this bill set total quotas for the quantity of imports from all countries; the 1985 bill specifically targeted South Korea, Taiwan, and Hong Kong and was thus dubbed "anti-Asian" by its critics.

Increasing pressure

### 1988

A massive omnibus trade bill won final approval in the Senate on August 3 and was signed into law on August 23.

Increasing pressure

The core of the measure (HR 4848-PL 100-418) focused on unfair foreign trade practices and relief for import-damaged domestic industries. It included provisions aimed at making trade a higher priority in U.S. policy making, less subservient to foreign policy and defense considerations.

Increasing pressure

This bipartisan legislation reflected congressional anger over accelerating trade deficits, currency imbalances, and the administration's reluctance to intervene.

Increasing pressure

A proposal by Gephardt to require cuts in U.S. imports from countries that ran trade surpluses with the U.S. and refused to moderate unfair trade practices was omitted from the final bill. But he was credited with helping pressure the administration and Congress into the more activist trade policy codified in the bill.

Increasing pressure

Final provisions of the bill required the president to report annually on trade agreements and expanded private sector advisory committees to consult on broad trade policy as well as on specific trade problems.

The bill directed the USTR to develop and coordinate international trade policy, international trade negotiations, and to be the principal trade spokesman.

*Increasing pressure*

The bill established principal U.S. negotiating goals in 17 areas, including agriculture, services, intellectual property, foreign direct investment, worker rights, and trade and monetary coordination.

*Increasing pressure*

Transferring from the president to the USTR the authority to decide whether a foreign practice hindering U.S. trade was unfair and should be investigated, the bill gave the USTR the authority to decide what action to take against an unfair foreign trade practice and to implement such action. These decisions were subject to presidential discretion.

*Increasing pressure*

The bill required the USTR to take retaliatory action against violations of trade agreements or other "unjustifiable" foreign trade practices, retaliation to be in an amount equivalent to foreign restrictions on U.S. commerce. The form of retaliation was discretionary, with preference given to tariff restrictions.

*Increasing pressure*

The bill imposed time limits for investigations, determinations, and retaliatory action. Among other things, the USTR was required to make a determination of unfairness and decide what action, if any, to take within 12 months of initiating investigations in subsidy and nontrade agreement cases, and within 18 months in trade agreement cases. The bill required that action to be implemented 30 days after a determination, although it could be delayed up to 180 days at the request of a petitioner in the case, or if the USTR determined progress was being made on the problem.

*Trade liberalization priorities ("Super 301"):*
The bill revised Section 301 of the Trade Act of 1974 to require the USTR to identify foreign trade practices whose elimination was likely to have the most significant potential for increasing U.S. exports; identify "priority" foreign countries, taking into account the number and pervasiveness of such practices; and estimate the amount by which U.S. exports would have increased the previous year if those barriers did not exist.

*Increasing pressure*

The bill also required the USTR to begin investigations into all priority practices in each priority country, seek a negotiated agreement to reduce those practices, and report the results to Congress. Failure to reach agree-

*Increasing pressure*

225

ment would mean continuation of U.S. unfair-trade-practice procedures as revised by the bill, with possible retaliation.

### 1989

The Bush administration named three countries, Japan, India, and Brazil, for action under "Super 301" of the 1988 trade act.

Increasing pressure

The administration announced a so-called structural impediments initiative (SII), under which it began holding talks with Japan on structural barriers to U.S. imports. By year's end, Max Baucus, chairman of the Senate Finance Committee's Trade Subcommittee, was warning that if the SII talks showed no progress, he would introduce legislation requiring that the administration expand Super 301 to apply to some structural barriers in Japan.

Increasing pressure

Super 301, a strengthened version of Section 301 of the 1974 Trade Act, required the USTR to identify trade liberalization priorities including "priority countries" (countries that engaged in those practices in a way that seriously thwarted U.S. imports). The law required the USTR to investigate the cited practices, try to negotiate agreements to eliminate them within three years, and determine what retaliation, if any, was appropriate if negotiations failed.

Increasing pressure

The decision to include Japan in the Super 301 list was made after a fierce internal debate within the administration. Treasury Secretary Nicholas Brady, Secretary of State James Baker, chief economic adviser Michael Boskin, and budget director Richard Darman all reportedly urged more leniency with Japan. Reportedly arguing for a stronger stance were Commerce Secretary Robert Mosbacher and USTR Carla Hills.

Increasing pressure

Japan was cited for prohibiting government purchases of foreign-broadcast, communications, and other satellites; for effectively barring government and university purchases of foreign supercomputers through government procurement processes; and for discouraging demand for wood products through building codes and product standards that favored other types of building materials.

Increasing pressure

South Korea, Taiwan, and the European Community were not on the list, though they were all mentioned by trade experts as possible Super 301 cases. Both South Korea and Taiwan saw designation itself as a form of retaliation and bargained successfully to stay off the list.

South Korea in April promised to cut tariffs on more than 200 agricultural products. By mid-May, Korean officials also promised to phase out import restrictions on more than 70 food items; to liberalize restrictions on grains and livestock feed; to let foreign travel and advertising agencies and pharmaceutical wholesalers do business in Korea; and to stop requiring foreign investors to export a specified amount of their products and meet other requirements. — Increasing pressure

Taiwan offered a detailed plan to boost domestic consumption and increase imports and agreed to crack down on its "movie television (MTV) parlors," which showed pirated U.S. films on videotape. — Increasing pressure

In addition to including Japan in the Super 301 list, the administration called for broad, top-level negotiations with Japan on structural barriers to trade. These barriers were deeply embedded ways of doing business that impeded U.S. imports but were not violations of international trade law. Two rounds of SII talks were held in 1989, led on the U.S. side by Hills, Baker, and Brady. — Increasing pressure

After the second round in November, the talks had accomplished less progress than hoped for by the administration. Additional talks were planned in January 1990, and members of Congress were expecting a midterm report on the negotiations in March 1990. — Increasing pressure

Senator Baucus, who held SII hearings in November, expressed impatience with the talks: "If SII appears to be lagging, I plan to introduce legislation to require Section 301 to be used against Japanese structural barriers should the SII fail." — Increasing pressure

SOURCE: *Congressional Quarterly Almanac*, various issues, Washington, D.C.: Congressional Quarterly Inc.

# PART FOUR

# Liberalizing Trade in a Multinational Setting

# 10

# The History and Prospects of GATT Agricultural Negotiations

*D. Gale Johnson*

The General Agreement on Tariffs and Trade (GATT) has provided the organizational structure for trade negotiations among the majority of the nations of the world for the past four decades. The most recent round of GATT negotiations began in September 1986 with a meeting of the ministers to GATT at Punta del Este, Uruguay. At that meeting, the general objectives of the round were agreed on as well as the subjects to be negotiated. Agriculture was included as one of the fourteen subjects.

Previous rounds of GATT negotiations had little success in liberalizing trade in agricultural products. One reason for the failure was that GATT had been effective only in negotiating reductions in tariffs. In agriculture, however, most measures that influence trade—the value of exports and imports—are not tariffs but are either domestic measures or border measures that are generally inconsistent with GATT principles. One of the basic principles of GATT is that the only acceptable border measures are tariffs or taxes; other measures such as import quotas, licensing, and the use of various standards to restrict imports have not been acceptable except under fairly specific conditions. Domestic measures that affect imports and exports, such as subsidies and deficiency payments, had not been considered subject to negotiation. GATT has rules governing the use of export subsidies, but these rules are so ambiguous that they have not been enforceable. In fact, the Common Agricultural Policy (CAP) of the European Community (EC) in its present form requires the use of export subsidies to make up the difference between the domestic prices and the lower world prices. Similarly, the United States has used export subsidies at various times and in violation of any reasonable reading of Article XVI of GATT, which deals with the use of export subsidies.

Thus, the ministers emphasized that the negotiations had to

231

strengthen the role of GATT and that the agricultural negotiations had to address issues before ignored. The strengthening of GATT's role implied modifying and making enforceable the provisions dealing with trade interventions other than tariffs. The areas that the agricultural negotiations were to tackle were, first, reduction in the use of domestic and export subsidies, second, improving market access, and, third, achieving harmonization of food, health, and safety regulations. The emphasis on regulation is important since such idiosyncratic health, sanitary, and safety regulations can be established that an exporter can meet them, if at all, only at great cost. Related trade barriers include packaging and marketing requirements that depart significantly from usual practice. Often such regulations, including those presumably for health and safety reasons, have no real purpose except to restrict imports.

Consequently, the objective of the GATT negotiation was to tackle all the major means by which domestic policies affect trade in agricultural products. In the case of agriculture, domestic policies had determined the nature of the interventions at the border. Up to the present, few countries have been willing to modify their farm programs to achieve more liberal trade in agricultural products. Agricultural trade measures have not been determined with any significant emphasis on their consistency with a liberal world trading order. Instead, countries have adopted measures to control trade as needed to carry out domestic farm price and income support programs at a minimum cost to the government. Consequently, the ministers were correct in emphasizing that all domestic farm programs with a significant effect on exports and imports had to be made a subject of negotiation. Otherwise, there was little reason to undertake the negotiation.

## The Special Role of the United States

The United States was primarily responsible for the creation of GATT, and it has had a major role in instituting each of the eight rounds of negotiations that GATT has undertaken. The United States merits considerable credit for the substantial liberalization of trade in industrial products since the end of World War II. That liberalization greatly assisted in the transformation of the East Asian economies that has occurred with such rapidity over the past three decades.

But as positive as its role may have been in liberalizing trade in industrial products, the United States bears much of the responsibility for the ineffectiveness of the agricultural trade negotiations and for there being no mechanism for restraining the major increase in agricultural protection over the past quarter-century. In the case of agriculture, the United States was not willing to apply the principles that it espoused for trade in industrial products to agricultural products. In other words, it was not willing to rely solely on tariffs as a means of protecting agriculture.

In the late 1940s when the GATT was being negotiated and later when it was implemented, the United States had price supports for many farm products. In several instances, especially for dairy products and wheat, these price supports were higher than world market prices. The United States was a net importer of dairy products. Since the United States had assented in a trade agreement to bind its tariff duties on dairy products, it was unwilling to increase the tariffs in violation of that agreement. Consequently, quotas were imposed to limit the dairy imports attracted by the relatively high domestic support prices. If imports had been permitted without further restraint, the cost of maintaining the dairy price supports would have increased, an outcome that Congress found unacceptable.

In the case of wheat, the support prices that exceeded world market prices severely limited exports and would have caused an unacceptably large increase in stocks owned by the government to maintain domestic market prices at the support level. As a result, the U.S. government resorted to export subsidies for wheat.

The general GATT principles were that both quantitative restrictions and subsidies, including export subsidies, were prohibited. Exceptions were made to these principles for agriculture, however, at the insistence of the United States (Johnson 1984). The exceptions included special treatment for quantitative restrictions on imports (import quotas) and for export subsidies.

The exception for quantitative restrictions for primary products was included in Article XI, paragraph 2. The article permitted the use of import restrictions on agricultural products "necessary to the enforcement of government measures," which operate to restrict the quantities of the domestic production of the product or to remove a temporary surplus of the product where the surplus is made available to domestic groups free or at below-market prices.

The following important guideline for the use of an import restriction other than a tariff was given:

> Moreover, any restrictions applied under (i) . . . shall not be such as will reduce the total of imports relative to the total of domestic production, as compared with the proportion which might reasonably be expected to rule between the two in the absence of the restrictions. In determining this proportion, the contracting party shall pay due regard to the

proportion prevailing during a previous representative period and to any special factors which may have affected or
may be affecting the trade in the product concerned.

What this guideline was intended to do was to say that if domestic
production were reduced by 10 percent, imports could also be reduced by 10 percent but by no more. And the general intention of
Article XI, paragraph 2, was that import quotas were to be used only
under specified conditions; when those specified conditions were not
met, import quotas or other quantitative restrictions were in violation
of GATT. The U.S. dairy program did not meet conditions imposed
by the restrictions; even with a relatively high price support, not the
slightest effort was made to restrict domestic production. Yet, at the
insistence of Congress, import quotas were imposed. In fact, in 1951
the United States was found to have violated Article XI because of its
import restrictions on dairy products. The United States was made
subject to retaliation provisions of Article XXXIII.

The Congress made known its unwillingness to have its actions
circumscribed by international agreement and subject to review by
an independent body. Instead of modifying programs to make them
consistent with GATT principles, Congress passed the infamous
Section 22, which was an amendment to the Agricultural Adjustment
Act of 1933. That section stated the following: "No trade agreement
or other international agreement heretofore or hereafter entered into
by the United States shall be applied in a manner inconsistent with
this section." The section required the president to impose quantitative restrictions or special fees in excess of regular tariff duties
whenever "any article or articles are being or are practically certain to
be imported into the United States under such conditions and in such
quantities as to render or to tend to render ineffective, or materially
interfere with" any U.S. farm program or "to reduce substantially the
amount of any product" subject to such a program (Dam 1970, 260–
61). After that amendment was passed, the United States imposed
import quotas on cotton, wheat, peanuts, oats, rye, barley, and
manufactured dairy products.

The sharp conflict between the requirements of Section 22 and
the requirements of Article XI caused the United States to ask for a
waiver of its obligations under that article in 1955. The waiver was
granted, without limit of time and without the necessity of justifying
the continuation of the waiver. This waiver was an enormous blow to
the effectiveness of GATT. Once the United States was relieved of any
necessity to abide by Article XI, hardly any country felt under
obligation to bring its farm programs in accord with it. So far as we

know, Canada is the only country that has consistently abided by the provisions of Article XI.

This was the first substantial weakening of the effectiveness of GATT in liberalizing trade in agricultural products. The second came three years later when the United States refused to endorse an absolute prohibition against export subsidies. When GATT was originally negotiated, export subsidies were permitted for primary products and for use under certain other designated purposes, but these exceptions were to end in 1958. Because a number of the U.S. farm programs relied on export subsidies to dispose of the difference between output and domestic consumption, however, the United States insisted that export subsidies continue to be permitted for agricultural products. Article XVI, which deals with such subsidies, was so loosely written that it has not been used to control or limit any agricultural export subsidy. Efforts to put some teeth into the article, such as those that followed the Tokyo Round, have been similarly ineffective.

These two actions by the United States can be held responsible for much of the current disarray in trade in agricultural products. Had these exceptions not been sanctioned and used by the United States freely and liberally over the years, the shape of the Common Agricultural Policy might have been very different. As a recent book on the CAP expressed it, "Ironically the Community's creation of the CAP in its current form, with its use of variable import levies and export refunds as its principal agricultural trade measures, was only possible as a result of earlier actions by, principally, the USA" (Harris, Swinbank, and Wilkinson 1983, 275). The authors made specific reference to the 1955 GATT waiver permitting the unrestricted use of import quotas and fees "to the extent necessary to prevent material interference with its domestic agricultural support programmes, so legitimizing the primacy of such programmes over international trade obligations."

It was then noted that when the United States refused to endorse an absolute prohibition against the use of export subsidies in 1958, the door opened to the extensive use of export subsidies by the EC "as a principal policy instrument."

It is a reasonable conclusion that the success of the Uruguay Round of GATT negotiations requires that the United States give up the waiver of its obligations under Article XI and that Section 22 be repealed or substantially modified. In its October 1989 proposal, the United States made explicit what was only implicit in its first proposal, that all waivers "that allow derogations from existing GATT rules for import access be limited." Similarly, export subsidies must either be prohibited or made subject to negotiations in a manner similar to negotiations on tariff duties.

## The First Round of Proposals

The first set of proposals for implementing agricultural policy and trade reform was submitted July 1987 through February 1988 by the United States, the EC, Japan, Canada, the Cairns Group (thirteen exporters of agricultural products), and the Nordic countries. An important aspect of the current negotiation is that several of the developing-country exporters have combined with Australia, Canada, and New Zealand to formulate a position favoring substantial reform of agricultural policies and of liberalization of trade in farm products.

A summary of the first set of proposals is now of historical interest only since a second round of proposals was tabled from October through December 1989. But in this case, history is of some importance since a comparison of the two sets of proposals indicates both where there had been shifts of position and where there had been little or no movement. Direct comparisons between the contents of the two sets of proposals are complicated by some differences in what the proposals had been requested to cover. The second set of proposals was guided by the Mid-Term Agreement for agriculture by the Trade Negotiation Committee in April 1989, with an emphasis on a long-term agricultural reform program and a timetable for implementation. The long-term objective was to achieve progressive reductions in agricultural support and protection, to correct and prevent restrictions and distortions in world agricultural markets. There was agreement that the proposals should consider ways of strengthening and making more effective GATT rules and disciplines. Negotiations should include all measures that directly or indirectly affect import access and export competition.

In spite of the differences in the coverage of the proposals, though, it is not difficult to discern the movement achieved between late 1987 and late 1989. A brief summary of the first set of proposals is presented in appendix 10A.

## The Second Round of Proposals

We include summaries of four of the second round of proposals in appendix 10B. The Nordic countries submitted a second proposal, and Switzerland and Austria also submitted proposals in response to the mid-term review. As noted earlier, the format of the summaries of the second proposals differs from the first.

236

A few words may help explain the summaries. The U.S. proposal emphasizes the replacement of all quantitative restrictions on imports, including variable levies, by tariffs—a proposal called "tariffication." At the beginning, the tariffs would be set at the difference between domestic and world prices that existed during 1986–1988. The tariffs would be gradually reduced over a decade to the final bound rates arrived at in the negotiations. The summary of the EC proposal includes a reference to SMU, that is, for the support measurement unit. It is a measure similar to the producer subsidy equivalent but excludes certain subsidies or transfers that do not have a significant impact on production decisions made by farmers. The Cairns proposal refers to a similar measure of protection, the aggregate measure of support (AMS).

The two summaries indicate that there have been compromises, especially by the United States and to a lesser degree by the EC. In its first proposal, the United States stated its objective as the elimination of all subsidies to agriculture that adversely affected production, consumption, and trade; this was essentially a free trade position. Many said this objective was unrealistic and, probably, one that the United States could not actually implement. In the second proposal, the aim is to "guide agricultural production and trade toward a market-oriented system governed by strengthened and more operationally effective GATT rules and disciplines and to integrate agriculture fully into the GATT." The second proposal spells out something on which the first proposal was silent, namely the U.S. waiver from Article XI of GATT and, in fact, calls for the elimination of Article XI(c). The movement on the part of the EC is perhaps more in the tone than in the substance. The SMU was to apply to a wider range of commodities than before. While condemning the concept of tariffication at one point, the proposal then indicates that the community is "prepared to include elements of tariffication." This concession was an apparent recognition that rigid import barriers need to be changed, at least in some cases, into transparent border measures—tariffs—and that the tariffs are subject to downward adjustment in the negotiations.

The Cairns Group probably made the fewest changes in its first proposal, partly because that proposal represented something of a middle ground between the position of the United States and the position of the EC, albeit closer to the general principles espoused by the United States. But the Cairns Group, while calling for substantial reductions in agricultural subsidies and border protection, did not call for zero protection as did the first U.S. proposal. In its first proposal, it called for banning all nontariff barriers, variable levies, and minimum import prices "not explicitly allowed in GATT." It maintained the same position in the second proposal, and the U.S. position is similar.

Japan moved some distance toward more liberal trade but not very much. In both proposals, Japan gave major emphasis to self-sufficiency in basic foodstuffs and argued that a country has the right to use domestic subsidies and border protection to achieve it. Unfortunately, Japan did not present any evidence that self-sufficiency would provide a significant degree of food security when it imports almost all its energy.

### Breakdown of Negotiations, December 1990

The Uruguay Round was scheduled to be completed by the end of 1990. Even with significant success in many areas of the negotiations, however, the failure to reach agreement on agriculture resulted in what seemed at the time an unsuccessful end of the negotiations. Numerous countries, including the Cairns Group and the United States, had threatened that if an acceptable agreement on agriculture could not be achieved, they would not approve any agreements in other areas. In contrast to prior negotiations, the United States carried out its statement that successful trade negotiation depended on successful negotiation on agriculture.

After nearly two years of limited movement in the agricultural negotiations, a mid-term review was held in Montreal in December 1988. As was true of much of the history of the negotiations, fundamental disagreements between the EC and the United States delayed achieving a mid-term agreement until April 1989. The agreement called for the participants in the negotiation to submit detailed proposals for achieving the long-term objective of "substantial, progressive reduction in agricultural support and protection" by December 1989. The detailed proposals were to cover the following areas:

- the terms and use of an aggregate measure of support
- strengthening and making more operationally effective GATT rules
- tariffication, decoupled income support, and other ways to reduce the trade-distorting effects of support and protection
- sanitary and phytosanitary regulations to minimize their use as trade protection

The proposals summarized in appendix 10B were made in response to the mid-term agreement. Wide disagreements are obvious on major issues, generally between the EC and Japan, on the one hand, and the United States and the Cairns Group, on the other hand.

The most critical difference between the U.S. and EC proposals, however, was the magnitude of the long-run reductions in protection. In a proposal made in October 1990, the United States called for a 90 percent reduction in export subsidies and a 75 percent reduction in import barriers and internal support over a ten-year period beginning in 1991. This proposal was intended to move the negotiations ahead by making it clear that the United States was not proposing elimination of all border measures or internal support.

The EC was either unable or unwilling to indicate what reductions in protection it was willing to offer until very nearly the zero hour. The EC submitted a proposal on agriculture on November 7, 1990, offering a 30 percent reduction in internal support for cereals, rice, sugar, oilseeds, livestock, and dairy products and a 10 percent reduction for other products, such as fruits, vegetables, and tobacco. These reductions were to be made over a ten-year period retroactive to 1986. The proposal went some distance, though far from the whole distance, in accepting tariffication in place of variable levies. The United States and the Cairns Group had proposed that all border measures be converted into tariffs; if this were done, then domestic prices and incentives would respond to changes in world market prices. If border protection comes from variable levies or import quotas, domestic prices are insulated from changes in world demand and supply. But the proposal was perhaps less forthright than it seemed. The tariffs were to consist of a fixed and a *variable* component. The variable component would represent a "corrective factor" that would take into account world market price fluctuations and exchange rate changes. Thus, the EC still clung to the view that it was appropriate and acceptable that EC farm prices should remain largely independent of world market prices.

What level of protection would have remained had the EC proposal been accepted? Even if one assumes that the 30 percent reduction applied to all farm products, which was not the case, the reduction was to be made from the 1986 levels. According to recent OECD estimates (1990, 177) the producer subsidy equivalent for the EC was 50 percent in 1986. A 30 percent reduction would be to a PSE of 35 percent; this is what it averaged for 1979–1985.

Some may have the impression that a PSE of 35 percent is not a particularly high rate of protection. But the PSE is not comparable to nominal protection, even when the only form of protection is a high support price. The measure of nominal protection is the percentage excess of domestic prices (or producer returns if there are deficiency payments) over border prices; the PSE is the percentage of total producer returns due to policy transfers. Consequently, a PSE of 50 percent means that half of producer returns result from policy protection. If the only policy transfers were through price supports or deficiency payments, the nominal rate of protection would be 100 percent—domestic prices or returns would be exactly double world market prices. A PSE of 35 percent is equivalent to a nominal protection rate of 54 percent. Thus it probably should have been expected that those looking for a significant improvement in market access would react skeptically to a proposal that set a tariff of 54 percent as its objective. The skepticism was likely enhanced by the inclusion in that tariff of a variable or corrective component that would change with world market prices and exchange rates.

## Reform Proposals

The domestic price and income support programs of the industrial economies adversely affect international trade in agricultural products because many, if not most, of the income transfers are tied to current production levels. In most cases, to maximize their incomes from production, including the incentives provided by the support programs, farmers increase their output beyond what they would produce if their only production incentive were either the current world market price *or* what the world market price would be if there were free or liberal trade in farm products. As long as such incentives are provided, governments have no choice but to intervene in agricultural markets and engage in various trade-disruptive devices, such as quantitative restrictions on imports or export subsidies. The subsidies need not be direct export subsidies; the U.S. deficiency payments have a significant effect on exports through their influence on agricultural output.

Both the U.S. and the Cairns proposal submitted in late 1989 called for the actual or near elimination of all forms of internal support directly tied to production or prices or, to put it differently, have significant trade-distorting effects. Neither proposal called for the elimination of all farm subsidies. Each proposal called for direct payments *and* deficiency payments linked to production to be phased out or reduced to nominal levels. This was contrary to some politically inspired statements that implied that the two proposals called for the elimination of all income transfers to farmers.

The proposals permitted two general types of subsidies. One type would be subject to commitments and GATT discipline; the other would be permitted if it were agreed that the income support measure was "not linked to production or marketing." Support policies directly "tied to production or prices" were to be phased out as stated in the U.S. proposal of October 1989, but a year later it was proposed that the most trade-distorting measures should be reduced by 75 percent over ten years, while less distorting measures should be reduced by 30 percent.

The Cairns and the U.S. 1989 proposals called for the elimination of quantitative import restrictions with their replacement by tariffs. Since many of the quantitative restrictions have been used to maintain large differentials between domestic and international prices, it was proposed that during the transition period tariff quotas would be established. At the beginning of the transition period, a tariff rate would be determined that equaled the difference between the average domestic and import prices for some base period such as 1986–1988. This tariff would be accompanied by a tariff quota, which would guarantee that at least as much would be imported as in a recent period or a minimum negotiated level of imports where the quota had been prohibitive. The tariff for imports within the quota would be at the bound rate that would prevail at the end of the transition period. Liberalization of import access would occur as a result of a progressive annual reduction of the over-quota tariffs to the final bound rates and the expansion of the initial tariff quotas by agreed minimum amounts. At the end of the decade, any remaining tariff quotas would be eliminated, and the final bound tariffs would be the only form of border protection.

The EC and Japan find this approach unpalatable. Both have attempted to provide a high degree of price stability for their farmers. A tariff, whether fixed or ad valorem, does not provide that stability. Any variation in international market prices is immediately transmitted to the domestic market. Their reluctance to consider this approach fails to take into account that much of the current instability of international market prices is the result of their farm support policies and similar policies in other countries. As indicated in chapter 11, international market prices would be much more stable with liberalization than is now the case. Moreover, the form of protection has a major effect on instability of prices in international markets. To a considerable degree, domestic price stability is obtained *at the cost* of international price stability. If the only form of agricultural protection were tariffs, even if the degree of protection were quite substantial, the international prices would be almost as stable as under free trade.

At the conclusion of the discussion of the reform proposals, a few words about permitted subsidies are in order. As noted, the permitted subsidies are those agreed to have no trade-distorting

241

effects because such payments are not related to current production. Examples of such subsidies include those for conservation and environmental protection, removing land from production, general public services (including research and extension), and domestic food aid. The purist can well argue that there is no such thing as a subsidy without trade-distorting effects. If the subsidy is large enough, additional resources can and have increased productivity of agricultural resources; payments for environmental protection could offset the adverse effects on production of limits on fertilizer or insecticide use. But these difficulties are not a valid argument for rejecting these aspects of the Cairns and U.S. proposals. It is a matter of degree. The trade-distorting effects, per dollar transferred, of the general category of permitted subsidies would be but a tiny fraction of the trade distortion from high price supports or deficiency payments tied to production.

Implicit in the U.S. proposal is an assumption that by "decoupling" its subsidies, it could obtain agreement for a significant continuing transfer of funds to farmers. These are the subsidies subject to discipline, presumably requiring that their trade-distorting effects be minimal. Decoupling, of course, refers to removing the connection between the subsidy and the current production activities. An example of a decoupled subsidy would be an annual payment per hectare of agricultural land; the payment would be independent of what use was made of the land or if no use were made of it. Or the payment could be made per unit of output produced in some past period with a prohibition against updating the base period.

Since over the past few years the United States has been gradually moving toward decoupled subsidies, it is perhaps not unreasonable that others do not consider the U.S. proposal on permitted or disciplined subsidies to be entirely without self-interest. It is obvious to all that for some time the United States has relied on direct payments to farmers to a much greater extent than any other major industrial nation. Most permitted or disciplined policies would require direct payments; they certainly cannot be financed by higher product prices. The European Community has been reluctant to rely on direct payments from the treasury rather than imposing the costs of farm support on the consumers. And many EC farmers are probably leary of receiving most of their income transfers in so open and politically vulnerable a manner.

## Could the United States Deliver on Its Proposal?

Skeptics in Europe and perhaps elsewhere have questioned the capacity of the U.S. administration to obtain approval for an agreement that eliminated almost all trade-distorting agricultural subsidies. A cynic might have responded that the EC could easily have tested this skeptical view by negotiating a substantial degree of liberalization and then seeing if the U.S. administration could deliver. If it could not, then the EC would be off the hook, so to speak. The negotiated liberalization would not be effected, and the EC could continue as it wished. But apparently the risk involved in this strategy was greater than the EC could accept.

In the United States, a trade agreement must be submitted to the Congress; thus a negotiated agreement can be rejected. But under the authority given to the president during the Uruguay Round, Congress could not amend or change a negotiated agreement. Its only authority would have been to reject the agreement, and both the House and the Senate would have to do so. This process is called the "fast-track procedure," presumably because if Congress could amend such an agreement, it would take years to complete.

When the negotiations in the Uruguay Round were started, the fast-track authority was granted for a period of four years. Because of the difficulties of reaching agreement on agriculture as well as on other matters, the authority expired in 1991 and was extended until mid-1993. The fast-track authority is essential for participation by the United States in trade negotiations. The United States is the only participant in GATT negotiations whose negotiators cannot bind its government to the agreement that is reached. Quite correctly, other countries would refuse to negotiate with the United States if the Congress could rewrite the agreement and thus force a reconsideration of the agreement.

There are those who have doubted that the United States could back up its proposals, assuming they became a part of the final agreement, and obtain congressional acceptance of an agreement that resulted in substantial reductions in agricultural protection. The two recent agricultural acts (1985 and 1990) have made significant progress toward less trade-distorting subsidies. While much more needs to be done, the freezing of crop yields used to determine deficiency payments and the 0–92 provision that allows farmers to obtain up to 92 percent of the deficiency payments they would otherwise be entitled to even if nothing were planted on their base acres constitute significant decoupling. A further step is to freeze the acreage bases so that farmers cannot respond to the subsidies by expanding their base acres; this is less important than freezing yields but still must be done if the decoupling is complete.

The 1985 farm bill reduced the nominal target prices for grains and cotton by 9 or 10 percent between 1986 and 1990; the real or inflation-adjusted reduction was 23 percent. The 1990 farm bill did not call for further reductions in the target prices for 1991–1995. This failure was the result of anticipating that efforts to limit the federal budget deficit would require reducing the costs of farm programs, and the supporters of the legislation did not believe that anticipatory reductions in cost would be reciprocated by an equivalent exemption from the budget cutting ax. Cost reductions were imposed; the estimated annual cost of $10.8 billion was reduced to $8.2 billion by several measures, but the most important was to reduce the acreage used in calculating deficiency payments by 15 percent. If deficiency payments were 40 percent of the target price, the reduction in payment acreage has the same effect as a 6 percent reduction in the nominal target price. If the general rate of inflation continues at about 4 percent annually, the reduction in real target prices will be a further 22 percent.

How much the further reduction in target prices would be reflected in a reduction in protection would depend on the trend in real international market prices. If these prices were approximately constant in real terms, then there would be a significant reduction in protection. Even if the long-run trend of a 1 percent annual decline occurred, there would still be a significant reduction in protection.

## What Are the Prospects?

It seems idle to speculate about the prospects for a successful conclusion for the agricultural negotiations. It is obvious that neither the EC nor Japan will modify its agricultural policies significantly to gain the advantages of achieving greater efficiency in obtaining a food supply. The political realities point to continued obeisance to the farm sectors, not just the farmers but the many firms and organizations with a stake in a large farm population and a high farm output.

What may have much greater weight is the realization that no agreements are possible without a successful conclusion to the agricultural negotiations. Some important Europeans may have thought the United States would blink, as it had in the past, and accept gains in other areas rather than let everything fall with agriculture. It should now be evident that the United States and the Cairns Group mean what they have been saying.

There may also be some concern that if the Uruguay Round fails, the whole GATT process will gradually be dismantled and that much of the progress in trade liberalization achieved over the past four decades will be lost. What will replace GATT? Probably bilateralism with increased threats to retaliate unless countries take desired actions. Disturbing also to the Europeans could be the creation of new regional trading blocs. They are in the process of gaining the full advantages of free trade in both services and trade, while retaining a degree of protection in certain sensitive areas, such as automobiles and some electronics. While by itself the North American free trade area would not constitute much of a threat to Europe's trade, a Pacific free trade area would be a matter of great concern.

Whether these possible outcomes are of sufficient concern to induce the compromises required to obtain an agreement on agricultural trade liberalization can be determined only as time passes.

### References

Dam, Kenneth W. *The GATT: Law and International Economic Organization.* Chicago: University of Chicago Press, 1970.

Harris, Simon, Alan Swinbank, and Guy Wilkinson. *The Food and Farm Policies of the European Community.* New York: John Wiley & Sons, 1983.

Johnson, D. Gale. "Domestic Agricultural Policy in an International Environment: Effects of Other Countries' Policies on the United States." *American Journal of Agricultural Economics* 66 (1984).

OECD. *Agricultural Policies, Markets and Trade: Monitoring and Outlook 1990.* Paris: OECD, 1990.

**Appendix 10A: A Comparison of GATT Proposals on Agricultural Trade for Several Countries and Groups, 1987–1988**

| Country or Group | Objective | Short-Term Measures | Long-Term Measures | Provisions for Developing Countries |
|---|---|---|---|---|
| United States (July 1987) | Complete elimination of policies or subsidies that adversely affect production, consumption, and trade of agricultural products for all commodities in all countries | None | Subsidies to be phased out over 10 years, except decoupled payments and bona fide food aid<br><br>Harmonize food and sanitary safety regulations to minimize trade effects<br><br>Use a standardized measure of government support afforded agricultural producers, such as the PSE, for negotiating commitments | Elaboration on U.S. proposal provides for special and differential treatment of developing countries according to economic or agricultural development. Subsidies are to be noncommodity specific for economic development. Bound tariffs to be used in lieu of import restrictions. |
| European Community (October 1987) | Reduction of policies that affect trade in key countries for all major commodities | Stabilize world markets for grains, sugar, and dairy using market-sharing agreements. Freeze | Reduce total support measures while maintaining market shares using request and offer approach | Special and differential treatment of developing countries allowed, based on needs |

| Cairns Group[a] (October 1987) | Elimination of policies affecting trade for all commodities in all countries | Freeze all access barriers, trade-affecting subsidies, and sanitary and food safety regulations operating as nontariff trade | support for grains, rice, dairy, sugar, beef, and veal at 1984 levels | CAP principles not negotiable | Longer adjustment periods for developing countries |
|---|---|---|---|---|---|
| | | | | International harmonization of sanitary and food safety regulations | |
| | | | | Improve GATT rules and principles to ensure continuation of negotiation process | |
| | | | | Use PSE or similar measurement adjusted for production control measures and world price and exchange rate fluctuations | |
| | | | | Ban all nontariff barriers, variable levies, minimum import prices, and other measures not explicitly allowed in GATT | |

*(Table continues)*

247

**Appendix 10A** (continued)

| Country or Group | Objective | Short-Term Measures | Long-Term Measures | Provisions for Developing Countries |
|---|---|---|---|---|
| | | barriers. Immediate across-the-board cuts in trade-distorting production and export subsidies by an agreed percentage and a commitment to increase market access by a determined percentage. Credit to be given in an intermediate-term program for short-term actions | Bind tariffs at low levels or eliminate. Prohibit use of trade-affecting subsidies and government support measures except trade-neutral ones that assist domestic consumption, research, extension, inspection, grading, market information, and the like | |
| | | Intermediate-term: During a 10-year period, countries will reach set targets of reduced total support levels and comprehensively deal with trade-affecting | Harmonize sanitary and food safety measures and minimize adverse trade effects where harmonization is not possible | |
| | | | Use PSE-type measurement for negotiations | |

| | | | |
|---|---|---|---|
| Canada (December 1987) | Support Cairns Group proposal | policy measures across a wide range of commodities according to a negotiated schedule of specific and monitorable commitments | Eliminate all special treatment provisions currently in place in the GATT | Consideration given to developing countries as provided for in Uruguay Round Declaration |
| | | Freeze all access barriers, trade-distorting subsidies, and sanitary and food safety regulations operating as nontariff trade barriers | Use Trade Distortion Equivalent (TDE) instead of PSE as the negotiable measurement of government support | |
| | | | Subsidies included in TDE to be reduced 50% over 5 years | |
| | | | Harmonize sanitary and food safety regulations and minimize adverse trade effects | |
| Nordic Group[b] (December 1987) | Reduction in trade-distorting policies for all countries us- | Immediate reduction or elimination of export subsidies and | Use TDE (with 1982–86 average as baseline) to target reform | None |

(Table continues)

**Appendix 10A** (continued)

| Country or Group | Objective | Short-Term Measures | Long-Term Measures | Provisions for Developing Countries |
|---|---|---|---|---|
| | ing short-term measures | other supply management programs that affect trade | measures and monitor progress | |
| | | Strengthen GATT rules and negotiate measures to improve market access | Harmonize sanitary and food safety regulations and minimize adverse trade effects | |
| Japan (February 1988) | Reduction of trade distortions recognizing the food security needs of countries | Freeze export subsidies at current levels and agree on phase out | Continue traditional request-offer approach for negotiating tariffs. Improve market access rules and refine rules on | Consider needs of developing countries when implementing agreements |

use of variable levy and minimum import price systems. Reduce trade effects of other subsidies and improve competitive environment

PSE- or TDE-type measures not necessary

Harmonize sanitary and food safety regulations and minimize adverse effects

a. Argentina, Australia, Brazil, Canada, Chile, Colombia, Hungary, Indonesia, Malaysia, New Zealand, Philippines, Thailand, and Uruguay.
b. Finland, Iceland, Norway, and Sweden.
SOURCE: U.S. Department of Agriculture, *Agricultural Outlook*, December 1988, pp. 34–35.

**Appendix 10B: Long-Term, Comprehensive GATT Proposals on Agriculture by Various Countries and Groups, 1989**

| | United States | Cairns Group | Japan | European Community |
|---|---|---|---|---|
| Date | October 25, 1989 | November 27, 1989 | November 27, 1989 | December 20, 1989 |
| Objective | Proposals aim "to guide agricultural production and trade toward a market-oriented system governed by strengthened and more operationally effective GATT rules and disciplines and to integrate agriculture fully into the GATT." | Proposals aim at "the establishment of a fair and market-oriented agricultural trading system"; "Aims at the full integration of trade in agricultural products into the generally applicable provisions with the GATT system." | Proposals aim "for substantial and progressive reductions in agricultural support and protection"; yet "full consideration should be given to the special nature of agriculture which is constrained by land and climatic conditions, and to the multifarious roles played by agriculture, such as food security." | Proposals aim "to reduce progressively support and protection to the extent necessary to re-establish balanced markets and a more market-oriented agricultural trading system." |
| Product coverage | All agricultural and fisheries products (HS chapters 1–23 and selected other | Product coverage would be left to the negotiations but should not prejudice | Major agricultural products having a certain volume of international trade | Cereals, rice, sugar, oilseeds, milk, beef and veal, pigmeat, eggs, and poultry |

| | | | | |
|---|---|---|---|---|
| | items including hides and skins, wool, and cotton) would be covered. | the objectives in the tropical products negotiations. | should be covered. Because of the substitutable nature of products, however, supports a product-sector approach rather than a product-by-product approach. | meat are priority commodities. Others should be included. Processed agricultural products should also be covered. |
| Import access | All waivers and derogations, protocols of accession, and grandfather clauses that allow derogations to existing GATT rules for import access would be eliminated. Variable import levies, voluntary restraint agreements, minimum import prices, and other import barriers not ex- | A prohibition would be placed on the introduction or continued use of all measures not explicitly provided for in the GATT, including nontariff barriers and other measures such as variable import levies and minimum import prices. All provisions for exceptional treatment would be eliminated | Proposals call for maintaining countries' right to use subsidies to support certain level (undefined) of self-sufficiency in "basic foodstuffs" for food security considerations. Proposals allow countries to use both domestic subsidies and market access barrier for food se- | Proposals caution that negotiations based in the main on frontier measures would inevitably lead to unbalanced and unacceptable results. Tariffication is not a viable alternative to present policies and would lead to a resurgence of the intervention of public authorities in the op- |

*(Table continues)*

**Appendix 10B** (continued)

| United States | Cairns Group | Japan | European Community |
|---|---|---|---|
| plicitly provided for in the GATT would be prohibited. | whether maintained under waivers, protocols of accession, or other derogations and exceptions. | curity considerations. | eration of agricultural markets. |
| GATT Article XI, 2(c) would be eliminated. | All tariffs on agricultural products would be bound at low levels or zero. | A "basic foodstuff" is a product that is a major source of nutrition to the nationals and is an important part of their daily calorie intake. | Proposals suggest an approach using an AMS/SMU for both support and protection to not isolate using one method for support policies and another on protection policies. |
| All tariffs would be bound on January 1, 1991, and then reduced over a 10-year transition period. | Phased elimination of voluntary restraint arrangements, consistent with the Punta del Este rollback commitment, would take place. | Contracting parties must notify GATT of the measures taken when applying or adjusting border measures and, upon request, discuss such measures with other contracting parties. | Proposals state the EC is prepared to include elements of tariffication. |
| Nontariff barriers would be replaced with a tariff-rate quota system on January 1, 1991, with their eventual removal at the end of the 10-year transition period. | Tariffs would be reduced by a formula approach supplemented with a request-offer process. | Except for bona fide food aid, the surpluses of basic foodstuffs concerned shall not be exported. | Border protection would be transformed into a fixed component and a variable component.

The fixed component would be reduced the same percentage as the SMU, and the variable |
| | A conversion of nontariff measures into tariffs accompanied by the progressive | | |

254

| | | | | |
|---|---|---|---|---|
| | | expansion of tariff quota levels when used as a transition mechanism is favored.<br><br>No explicit mention is made of GATT Article XI, 2(c). | GATT disciplines on variable levies and minimum import prices should be clearly stipulated.<br><br>A working group of should be established to review and clarify GATT Article XI, 2(c), specifically as it defines *government measures, production restriction, like product,* and *perishability.* | component would act as a corrective factor that would compensate for exchange rate and world market price fluctuations.<br><br>Article XI, 2(c) would be retained and modified. |
| Export competition | Current list of prohibited subsidies in the Subsidies Code to agriculture would be applied.<br><br>Proposal sets out a 5-year phase-out period for export subsidies.<br><br>Bona fide food aid would be exempt | Proposals prohibit new export subsidies and phases out existing ones.<br><br>All food aid should be provided on a grant basis.<br><br>Proposals suggest amending GATT Article XVI and the relevant GATT codes. | Export subsidies should be progressively reduced and eventually eliminated.<br><br>Proposals call for amending GATT Article XVI and the Subsidies Code to reflect elimination of export subsidies. | Commitments on export subsidies would be included in commitments on the SMU.<br><br>The amount granted to exports could not exceed that levied on imports. |

*(Table continues)*

**Appendix 10B** (continued)

| | United States | Cairns Group | Japan | European Community |
|---|---|---|---|---|
| Export restrictions and prohibitions | from prohibition.<br><br>GATT Article XI, 2(a), would be removed.<br><br>Differential export taxes would be progressively reduced and eliminated. | Group is prepared to negotiate.<br><br>Measures applied consistently with GATT Article XX, should not suffer prejudice. | GATT Article XI, 2(a) should be reviewed to provide a "clearer definition" of the term *critical shortage*. | No explicit mention is made in proposal. |
| Internal support | Proposes a three-tiered approach.<br><br>Policies to be phased out (those directly tied to production or prices) over the transition period.<br><br>Policies to be strengthened through GATT rules and disciplines (generally available input and investment subsidies, all other not specified in the other two categories). | For commodities for which an AMS can be calculated, target reductions would be agreed to with annual commodity-specific cuts in produce support prices and an AMS expressed in total value terms.<br><br>For commodities for which an AMS cannot be calculated, equivalent commitments would apply with cuts in pro- | Domestic support for agriculture should be clearly distinguished from export subsidies.<br><br>Domestic support policies with no trade-distorting effects or those for which such effects are negligible should be allowed.<br><br>Domestic subsidies, other than those permitted, should be included in commit- | Commitments on support policies would be included in commitments on the SMU.<br><br>Deficiency payments would be converted to tariffs and reduced. |

| | | | |
|---|---|---|---|
| | Proposals list permitted policies (income support policies not linked to production or marketing): Environment and conservation, disaster assistance, certain marketing programs, research and extension, and education.<br><br>Commitments on internal support would be implemented over a 10-year period.<br><br>Policies to be disciplined would be reduced on an AMS basis. | ducer support prices and budgetary expenditures.<br><br>Other forms of support that have a lesser impact on trade (input subsidies) would be subject to annual reductions in total budgetary expenditures.<br><br>Clearly defined rules and disciplines would be created on three policy categories: prohibited, permitted but subject to discipline, and permitted. | ments subject to reduction using an AMS.<br><br>Proposals call for establishment of a working group to examine how and by what standard distinction should be made between permissible policies and policies that should be subject to disciplines.<br><br>Specific commitments should be made on an AMS itself and not on specific policies. | |
| Sanitary and phytosanitary | Proposals provide for a mechanism for notification, consul- | Proposals would define more clearly, interpret, and modify | Proposals seek to achieve greater harmonization of sani- | Proposals seek agreement on a common interpretation |

(Table continues)

257

**Appendix 10B** (continued)

| United States | Cairns Group | Japan | European Community |
|---|---|---|---|
| tation, and dispute settlement that would ensure that measures taken to protect animal, plant, and human health are based on sound scientific evidence and recognize the principle of equivalency.<br><br>Proposal offers specific amendments to GATT Article XX(b) to be fully in effect in 1991. | Article XX to require sanitary and phytosanitary measures to be based on scientific evidence and recognize the principle of equivalency.<br><br>Consultations should begin immediately to draw up a list of topics for ad hoc negotiations concerning significant issues deriving from sanitary and phytosanitary regulations.<br><br>Agreed-upon methodologies for risk assessment should be developed. | tary and phytosanitary measures based on sound scientific evidence, secure transparency through improvement of notification procedures, and improve consultation and dispute settlement procedures.<br><br>Harmonized measures should be based on guidelines or standards examined and drawn up by international scientific organizations on the basis of sound scientific evidence. | of GATT rules in this area, to harmonize regulations and measures based on recognition of international standards and using suitable principles of equivalency.<br><br>Short-term implementation should focus on identifying sanitary and phytosanitary elements of international standards and suitable issues for ad hoc negotiations. |

| Special and differential treatment | Proposal urges criteria related to the level of agricultural and general development be taken into account.<br><br>Less-developed countries would be allowed to maintain agreed-upon final bound tariffs at moderate levels commensurate with a particular country's demonstrated need.<br><br>Less-developed countries would be allowed to maintain certain subsidies for the purpose of long-term agricultural development.<br><br>For products of priority interest to developing countries, | Measures that encourage agricultural and rural development in developing countries should not be subject to reduction commitments.<br><br>Proposals recommend longer time frames for implementation and completion of reform commitments.<br><br>The depths of cuts in barriers to imports for developing countries would be lower.<br><br>For products of priority interest to developing countries, accelerated reductions in barriers and internal support should be provided. | A longer time frame should be given to developing countries in achieving the objectives of the Uruguay Round.<br><br>Proposals allow for flexibility in fulfilling commitments in the reduction of support and protection for developing countries.<br><br>Proposals recognize the variety of stages of economic and social development among developing countries. | A degree of flexibility in the application of whatever rules will be adopted for the reduction of support and protection.<br><br>Flexibility would vary according to the actual level of development of the country concerned.<br><br>Flexibility could also be applied to the concerns of net food-importing countries. Possibly a limited number of products and the magnitude of reductions or longer time frames would be implemented. |
| --- | --- | --- | --- | --- |

*(Table continues)*

**Appendix 10B** (continued)

| United States | Cairns Group | Japan | European Community |
|---|---|---|---|
| accelerated reductions in barriers and internal support should be provided. | Commitments to reduce internal support in developing countries would not be required in the negotiations.<br><br>Concerns of the net food-importing countries and non-trade concerns should be taken into account. | | |

SOURCE: U.S. Department of Agriculture.

# 11
# Effects of Trade Liberalization on World Prices for Agricultural Products

*D. Gale Johnson*

Since World War II, negotiations on international trade within the structure of the General Agreement on Tariffs and Trade (GATT) have been very successful in reducing the barriers to trade in manufactured products. This success does not mean that free trade has been created or that significant sectors, such as textiles, do not still have important impediments to trade. In spite of the remaining barriers to trade, however, the world's exports of manufactured products have expanded at a much faster rate than the world's output of manufactured products.

Unfortunately, past GATT trade negotiations have not been successful in reducing the barriers to trade in agricultural products. Instead, the degree of protection of agriculture in the industrial market economies during the 1980s was substantially greater than in the 1950s. Consequently, world trade in agricultural products grew relatively slowly, at a rate only somewhat more than the growth of world production. But even that performance was due, at least in part, to the failures of the agricultural policies of the centrally planned economies and to the large-scale subsidization of exports by the European Community and the United States. Exports were subsidized because the high support prices encouraged greater agricultural output than domestic markets could absorb, and, in the case of the European Community for most farm products and in the United States for dairy products and sugar, high consumer prices discouraged consumption. As a result, exports from these countries were larger than they would have been with lower rates of protection.

Liberalization of trade in agricultural products would affect international market prices. The attractiveness of trade liberalization to farmers and their governments depends on the size of the international price effects that would result from either partial or full trade liberalization. The larger the increase in international market prices, the smaller would be the reductions that would have to occur in domestic prices as protection of domestic agriculture is reduced. The measures of protection are related to the difference between domestic returns and the international market prices for farm products. Increases in international market prices would require smaller reductions in prices and returns in the domestic market to meet a promised reduction in the degree of protection.

It is important that policy makers understand the major effects of liberalized trade in agricultural products. Individual countries are reluctant to liberalize unilaterally, since their exports and imports could then be affected by the protectionist devices of other countries. If a country significantly reduces its import barriers on a farm product, for example—in the absence of limitations on the export subsidies that could be paid to an exporter—imports could increase substantially and domestic prices could be doubly adversely affected: first by the direct effects of the reduction in protection, assuming that world prices were not affected, and second by an increase in export subsidies targeted for its market. This possibility explains why substantial reductions in protection of agriculture will occur primarily as a result of multilateral negotiations rather than by unilateral actions. Unilateral actions in response to domestic political circumstances, of course, can affect the degree of support provided to agriculture. Consumer resistance to high prices or taxpayer resistance to high budget costs may induce governments to permit price supports to fall in real (inflation-adjusted) prices by holding nominal prices constant or by letting them fall gradually. Such developments have occurred in a number of industrial countries since the mid-1980s in apparent response to the sharp increase in consumer and taxpayer costs in the early 1980s. This chapter, however, emphasizes the effects of multilateral reductions in the degrees of protection and not the probability of such reductions actually occurring or the nature of the forces that might induce such an outcome.

## Projecting Price and Trade Effects

Most major studies of the effects of trade liberalization have been partial equilibrium models. That is, they have looked at agriculture as a separable part of the economy—what happens to agricultural prices and incomes and to resource use has no effect on prices in the rest of the economy. The other approach, which has had much more limited application because of the required amount of data, is the general equilibrium approach. This approach considers agriculture an integral part of the economy and traces through the effects of changes in agricultural prices and incomes on prices, incomes, employment, and resource use in the rest of the economy. The general equilibrium approach considers the effects of trade liberalization on the exchange rate, while the partial equilibrium approach does not. The partial equilibrium studies provide estimates of the price effects of particular commodities; the general equilibrium studies emphasize the change in employment, foreign trade balance, and real national incomes as well as price changes.

The studies of price and trade effects require certain basic information for the commodities and countries included in the studies, such as the measure of protection for each commodity and country and the appropriate elasticities of supply and demand. If some countries are not included directly in the analysis, assumptions must be made concerning how their imports and exports would change in response to changes in international market prices. Generally, the centrally planned economies have not been included among the countries expected to liberalize their trade, but changes in their trade in response to changes in international prices are included.

The studies generally estimate the degree of protection for one period of time, either for a year or for the average of two or three years. The different studies have not used the same years for their base period; consequently, care must be taken in comparing the projected effects of the studies. Differences in price effects arise mainly as a consequence of the degree of protection in the base period. The rates of protection for temperate-zone products were much lower during the late 1970s and early 1980s than during the mid-1980s.

Studies may also differ somewhat in their assumptions of price elasticities of demand and supply. There does not exist a generally agreed-upon set of such estimates for each of the important countries, so that some difference in results may emerge due to differences in the elasticities. But the differences in elasticities appear to be a relatively small source of differences in outcomes. The major differences appear to stem from the different national protection levels in the various base periods used in the analyses. Fluctuations in international market prices rather than significant changes in domestic farm programs largely account for the differences in the estimates of protection. The great increase in measured protection between 1980–1982 and 1986 was caused by the decline in world prices rather than by any significant increase in domestic prices or other incentives for production. Similarly, the reduction in protection that took place between 1986 and 1989 was attributable to increases in world market prices. The increase in international market prices of the major grains (wheat, maize, and rice) between 1986 and 1989, for example, was from 22 to 52 percent, with rice having the largest increase.

## Protection Levels in the Industrial Market Economies

Our objective here is to place the studies of the effects of agricultural trade liberalization in historical perspective by providing data on the changes in the degree of protection of farm products since the mid-1950s. But before presenting any data, we should indicate how protection is measured. Several measures are now commonly cited, and it is necessary to use each with caution to prevent confusion.

The simplest measure of protection is called nominal protection. In its purest form, it represents the difference between the domestic price of farm products and the international price. If the product is imported, the appropriate international price is the import price with proper adjustment for quality to achieve comparability with the domestic production. If it is an export product, the international price would be the export price, again with care taken to ensure comparability of quality. Where the import price is used, it should be cost, insurance, and freight (CIF) or the actual price paid by the importer at the country's border. The export price should be the FOB (free on board) price at the major port or the actual price received by the exporter. As these definitions indicate, producers in a country that imports have a degree of what might be called natural protection— the import price is always higher than the export price for a product of the same quality.

As farm policies have become more complex with the introduction of direct or deficiency payments, the difference between the domestic and the international price may not fully reflect the excess returns to the producers. In the United States, for example, the domestic price of corn or wheat is at the world price, but farmers receive a deficiency payment that is the difference between a target price and the market price. Consequently, the deficiency payment represents the protective component. Geoff Miller of Australia has called his concept the "price adjustment gap" (Miller 1987), since it represents how much the returns per unit of output would have to be reduced to eliminate all the difference between what the domestic producer received and the appropriate international market price. We shall call this measure the nominal protection coefficient, however, with the understanding that not only the market prices but also any subsidy payments associated with output are included in the domestic returns compared with the international prices to determine the degrees of protection.

The Organization for Economic Cooperation and Development (OECD) has made extensive use of the producer subsidy equivalent (PSE), a measure first proposed by Timothy Josling (1975). It differs from the nominal protection coefficient or the price adjustment gap in two main ways. First, the PSE includes a wider range of subsidies or transfers to agriculture, and, second, it calculates the value of the transfers or subsidies as a percentage of the total adjusted income of the producer. The total adjusted income includes the government policy transfers to agriculture whether received directly by the producer or not. Policy transfers that are not a component of the return received by producers include the governmental cost of agricultural research and extension and transportation and marketing subsidies.

The method of calculation of the PSE gives a very different nominal figure from the nominal protection coefficient. A PSE of 50, for example, means that half the adjusted producer income came from government transfers. If the entire government policy transfer consisted of either a variable levy or tariff or a deficiency payment, the nominal protection coefficient would be 100 percent or exactly double the PSE measure of 50 percent. The PSE measure has a practical upper limit of 100 percent, which would be reached when the government policy transfers exactly equaled the adjusted producer return. This limit has been exceeded in Japan, where the PSE for barley in 1987 was 107 percent (Webb et al. 1990, 161).

Some have complained that the OECD has gone rather too far in attributing a wide range of subsidies to agriculture and that its PSE calculations have included subsidies that do not increase farm returns or have significant trade-distorting effects. Expenditures on research and extension do not go directly to farmers, and theory tells us that in the long run almost all the benefits go to consumers rather than to farmers as producers. Actually, the expenditures on research, extension, and inspection services make a very small contribution to total policy transfers. More important may be the use of budgetary expenditures as the measure of the amount of the policy transfers. In many if not most cases, administrative expenses absorb a significant part of the total budget. In addition, requirements imposed on the recipients may significantly reduce the amount of the actual benefit the farmers receive.

The European Community has proposed the concept of aggregate measure of support (AMS), which would include only those policy transfers that directly affect international trade. It is our view that a too-inclusive measure of subsidies could have undesirable consequences if the commitments made in the GATT negotiations are in terms of reductions in PSEs or AMSs, since governments could meet some of their commitments by eliminating expenditures on programs that may have significant social value but contribute little to farm income and thus have little or no trade-distorting effect.

This is a rather lengthy introduction to table 11–1, which presents estimates of nominal protection for 1956, 1965–1967, 1979–1981, and 1984–1986 for most of the industrial economies important in international trade in agricultural products. The first two columns list the percentage differences between prices received by farmers and the international price. The last two columns, which were derived from estimates of producer subsidy equivalents, have been adjusted to make the PSEs more comparable to nominal protection coefficients or, more accurately, the price adjustment gap, since direct payments to farmers have been included in the measure of protection.

The degree of protection has obviously increased significantly over time. It increased generally from the mid-1950s to the mid-1960s and had further increased substantially by the end of the 1970s. But the upward trend did not stop there, as evidenced by the last column with estimates for 1984–1986. Since 1986, agricultural protection has decreased somewhat but, except for New Zealand, remains at a level higher than in 1979–1981. New Zealand radically reformed its agricultural price and income policies, as well as most of its macroeconomic policies in 1984, and by 1987 its rate of nominal protection had declined to less than 8 percent. These changes were unilateral, making New Zealand one of most open agricultural economies in the world.

### Effects of Trade Liberalization

We have not undertaken a new or independent study of the effects of trade liberalization on international market prices for the major farm products. Instead, we will summarize the results of the existing major studies. As will be shown, when the studies assume similar rates of protection, the estimates of the effects on international market prices are quite comparable.

As table 11–1 shows, the estimated price effects of liberalization of agricultural trade would be smaller in a study that used the 1980 (or 1979–1981) protection rates than a study that used the protection levels of 1984–1986. And this, of course, is exactly how the results compare. The higher the rates of protection in the base period, the larger are the effects of trade liberalization on international market prices.

266

## TABLE 11–1

ESTIMATES OF NOMINAL PROTECTION OF AGRICULTURAL PRODUCTS IN
VARIOUS INDUSTRIAL COUNTRIES, SELECTED YEARS 1956–1986
(percent)

|  | 1956 | 1965–67 | 1979–81 | 1984–86 |
|---|---|---|---|---|
| Australia | n.a. | n.a. | 5 | 11 |
| New Zealand | n.a. | n.a. | 18 | 21 |
| United States | 2[a] | 8[b] | 19 | 36 |
| Canada | n.a. | n.a. | 25 | 54 |
| Austria | n.a. | n.a. | 57 | 68 |
| European Community | 16[c] | 52[c] | 60[d] | 64 |
| Denmark | 3 | 5 | n.a. | n.a. |
| Ireland | 4 | 3 | n.a. | n.a. |
| Netherlands | 5 | 37 | n.a. | n.a. |
| Belgium | 5 | 54 | n.a. | n.a. |
| Italy | 16 | 64 | n.a. | n.a. |
| France | 18 | 47 | n.a. | n.a. |
| West Germany | 22 | 54 | n.a. | n.a. |
| United Kingdom | 32 | 28 | n.a. | n.a. |
| Sweden | 27 | 54 | 128[e] | 79 |
| Japan | 42 | 76 | 143 | 277 |

n.a. = not available.
a. 1955.
b. 1965–1969.
c. EC-6.
d. EC-10.
e. Protection level is for the Nordic countries, which include Norway, Finland, Sweden, and Switzerland.
SOURCES: Gavin McCrone, *The Economics of Subsidizing Agriculture* (London: George Allen & Unwin, 1962), p. 51; Richard W. Howarth, *Agricultural Support in Western Europe* (London: The Institute of Economic Affairs, 1971), p. 29; and Eric Saxon and Kym Anderson, *Japanese Agricultural Protection in Historical Perspective*, Pacific Economic Papers, no. 92 (Canberra: Australian National University, 1982), p. 29. The McCrone and Howarth estimates have been adjusted to measure protection in terms of international prices instead of domestic prices. Masayoshi Honma and Yujiro Hayami, "Structure of Agricultural Protection in Industrial Countries," in Kym Anderson and Y. Hayami, *The Political Economy of Agricultural Protection* (London: Allen & Unwin, 1986) and OECD, *National Policies and Agricultural Trade*) (Paris: OECD, 1987), p. 134. The PSEs have been converted to nominal protection coefficient by dividing the PSE by 100-PSE and multiplying by 100. OECD, *Agricultural Policies, Markets and Trade: Monitoring and Outlook 1988* (Paris, OECD, 1988) and ibid, 1989. Economic Research Service, U.S. Department of Agriculture, *Estimates of Producer and Subsidy Equivalents: Government Interventions in Agriculture, 1982–86*. ERS Staff Dept. No. AGES 880127, April 1985.

The other important element that creates differential outcomes is the assumption concerning the countries that liberalize their trade in farm products. Generally speaking, the studies include the industrial market economies and also, in some cases, the developing market economies. To our knowledge, none of the studies have assumed that the centrally planned economies of Europe and Asia would liberalize. Where both the industrial market economies and the developing market economies are included, the international price effects of trade liberalization are smaller than when only the industrial market economies liberalize. The reason for this outcome is that the developing countries tend to tax agriculture and to subsidize one or more foods through price controls, subsidies, or an overvalued currency. The current policies of the developing countries result in less food production and more food consumption than what would occur under free trade. Thus, if the developing countries as a group liberalized their trade in farm products, international prices would be lowered somewhat compared with what would occur with a continuation of existing policies.

The studies of the effects of trade liberalization on international market prices differ in the base period uses. As noted above, the levels of protection of farm products in the industrial countries have varied over time. Magiera and Herlihy (1988) analyzed five different projections of the world price effects of trade liberalization to determine if the models were telling essentially the same story. The other studies analyzed were by OECD; by Rod Tyers and Kym Anderson in work undertaken for the World Bank using protection levels for 1980–1982 and projected levels for 1995, assuming that recent trends in protection persisted; and by the International Institute of Applied Systems Analysis model, which projected prices and protection levels to the year 2000. The USDA model has the unromantic name Static World Policy Simulation Model, with the acronym SWOPSIM. SWOPSIM was used to duplicate each of the other four projections by using the base data on production, consumption, and trade and protection levels used in each of the studies. Various aspects of the results were compared, but our interest is in the comparability of the projections of world price effects when the base data and protection levels are made comparable.

Magiera and Herlihy (p. 1) concluded that for world prices, the models are telling us basically the same story. Differences in world price changes between the models can be explained primarily by differences in the protection levels used in the models. Differences in world price changes within each of the models are very similar and can be explained "by differences in protection levels between sectors, by base period data, and by an understanding of a few key commodity linkages."

Table 11–2 presents the Tyers and Anderson projections for conditions that prevailed in 1980–1982 as well as for two later periods. As noted, in 1980–1982 rates of protection in the industrial market economies were relatively low, at least compared with rates during the rest of the 1980s. The price effects of free trade in the industrial market economies were projected to be relatively modest—with an average for the commodities included of 16 percent. For rice the price increase attributable to free trade in the industrialized market economies was projected at 11 percent.

The results of increased protection are shown in the estimates of the price effects of trade liberalization for 1988–1990 and 1995. Before turning to the findings, we should note that the levels of protection for these two periods were based on projected rather than on actual rates. Moreover, the results for 1988–1990 are not comparable to those for either 1980–1982 or 1995. The 1980–1982 and the 1995 figures are long-run equilibrium results, assuming that the full effects of trade liberalization have occurred. The 1988–1990 estimates are the short-run effects of starting with a phased liberalization in 1988. The results of trade liberalization if only the United States liberalized occur because it is assumed that the U.S. accumulated stocks of major crop products would be released onto the market and the supply-management programs would be phased out. The effects of these two changes would have been to increase the free or available supply of major crops on the world markets significantly.

Because of the assumed increase in protection between 1980–1982 and 1995, the weighted average price effects of full liberalization by the industrial market economies in 1995 is projected to be nearly double the 1980–1982 effects—an increase of 30 percent in world market prices compared with 16 percent. The results for 1988–1990 indicate that the effects of trade liberalization during the first few years would be quite modest. The projected increase in the world market price of rice in 1995 was 18 percent. The largest increase would be for dairy products (95 percent), followed by ruminant meat (43 percent).

The projections of Roningen and Dixit of the U.S. Department of Agriculture are presented in table 11–3. They project the levels of protection and the demand and supply conditions as of 1986. Protection levels were high in 1986 for several crop products owing to the disposal of stocks by the United States following the 1985 farm bill. The international price of rice was significantly depressed by the U.S. action, and the projected increase in international rice prices reflects

## TABLE 11–2

### REAL INTERNATIONAL PRICE EFFECTS OF A PHASED LIBERALIZATION OF FOOD MARKETS IN INDUSTRIAL MARKET ECONOMIES, SELECTED YEARS, 1980–1995

(percent difference)

| Liberalization | Wheat | Coarse Grain | Rice | Ruminant Meat | Nonruminant Meat | Dairy Products | Sugar | Weighted Average |
|---|---|---|---|---|---|---|---|---|
| EC-12 | | | | | | | | |
| 1980–1982 | 6 | 5 | 3 | 22 | 4 | 33 | 8 | 11 |
| 1988–1990 | 23 | 6 | 7 | 18 | 4 | 29 | 6 | 15 |
| 1995 | 23 | 5 | 9 | 26 | 4 | 59 | 18 | 22 |
| EFTA | | | | | | | | |
| 1980–1982 | 1 | 1 | 1 | 3 | 0 | 6 | 0 | 1 |
| 1988–1990 | 1 | 0 | 0 | 3 | 0 | 6 | 1 | 1 |
| 1995 | 1 | 0 | 0 | 5 | 1 | 13 | 3 | 2 |

| | | | | | | | | |
|---|---|---|---|---|---|---|---|---|
| Japan | | | | | | | | |
| 1980–1982 | 1 | 1 | 6 | 5 | 4 | 11 | 2 | 3 |
| 1988–1990 | 1 | 1 | 6 | 6 | 5 | 15 | 2 | 4 |
| 1995 | 2 | 1 | 9 | 13 | 6 | 28 | 2 | 7 |
| United States | | | | | | | | |
| 1980–1982 | −18 | −4 | 0 | 3 | −1 | 28 | 3 | 4 |
| 1988–1990 | −10 | −10 | −13 | −2 | −4 | 3 | 0 | −10 |
| 1995 | 2 | −6 | −1 | 6 | −2 | 27 | 3 | 4 |
| All industrial market economies | | | | | | | | |
| 1980–1982 | 10 | 3 | 11 | 27 | 8 | 61 | 11 | 16 |
| 1988–1990 | −5 | −2 | 0 | 22 | 4 | 40 | 7 | 8 |
| 1995 | 25 | 3 | 18 | 43 | 10 | 95 | 22 | 30 |

NOTE: The results for 1980–1982 and 1995 are derived from a long-run equilibrium solution of the model, thereby not including transient dynamic effects, whereas the 1988–1990 results are from the dynamic version of the model so as to show the short-run effects of a phased liberalization beginning in 1988.

SOURCE: Rod Tyers and Kym Anderson, "Liberalizing OECD Agricultural Policies in the Uruguay Round: Effects on Trade and Welfare," *Journal of Agricultural Economics* 39 (May 1988).

TABLE 11–3

WORLD PRICE EFFECTS OF LIBERALIZATION ON VARIOUS COMMODITIES, 1986–1987

(percent)

| Commodity Group | Unilateral Liberalization | | | | | | | Multilateral Liberalization by Industrial Market Economies |
|---|---|---|---|---|---|---|---|---|
| | United States | Canada | EC | Other Western Europe | Japan | Australia | New Zealand | |
| Ruminant meat | 3.8 | 0.4 | 13.5 | 1.5 | 1.8 | 0.2 | 0.2 | 21.0 |
| Nonruminant meat | 3.0 | .5 | 5.8 | 1.0 | 2.3 | .1 | 0 | 12.4 |
| Dairy products | 23.5 | 4.1 | 31.6 | 6.2 | 4.5 | .7 | .5 | 65.3 |
| Wheat | 10.6 | 4.1 | 19.1 | 1.6 | 2.5 | 1.6 | 0 | 36.7 |
| Coarse grains | 11.6 | 2.2 | 11.5 | 1.5 | .6 | .2 | 0 | 26.3 |
| Rice | 2.9 | .4 | 3.2 | .2 | 19.6 | .2 | 0 | 26.2 |
| Oilseeds and products | −2.6 | .5 | 7.9 | .2 | .4 | 0 | 0 | 6.4 |
| Sugar | 22.8 | .4 | 18.6 | 3.3 | 6.4 | 1.1 | 0 | 52.7 |
| Other crops | 4.0 | 0 | 3.3 | .1 | .7 | −.1 | 0 | 7.7 |
| Aggregate | 5.9 | 1.2 | 10.6 | 1.4 | 3.6 | .3 | .1 | 22.0 |

NOTE: Unilateral liberalization means that each country removed its support while others maintained theirs. Multilateral liberalization means that all industrial market economies simultaneously removed their agricultural support.
SOURCE: Vernon O. Roningen and Praveen M. Dixit, *How Level Is the Playing Field? An Economic Analysis of Agricultural Policy Reforms in Industrial Market Economies.* Economic Research Service, USDA, Foreign Agricultural Economic Department no. 239, December 1989.

to some degree the distortion introduced by the change in U.S. policy for farm price supports.

Free trade in the industrial market economies was projected to increase average international market prices for the nine commodity groups by 19 percent. For rice, the projected increase was 24 percent. The largest increases were for dairy products (49.8 percent) and sugar (38.9 percent). The table also shows the projected effects of unilateral free trade on international market prices for seven countries or groups of countries. The projected increase in prices resulting from each country or group's unilaterally eliminating its trade barriers approximates the adverse effects of the agricultural trade policies of each country or region on international trade in farm products. The effects result from the degree of protection and the size of the economy. Consequently, while Japan has by far the highest rates of protection of agriculture, that protection has a smaller effect on international market prices than the policies followed by the United States or the European Community. The EC-12 accounts for about 45 percent of the total price effects, the United States for 27 percent, and Japan for 19 percent.

## Liberalization and Price Stability

We have considered the effects of trade liberalization or free trade on the international market. But another very important effect of trade liberalization is the reduction of price instability in international markets. Most governments follow policies designed to stabilize the prices received by their farmers. As a consequence of these policies, the variability of international market prices increases significantly (Johnson 1975). Governments generally stabilize the domestic prices by varying imports and exports; price stability achieved solely or primarily by storage becomes very expensive. Stabilizing prices by equating supply to demand at the established price causes increased instability in international markets for two reasons. First, all the domestic shocks, such as variations in production due to weather or disease or in demand due to the state of the domestic economy, are transmitted to the international market. Thus, if adverse weather causes a shortfall in production in a given country, by stabilizing prices to its producers and consumers, that country absorbs none of the consequences domestically, forcing the full adjustment on the international market. In other words, domestic consumers do not face higher prices with the production shortfall and thus do not reduce their consumption, nor do producers increase their inputs the following year because their price will not change under the price policy. If the crop is relatively large owing to weather, the effects are the opposite—consumption does not increase with greater availability, nor are farmers induced to adjust production in the subsequent year—and all the extra output is "dumped" on the world market, so to speak.

In addition, domestic price stabilization prevents the country from absorbing any of the shocks that affect supply and demand outside its own borders. Thus, if India and China have poor grain crops in a given year, consumers and producers in the European Community and Japan would not change either their consumption or their production in response to the higher world market prices. The reason is very simple: so far as Europe and Japan are concerned, prices have not changed. As a result, world market prices will rise much higher when India and China have poor crops, because all the response to the reduced production in terms of consumption adjustments must occur in countries of the world outside Japan and the EC. Similarly, there would be no production response in Japan or the EC in the subsequent year because of this year's shortfall in world grain production. The sharp increase in world grain prices in 1972–1973 happened primarily because of the price policies of governments and not because of production shortfalls.

Tyers and Anderson have estimated the effects of free trade on world price variability for farm products. Their results for 1980–1982 and 1995 are given in table 11–4. The data are the coefficients of variation of international market prices. The coefficient of variation is the standard deviation divided by the mean; thus it is a measure of the relative amount of variation. If the coefficient of variation is 0.30, in two years out of three the price will differ from the mean by 30 percent or more.

The first two lines of the table present the estimates of the variability of world market prices with the price policies of the industrial market economies as of 1980–1982 and for the projected levels of protection for 1995. The other lines provide projections of what the variability would have been in 1980–1982 if different countries or groups of countries had unilaterally liberalized their trade in agricultural products and if all the industrial market economies had done so together. In all cases, if any one of the industrial market economies alone liberalized or did so as a group, the variability of prices would have been reduced. The reduction in variability is greater when all the industrial market economies liberalize than if only one industrial economy does. In the case of rice, if only the industrial economies liberalize, the coefficient of variation declines by more than 25 percent. For the entire group of farm commodities, the

## TABLE 11–4
### Effects on International Price Instability of Liberalizing Food Markets in Industrial Market Economies, 1980–1982 and 1995
(coefficient of variation around trend levels)

| | Wheat | Coarse Grain | Rice | Ruminant Meat | Nonruminant Meat | Dairy Products | Sugar | Weighted Average[a] |
|---|---|---|---|---|---|---|---|---|
| 1980–1982 | .58 | .53 | .38 | .24 | .08 | .26 | .36 | .34 |
| 1995 | .76 | .68 | .39 | .31 | .10 | .22 | .32 | .40 |
| Coefficient in 1980–82 in the absence of domestic stabilization by | | | | | | | | |
| EC-12 | .39 | .45 | .32 | .15 | .08 | .13 | .28 | .26 |
| Japan | .54 | .51 | .33 | .09 | .07 | .18 | .33 | .28 |
| United States | .60 | .64 | .36 | .17 | .10 | .27 | .31 | .35 |
| All industrial market economies | .33 | .47 | .28 | .07 | .08 | .11 | .25 | .23 |

a. Based on weights derived from the shares of each commodity group's exports in total GLS exports.

SOURCE: Rod Tyers and Kym Anderson, "Liberalizing OECD Agricultural Policies in the Uruguay Round: Effects on Trade and Welfare," *Journal of Agricultural Economics* 39 (May 1988).

reduction in price variability through trade liberalization was projected to be more than 40 percent—a very substantial increase in price stability. Although the reduction in price variability is an important consequence of trade liberalization, governments ignore that effect. Perhaps reducing price variability undermines to some degree the basis for domestic price stabilization policies. Governments, especially those in the European Community and in Japan, justify such domestic programs on the grounds that international market prices are unstable. In this justification, they obviously ignore the fact that their domestic policies are an important source of price instability. The results in table 11–4, for example, indicate that if the EC-12 alone liberalized their agricultural markets, the decrease in world price instability would be from a coefficient of variation of 0.34 to 0.26, a reduction of almost 25 percent. If Japan alone liberalized, the reduction would be 18 percent.

Tyers and Anderson (1992, 226) have also estimated the effects on world price variability if both the developed and the less-developed countries liberalized trade in farm products. They projected for 1980–1982 a further substantial reduction in price variability. If both groups of countries liberalized their rice policies, for example, the coefficient of variability was projected to be 0.09 compared with 0.38 with current policies and 0.28 if only the developed countries liberalized. For both wheat and coarse grains, liberalization by the less-developed countries would have resulted in price variability reductions of half or more compared with liberalization by the developed countries alone.

## Costs and Benefits of Farm Price Programs

A generally neglected consequence of the farm price programs of an individual country or group of countries is that a substantial fraction of the consumer and taxpayer costs of each program is required to offset the negative effects on international market prices of the programs of other countries. In other words, the lower world market prices that result from trade interventions increase the cost of achieving a given level of gross income for farmers in a particular country. The fact that the general effect of national programs on world market prices is about 15 percent may seem quite modest. But an increase of this magnitude in world market prices would have provided an increase in the gross income from sales of farm products to the nonfarm economy of about $13 billion in 1988 in the United States. In that year, the total direct government payments to farmers was little more than that, namely $14.5 billion. Since all the direct government payments were paid to producers of crops, the distribution of the increase in income through higher market prices would be different from that of the government payments. Approximately a third of the income increase would go to producers of livestock products that do not have price supports or deficiency payments. But the main point of this example is that short-run effects of lowered world market prices are large relative to the increases in farm income resulting from the deficiency payments in the United States.

Tables 11–5 and 11–6 are modifications of tables developed by Roningen and Dixit (1989). Table 11–5 provides estimates of the producer benefits from the agricultural support programs (the first column) and the costs that these programs impose on consumers and taxpayers and the total costs (columns 2, 3, and 4, respectively). The last column indicates the percentage of the costs of the support program that actually results in benefits to producers. For all industrial market economies, only 71 percent of the transfer cost is received by producers. But this percentange is a clear overestimate of the increase in net incomes of farm operators. If some farm land is owned by individuals who do not operate farms, part of the transfer payment goes to such owners. If farm production and the purchased inputs increase as a result of the higher prices, some of the transfer is dissipated by such expenditures. But even if it is assumed that all the producer benefit constitutes an increase in net income, for each dollar received by farmers, consumers and taxpayers are charged $1.42.

Table 11–6 gives estimates of how much the agricultural support programs of individual nations or groups cost producers in other countries. The costs to other producers are based on the effects of a particular agricultural support program on world market prices. Of course, it may not be fully accurate to say that the adverse effects on a second country are borne by producers. More likely, most costs are in turn imposed on consumers and taxpayers, at least in the industrial market economies.

Consider the agricultural support program of the United States. As indicated in table 11–5, that program transferred $26.3 billion to farmers in 1986–1987. The effects of this transfer on producers in all the countries and regions to the right of the United States at the top of the table, however, were negative. The sum of the negative effects was $17.4 billion, of which $4.3 billion was imposed on producers in developing countries. In the case of Canada, the negative effect on producers in other countries was the same as the transfers to Canadian farmers—a negative $3.8 billion compared with a transfer of $3.7 billion.

The sum of the transfers to producers in the industrial market

# TABLE 11-5

## THE ANNUAL BENEFITS OF AGRICULTURAL SUPPORT TO PRODUCERS AND COSTS TO CONSUMERS AND TAXPAYERS IN INDUSTRIAL MARKET ECONOMIES, 1986–1987

### (billions of dollars)

| Country or Region | Producer Benefits | Consumer Costs | Taxpayer Costs | Total Costs[a] | Producer Share of Transfers (percent) |
|---|---|---|---|---|---|
| United States | 26.3 | 6.0 | 30.3 | 36.3 | 72 |
| Canada | 3.7 | 2.3 | 3.8 | 6.1 | 61 |
| EC | 33.3 | 32.6 | 15.6 | 48.2 | 69 |
| Other Western Europe | 8.8 | 4.3 | 6.3 | 10.6 | 82 |
| Japan | 22.6 | 27.7 | 5.7 | 33.4 | 68 |
| Australia | .6 | –.5 | 1.1 | 0.6 | 86 |
| New Zealand | .2 | –.2 | .5 | 0.3 | 96 |
| Industrial market economies | 95.4 | 72.4 | 63.1 | 135.5 | 71 |

NOTE: Estimates based on unilateral liberalization by the countries or regions.

a. Total cost is the sum of producer benefits (+), consumer costs (–), and taxpayers' costs (–), and includes transfers to other groups, for example, quota holders.

SOURCE: Vernon O. Roningen and Praveen M. Dixit, *How Level Is the Playing Field? An Economic Analysis of Agricultural Policy Reforms in Industrial Market Economies.* Economic Research Service, USDA, Foreign Agricultural Economics Department no. 239, December 1989.

TABLE 11–6

COSTS AND BENEFITS OF AGRICULTURAL SUPPORT TO PRODUCERS, 1986–1987

(billions of dollars)

| From Policies of Country or Region | United States | Canada | EC | Other Western Europe | Japan | Australia | New Zealand | Developing Exporters | Centrally Planned Economies | New Industrial Asia | Developing Importers | Total Costs to Others |
|---|---|---|---|---|---|---|---|---|---|---|---|---|
| U.S. | 26.3 | -0.7 | -7.2 | -0.8 | -0.5 | -0.6 | -0.5 | -1.1 | -2.7 | -0.1 | -3.2 | -17.4 |
| Canada | -.7 | 3.7 | -1.2 | -.2 | -.1 | -.1 | -.1 | -.2 | -.6 | 0 | -.6 | -3.8 |
| EC | -8.1 | -1.6 | 33.3 | -1.2 | -.8 | -1.2 | -1.1 | -2.4 | -4.9 | -.2 | -5.2 | -26.7 |
| Other Western Europe | -1.1 | -.2 | -1.7 | 8.8 | -.1 | -.1 | -.1 | -.3 | -.7 | 0 | -.6 | -4.8 |
| Japan | -1.2 | -.1 | -2.0 | -.2 | 22.6 | -.2 | -.1 | -1.3 | -1.9 | -.2 | -2.9 | -10.3 |
| Australia | -.2 | -.1 | -.3 | 0 | 0 | .6 | 0 | -.1 | -.1 | 0 | -.2 | -.9 |
| New Zealand | -.1 | 0 | -.1 | 0 | 0 | 0 | .2 | 0 | 0 | 0 | 0 | -.1 |
| Total[a] | -11.3 | -2.7 | -12.5 | -2.5 | -1.5 | -2.3 | -2.0 | -5.3 | -10.9 | -.5 | -12.6 | -64.0 |

NOTE: Benefits (+) of support defined as lost producer surplus from unilateral liberalization scenarios of countries or regions on left.

a. Total is the costs of others' policy.

SOURCE: Vernon O. Roningen and Praveen M. Dixit, *How Level is the Playing Field? An Economic Analysis of Agricultural Policy Reforms in Industrial Market Economies.* Economic Research Service, USDA, Foreign Agricultural Economics Department, no. 239, December 1989.

economies was estimated to be $95.4 billion; the negative effect on producers in countries or regions adversely affected by each agricultural support program was estimated at $64.0 billion. Consequently, the net transfer to producers through agricultural support measures was estimated at $31.5 billion—at a cost of $135.5 billion to consumers and taxpayers in the industrial market economies.

To complete the story, let us note that the agricultural support policies of the industrial countries do benefit consumers in developing countries and in the centrally planned economies by perhaps $30.5 billion. But these benefits only slightly exceed the losses to producers in the same countries.

The data in tables 11–5 and 11–6 make it very clear that a cooperative undertaking to increase prices received by farmers would impose far fewer costs on consumers and taxpayers. One form, and the preferred form, of that cooperative effort would be to agree to multilateral liberalization of agricultural trade and a staged reduction in the protection of agriculture.

## Conclusion

Studies of the effects of domestic farm price-and-income programs on world agricultural markets agree that these policies significantly depress world market prices. These effects vary from time to time, since the degree of protection has not remained constant. The studies show that if all the industrial market economies fully liberalized their trade in farm products, world market prices would increase by a significant percentage. If the developing countries also liberalized, the increase in world market prices would be even larger than if only the developed countries did so.

Thus, perhaps half to two-thirds of Taiwan's nominal protection coefficient of 33 percent for 1985–1987 reflects the degree to which world market prices have been depressed by national farm policies. In other words, if there were free trade in farm products, the increase in world market prices would mean that Taiwan's prices would be no more than 12 to 16 percent higher than the world prices.

The other important result from the studies is that the domestic farm policies of both industrial and developing economies have significantly increased the variability of world market prices. Trade liberalization would result in much more stable prices and greater food security for all nations in the world.

## References

Dam, Kenneth W. *The GATT: Law and International Economic Organization.* Chicago: University of Chicago Press, 1977.

Johnson, D. Gale. *World Food Problems and Prospects*. Washington, D.C.: American Enterprise Institute, 1975.

———. *World Agriculture in Disarray*. London: Macmillan & Co., 1991.

Josling, Timothy E. *Agriculture Protection and Stabilization Policies: A Framework of Measurement in the Concept of Agriculture Adjustment*. Rome: Food and Agriculture Organization, 1975.

Magiera, Steven L., and Michael T. Herlihy. "Comparing World Price Changes from Trade Liberalization Models." Paper prepared for the International Trade Research Consortium, "Bringing Agriculture into the GATT: Assessing Benefits of Trade Liberalization." Annapolis, Maryland, 1988.

Miller, Geoff. *The Political Economy of International Agricultural Policy Reform*. Canberra: Australian Government Publishing Service, 1987.

OECD. *Agricultural Policies, Markets and Trade: Monitoring and Outlook 1987*. Paris: OECD, 1987.

———. *Agricultural Policies, Markets and Trade: Monitoring and Outlook 1990*. Paris: OECD, 1990.

Roningen, Vernon O., and Praveen M. Dixit. *How Level Is the Playing Field? An Economic Analysis of Agricultural Policy Reforms in Industrial Market Economies*. Economic Research Service, USDA, 1989.

Tyers, Rod, and Kym Anderson. *Disarray in World Food Markets—A Quantitative Assessment*. Cambridge: Cambridge University Press, 1992.

Webb, Alan J., Michael Lopez, and Revata Penn. *Estimates of Producer and Consumer Subsidy Equivalents in Agriculture, 1982–87*. Economic Research Service, USDA, *Statistical Bulletin*, 1990.

# 12

# Modifications of Agricultural Policies Required by Freer Trade

*D. Gale Johnson, Chi-ming Hou, and Chaw-hsia Tu*

The United States was the principal author of the documents that became the General Agreement on Tariffs and Trade (GATT). One of the basic purposes of GATT was to codify the principles that defined liberal international trade. The principles are those of liberal trade regimes rather than of free trade. While the long-run objective of those who promulgated GATT may have been to achieve free trade, it was instituted to define the types of interventions at the border and in markets that are consistent with nondiscriminatory and relatively liberal international trade.

According to GATT principles, the only acceptable border measure is a tariff, tax, or duty. Quantitative restrictions, such as import quotas, were unacceptable, as were export subsidies. Quantitative restrictions were rejected because they prevent domestic markets from responding to changed supply and demand conditions in international markets and because allocating quotas among exporters is discriminatory behavior. Export subsidies were to be banned because they are used to increase exports and to gain world market share, not on the basis of low production costs but on the exercise of monopoly power if the subsidy is by a firm or on the intensity of political interest in expanding exports if the subsidy is by a government. Both quantitative import restrictions and export subsidies result in different and less efficient allocations of the world's resources than would prevail in their absence.

The full text of paragraph 1 of Article XI, which is entitled "General Elimination of Quantitative Restrictions," is:

> No prohibition or restrictions other than duties, taxes or other charges, whether made effective through quotas, import or export licenses or other measures, shall be instituted or maintained by any contracting party on the importation of any product of the territory of any other contracting party

or on the exportation or sale for export of any product destined for the territory of any other contracting party.

It is worth noting that Article XI also included a blanket proscription of prohibitions or restrictions on the exports of any product, though the proscription applies only to exports to other contracting parties, that is, other countries that are members of GATT.

Unfortunately, at the insistence of the United States, a paragraph was added to Article XI that provided for exceptions to the general principle opposing quantitative restrictions in the case of primary products. This paragraph, which was added very early, was designed to be consistent with the actual practice of U.S. farm programs in the late 1940s. At that time, some commodity programs required the use of quantitative import restraints, since the price supports exceeded the world market prices. Without the import restraints, given the commitment that the government had either to purchase or to provide a loan to the farmers on whatever amount of the commodity that could not be sold at the support price in the market, it would have been very costly to accept all the imports that would have been offered.

The exception governing quantitative restrictions on the importation of primary products was not intended to be universal or open ended. These restrictions were to be limited to three general cases, of which the first was by far of greatest practical significance:

- If there were a domestic program that limited the amount of a product that could be produced or marketed, a quantitative import restriction could be imposed, but the percentage reduction in imports could be no greater than the percentage reduction in domestic production or marketing.
- If there were a domestic program to remove a temporary surplus of a commodity by sale at a low price or by distribution free of charge, imports could be restricted by a quantitative measure.
- If an animal product is directly dependent on an imported product, then if the production of the animal product is limited, the amount of imports could be controlled.

In actuality, only the first of these exceptions has been important or, more accurately, potentially important. Except for Canada, no country has made a serious attempt to abide by the exceptions provided in Article XI. This statement does not mean that there has been little or no use of quantitative import restrictions. Quite the contrary: except for Canada, the countries that have made frequent and long-term use of import quotas or variable levies, which are similar to import quotas in effect, have not met the conditions described in the article.

The United States bears much—some might say all—of the responsibility for this state of affairs. In 1951, a complaint was lodged in GATT against the United States because it had import restrictions on dairy products but had not even a pretense of a restraint on domestic production. The United States lost that case, and the Netherlands was permitted to limit its imports of wheat flour to 60,000 tons per year (Dam 1970, 260).

The passage of Section 22 of the Agricultural Adjustment Act of 1933 made it, in effect, impossible for the United States with its farm commodity programs current at the time to abide by the terms of Article XI(c). The legislation required the administration to impose quantitative restrictions or added duties (above those agreed in international negotiations) whenever "any article or articles are being imported into the United States under such conditions and in such quantities as to render or tend to render ineffective, or materially interfere with" any U.S. farm program or "to reduce substantially the amount of any product" subject to such a farm program. Section 22 was to take precedence over any international agreement that had been signed by or was to be signed by the United States.

Section 22 required the administration to request a waiver of its obligations under Section XI. This waiver was granted in 1955, without limit on time and without any requirement that the United States justify its continuation. At the time the waiver was granted, the United States had import quotas on cotton, wheat, peanuts, oats, rye, barley, and manufactured dairy products that did not meet the conditions of Article XI. There were also import quotas on sugar, which were probably consistent with Article XI 2(c) at the time. The import quotas on sugar still exist and are no longer consistent with Article XI(c), since the United States does not limit the output of domestic sugar in any way. There remain, in addition to the import quotas on sugar, quotas on peanuts and manufactured dairy products, as well as legislative authority for import quotas on beef.

If there is to be a successful conclusion to the GATT negotiations on agricultural products, the United States must give up its 1955 waiver. Consequently, as a minimum, it must make its farm programs consistent with Article XI. As the domestic farm programs were constituted in 1993, the only ones that would require significant changes to comply with Article XI are the dairy, sugar, and peanut programs. The programs that rely on deficiency payments—grains and cotton—do not require quantitative restrictions on imports, since the domestic prices are at the world market levels. There is no price support program for beef, and thus the import quotas on beef could be removed without causing a conflict with a domestic price support program.

In the proposals that it made in 1989, the United States took the position that Article XI 2(c) should be eliminated from GATT, thus removing the right to use quantitative import restrictions under any circumstances. There is strong resistance to such action, especially by Canada and potentially by the European Community (EC), if the variable levy were defined as a quantitative import restriction.

### Export Subsidies

Article XVI of GATT states the general principle that export subsidies are unacceptable:

> From January 1, 1958, or the earliest practicable date there-after, contracting parties shall cease to grant either directly or indirectly any form of subsidy of any product . . . which subsidy results in the sale of such product for export at a price lower than the comparable price charged for the like product to buyers in the domestic market.

As originally written, the words quoted were to apply to all products. Unfortunately, since the United States was paying export subsidies on wheat, cotton, and dairy products at the time, it insisted that the clause "other than a primary product" be inserted between "any product" and "which subsidy results." Subsequently, this unwillingness to modify its domestic farm programs so that export subsidies were not required turned into an enormous blunder, since without the acceptance of export subsidies for primary products, the Common Agricultural Policy of the European Community could not have taken its present form with its heavy reliance on export subsidies.

The United States continued to use export subsidies until 1973 and then abandoned them until 1985, when a combination of a high foreign exchange value of the dollar and high price supports resulted in a substantial decline in the value of exports of farm products. The export subsidies were targeted to specific markets, where competition with the European Community was keen. A large percentage of the subsidies were expended for wheat and its products, and the beneficiaries were primarily the Soviet Union, China, and North African and Middle Eastern countries. The export subsidies are in no way critical to the operation of any domestic farm program except the dairy program. For wheat, cotton, and other grains, price supports have not been a barrier to exports under the 1985 Agricultural Act. In that act, the price supports were set relatively low for the grains, and for cotton the concept of a marketing loan was introduced.

Because the marketing loan rate is based on actual market prices, it cannot interfere with exports or domestic sales. It is below the price support rate, which is used only to determine the amount paid to farmers for the cotton output that met the conditions of full participation in the cotton price-and-income-support program. The marketing loan rate is used to determine how much the farmer must pay to the government to cover his price support loan at the time the cotton is actually sold. The marketing loan concept is simply a way of increasing the size of the deficiency payment when market prices fall below the price support level. Marketing loans have not been used for grains and soybeans, but if price support levels are kept at approximately the recent nominal levels, the price supports would have little or no effect on exports. The price support levels do have some effect on the level of stocks held by the economy, even when the government has acquired limited quantities. The availability of the price support loan reduces the risks of holding stocks by providing a floor under prices. If the marketing loan were introduced, this floor would no longer be available, stocks of grain and soybeans held by the marketing system would be reduced, and market price variability would be increased somewhat.

To summarize, except for the dairy program, export subsidies do not have a critical role in any of the current farm price-and-income-support programs. And if price supports for dairy products were lowered moderately so that output was reduced by about 5 percent from its current level, export subsidies would not be required. The primary rationale for the export subsidies on grain has been and continues to be to create financial difficulties for the European Community. Success in the Uruguay Round of GATT negotiations, we hope, will reduce the expected value of such behavior.

## Domestic Subsidies

Article XVI(a) also includes a general admonition against any subsidy "including any form of income or price support, which operates directly or indirectly to increase exports of any product from, or to reduce imports of any product into, its territory." Such subsidies have not been prohibited, however, and all the section requires is that any government providing such subsidies should inform other contracting parties of the "extent and nature of the subsidization" and of its potential effects on either exports or imports. If there is a determination that the subsidies present a "serious prejudice to the interests of any other contracting party," the country is obligated, if requested, to discuss the possibility of limiting the subsidization. So far as we know, this part of Article XVI has never been invoked: no country or economic entity has participated in discussions about the possibility of limiting its subsidies except during the several general rounds of negotiations that have been held. And as has been noted in chapter 11, the past negotiations have not resulted in a general reduction in agricultural subsidies. On the contrary, since the 1950s the average rates of protection in agriculture in the industrial market economies have increased.

In the Uruguay Round, however, some industrial countries have made proposals related to both the nature and the level of domestic subsidies to agriculture. In the proposals submitted in late 1989, there was general agreement that all forms of subsidies should be taken into account in measuring the degree of protection and in the commitments made to reduce protection rates. But in addition, views were expressed that not all subsidies had the same effects on the interests of other countries. Subsidies could be said to fall into three categories, with each category subject to different conditions: (1) subsidies such as price and income support that directly affect current levels of production or consumption and thus the quantities exported or imported; (2) subsidies that have an indirect effect on production, such as input and credit subsidies, and thus on imports and exports; and (3) subsidies and income support policies not linked to production or marketing. Generally, there was agreement that the first types of subsidies—such as price supports, deficiency payments, or transportation subsidies—were subject to negotiation with the long-run objective either to cut to low levels or to entirely eliminate. The second category would continue to be permitted but would be subject to discipline and negotiation, with agreement on periodic reductions in budgetary expenditures.

The third category includes what are called "decoupled subsidies"—subsidies that are neither directly nor indirectly related to current or prospective levels of production and marketing. According to some participants, an important objective of the Uruguay Round was to reach agreement on the particular subsidies that could be continued for an extended time because of their minimal impact on production, consumption, and trade. The United States and the Cairns Group propose that the third category be classified as permitted policies; subjected only to periodic review to certify that these policies were not being subverted to provide incentives for current production, the subsidies would be permitted indefinitely. The decisions concerning which policies were to fall into the permitted category were to be determined by negotiations. The United States proposed several programs as meeting a reasonable requirement of not influencing current production or marketing or that should be permitted to be continued because of their broad social values: decoupled direct income payments to producers; payments for conservation and environmental protection plans and practices; disaster assistance; domestic food aid (low prices to low-income consumers or direct food transfers); research, extension, and education; land retirement programs; and programs to stockpile food if there is no provision for direct price or income support.

The Cairns Group was not specific in describing methods of support or income transfers that could be considered not to distort trade. Their proposal was put as follows:

> Some forms of support considered not to be linked to production or trade because they meet clearly-defined and multi-laterally-agreed criteria, would be exempted from the reform commitments. Surveillance of the use of these policies will be required to ensure that recourse to them does not create new trade distortions. In that event, disciplines may need to be considered.

Obviously, agricultural research, extension, and education have actual or potential effects on agricultural output. In some cases, research is very directly oriented to increasing the yield potential of a particular crop, such as work on plant breeding or protection. But it seems reasonable to classify such efforts as permitted and without specific trade effects because it is through such efforts that it has been possible to achieve a record of significant declines in the real prices of most agricultural products during the twentieth century. In contrast to the agricultural price-and-income-support programs, expenditures on research, extension, and education have a high positive social rate of return as measured by relationships between the increases in national output and the costs involved. Further, the evidence is clear that in the long run the benefits of improved technology are realized primarily by consumers and not by individuals as producers. In addition, most of the results of agricultural research are public goods and are available to countries other than the ones responsible for the original work. While there may be some time lag in the transfer of knowledge, in a matter of a few years most research results in agriculture that have wide applicability are internationalized.

Some of the transfer programs would require close monitoring to prevent their use for significantly increasing the productivity of agriculture. Conservation programs, for example, can be used to increase the productivity of land. Very large areas of farmland in the United States have been drained, paid for in considerable part by subsidies in a conservation program. The drained land had a significantly greater production potential than it had before it was drained.

But the major area of disagreement will arise over whether subsidies to current agricultural resource owners are truly "decoupled"—subsidies with no effect on current production of farm products. Agreement on such a category of subsidies has been desired by several of the countries so that they can minimize the opposition to reducing the degree of protection that they provide to agriculture. Such a reduction will result in income losses and, especially, a decline in asset values. This decline will occur in the value of land and production quotas and where the protection rates have been high, the decline in asset values could be large relative to the total value of assets in agriculture—in some cases a quarter or more of the total. Such declines, if they were to occur without some form of compensation, are unlikely to be politically acceptable. Thus policy makers have searched for a negotiated agreement on mutually acceptable subsidies considered to have minimal or no trade-distorting effects and that can be used to compensate resource owners for the losses in asset values.

It is clearly possible to compensate resource owners fully for the losses that would occur during the transition from existing protection to low or zero protection at a financial cost significantly less than what consumers and taxpayers would incur if the protection levels were to remain unchanged. There are two main reasons why this is true. One is that there are significant dead-weight losses due to the responses of farmers to protection—some resources are used in agriculture that would have a higher real product if used elsewhere. Put another way, protection causes agricultural output to be larger than it would be if resources of an economy were used efficiently. The second reason is that there is considerable evidence that the rate of discount used to capitalize the income attributable to government price-and-income-support programs is much higher than the rate of interest at which governments can borrow. Generally speaking, the value of a production quota, such as the quotas for milk and poultry production in Canada or tobacco in the United States, represents approximately the value of four years' real net income due to the quota (Johnson 1991, chap. 9). In other words, when the real rate of interest is 5 percent or less, the rate of discount for income due to the governmental programs is about 20 percent. Consequently, based on the response of farmers to such programs, the compensation for eliminating the income and price support would be a sum equal to four years' net increase in income.

But the cost to consumers and taxpayers would generally be less than their combined costs for four years. The increase in annual net income to agricultural resource owners attributable to the price support programs is significantly less than the annual cost of the programs to consumers and taxpayers. This would be the case even if a country eliminated such programs unilaterally because of the substantial dead-weight costs of such programs and the alternative value of the resources that the subsidies have attracted into agricultural production. It is estimated in table 11–5, assuming unilateral trade liberalization for each country or region, that farm resource owners receive only 71 percent of the costs borne by taxpayers and consumers in the industrial market economies.

In addition, as indicated in table 11–6, at least a third of the costs of the income transfer programs in the industrial market economies is due to the policies of other countries through the international price effects of those policies. Consequently, if there were multilateral liberalization, the amount of the required transfer to compensate agricultural resource owners fully for the income loss caused by free trade would be significantly less than the sum of four years of costs to consumers and taxpayers. A large net gain would thus accrue to each of the economies by reducing or eliminating protection even when resource owners are fully, even generously, compensated for the loss in the value of their assets. Therefore, it is important that the GATT negotiations reach agreement on subsidies or income transfers used primarily to compensate resource owners for the loss of asset values due to the reduction in protection. Moreover, losses to labor may not be reflected in the loss in asset values, and subsidies should be permitted to provide for retraining, including income forgone during the retraining period, and costs of transferring to another job outside of agriculture. But the costs of such subsidies are likely to be small compared with the costs of compensating for the losses in asset values.

But there should be some limit of time on the payment of subsidies that compensate for losses in asset values. Without a time limit, at some point taxpayers will have paid out more than the value of the gains to consumers and taxpayers from reducing protection. One important defect of the U.S. proposal is that there is no time limit on such subsidies. Unless there is a limit, a time will come when the majority of the payments go to individuals no longer engaged in agriculture: that is, if payments are made to resource owners on the basis either of some past level of production or of resource ownership as of a given date (for example, the amount of land owned or operated). This has occurred in the United States for quotas for producing tobacco (Johnson 1991, chap. 9). Most quotas for producing certain types of tobacco are now rented from those who own the quotas but are not farmers themselves. Consequently, many current producers of tobacco receive little or no benefit from the tobacco programs. Such a situation is neither good social nor good economic policy; obviously, it appears to be good political policy.

The U.S. proposal for decoupled subsidies would be strengthened if it were subdivided into those subsidies intended to be permanent and accepted as unrelated to current production and marketing decisions of farmers and those made to compensate resource owners for the losses incurred through the reduction in protection. The compensation for losses in asset values and in labor income should be made over a limited time. While the clearest and most definite approach would be to make the compensation in one lump sum, it may be necessary to spread the payment out over several years for budgetary reasons. Where part of the income transfer due to protection has been through higher consumer prices, it might be necessary to spread the payments over as much as a decade. In the United States, however, where most of the income transfer has been through deficiency payments, the period could be as short as five years.

A primary reason for limiting the period during which payments are made and making it as short as possible is that governments are not trustworthy when it comes to agricultural policies. Their word is not their bond and is all too likely to be changed just before the next election. It is absolutely essential that owners who have resources committed to agriculture or are considering such a commitment believe beyond any doubt that the planned reduction in protection will occur and that the compensation payments are fixed in amount and duration and will not be changed. With uncertainty on either of these points, more resources will be devoted to agriculture than would be viable if the trade liberalization were carried out as planned. In other words, the failure of governments to live up to their commitments is a source of inefficiency in the use of resources. One might argue that the government is not going back on its word if it pays more to the farmers and over a longer period of time than originally stated, but this view is erroneous. First, other parties are affected by the commitment, specifically, taxpayers and consumers; and second, those who accepted the word of the government and made decisions on that basis lose income or asset value.

Thus the effectiveness of decoupled payments used to compensate resource owners for losses in asset values and for relocation and training costs for workers depends on the certainty that the payments will be so much and not more. If such certainty can be achieved, the compensation may have its desired effect, namely, that of making it possible to gain a significant degree of trade liberalization over time.

## Modification of U.S. Farm Programs

The modifications of farm programs can be considered in two phases—the transition period to the agreed-on degree of protection and the long run. We shall first consider the transition period.

The changes during the transition period depend on the specific nature of the existing farm price-and-income-support programs. Two different broad types exist. In one, the government intervenes to increase the market price of the product through controlling imports and, in some cases, using export subsidies to dispose of unwanted output. This group includes programs for dairy products, sugar, and peanuts. In the other, the income transfers occur through deficiency payments that equal the difference between a target price and the market price multiplied by some quantity of output as determined for each farm by the terms of the income support program.

The first group of programs relies on quantitative import restrictions or import quotas to maintain the domestic price above the import price. The United States, proposing that the import quotas no longer be an acceptable form of protection, has suggested that Article XI 2(c), which states conditions under which import quotas for farm products can be applied, be deleted from GATT. The import quota would be replaced by a tariff quota and by a tariff rate equal to the difference between the domestic price and the import price during an agreed-on recent period. The tariff quota would permit a volume of imports during the first year of at least the same amount as that permitted by the import quota; additional imports could occur at the tariff rate determined as indicated. There would be negotiations concerning the rate at which the tariff quota would be increased annually, with its being entirely phased out within a decade. The tariff would be reduced annually so that by the end of a decade, it would be at the negotiated and bound level.

For this group of commodities, there are three main options. One would be to abandon the price supports immediately and introduce the compensation scheme for resource owners and workers. A second would be to lower the price supports substantially and introduce deficiency payments for a time, perhaps five years, and then introduce the compensation scheme for resource owners and workers. Presumably, the second option would permit a more accurate estimate of the losses likely to be incurred by resource owners due to trade liberalization than would be possible at the beginning of the transition period. When associated with high price protection, the delay might make the compensation scheme more politically acceptable. The target price used to determine the deficiency payment should be reduced during the five-year period according to a negotiated schedule.

The third approach would be to continue with price supports, gradually reducing them from their current level over a five-year period in a manner consistent with the reduction in the tariff on imports in excess of the tariff quota. At the end of the five years, the compensation scheme for resource owners and workers would be started and completed in the following five years.

For the second group of commodities—namely, wheat, feedgrains, rice, and cotton—the transition would require the gradual elimination of export subsidies and a gradual reduction in target prices as determined by the GATT negotiations. The elimination of the export subsidies, which have been important only for wheat, would have little effect on domestic market prices since the export subsidies have had only modest effect in increasing wheat exports. The reduction in target prices would cause some loss of income to resource owners, and in this case it might be desirable to pay part of the compensation during the first year or two of target price reductions and before the actual amount of the compensation has been determined. The amount paid during this period would be a part of the total compensation.

The amount of the compensation depends on several variables, as noted earlier. On the one hand, it is necessary to estimate what share of the costs imposed on consumers and taxpayers by the programs actually ends up as added net income to resource owners, as well as the discount rate used to convert the expected income stream into asset values. On the other hand, an estimate must be made of the increase in international market prices that can reasonably be assumed as a result of the degree of trade liberalization actually achieved. Such an estimate can be made with greater accuracy after three or four years of experience with reduced protection. It is understandable why producers would not want to accept an estimate of the international price effects based on models that used data entirely from the preliberalization period.

In the long run, or after the transition to the negotiated level of protection, the farm products that now have price-and-income-support programs would have to operate on the same basis as the poultry, pork, beef, and most fruit and vegetable producers now do, that is, without the intrusion of price supports or other significant governmental intervention. Producers of the above products have not gained from the price supports on the grains; in fact, in some conditions the price supports for the grains have increased income instability for livestock producers. This outcome has occurred when a change in the demand for a livestock product was not reflected in the prices of the grains, because the price was at the price support level and the adjustment to the demand change occurred through changes in stocks. In the absence of the price supports, the price of grains would have reacted to the change in the demand for livestock and thus somewhat dampened income variability in livestock production.

Of course, the U.S. proposal for dealing with import quotas may not be adopted. If not, then the likely alternative would be a negotiated annual increase in the size of each import quota, culminating in approximately the level of imports at the agreed amount of protection for each commodity affected. The proposals made for the transition period with a tariff quota could work equally well for a gradual increase in the quantities permitted under import quotas.

One possibility not considered above is that the European Community and the United States reach agreement to exclude a wide variety of farm subsidies from the negotiations because they are not related to current production levels. In other words, the United States may claim that its current programs for food grains, feed grains, and cotton meet the criteria for permitted programs and that only modest changes would be required to remove the remaining trade-distorting effects: for these programs decoupling has already been achieved. Similarly, the European Community has proposed reforms of its Common Agricultural Policy that provide for significant reductions in farm prices to be replaced by large payments distributed according to the area a farmer devotes to specific crops. Since the payment is not directly related to current production, it is argued that such payments are decoupled and thus should be permitted. Such a resolution of the conflicts between the United States and the European Community should not be greeted with enthusiasm by other producers of temperate-zone agricultural products.

In its October 1989 submission on comprehensive long-term agricultural reform, the United States presented what it considered the characteristics of permitted policies. Three descriptions were presented that bear a close resemblance to what U.S. negotiators may well argue describe the major features of the U.S. income-and-price-support programs for the major crops. The three permitted policies include:

- direct-income payments to producers that are not tied to current production, prices, the cost of production, or marketing of agricultural commodities
- programs for the development and implementation of bona fide conservation and environmental plans and practices
- programs to remove land or other production factors from agriculture or to facilitate the transition process

If others accept these measures as permitted policies, the United States will undoubtedly argue that there needs to be little or no change in its programs for the grains and cotton. As noted in chapter 5, the yields used to calculate deficiency payments have been frozen. The acreage bases for individual farms have not been frozen, but to correct this would affect relatively few farmers, though these must be politically well-placed farmers or the change would already have been made.

Is it likely that the other contracting parties will accept this U.S. position, assuming that it is the position? I think not, and I hope not. Let me first say why I hope not. Continuation of the current programs, as authorized by the 1990 farm bill, does not make U.S. agriculture market oriented. The provisions of the farm programs may have several decoupled provisions, but for the farmers who farm 75–90 percent of the base acres, other program features seriously inhibit their production decisions. If, for example, a farmer chooses the 0–92 provision and plants none of the program crops, he is prohibited from planting soybeans. He can plant a so-called minor oilseed crop, such as sunflowers or flax, which are both less profitable and less familiar. If the acreage retirement programs are not phased out in response to a trade agreement, it is unlikely that they will be so in the foreseeable future. There are two important negative implications of making these programs permanent.

The first is that governmental expenditures of $6–13 billion will continue indefinitely for the deficiency and other payments needed to maintain the acreage reduction features of the program. The programs are voluntary; consequently, each year the payments must be large enough to induce farmers to set aside the desired amount of cropland.

Only a part of the deficiency and related payments is retained by farm operators as net income. A significant part goes to landowners who are not farm operators as well as to farmers in compensation for the costs of properly caring for the idled land. Part is also required for the adverse effects of the land idling on the efficient use of machinery and other fixed resources.

The second implication is that the comparative advantage of U.S. agriculture will continue to be eroded by increasing production costs and by inhibiting farmers from producing those crops where they have the greatest comparative advantage. It is generally agreed that the feed grain and cotton programs have caused the United States to lose market share for soybeans, because the subsidies for feed grains and cotton have induced farmers to limit their soybean acres because of the artificial profitability created for corn and cotton by the programs. Cropland has been idled that could have been profitably used for soybeans, but incentives made participation in the feed grain and cotton programs, which required idling land, even more profitable than growing soybeans.

I am not arguing here that the continuation of the grain and cotton programs as permitted programs would result in greater exports (or fewer imports) than would occur if U.S. farmers responded solely to market incentives. In fact, it is probable that the supply management programs have reduced U.S. exports through the combined effects of acreage reductions and diminished efficiency of production.

I doubt if the other countries would accept a continuation of the U.S. grain and cotton programs as meeting the objective of trade liberalization, even if the United States were to agree to forgo the use of export subsidies and would eliminate its largely meaningless import quotas on cotton. The continuation of the U.S. programs would make it politically impossible for the European Community to liberalize the Common Agricultural Policy significantly. Equally detrimental to the creation of a market-oriented agriculture in the EC would be the further extension of supply management programs. In any case, it appears that the EC is gradually adopting the basic features of the U.S. farm programs (having already applied output quotas for dairy products), is well on its way to restricting acreage for major crops, and is introducing the concept of a high price for a given amount and a lower export price for production or marketing in excess of that amount. But as argued earlier, these programs do not remove the excess resources from agriculture. They may serve to inhibit further output increases or even to reduce output slightly, but they do not result in the output levels that would prevail if production responded solely to market incentives based on international market prices. Thus, the cost of the U.S. position may well be a reform of the Common Agricultural Policy in a direction nearly as distorting as the present one.

## Some Long-Run Effects of Trade Liberalization

If price supports are no longer used for crop products, farm operators will have to adjust their mode of operation. The production of these products will be subject to greater risks from increased price variability. Price variability, however, has not been the sole and probably not the most important source of risk for farmers. Two other sources have been at least as important—variability of interest rates and variability of output due to natural factors. The significant financial difficulties of many farmers during the first half of the 1980s was not attributable to price variability but primarily to unanticipated increases in interest rates.

Farmers can operate with greater price risks than they have had in recent years and do so profitably. They can use futures and options markets to reduce some risks, and they can adjust their portfolios of assets and liabilities to the expected degree of price risk. In fact, compensation for reduced asset values could ultimately improve the capacity to absorb risks. The value of farm land would be written down but by not more than the liquid assets acquired through the payments. In the long run, the amount of debt incurred to purchase farmland or to enter the production of products now subject to quotas would be substantially reduced, thus lessening the exposure to both interest rate and output price risks.

In 1990, just 14.1 percent of all farms received 73 percent of all direct payments made to farmers, at an average of $21,100 (ERS, 1991). Their average net cash income from farming was $162,000, and, in addition, they averaged $21,200 from nonfarm sources for a total net cash income per farm of $183,200. These are obviously a rather sophisticated group of farm operators with the capacity to adjust to changing conditions. If they are fully compensated for the loss in the value of their assets and earning capacity because of trade liberalization, we can be confident that they will adjust to the new conditions and do so with little loss in incomes. They will lose some current income, since the earnings on the newly acquired liquid assets from the compensation scheme are unlikely to be as high as the rate at which the net benefits of the government programs have been capitalized. But this difference should be no more than a few thousand dollars, perhaps $10,000 at a maximum, for this elite group of farm operators.

## Modification of Taiwan's Farm Programs

The Republic of China on Taiwan has repeatedly made it clear that it has adopted economic liberalization and economic internationalization as guiding principles of policy; that it wants to join the General Agreement on Tariffs and Trade; that it would make every effort to reduce trade frictions between the ROC and the United States; and that when the opportunity presents itself, the ROC would want to enter into a free trade agreement with the United States. In our view, all these objectives are in the national interest of the ROC and should be pursued vigorously.

But to achieve each of the above objectives, the ROC needs a more liberal agricultural trade policy—and behind it, a more liberal agricultural policy, particularly if the basic principles of the GATT are to be observed.

Currently, the farm policy of the ROC consists mainly of subsidies, price supports, quantitative import restrictions, and tariffs. The production and marketing of hogs and vegetables have been subsidized, though the proportion of subsidy to farmers has been minimal in recent years; preferential interest rates on loans are available for agricultural production; irrigation, electricity, housing, and insurance are subsidized; certain taxes are waived, including capital gains tax, inheritance tax, and farmland tax; agricultural research and extension are provided; and rural infrastructure has been strengthened.

A guaranteed price program is in force for rice, sugar, major grains (corn, sorghum, and soybeans), and some minor products. Quantitative import restrictions are imposed on a number of products including peanuts, red beans, edible offal, garlic bulbs, fresh milk, and several kinds of fish. These import restrictions also apply to rice and sugar.

The average nominal tariff rate on agricultural products was 21.6 percent in 1991. It should be noted that not all farm policies are inconsistent with the principles of GATT. Domestic subsidies are acceptable to the GATT, but price support and quantitative import restrictions are not. A modification of farm policy is certainly called for if the ROC wants to conform with the GATT principles.

It is true that at this time it is still not certain what the Uruguay Round will come up with. The draft final act proposed by Secretary Arthur Dunkel of the GATT in December 1991 suggested a compromise concession of opening domestic market schedules to all parties based on the proposal submitted by the United States and the European Single Market. A compromised proposal means that the pace of trade liberalization of international agricultural products has been slowed down in comparison with the U.S. proposal. But the principles of liberalization proposed by the United States were maintained and accepted by most parties. Import quotas and price supports, for example, should no longer be acceptable forms of protection. All parties to the negotiation acknowledge that the norms of the GATT must be modified to reduce protection and enhance GATT's surveillance. Instead of import quotas, the GATT would substitute a tariff quota or a tariff rate equal to the difference between the domestic price and the import price. Moreover, tariff protection would fall by 36 percent.

Since such moves toward freer agricultural trade policy would be made over a seven-year period, allowing domestic agricultural production to adjust to world competition, the possible negative effects of liberalization policy will be reduced. Because the average protection levels of agricultural products in Taiwan are not very high, Taiwan has no reason to fear such competition and thus to exempt itself from the obligations to reduce protection on agricultural products. Considering the institutional factors that impede the adjustment of Taiwan's domestic industries, though, the possible influence on domestic production may be much higher than usual. We therefore suggest that the government try to speed up removal of these institutional impediments.

Contemporary agricultural development in Taiwan has been encountering various difficulties and challenges. Most difficulties are closely related to the rigid farmland tenancy system and the structural problems of an economy in a rapid transformation, that is, from an agricultural economy to an industrial one. Consequently, the government needs to draw up a new farmland reform program to relax the inflexible land tenure system and also map out an adjustment assistance policy to remove or reduce resistance to further liberalization. These institutional modifications and assistance policies do not obviate the obligation to open up domestic markets as requested by the GATT, but these policies should be in force before, or at least no later than, the implementation of the liberalization policy requested by the GATT.

**Encouragement of Larger Farms and Reform of Farmland Tenancy.** It is obvious that the average farm of 1.2 hectares in Taiwan is too small to be cultivated efficiently. Such small-scale farm operations and the rigid farmland tenancy system, however, were closely related to the land reform in Taiwan in the early 1950s. This reform has been evaluated by most economists as a successful method for rebuilding a reasonable relationship between farmer and landlord. Labor productivity increased to some extent by redistributing land ownership through strict qualifications for purchasing land, which basically benefited the farmer. Labor productivity, however, improves from this approach only when the society has a peasant economy, where overpopulation relative to the available land-capital resources exists as the main problem of underdevelopment. In the long run, the strict land tenancy system may hinder the mechanism by which the small cultivator avails himself of technology, and it may therefore impede the farmer's efforts to increase labor productivity further.

In the 1960s, when wage rates were driven up by the very fast growth of the industrial sector, the surge of labor costs and hence the costs of farm production undermined the competitive edge of farm products in the world market, and farm income therefore grew relatively slowly. To promote the working efficiency of the small farm, the government has encouraged group farming and farm mechanization to realize economies of scale. Fear that the government would invoke land reform regulations to force landowners to give up their land ownership, however, has caused many part-time farmers to leave their land to an overseer instead of leasing it to other farmers. The results of encouraging enlarged farmland are thus unsatisfactory.

In 1982, a second phase of farmland reform was again designed to promote land use, labor productivity, and a large farming scale. The 37.5 Percent Rent Reduction Act of the land reform in 1950 was amended to give entrusted farming and custom farming a stronger legal basis; the act clearly stated that these types of farming would not be subject to the provisions of the Rent Reduction Act. Because of farmers' lack of confidence in the program, however, the results were considered unsatisfactory again, and farm size rose only from 1.07 hectares in 1982 to 1.21 hectares in 1988. The small-scale farm is closely related to the farmland tenancy system and is therefore a major obstacle to reducing costs to dometic producers.

**Restructuring the Farm Labor Force and Increasing Farmers' Income.** Since the late-1960s, farm income has risen slowly in comparison with that of nonfarm families. In 1970, the per capita income of farm families was down to 60 percent of that of nonfarm families, or 70 percent of that of workers' families. Since then, various support policies were implemented to raise farm income. By 1989, per capita farm family income had recovered to 73 percent to that of nonfarm families.

Since farmers' incomes are consistently lower than nonfarmers' incomes, agricultural labor, especially the young labor force, moved toward the industrial and service sectors to seek better jobs. This migration of the young created a major difficulty, an aging farm labor force, that could be met only if technology production increased faster than the surging wage rate. In 1991, more than 31 percent of the farm labor force was over fifty-five years old. It is clear that the capacity of these workers to adjust to a free-trade policy is quite limited by both willingness and ability. Their resistance to open-market policies, therefore, presents an obstacle to the government's effort to introduce freer trade.

The government has recognized both problems, the rigid land tenancy system and the aging farm labor force. The new farmland law prepared by the Council of Agriculture is in the process of getting approval from other departments. It will provide more flexible conditions for farmland transactions and tenancy. In order to solve the problem of low incomes for farmers and an aging farm labor force, the Council of Agriculture has also proposed an adjustment program to encourage early retirement, to establish a pension system, and to strengthen on-the-job training by fostering viable farmers, with the hope that these measures will restructure the labor force on farms and therefore increase farm productivity and income.

These policies should all be accepted by the GATT and increase the capacity of domestic producers to make necessary adjustments. We hope that they will be put into action as soon as possible, since they provide the structure for increasing farmers' income and productivity. They also serve the purpose of finishing the preparation for further liberalization of domestic policy.

While removal of domestic institutional impediments will improve labor productivity by enlarging the operational size of farms, the protection of such products as rice, corn, sorghum, soybeans, sugar, and fresh milk—which still enjoy price supports or import controls—will influence what a farmer chooses to produce. It is necessary that policies applied to these products be liberalized further, as is suggested elsewhere in this book. Consequently, the quantitative import restriction on rice, sugar, and fresh milk should be relaxed, and price support on grains should be reduced gradually.

As old policies are phased out, perhaps a tariff quota and a tariff rate equal to the difference between the domestic price and import price could be put in place, and the tariff would be reduced and the tariff quota would be increased annually as required by the GATT. As for the timing of such policy changes, because the final outcome of the tenancy system reforms may take time to be revealed, the reduction of price supports should take place over some time, and direct transfer payments to farmers may need to be distributed as a bolster for farmers' incomes, which will have been lowered by the reduction in price support. Price supports, then, may stay at their current level at the beginning of the first five-year transition period, then diminish in a manner consistent with the agreement reached by the Uruguay Round. Whenever the reductions in price support begin, the compensation scheme for resource owners (for example, land owners, fertilizer suppliers, food manufacturers) and farmers would be started and completed in the second period of reforms. The amount of the compensation for resource owners and workers can be estimated in the way outlined in chapter 7 where table 7-5 shows the total cost to consumers and taxpayers under the protective program in 1988 and can be used for approximate maximum figures of such compensation. Or more precisely, the compensation should be no more than 71 percent of the total cost to consumers and taxpayers, since that is the portion the resource owners and workers usually received under protective policy.

In the long run, if price supports are no longer used for agricultural products, the crops that farm operators choose to grow will be more varied. More capital-, labor-, or technology-intensive products, such as fruits, flowering plants, and livestock, will be chosen as substitutes for products such as grains, which are more land intensive and in which Taiwan has a comparative disadvantage. Both the import of grains and the export of nongrain agricultural products may therefore increase as a result of such liberalization of agricultural policy. But in total, the increase of imports of agricultural products will exceed the increase of exports of some products and will therefore relieve some of the price pressure on land in Taiwan.

## References

Dam, Kenneth W. *The GATT: Law and International Economic Organization*. Chicago: University of Chicago Press, 1970.

Economic Research Service (ERS), U.S. Department of Agriculture, *Economic Indicators of the Farm Sector: National Financial Summary, 1990*. ECIFS 10.1, 1991.

Johnson, D. Gale. *World Agriculture in Disarray*. London: Macmillan & Co., 1991.

Webb, Alan J., Michael Lopez, and Renata Penn. *Estimates of Producer and Consumer Subsidy Equivalents: Government Intervention in Agriculture, 1982–87*. Economic Research Service, U.S. Department of Agriculture. Statistical Bulletin no. 1803, 1990.

# 13
## Adjustments Required in Agriculture by Trade Liberalization

*D. Gale Johnson*

A rough indication of the adjustments to trade liberalization that an agriculture and its sectors must make is visible in the level of protection existing before liberalization occurs. In other words, the higher the level of protection—that is, the greater the difference between domestic prices, including deficiency payments, and international market prices—the greater the required adjustment. A large difference implies that the costs of producing the product are high relative to the international market prices.

If we accept that conclusion, allowing for some exceptions noted later, our American readers surely will be surprised to learn that low levels of protection would require greater adjustments in the agriculture of the United States than in Taiwan. This conclusion results from a cursory examination of table 13-1, which gives a measure of the level of protection of individual agricultural products for the United States and Taiwan and an average for all the products for which protection levels have been calculated. The protection estimates used are based on the producer subsidy equivalents (PSEs), as published by the United States Department of Agriculture, converted to nominal levels of protection. The estimates included in the table are averages for 1984–1987. This period includes two years, 1984 and 1985, when international prices were relatively high; and two years, 1986 and 1987, when these prices were relatively low. Consequently the data for these years are assumed to approximate the average level of international market prices that could be called normal for the period prior to trade liberalization.

The data in this table indicate that for 1984–1987 the average level of nominal protection was greater in the United States than in Taiwan. Although the data used for this comparison are published by the U.S. Department of Agriculture, the results of the comparisons would not have been obvious from the political rhetoric about the agricultural trade controversies of the late 1980s.

TABLE 13–1

NOMINAL PROTECTION COEFFICIENTS (NPC) FOR AGRICULTURAL
PRODUCTS, TAIWAN AND THE UNITED STATES, 1984–1987 AVERAGE

| | NPC | | % of Value to Producers[a] | |
|---|---|---|---|---|
| Specific product | Taiwan | United States | Taiwan | United States |
| Beef and veal | 25 | 11 | 0.8 | 20.2 |
| Chicken | 58 | 16 | 10.4 | 7.5 |
| Corn | 286 | 56 | 2.3 | 20.1 |
| Milk | 86 | 145 | 1.4 | 16.8 |
| Pork | 2 | 7 | 40.0 | 9.0 |
| Rice | 54 | 114 | 32.6 | 1.5 |
| Sorghum | 330 | 49 | 0.9 | 1.9 |
| Soybeans | 161 | 10 | 0.2 | 9.9 |
| Sugar | 113 | 252 | 8.9 | 1.6 |
| Tobacco | 121 | n.a. | 2.4 | n.a. |
| Wheat | 246 | 107 | 0.1 | 9.2 |
| Barley | n.a. | 253 | n.a. | 1.3 |
| Oats | n.a. | 11 | n.a. | 0.6 |
| All products | 32 | 41 | — | — |

n.a. = not available.
a. Based on eleven commodities for Taiwan and twelve for the United States.
The percentages reflect the value to producers, which equals policy transfers
to producers plus the market value.
SOURCE: U.S. Department of Agriculture.

The difference in average nominal protection levels is not great—
33 percent for Taiwan and 40 percent for the United States. The
nominal protection coefficient is a measure of the excess of the
domestic return to producers over what the value of production
would be if valued at the relevant international market price.[1] Given

---

[1]The nominal protection coefficient, as we are using it, is based on the
return per unit of output received by producers. The return is the market
price plus any payments that are a function of current or recent past
production. Thus directly using PSE estimates to calculate nominal protection coefficients is not quite accurate if there are any nonmarket
transfers. If there are nonmarket or nonprice transfers, the nominal
protection coefficient is overestimated. The conversion of PSEs to nominal protection coefficients has been calculated as follows:

$$\frac{PSE}{100\text{-}PSE} \times 100$$

that the estimate we are using is based on PSEs, the value of the transfer to producers includes some components not actually received by the farmers: for example, the cost of administering some farm programs and transportation subsidies that are already reflected in whole or in large part in the prices received by farmers. The nominal protection coefficient as normally calculated does not include these nonmarket or nonprice elements. The relative importance of the transfers not received by farmers or already reflected in market prices is somewhat greater in the United States than in Taiwan, but not by enough to significantly modify the comparisons we make.

Some individual protection coefficients show rather striking disparities in the levels of protection. One of the comparisons is for rice. Given the enormous differences in the sizes of farms and the high technology of rice production in the United States, it might be expected that the protection level in Taiwan, of necessity, is higher than in the United States. The opposite is the case, and not by a little. The estimated nominal protection levels for 1984–1987 were 52 percent for Taiwan and more than double that for the United States—108 percent. Thus the return to the Taiwanese rice producer was approximately 50 percent greater than the international market price, while in the United States the domestic return per unit of production was approximately twice the international price.

The comparison of protection rates for sugar reveals an even greater discrepancy. While Taiwan provided a high rate of protection for its sugar—98 percent for 1984–1987—the United States gave its sugar producers a much higher level of protection—an average of 233 percent. For these years the producer price per unit of production in Taiwan was about double the world market price minus the nonprice

---

When there are nonmarket transfers included in the PSEs, the nominal protection coefficient compares the domestic return (including any deficiency payments) less the nonmarket transfers per unit of product to the international market price. Assume that the PSE is fifty and that 20 percent of the policy transfer is nonmarket and 80 percent is through price enhancement in the market. According to the formula given above, the nominal protection coefficient is one hundred, but the domestic price exceeds the world market price by 80 percent and not 100 percent. Of the policy transfer of $50 per ton, $40 is transferred through the market and the remaining $10 by nonmarket transfers, and the world price is $50. The conversion formula given above indicates that the nominal protection coefficient is one hundred. The domestic price (return), however, is 80 percent greater than the world market price. This difference arises because not all the policy transfers accrue as added gross returns to the producers.

transfers per unit of production. In the United States the comparable domestic return per ton of sugar was more than three times the world price minus the nonprice transfers per unit of production. But if one excludes the nonprice transfers, the producer price in Taiwan averaged 88 percent more than the world market price. In the United States the farm price of sugar was 267 percent of the world market price on the average for 1984–1987.

In both Taiwan and the United States the protection of pork is low or nil. The estimate of the PSEs includes only nonprice policy transfers. Milk production in Taiwan is at a low level, and on a per capita basis, it is only 3 percent of the U.S. production. But the rate of nominal protection based on the PSE calculations was significantly lower in Taiwan than in the United States from 1984 to 1987—85 percent, compared with 143 percent. Of course, there are producers with higher rates of nominal protection in Taiwan than in the United States. These include the grain crops other than rice—corn, sorghum, wheat, and soybeans. But the level of production of this group of farm crops is very low in Taiwan. In 1987 the aggregate production of the four crops was only 378 thousand tons. This compares with rice production in Taiwan in the same year of 1,748 thousand tons, and grain production in the United States of nearly 280 million tons plus 52 million tons of soybeans. As a share of the value of production for the commodities included in the PSE calculations, the feed grains, wheat, and soybeans composed 3.5 percent in Taiwan compared with 43.0 percent in the United States.

### Some Refinements on Production Adjustments

Earlier it was noted that based on the lower average level of nominal protection in Taiwan than in the United States, one could conclude that fewer adjustments to multilateral free trade would be required of Taiwanese agriculture than of U.S. agriculture. This conclusion, however, is only a rough guide to the probable required adjustments.

Another factor is that the estimates of nominal protection are based on international market prices that prevailed when levels of protection, particularly in the industrial market economies, were quite high. As shown in chapter 11, trade liberalization would result in significant increases in world market prices. But the price increases would not be uniform. For example, most of the projections indicate that the increases in international prices of milk and sugar would be 50 percent or more, depending on the base year used in the study.

Nevertheless, the increase in world market prices for rice would be modest, especially if the developing market economies liberalized their trade. If the milk price in international markets were to increase by 50 percent relative to its 1987 level and the price to producers in Taiwan remained as it was in 1987, the nominal protection of milk would decline to 15 percent. This level of protection could probably be accommodated in a decade, especially if uncoupled transition payments prevented any loss in the net asset position of milk producers. This level of protection of dairy products could also be considered low in comparison with the negotiated levels for the European Community or the United States.

There is a second factor for which adjustment must be made to the inferences based solely on the nominal protection coefficients. Not all the gross policy transfers have been translated into the incomes of the resources devoted to the commodity; some of them have been required to compensate for the production inefficiencies caused by the programs and to pay the administrative costs of the programs. In the United States the feed grain, wheat, and cotton programs have required that farm operators idle large amounts of land in order to be eligible for price supports and to receive the various payments. In 1988, U.S. farmers "set aside" or idled 21.5 million hectares of cropland. This was 18 percent of the actual amount of cropland harvested in that year. An unknown percentage of the total policy transfers that went to agriculture during that year was required to compensate farmers for leaving a large amount of land idle. When the land is idled, other resources such as machinery and management are also used less fully.

The high rates of nominal protection for the grains in the United States are due in considerable part to the inefficiencies of attempting to limit crop production by reducing the amount of land devoted to the particular crops. Recent costs of production are thus not relevant to what the costs would be if there were trade liberalization and the acreage restriction programs for grains and cotton were abandoned.

The adjustments that would be required of the agricultures of Taiwan and the United States will be determined by several variables—the current levels of protection, the effects of trade liberalization on the international market prices of each commodity, and the particular features of the existing farm price-and-income-support programs. Where all or most of the policy transfers occur because of higher product prices, the first two variables would determine the magnitude of the price adjustment to be faced by producers. This is the probable situation for Taiwan's farmers and for U.S. producers of dairy products and sugar.

The third variable would be significant for producers of commodities subject to acreage restrictions. But the output and resource adjustments are not solely determined by the price adjustment and the reduction in costs that come from eliminating arbitrary decisions on the amount of land to be cultivated or the crop to which it is allocated. The supply conditions for the resources used in producing each product would influence how the price and cost changes affect production.

Resources that have an inelastic supply in the production of a commodity will affect the output response.[2] The resource with the most inelastic supply to agriculture is land. This resource has gained the most in increased annual returns and prices from agricultural protection. It will lose the most with the reduction of protection. But since its supply with respect to rent or return is low, the amount of land devoted to crop production will change little, if at all, as output prices decline.

Where land is of little importance in production and the majority of inputs are purchased, such as feed, capital, and hired or family labor—which has good alternative earning opportunities—the supply of the product is quite responsive to changes in prices.

Given the relationships noted, a given percentage output price change will have a smaller percentage effect on the output of rice than a similar price change would have on the production of chickens. Land is an important input in the production of rice, although almost all the inputs used to produce broilers are variable over a period of a few years.

### Estimated Output and Trade Effects of Liberalization

Using models of the effects of trade liberalization, economists at the U.S. Department of Agriculture have projected changes in production and trade. The estimates have been published in considerable detail for the United States and other industrial market economies as well as for Taiwan and other East Asian economies.

Table 13–2 gives estimates of the effects of trade liberalization on nine output categories for the industrial market economies, developing exporters, centrally planned economies, newly industrialized Asia (including Taiwan), and developing country importers. The output changes are based on the price effects projected to result from multilateral trade liberalization, as shown in the last column of table 13–3.

---

[2] An inelastic supply means that the quantity of resources supplied changes little with a change in price. The extreme case is where the supply is fixed regardless of the price.

TABLE 13-2

AGRICULTURAL OUTPUT CHANGES FROM MULTILATERAL LIBERALIZATION OF INDUSTRIAL MARKET ECONOMIES, 1986

(percent)

| Commodity Group | United States | Canada | European Community | Other Western Europe | Japan | Australia | New Zealand | Developing Ex-porters | Centrally Planned Economies | New Industrial Asia | Developing Im-porters |
|---|---|---|---|---|---|---|---|---|---|---|---|
| Production output | | | | | | | | | | | |
| Ruminant meat | 4 | 3 | −15 | −24 | −13 | 8 | 11 | 5 | 0 | 1 | 4 |
| Nonruminant meat | 0 | −2 | 0 | −9 | −15 | 7 | 8 | 3 | 0 | 2 | 2 |
| Dairy products | −5 | −4 | 0 | −17 | −18 | 8 | 15 | 6 | 2 | 0 | 4 |
| Wheat | −6 | −3 | −16 | −13 | −61 | 10 | 23 | 4 | 1 | 2 | 6 |
| Coarse grains | −4 | −15 | −4 | −10 | −71 | 5 | 11 | 4 | 0 | 0 | 3 |
| Rice | −11 | 2 | −32 | 5 | −48 | 3 | 0 | 3 | 0 | 0 | 4 |
| Oilseeds and products | 2 | 1 | −16 | 0 | −16 | 0 | −1 | 0 | 0 | 0 | −1 |
| Sugar | −42 | −10 | −3 | −26 | −34 | 14 | 9 | 8 | 0 | 2 | 5 |
| Other crops | −7 | 5 | −11 | 0 | 0 | −1 | 0 | 0 | 0 | 0 | 0 |
| All farm output | −1 | −2 | −7 | −13 | −32 | 7 | 10 | 3 | 0 | 1 | 2 |

SOURCE: Vernon O. Roningen and Praveen M. Dixit, *How Level is the Playing Field? An Economic Analysis of Agricultural Policy Reforms in Industrial Market Economies*, Economic Research Service, USDA, Foreign Agricultural Economics Department, no. 239, December 1989, p. 23.

TABLE 13–3

Projected Agricultural Output Changes from Trade
Liberalization for Three Scenarios for Taiwan

(percent)

| Commodity Group | Industrial Market Economies–1[a] | Industrial Market Economies–2[b] | Global[c] |
|---|---|---|---|
| Meat | 1.1 | 2.3 | −2.2 |
| Dairy | — | — | — |
| Wheat | 3.5 | 5.8 | 5.0 |
| Coarse grains | 1.8 | 3.4 | −4.4 |
| Rice | 1.0 | 1.2 | −3.2 |
| Oilseeds | — | 0.1 | 9.3 |
| Sugar | 2.0 | 2.5 | −4.9 |
| Other crops | 0.1 | 0.2 | −10.0 |
| Aggregate | 1.1 | 1.9 | −1.8 |

a. Trade liberalization by industrial market economies, with developing market economies adjusting domestic market prices by $0.50 for each $1.00 change in world prices.
b. Same as IME–1, except developing market economies fully transmit the world price change to the domestic market.
c. Both industrial market and developing market economies fully liberalize agricultural trade.
Source: Barry Krissoff, John Sullivan, John Wainio, and Brian Johnston, *Agricultural Trade Liberalization and Developing Countries*, USDA, Economic Research Service, Agriculture and Trade Analysis Division, May 1990, pp. 27–29.

For the United States, the projected output effects are 7 percent or less for all output categories except rice and sugar, where the projected reductions in output were 11 and 42 percent, respectively. The only major adjustment required is for sugar. The rice adjustment could come about through a small reduction in the area of rice harvested and through a decline in rice yields. The total area of rice harvested has been about 1.25 million hectares in recent years. The estimated effect on all farm output would be essentially no change— a reduction of 1 percent.

The effect of industrial market economies' liberalization on agriculture in the new Asian industrial countries would be modest. In this projection it is assumed that the new Asian industrial countries would fully reflect the changes in international market prices in their domestic farm prices. Thus, on average, prices received by farmers in these countries would increase, and the rate of protection would change little.

TABLE 13–4

PROJECTED OUTPUT EFFECTS OF AGRICULTURAL TRADE
LIBERALIZATION BY INDUSTRIAL MARKET ECONOMIES AND GLOBAL
MARKET ECONOMIES, TAIWAN AND UNITED STATES, 1986

| | Taiwan | | United States | |
|---|---|---|---|---|
| Commodity | IME-1 | Global | IME-1 | Global |
| Beef | 2.2 | −6.3 | 3.3 | −0.6 |
| Pork | 1.8 | 2.8 | 2.4 | 1.9 |
| Mutton and lamb | 7.0 | 10.1 | 8.4 | 3.0 |
| Poultry—meat | 0.8 | −15.5 | −0.9 | −1.4 |
| Poultry—eggs | −0.3 | −0.2 | −2.1 | −2.3 |
| Dairy—fresh mills | | | −1.0 | −1.2 |
| Dairy—butter | | | 8.4 | 5.5 |
| Dairy—cheese | | | −10.0 | −10.2 |
| Dairy—mills powder | | | 12.2 | 8.0 |
| Wheat | 3.5 | 5.0 | −5.3 | −10.9 |
| Corn | 4.2 | 34.8 | −2.9 | −3.7 |
| Other coarse grains | −1.2 | −51.3 | −10.1 | −11.5 |
| Rice | 1.0 | −3.2 | −12.6 | −13.8 |
| Soybeans | −1.2 | −25.7 | 2.5 | 2.9 |
| Soymeal | −0.1 | 10.4 | 0.1 | 0.7 |
| Soyoil | −0.1 | 10.4 | 0.1 | 0.7 |
| Other oilseeds | 2.0 | 11.8 | 12.4 | 13.8 |
| Other meals | −1.2 | 4.0 | −3.4 | 1.3 |
| Other oils | −1.2 | 4.0 | −3.4 | 1.3 |
| Cotton | 1.2 | 0.8 | −9.7 | −14.4 |
| Sugar | 2.0 | −4.9 | −43.2 | −44.4 |
| Tobacco | 0.1 | −10.1 | −0.6 | −0.8 |
| Aggregate | 1.1 | −1.8 | −1.5 | −3.0 |

SOURCE: Computer output, *Agricultural Trade Liberalization and Developing
Countries*, study by the Economic Research Service and U.S. Department of
Agriculture.

In another model run, it was assumed that the developing market
economies liberalized their trade in agricultural products (Krissoff
1989). Two assumptions were made concerning the nature of the
liberalization by the developing market economies. In one it was
assumed that both producer and consumer prices would be liberalized—that is, equal to border prices that were directly linked to world
market prices. In the other it was assumed that in addition to trade
liberalization, exchange rates were aligned to remove all cases of

311

TABLE 13–5

Projected Effects of Agricultural Trade Liberalization on
Agricultural Trade Balances, Consumer and Producer
Surplus, and Total Welfare, Taiwan, 1986
(millions of U.S. dollars)

| | IME-1 Scenario[a] | IME-2 Scenario[a] | Global |
|---|---|---|---|
| Agricultural trade balance | −52 | 68 | −115 |
| Consumer surplus | −374 | −575 | 530 |
| Producer surplus | 212 | 329 | −268 |
| Total welfare | −254 | −273 | −58 |

a. For description of scenarios, see table 13–3.
Source: Barry Krissoff, John Sullivan, John Wainio, and Brian Johnston, *Agricultural Trade Liberalization and Developing Countries*, U.S. Department of Agriculture, Economic Research Service, Agriculture and Trade Analysis Division, May 1990, p. 35.

overvaluation or undervaluation. In the first model run, the average increase in world market prices for farm commodities was 16 percent; in the second model run the increase was 8 percent. The reason for the smaller price effect in the second case was that the majority of the developing market economies would undergo devaluations, resulting in price increases for both their producers and consumers. The one would increase production and the other would reduce consumption, thus moderating the increase in world market prices.

Three projections were made of the effects of trade liberalization on changes in trade, on total agricultural production, and on producer, consumer, and total welfare in Taiwan (Krissoff 1990). These projections are presented in table 13–5.

The change in total welfare is not equal to the net changes in consumer and producer surpluses. This is because the government of Taiwan realizes net revenue from its agricultural programs when customs receipts are included. On balance, trade liberalization of both industrial and developing market economies would probably have little direct effect on the total welfare of the Taiwan economy. There would be a transfer from producers to consumers, but the net effect of that transfer could be fully offset by transition payments equal to the loss in the value of assets used in agricultural production caused by liberalization.

### References

Johnson, D. Gale. *World Agriculture in Disarray*. London: Macmillan & Co., 1991.

————. *World Food Problems and Prospects*. Washington, D.C.: American Enterprise Institute, 1975.

Josling, Timothy E. *Agriculture and Britain's Trade Policy Dilemma. Thames Essay no. 2*. London: Trade Policy Research, 1970.

Krissoff, Barry, John Sullivan, and John Wainio. "Opening Agricultural Markets: Implications for Developing Countries." Paper presented at the meeting of the Canadian Agricultural Economics and Farm Management Society, Montreal, Canada, July 9–12, 1989.

Krissoff, Barry, John Sullivan, John Wainio, and Brian Johnston. *Agricultural Trade Liberalization and Developing Countries*. U.S. Department of Agriculture, Economic Research Service, 1990.

Miller, Geoff. *The Political Economy of International Agricultural Policy Reform*. Canberra: Australian Government Publishing Service, 1987.

Roningen, Vernon O., and Praveen M. Dixit. *How Level Is the Playing Field? An Economic Analysis of Agricultural Policy Reforms in Industrial Market Economies*. Economic Research Service, USDA, Foreign Agricultural Economics, no. 239. December 1989.

Tyers, Rod, and Kym Anderson. *Disarray in World Food Markets—A Quantitative Assessment*. Cambridge: Cambridge University Press, 1992.

Webb, Alan J., Michael Lopez, and Revata Penn. *Estimates of Producer and Consumer Subsidy Equivalents in Agriculture, 1982–1987*. ERS, USDA, Statistical Bulletin no.803. April 1990.

# 14
## Adjustment Policies to Assist Farmers

### D. Gale Johnson

In chapter 12, we discussed the changes required to make the agricultural policies of the United States and Taiwan consistent with low levels of protection. We suggested certain transition programs that would assist owners of farm resources while asset values were reduced because of lower output prices. In chapter 13, we discussed the probable adjustments in output and resource use that might be required of the two agricultures. Although the required resource adjustments for agriculture as a whole would be relatively small, some sectors of agriculture in each country would need significant resource adjustments. This chapter suggests how governments could assist farmers in making these adjustments over the long term. Not only will the value of certain farm resources, especially land and buildings, decline because of trade liberalization, but some resources will be withdrawn from agriculture; farm size and organization will have to be adjusted to adapt to the new conditions.

### Protection and Excess Resources

Protection encourages the retention of excess resources in agriculture. A greater level of output is encouraged when prices are maintained at a higher level than they would be with low or no protection. Protection may do this indirectly as well, as in the United States, by adopting measures that pay farmers to keep certain resources idle to minimize the budgetary costs of the price programs. But the idling does not eliminate the excess resources; the idled resources remain and can and will return to increase agricultural production if the governmental intervention is reduced or eliminated.

Protectionist policies, whether in agriculture or elsewhere, are intended to reduce the need for a sector to adjust to changing conditions. In response to the changes in economies that have achieved high and growing levels of income, agriculture must undergo major changes. The protectionist instruments available to government are not powerful enough to prevent a considerable amount of adjustment in resource use. The most troublesome feature of the required adjustment in agriculture is its relative decline as the source of national output and employment of labor. It is not only that labor employment must decline relatively, but in Taiwan, the United States, and all other countries with similar income levels, the absolute level of labor employment has fallen sharply over the past three decades. Between 1960 and 1989, farm employment declined by 40 percent in Taiwan and by 42 percent in the United States. Given the differences in resource endowments, these are remarkably similar responses to economic growth.

Protection can perhaps slow the adjustment process, but the available evidence shows that only limited success has been achieved in any country and that at high cost to consumers and taxpayers. Table 14–1 presents data on the annual rate of decline of farm employment for selected periods since 1955 in agriculture for Taiwan and the United States and for other important agricultural countries. In addition, for the countries for which data are available starting in 1955, the percentage rates of decline in farm employment for the entire period are given. It is evident from the table that high rates of agricultural protection did not prevent rapid declines in farm employment. Japan has had high rates of agricultural protection since the mid-1960s (see table 11–1) and yet in both the 1960s and the 1970s the annual rate of decline in farm employment ranged from 4.2 percent to 4.5 percent. Such annual rates over a decade result in a decline of approximately 35 percent.

Although nominal protection for agriculture in the European Community (EC) has been significantly higher than in Canada, Taiwan, and the United States, the EC has had rates of farm employment decline that are as high or higher. Thus the Common Agricultural Policy has failed to achieve its objective of maintaining a large and viable farm population and preventing an exodus from rural to urban areas. Actually, the rural populations in Western Europe have not declined in absolute numbers in the past two decades. The growing importance of part-time farming, which the improved transportation and the increased nonfarm job opportunities in rural areas have made possible, has prevented a significant actual decline in the rural population (Johnson 1991). While the rural population in Canada and the United States increased between 1960 and 1980, the absolute levels of the rural populations in Japan and France declined slightly during the 1960s. In both France and Japan, however, the

315

TABLE 14–1

ANNUAL RATES OF CHANGE IN FARM EMPLOYMENT FROM 1961 TO 1989
BY PERIODS AND INDEX OF CHANGE FROM 1960 TO 1989

| | 1961–70 | 1971–80 (percent) | 1981–89 | 1989 (1960 = 100) |
|---|---|---|---|---|
| Australia | −0.4 | −0.6 | 0.5 | 94 |
| Canada | −2.7 | −0.4 | −0.5 | 70 |
| New Zealand | −0.4 | 0.6 | 0.5 | 107 |
| United States | −4.4 | −0.1 | −0.9 | 58 |
| Taiwan | −0.4 | −2.7 | −2.1 | 60 |
| European Community (9)[a] | −4.6 | −3.4 | −3.3 | 33 |
|   Belgium | −5.0 | −4.3 | −1.5 | 56 |
|   Denmark | −3.2 | −4.1 | −1.8 | 40 |
|   France | −4.1 | −3.9 | −3.2 | 33 |
|   W. Germany | −4.6 | −4.4 | −3.6 | 29 |
|   Ireland | −3.2 | −3.0 | −2.7 | 42 |
|   Italy | −5.2 | −2.9 | −4.3 | 29 |
|   Netherlands | −3.4 | −1.6 | 0.6 | 64 |
|   United Kingdom | −3.6 | −2.0 | −1.6 | 49 |
| Austria | −4.8 | −4.0 | −2.1 | 34 |
| Finland | −4.5 | −4.1 | −4.0 | 29 |
| Norway | −3.6 | −2.5 | −2.0 | 58 |
| Sweden | −5.8 | −2.8 | −4.3 | 28 |
| Switzerland | −3.7 | −2.0 | −1.1 | 62 |
| Japan | −4.5 | −4.2 | −2.4 | 33 |

a. Includes Luxembourg not listed separately.
SOURCES: OECD, *Labour Force Statistics*, Paris: OECD, 1957–1967, 1964–1984
and 1969–1989.

population of rural areas stabilized in the mid-1970s and has not declined since.

Agriculture now accounts for significantly less than half of the employment in rural areas in most industrial countries. Consequently, the future development of rural areas, and the population and employment, will depend much more on factors that make rural areas attractive for nonfarm employment than on agricultural programs. Farm employment as a percentage of total employment in rural areas of the United States, Canada, France, and Japan range from 11 percent to 26 percent. Rural population in the United States increased from 54 million in 1950 to almost 60 million in 1980, while farm employment declined by 4 million—that is, by about 60 percent.

## Limiting Excess Supply with Excess Resources

Our discussion will be advanced by clarifying the terms *excess supply and excess resources*. Excess resources are the resources greater than could earn a return comparable to what similar resources earn in the rest of the economy if the prices received and paid by farmers were those that would prevail in a free-trade regime. Resources used in agriculture are assumed to be fully employed, though not necessarily in agriculture. Many resources are most profitably used by combining work in agriculture with some other employment. This occurs with part-time farming.

The excess resources have the capability of creating excess supply—a supply greater than can be absorbed by markets at the prices to which governments have committed themselves. This capacity may or may not be realized in full. In the EC generally and in the U.S. dairy and sugar industries, the excess resources were used to produce an excess supply by the output prices provided. For several crop products, the United States has engaged in supply management by limiting the quantity of one input—land—which could be used for production. In recent years, the EC has reduced excess supply by utilizing output quotas for dairy products and sugar. But most of the excess resources remain in agriculture and would be quickly translated into excess supply if production restraints were removed.

There is a difference between excess resources and excess supply. Excess supply could be eliminated by a government program that would result in selling output at the prevailing prices or at prices prevalent in a free-trade world. But the important point is that eliminating excess supply by output quotas or input limitations does not result in the elimination of excess capacity. The capacity to produce is not reduced by such governmental programs. Once the restraints are removed, if the same price incentives are maintained the excess resources will be transformed into excess supply.

The price and income policies of North America, western Europe, and Japan may have had some limited effect in reducing excess supplies but have been unsuccessful in eliminating excess resources. There is clear evidence that these policies have caused the high governmental and consumer costs. One reason for the high cost is the necessity to compensate the excess resources that have been retained in agriculture. The land set-aside programs in the United States, for example, compensate land owners for land left idle. Not only are the owners compensated, but they are compensated as though the land were used to produce and sell a crop at the artificially high price.

But land and farm labor are not the only excess resources in our modern industrial economies. An important reason for the high cost of farm price programs and income support programs is that farmer-supplied inputs have become the minority in agricultural production. A large part of the transfer—the cost of excess resources in agriculture—goes toward pulling resources from the nonfarm economy into agriculture. The share of intermediate consumption—current inputs of nonfarm origin—were the following approximate percentages of the value of farm production in the early 1980s (Johnson 1991):

| Country | Percentage |
| --- | --- |
| EC-10 | 50 |
| Japan | 42 |
| United States | 47 |
| Taiwan | 49 |

The share of intermediate consumption in total farm output fails to reflect the full significance of inputs of nonfarm origin as sources of output expansion and of claims on income produced in agriculture. In the United States, the net return to farmland, owned capital, and all labor and management averaged approximately a quarter of the value of farm output during the 1980s. This is true after all expenditures on livestock and feed are subtracted from the measure of farm output. Similar calculations for four EC members (Denmark, Germany, the United Kingdom, and France) indicate that the returns to farmer-owned resources as a percentage of the value of farm output range from approximately 18 percent in Denmark to 36 percent in France. Consequently, all inputs of nonfarm origin—capital inputs as well as current purchased inputs—account for between 65 percent and 80 percent of total inputs used in agricultural production. Thus, a large percentage of the total transfers to agriculture pays for nonfarm inputs rather than increasing the returns for farmer-owned resources.

Another reason for emphasizing the importance of nonfarm inputs is that these inputs are important in explaining the growth of farm output in recent decades. Higher farm output prices would increase the returns to farmer-owned inputs only if the supply response to the higher prices was very low. In other words, if the higher prices did not bring forth increased output, then the income transfers would go primarily to the owners of farm resources—land, labor, and management. But, as we have seen, the majority of the costs of producing farm products are due to expenditures on inputs of nonfarm origin. The continuous escalation of the costs of farm-price and income-support programs has resulted from the farmers' ability to expand production in response to those programs. That ability to expand output is due to improved technology and the increase in the availability of inputs of nonfarm origin. Improvements in technology are, in considerable part, due to the response of research institutions and producers of farm inputs to the above-equilibrium returns guaranteed by the farm policies.

### Adjustment Policies

The transition payments described in chapter 12 are designed to minimize the impact of trade liberalization on asset values of resources used in agriculture.[1] Compensating for the fall in the value of assets that have limited use outside of agriculture—particularly land, buildings, and specialized farm machinery—represents an adequate response to the effects of trade liberalization. Since such assets do not have a significant alternative use, they will continue to be used in agriculture, as in the case of land, or will be worn out and not replaced, as in the case of machinery.

The adjustment problem also exists for transferable resources whose incomes are adversely affected by trade liberalization. The most important resources in this category are labor and management in two senses. First, the brunt of the quantity adjustment in the farmer supplied inputs will fall on labor and management, since the amount of land devoted to agriculture is unlikely to change significantly. Thus, the elimination of excess resources and excess supply will require a greater decline in labor and management than the actual decline in output that would occur. It may be noted that a significant share of the resource adjustment will occur through reduction in the use of nonfarm inputs, such as fertilizer, pesticides, energy, and farm machinery. As noted earlier, these inputs are now significantly more important than the sum of the farm-supplied inputs. Second, the decline in the current return to labor and management will not immediately bring about a full supply adjustment that would provide such labor and management with the relative income position they had before trade liberalization. Although it is true that in the long run the supply of labor and management to

---

[1]Where there are specialized production facilities used in the processing and marketing of a farm product whose output would be significantly reduced by trade liberalization, it may be politically expedient to compensate for the losses in such nonfarm assets. This could be important for both Taiwan and the United States in regard to sugar processing facilities.

agriculture is elastic, in the short run this is not the case. Not all farm workers and managers would have an equal ability to adjust to the new conditions. Young men and women could adjust quickly by transferring to nonfarm jobs. Older farm workers and managers who have a lot of acquired human capital that is specialized to farming, however, may face significantly lower incomes not only in the short run but for the remainder of their working lives.

The adjustment policies have several components. The first, and perhaps the most important, is that the government should be honest with farmers, and provide them with all of the information it has on the anticipated effects of trade liberalization. Government departments and ministries dislike being the bearers of bad news but must when necessary. The second is that the government must make its position credible and convincing. That is, the government must intend to carry out its commitments to liberalize trade in agricultural products and must not waver as time passes. This may be the most difficult condition of all.

The adjustment process will be substantially eased if these two conditions are met. Since the movement to the agreed level of liberalization will occur over an extended period, probably a decade, the adverse income effects in the first year or two will be modest. As a result, immediate adjustment of resources is not required of most farm families. There will be time to plan appropriate strategies to meet the new conditions in the optimum manner.

The third component is to provide adjustment assistance to farm workers and operators to prepare them for acceptable nonfarm jobs. This assistance could range from additional education and training for the acquisition of skills that are in demand to relocation allowances for those who must move to search for new jobs.

The fourth component is a transfer or payment program for those who because of age or disability, cannot find nonfarm positions that will pay as much as farm positions, even after the full adjustment to trade liberalization. Here there are a number of alternatives. One is to make annual payments that represent the difference, within a particular class of workers between earnings before trade liberalization, earnings during the transition period, and earnings when trade is liberalized to the agreed on degree. These payments should be continued to the normal retirement age, when social security becomes available. The base for calculating the payment should be adjusted to real terms to reflect changes in real earnings for comparable persons in the nonfarm sector.

The significance of the third and fourth components will depend on the state of employment opportunities in general and in rural areas in particular. The stronger the demand conditions for labor, the less adjustment assistance workers will need and the less costly the transfer payments will be for those who would suffer a significant income loss by accepting nonfarm jobs.

The objection may be raised that administering the adjustment assistance and transfer programs fairly and equitably will be difficult. When we view the complexity of our farm programs and the ambiguities that are involved in their administration, we must conclude that we clearly have the capacity to administer the adjustment assistance and transfer program with at least the same degree of precision and fairness as we administer the present farm income and price support programs.

## Employment Effects in the United States

The data on the total number of farms in the United States and Taiwan give a misleading indication of the number of farm operator families who would need any form of adjustment assistance. The majority of the families living on farms do not depend on agriculture for a significant portion of their net family incomes.

Table 14-2 presents data on the amounts of income from farm and off-farm sources, with the farms classified by the value of sales. About 25 percent of the 2.2 million farms received 50 percent or more of their incomes from farm sources in 1990. The next lower sales class, with sales of $20,000 to $39,999, obtained less than 25 percent of its income from farming and could suffer only a small loss from trade liberalization. In 1990, the 25 percent of the farms with half or more of their income from farm sources received 92 percent of all direct government payments. The 58 percent of farms with sales of less than $20,000 received only 2.6 percent of all direct government payments.

The farm operators and family members on approximately 750,000 farms would lose some income from their labor and management after trade liberalization. This would involve approximately a million family workers. In addition, this group of farms provides employment for most of the hired workers on the approximately 1.5 million farms in the United States. For reasons that are somewhat difficult to accept, the farm price support programs are applied to several crops, such as grains and cotton, that use relatively little farm labor per unit of output and exclude products that are labor intensive or that use substantial quantities of labor per unit of output, such as fruits and vegetables. As of the mid-1980s, only a third of all farm labor directly applied to current production was used to produce the

TABLE 14–2

AVERAGE CASH INCOMES OF FARM OPERATIONS IN THE UNITED STATES BY MAJOR SOURCES AND GOVERNMENT PAYMENTS BY VALUE OF SALES, 1990

(dollars per farm)

| Value of Sales (thousands) | Number of Farms (thousands) | Net Farm Income | Off-Farm Income[a] (thousands) | Total Income | Government Payment[b] |
|---|---|---|---|---|---|
| 500 or more | 43 | 634.5 | 26.3 | 660.8 | 33.0 |
| 250–499.9 | 64 | 158.3 | 27.6 | 185.9 | 33.3 |
| 100–249.9 | 214 | 70.4 | 18.1 | 88.5 | 15.1 |
| 40–99.9 | 306 | 25.9 | 25.3 | 139.7 | 5.8 |
| 20–39.9 | 259 | 9.1 | 31.9 | 41.0 | 2.0 |
| < 20 | 1,457 | -0.4 | 35.2 | 34.8 | 0.2 |
| Total or average | 2,140 | 28.9 | 32.3 | 60.2 | 4.3 |

NOTE: The rental value of housing and value of consumption of owned products are excluded but would increase net income per farm by less than $3,000.

a. Some farm operations have more than one family sharing the income from farming; the off-farm income is only for the principal farm operator family. The total income per farm is somewhat greater than the average total income for a farm operator family on the largest farms.

b. Included in net farm income.

SOURCE: U.S. Department of Agriculture, Economic Research Service, *Economic Indicators of the Farm Sector: National Financial Summary, 1990.* ECIFS10-1. November 1991.

crops, such as grains, cotton, tobacco, sugar, and dairy products, that had significant levels of protection. As a result, probably no more than a million farm workers—including farm operators, family members, and hired workers—would be adversely affected by trade liberalization.

Most important is not the number of workers adversely affected in the short run but the reduction in the number of workers required to return the income level for labor and management to what it would have been if previous levels of protection had been maintained. The data in chapter 13 (table 13-4) indicate that U.S. farm production of the highly protected crops and dairy products would decline by about 5 percent with multilateral trade liberalization. The demand for labor at existing rates of return (for producing the protected crops and dairy products) would decline somewhat more than this, since the amount of land used for production would increase, and existing capital would continue to be fully utilized. If we assume that approximately a million farm workers are involved in producing the products of the highly protected sector and that the demand for labor and management at existing rates of return would fall by twice the reduction in output, a reduction in employment by 100,000 would be necessary. In other words, trade liberalization would require a transfer of 100,000 workers—over and above those who would ordinarily transfer during that period—to nonagricultural employment. During the 1980s, civilian employment in the United States increased at an annual rate of 1,800,000. We do not want to minimize the difficulties any one individual may face in changing jobs, but the drawbacks of labor transfer during trade liberalization would be minimized by the creation of new jobs. If all of the agricultural labor adjustment occurred in four years, this would be only a little more than 1 percent of the rate at which new jobs have been created. This rough calculation ignores the probable creation of jobs in the other sectors of agriculture, where output would increase and, with it, the demand for labor.

The significance of a required additional decline in farm employment over a period of years is also evident when comparing the figure to the actual annual rates of reduction in farm employment in recent decades. The declines in U.S. farm employment during the 1970s and 1980s were historically low. In the 1970s, the annual decline was only 10,000, but increased to 26,000 in the 1980s. During the 1960s, however, the annual decline in farm employment was 200,000. The large difference was due to a substantial but significantly declining difference between farm and nonfarm incomes during the 1960s. In 1960, the net cash income of a farm operator household was 0.61

relative to the U.S. population; by the late 1960s, this ratio was approximately 0.90. The ratio increased during the 1970s and actually exceeded unity from 1972 to 1976. The ratio declined in the early 1980s, reaching a low of 0.76, but again exceeded unity in 1985 and 1986. It appears—from the limited decline in farm employment and the relative income position of farm operator households—that there was little incentive for outmigration from agriculture during the 1970s and 1980s. An additional transfer of 100,000 farm workers to nonfarm jobs could probably be achieved with little difficulty, judging from a similar experience in the 1960s.

Although most of the labor transfer required by trade liberalization would probably occur with little disruption or difficulty, we should not neglect efforts to assist the transfer. To obtain political support for trade liberalization, all reasonable and cost effective means should be taken to minimize individual hardships. In addition, equity would hardly be served by spending billions of dollars to compensate owners of land and production quotas while doing nothing to assist the labor transfer.

### Employment Effects in Taiwan

In chapter 13, the results of projections of the effects of agricultural trade liberalization on agricultural output in Taiwan were presented. These projections indicated that Taiwan's total agricultural production might either increase very slightly and decline very slightly. This does not mean, however, that there would be no adjustment problems within agriculture. Since Taiwan has a lower rate of nominal protection than the United States and since it also has interfered less with resource allocation within agriculture, Taiwan could have fewer adjustment problems than the United States. This is a surprising conclusion, but it has a basis.

Even if total agricultural output in Taiwan increases a little or remains approximately constant, however, resource adjustments could not necessarily be avoided. If total agricultural output remains approximately constant, the output of some sectors would increase and the output of others would fall. Generally speaking, in the case of Taiwan the sectors that would face downward output and resource adjustments are other coarse grains, soybeans, sugar, beef, tobacco, and poultry meat. Although dairy products are relatively protected in Taiwan (though less than in the United States), the increase in international market prices that would result from global trade liberalization could well be enough so that the dairy sector would no longer be protected with market prices similar to the prevailing ones.

Except for chicken and sugar, the other products listed are relatively unimportant in Taiwanese agricultural output. These products accounted for only 4.4 percent of the value of output of the products included in table 13-1 and much less than that if the value of fruit and vegetable output were included in total agricultural output. Chicken and sugar, however, do account for about 19 percent of total sales.

Taken together, rice and sugar accounted for 41.5 percent of the value of output of the commodities in table 13-1 while beef, milk, and pork accounted for 44.4 percent. If the two groups of products were equally labor intensive, then one could assume that the employment effects would be approximately offsetting. Rice and sugar, however, probably are more labor intensive than pork and beef. Consequently, labor employment in agriculture might be reduced because of trade liberalization. The extent depends on differences in labor intensity.

In the absence of actual data on labor intensity, let us assume that the labor intensity for chicken and sugar is 1.2 times the national average for agriculture and that the labor intensity for pork is 0.8 times the national average. Assume also that the output of the first group will fall by 10 percent and the output of the second group will increase by 10 percent, thus keeping total agricultural output approximately constant. The decline in output of chicken and sugar would result in a decline of 1.5 percent in labor use. If the output changes for each group were 20 percent instead of 10 percent, the decline in labor use would be about 3 percent.

In 1988, total farm employment in Taiwan was 1,112,000. If trade liberalization were to result in a 3 percent decline in employment, the decline would be 33,000. Between 1980 and 1988, farm employment declined at an annual rate of 20,600. Thus, if the required labor reduction were spread over a decade, the rate of decline of agricultural employment would be 3,300 greater for the 1980s and about 16 percent greater annually. Compared with the annual decline in farm employment in the 1970s of 40,400, however, the increase in the annual rate would be only 8 percent.

## References

Johnson, D. Gale. "Policy Options and Liberalizing Trade in Agricultural Products: Addressing the Interests of Developing Countries." Paper no. 88:02, Office of Agricultural Economics Research, University of Chicago, 1988.

————. *World Agriculture in Disarray.* London: Macmillan & Co., 1991.

# PART FIVE
# A New Consensus

# 15
## Reaching a New Consensus
*Chi-ming Hou and D. Gale Johnson*

There were major conflicts between the United States and Taiwan over agricultural trade during the 1980s. These were resolved, and new ones have not arisen. More important, it can be said that a new consensus on agricultural trade has been reached. Taiwan and the United States agree that trade liberalization generally and for agricultural products specifically is in their joint and separate interests. The United States has been a major force pushing for the liberalization of trade in agricultural products in the Uruguay Round. In doing so, it has recognized that several of its domestic farm programs must be significantly modified. Taiwan has applied for membership in GATT with the full understanding that it must accept and comply with whatever agreements are reached concerning the conduct of agricultural trade.

It is now generally recognized that agricultural policies must become much more market-oriented if trade in agricultural products is to be liberalized. There has long been a reluctance to admit that trade barriers were a necessary adjunct to domestic agricultural policies that required direct intervention in agricultural markets. Without such recognition no progress could be made in reducing the barriers to trade in agricultural products. Since 1950, both Taiwan and the United States have had farm price support and subsidy programs. As shown in chapters 7 and 8, the cost to consumers and taxpayers in both countries exceeds by a significant margin the increase in the net income of farmers.

### Costs of Agricultural Policies

It was estimated for Taiwan that for each dollar of increase in the net income of farmers, consumers and taxpayers paid $1.37 in 1988. In the United States it cost approximately $1.20 to increase producers' incomes by $1.00.

The excess of costs to consumers and taxpayers over the gains to farmers is not the only price of the farm programs. These programs require that governments intervene in their trade in agricultural products. The interventions are often, one might say generally, contrary to the principles of liberal trade as reflected in the General Agreement on Tariffs and Trade (GATT). Taiwan is not yet a member of GATT, but it has applied for membership and has the support of the United States for its application. By its application Taiwan has clearly indicated a desire to bring its domestic and trade policies in line with the principles of GATT. Unfortunately, GATT permits a number of special exceptions for agriculture to its two important general principles: that the only acceptable import barriers are tariffs or duties, and that export subsidies are not permitted. The clauses that permit export subsidies for agricultural products are so poorly written that no significant restraint has been placed on their use. Proof of this is found in the billions of dollars the European Community expends annually on export subsidies and in the smaller but significant expenditures by the United States, presumably in retaliation for the EC subsidies, but with major adverse effects on other exporters of farm products.

The farm programs have required interventions in agricultural trade that are contrary to the principles of a liberal trade regime and that have direct consequences to other countries. Therefore an added cost of farm programs has been the creation of ill feelings in one's trading partners. It is evident from various chapters in this book—especially chapters 4, 7, and 9—that the response of the United States to various trade measures taken by Taiwan to support farm prices resulted in significant tensions in the political and economic relationships between the two. These costs were considered of such importance to the government of Taiwan that on a number of occasions the objectionable trade measures were modified.

The farm programs and trade policies of the United States impose costs by affecting relationships with countries that are important in its foreign policy. A few examples will suffice. First, in 1986 the United States modified its rice price-support policy by increasing the deficiency payment and making it possible for producers to export at a very low price without reducing their return. This measure sharply reduced the international market price for rice, and heavy costs were imposed on an important ally—Thailand. Second, the sugar program has, contrary to Article XI of GATT, discriminated strongly in favor of domestic production and against foreign production since the early 1980s. Imports of sugar were reduced sharply, by as much as 75 percent, compared with the level in 1980. This reduction imposed substantial costs on exporters, including developing countries in the

Caribbean and in Central and South America. For many of these countries, the loss of sugar exports was far more important than all other efforts by the United States to aid in their economic development. Australia is a low-cost producer of sugar, and it also lost a large share of its market in the United States.

A third and last example, chosen from an extensive list, involves the U.S. response to a modest hog subsidy program in Canada that resulted in the imposition of an extra duty on the importation of live hogs and subsequently on pork products. The action generated ill will, and the Canadian government responded by imposing an added duty on corn imported from the United States—a duty more or less equal to the size of the deficiency payment on corn. Compared with the relative size of the subsidy on hogs, the United States subsidy on corn was several times as great. It is true that the duty on Canadian exports of hogs and pork was not the direct result of a U.S. farm program for hogs—there is no program for hogs or pork—but of the enforcement of antidumping legislation. But when the United States also subsidizes exports, one can understand why animosity is created when antidumping duties are imposed.

Because of the enormous size of its economy and its role in international trade, the United States need not and has not responded to the objections of its trading partners in the same way Taiwan has responded to pressure from the United States. But it is likely that one reason the United States pressed for the elimination of all agricultural subsidies in its first proposal for the Geneva Round of trade negotiations was the positive effect on its international relationships. The current agricultural and trade policies find the United States engaging in behavior many other friendly nations find objectionable, and doing so for the presumed benefit of only a tiny minority of its population— namely, those living on farms and earning a significant share of their income from farming. The population on these farms accounts for no more than 1 percent of the nation's population. Of course, others gain from the farm programs—such as those who supply inputs to agriculture and who own farmland that they rent to others.

## Benefits of Agricultural Programs

The farm and associated trade programs would not exist unless some participants in the political process received significant benefits. Chapters 6, 7, and 8 provide analyses of the political processes by which farmers, who now represent a small minority of the total population in the industrial economies, are able to obtain programs that they believe are in their interest. A strong case has been made that in the 1980s and early 1990s the farm and trade policies contributed little to the return to labor and capital engaged in farming. Nevertheless, the agricultures of the United States and Taiwan, especially the latter, have been subjected to great pressure to adjust since 1950. The agricultures of both economies have come through this period remarkably well. Although it is not possible to determine how effective the farm programs were in assisting this adjustment and minimizing the effects on farm incomes, we believe that the economic policies followed were remarkably successful. The success was that of achieving a large transfer of labor out of agriculture while farm people shared fully in the economic growth generated by the economies. In addition, agricultural output continued to grow while the real costs of farm products declined significantly over that period of time.

The magnitude of the adjustment imposed on agriculture by economic growth is most appropriately indicated by the decline in farm employment. In Taiwan, farm employment declined from 56 percent of the national total in 1952 to 13 percent in 1990, while the absolute numbers employed in farming fell from 1.64 million in 1952 to 1.06 million in 1990, a decline of 35 percent. In the United States the change in the fraction of the labor force engaged in agriculture was much smaller—from 11 percent in 1952 to 3 percent in 1990. But the percentage fall in absolute farm employment was much greater, at 55 percent.

Farm people's adjustments to the changes they had to make to share in economic growth compare interestingly with those developments. While in the United States the number of farms decreased at roughly the same rate as the farm labor force—by 60 percent—in Taiwan there were more farms in 1990 than in 1952. In both economies a significant part of the transfer of labor from farming to other activities occurred through increases in part-time farming. As of the 1990s, the majority of the workers living or working on farms combined a nonfarm job with their farming activities.

In Taiwan, the population living on farms increased from 1952 to 1970 and then declined to slightly below the 1952 level in 1990. In the United States, however, the farm population declined by about 80 percent, and by 1990 it accounted for only 2 percent of the national population. The labor adjustment that occurred through outmigration from farms, either through a physical move or through abandoning agricultural activities while living in the same residence, was greater in the United States than in Taiwan. There the shift in labor was primarily through off-farm activities.

It must be noted, however, that Taiwan's agricultural labor adjustment still has some distance to go. This will be true whether there is further liberalization of agricultural trade or not. There is a high and inescapable relationship between the level of real per capita incomes and the percentage of the labor force employed in agriculture. As real per capita incomes continue to increase in Taiwan, the percentage of the labor force in farming will continue to decline. This adjustment process carries two pieces of good news. First, if the percentage of the labor force engaged in agriculture were to fall to only 3 percent while real per capita gross national product approached the current U.S. level of $20,000 (1990 U.S. dollars)—as it may well do early in the next century—then the extent of the adjustment required would be little more than what actually occurred during the 1980s, and it would be less than during the 1970s. From 1980 to 1990, agriculture's share of national employment fell from 19.5 to 12.8 percent; from 1970 to 1980, from 36.7 to 19.5 percent.

Second, the process of transferring workers from agricultural to nonagricultural activities is now much less difficult than it was in earlier decades. One reason for this is that in Taiwan many more nonagricultural positions are now available than were in 1960, 1970, or 1980 for each farm worker wishing to leave farm employment in whole or in part. When farm employment was 40 percent of the total, reducing farm employment by 100,000 workers meant that nonfarm employment had to increase by 4 percent to absorb the transfer without an increase in unemployment. In 1990 a reduction of 100,000 farm workers required an increase of only 1.4 percent in nonfarm employment. Viewed slightly differently, in the late 1960s a decline of 6 percent in farm employment through transfer to nonfarm jobs required nonfarm jobs to increase by 4 percent. In 1990 a reduction of farm employment by almost 10 percent could be accommodated by an increase in nonfarm jobs of only 1.4 percent.

Most of the adjustment of the farm labor force that is required by economic growth has already occurred in both Taiwan and the United States. The years of greatest difficulty in potential costs to farm people are already behind us. This does not mean that the required further adjustments will be without cost or difficulty. A major reason why the adjustment of the farm labor forces occurred so rapidly and with little or no loss in the relative income position of farm families was the rapid increase in the integration of rural life into the economy and society as a whole. Between 1950 and 1990, most of the differences between rural and urban life disappeared. This was the result of many positive general developments that accompanied economic growth—increased availability and greatly reduced costs of communication and transportation, the near elimination of differences in infrastructure, and both public and private services between rural and urban communities. The disparity in educational opportunities has in particular been reduced. In both Taiwan and the United States these differences have been nearly eliminated for today's children and youth. Unfortunately, some of the differences in incomes of farm families today represent the heritage of differences in educational opportunities of the 1950s and 1960s.

Although farm price support and subsidy programs are ineffective in increasing the earnings from labor and management employed in farming, there are interests that either gain from these programs or would lose from their sudden abandonment. If the farm programs were eliminated all at once rather than gradually, farm operators and workers would suffer short-term losses, even if their current returns are the same as they would have been had the farm programs never existed. The reason is that the programs have induced more human and physical capital resources to remain in farming. The paucity of gain in income or returns from the programs, however, does not protect against temporary losses during the period of adjustment to the new circumstances.

It is understandable that those who are now farming would support the continuation of existing price and subsidy programs, even though they now gain little or nothing. No farmer can with equanimity face the loss of direct payments of 20–50 percent of net farm income, as do thousands of farmers in the United States. Nor can he look with favor on an immediate one-fourth reduction in the price of rice, as could occur in Taiwan with trade liberalization. Policy makers in both Taiwan and the United States have long ignored the difficulty of abandoning subsidy programs when the net continuing benefits are nil.

Others support the continuation of the farm programs—namely, those who supply farmers with inputs. High price supports encourage farmers to produce a larger output through greater purchases of nonfarm inputs, such as fertilizers, insecticides, veterinary services, tractors, and trucks. Thus the producers and suppliers of these inputs know they will suffer short-term losses if the farm subsidies are eliminated all at once. And even though a gradual elimination of the programs would permit most suppliers to escape with minimal losses, it would still be necessary for them to adjust. Consequently most will use their political power to encourage continuation of programs, even though their current benefits are small.

### Land Owners Do Gain

In almost all countries the elimination of agricultural protection will result in both short-term and long-term losses for the owners of farmland. This is inescapable, since nearly all the increase in net income to agriculture has gone to the owners of land. As noted earlier, the supply of land increases little in response to higher rents, while the supply of both labor and capital respond to higher returns. The elimination of the protection for U.S. agriculture would result in significant reductions in the values of farmland, the size of the reductions varying with the use of the land. Because the farm programs require the idling of millions of hectares of farmland, it is difficult to estimate the effects of trade liberalization on the value of farmland.

The reduction in farmland values in the United States could be at least 10–15 percent of current values. This implies a reduction in annual returns to land of $10–15 billion and a fall in land values of $50–75 billion, as a rough approximation. Land owners obviously would not accept such a reduction without making an effort to prevent it.

Considerable evidence shows that farm resource owners do not capitalize the current annual flow of return from a governmental subsidy program at the same rate as they do returns generated directly from the market. The discount rates used in North American agriculture are such that the increase in market value of the asset is equivalent to no more than four or five years of annual returns (Johnson 1991, chap. 9). This means that the discount rate being used is 20–25 percent, at least double the market rates of interest. It also means that landowners could be fully compensated for the loss in the value of their assets for an amount that is substantially less than the present value, calculated at the rate the federal government can borrow, of the net annual costs of the farm subsidy programs.

If the restraints on the buying and selling of farmland were removed in Taiwan at the same time as price and trade liberalization occurred, land values would probably increase rather than decline. While farmland values in Taiwan are much higher than in the United States, the controls that restrict selling farmland for nonagricultural uses or to nonfarmers have caused lower land prices than would prevail in a relatively free land market. The factors that limit the renting of farmland have also depressed land prices. Consequently, changing the regulations affecting the buying, selling, and renting of land would offset more or less fully the effects of liberalization on land values. Some would argue that the land market should be liberalized in any case. Obviously, liberalizing the land market simultaneously with liberalizing price and trade would protect landowners against a decline in the value of their most important financial asset— the land.

The protection of agriculture has increased the annual return to farmland in Taiwan, but because of the restraints imposed on the land market these returns have not been fully reflected in the value of land. For this reason the elimination of protection would not have a significant influence on the value of land if there were a simultaneous reform of the land market.

### Adjustment Assistance and Decoupled Payments

The cost to taxpayers and consumers exceeds the benefits to farmers from the farm price-and-subsidy programs, in both Taiwan and the United States. This is true partly because the structure of the programs either relates benefits to output or provides such incentives for increasing output that efforts are made to restrict it, to avoid unwanted output and higher costs to the government for its disposal. The measures to restrict output, such as set-asides in the United States, increase farmers' costs and cause resources to be idle.

In recent years the concept of decoupled payments has emerged as a way of achieving three different objectives. First, they increase the fraction of the costs incurred by taxpayers and consumers that is retained by farmers. Second, they minimize, if not entirely avoid, the influence of payments on the amount of farm production. Third, related to the second, the use of decoupled payments makes it possible gradually to reduce protection at the border, and in the process to provide consumers with the opportunity to broaden the alternatives available to them. By reducing protection while continuing to maintain the income of farm families in a manner accepted by the international community, an economy contributes toward the reduction of tensions in international trade.

An important aspect of the negotiations during the Uruguay Round since 1986 concerned reaching agreement on what constitutes decoupled payments. The underlying concept of decoupled payments is that the payments should not influence production decisions of farmers in choosing either which products to produce or the amount to produce. It is generally agreed that if payments are determined solely on the basis of past behavior—such as the amount of land devoted to rice production, the number of cows milked, or the amount of milk produced in a five-year period—the payments would have no effect on current production and would thus meet the requirements of decoupled payments. With a program of assistance based on decoupled payments, a farmer will make production decisions based on current market prices for outputs and inputs.

The advantage of decoupled payments is that they permit an

economy to have low protection at the border while providing farmers with adequate time to adjust to the price changes that would follow trade liberalization. If one's only evidence about the ability of farmers to adjust to changing conditions were the rhetoric of the political debate on farm policies, then one would assume farmers have a very limited ability or willingness to adjust. The descriptions of the agricultures of Taiwan and the United States given in chapters 2 and 3 and elsewhere totally belie this conclusion. Farm people and the institutions that serve them have adapted quickly and well to the enormous changes they have had to cope with from 1940 to 1990.

In our view, the decoupled payments should be gradually phased out over a decade. This does not mean that the phaseout should be at a constant rate over the decade. Since much of the production adjustment will occur in the early part of the adjustment period, there is good reason to maintain the level of the decoupled payments for the first three to five years and then to reduce them during the latter half of the decade.

If the majority of the decoupled payments are continued indefinitely, the payments will increasingly go not to persons engaged in farming activities but to those who owned farmland when the payments were started and subsequently retired or left farming for other reasons. That is what has happened to payments under the tobacco programs in the United States. For certain types of tobacco the majority of the recipients are individuals whose only connection with the crop is ownership of farmland with a quota that permits tobacco production. Those who rent and farm land with a tobacco quota pay a rent to the landowner for the right to produce tobacco. Thus they gain little or nothing from the costs imposed on consumers and taxpayers as a result of the tobacco program.

If the decoupled payments are continued indefinitely, new entrants into farming will have to pay for the very right to farm. The families who were farming when decoupled payments started will capture most of the present value of all future payments. Those subsequently entering farming will view the price for receiving decoupled payments in the future in much the same way as they view the price of land—a necessary cost of being a farmer. It will make no difference if they rent some or all of the land they farm; either the payment will go directly to the owner of the land, or the annual rent will include an amount equal to the annual payment plus the true rent, based on the current productivity of the land. This conclusion can be derived from Canada's experience with output quotas for dairy and poultry products. The cost of purchasing the right to produce poultry exceeds the physical capital requirements (Johnson 1991, 201).

We do not imply that any system of decoupled payments will obviate all the pain of adjustment to the gradual reduction of agricultural protection. Nor do we imply that the difficulties of adjustment in Taiwan will be less than those in the United States because the average level of agricultural protection is lower in Taiwan. Since the percentage of the labor force engaged in agriculture in Taiwan is substantially higher than can be sustained in the long run and further adjustment to higher earnings for labor through part-time farming has become increasingly difficult, the future prosperity of agriculture depends upon significant increases in the average size of farms. The number of farm operating units must decline over time, and substantially so. This process will have to occur whether or not agricultural protection is reduced. There is a limit to the extent that part-time farming can reduce the labor engaged in farming without adversely affecting costs of production. That would require an increase in agricultural protection, either through higher prices or through a variety of subsidy programs.

## Taiwan Agriculture Faces Difficult Adjustments

It has been shown in earlier chapters that the level of agricultural protection in Taiwan during the mid-1980s was lower than in the United States, though in 1990 the protection levels were the same. This raises a serious question. Was it fair for the United States to put such great pressure on Taiwan to liberalize its imports or to reduce its export subsidies? That the average level of agricultural protection is relatively low does not mean that liberalizing agricultural trade would occur without inflicting significant costs upon Taiwanese farmers. But in our view, the magnitude of the adjustments and the costs of those adjustments will not be greater than what has actually occurred over the past two decades.

Without trade liberalization, agriculture in both Taiwan and the United States must continue to adjust to the consequences of economic growth. In both economies the share of agriculture in employment and national income must decline if farm people are to share in the increased levels of per capita incomes. This means for Taiwan that either the size of farms must increase or the percentage of full-time farms must decline for the indefinite future. The adjustment to trade liberalization will be of the same general kind—adjustments that permit an increase in the amount of land and capital per worker engaged in farming. Increased returns to farm labor result from increasing the resources per worker and making changes in productivity. These changes have occurred in the past at a rapid rate. Even with trade liberalization, the required reductions in the labor engaged in farming in Taiwan will be less than in the 1960s, 1970s, and 1980s.

## Reference

Johnson, D. Gale. *World Agriculture in Disarray.* London: Macmillan & Co., 1991.

# 16
## Afterword

*Yu Yu-hsein*

Since the early 1970s, agricultural trade between the United States and the Republic of China has increased in volume, particularly in recent years. For the year 1990, for example, the two-way trade in agricultural products chalked up more than $2.7 billion, making the ROC the sixth largest market for exported U.S. farm commodities. In the meantime, the United States has become the second largest importer of agricultural products from Taiwan. Since 1978, agricultural trade has been top on the agenda of trade negotiations between the two countries, mainly as a result of a growing trade volume, trade liberalization, and the desire of the United States to enhance farm exports through negotiation.

The concerned parties, however, have failed to reach consensus on agricultural trade liberalization since the Uruguay Round of multilateral negotiations was launched in 1986 under GATT auspices. But what is clear to everyone is the trend toward a more liberal trading pattern for agricultural commodities. As is obvious from various policy measures, the government of the ROC is committed to opening the domestic market to farm imports and to continuing to lower tariff rates. Those developments coupled with the application for membership in GATT are bound to place a heavy burden on Taiwan's agricultural sector.

While it has enjoyed a huge surplus in total trade with the United States for some time, the ROC has in recent years seen a growing deficit in agricultural trade, which amounted to more than $2 billion in 1990.

The United States has been the biggest supplier of farm products for the ROC. Of the $5.8 billion in farm imports for 1990, the United

---

We are pleased to close our book with the remarks made by Dr. Yu Yu-hsein at the Sino-American Conference on Agricultural Trade Policy in Taipei on June 28, 1991. These remarks are an important addition to the work of the joint team that undertook this study.

States accounted for 41 percent. The major commodities supplied by the United States are feed grain, wheat, soybeans, timber, and fruits. A recent development worth mentioning in this regard is the decreasing proportion of feed grain and soybeans, which, however, still stood at 54 percent in 1989, together with a marked increase in the importance of fruit, beef, and processed items.

On the export front, the United States has been the second largest market, receiving 9.4 percent of the total farm exports from the ROC, valued at $3.5 billion in 1990. The commodities exported to the United States, including fishery products, frozen vegetables, mushrooms, and bamboo shoots, were worth $327 million in 1990, a drop of 18 percent from the previous year.

As far as agricultural trade is concerned, "Buy American" has been a top priority. Statistics indicate that on the average each person in the ROC imported $101 worth of U.S. farm products in 1990, which was the highest among all U.S. customers. Each year at least one special mission is sent to the United States to purchase various farm products. A study by the U.S. Department of Agriculture (USDA) shows that the ROC has a market openness degree of 44.3 percent, ranking behind such nonagricultural countries as Hong Kong, Singapore, and Saudi Arabia but far ahead of Japan, South Korea, and Spain. Moreover, according to the USDA, the ROC's support for agriculture in terms of producer subsidy equivalent registered only 25 percent in 1987, which was much lower than the 79 percent for Japan, 62 percent for South Korea, 52 percent for the European Community, and 33 percent for the United States.

In the expectation that the agricultural sector will suffer as a result of various unfavorable developments, Taiwan has formulated a series of coordinated measures. One of the most important is the identification of priority industries, which should meet such criteria as market potential, high value added, and minimal environmental costs. Only products that provide major food supplies, involve large numbers of farmers or huge acreage, or have no alternative crops will receive government protection.

Another measure consists of a feasibility study to determine when to introduce the so-called decoupling policy. Emphasis will be placed on the enhancement of market competitiveness and the phase out of price supports. A third program would focus on various initiatives to promote trade. Tariff rates will be reviewed, and adjusted accordingly, for different products. Market access may vary from commodity to commodity. An early warning system will be set up for farm imports to minimize an adverse impact on domestic products. Farmers may get government relief from damage done by farm

341

imports, and a set of regulations has also been published to crack down on smuggling to protect the interests of farmers.

It is a challenge to foster the growth of the agricultural sector when that sector must often subordinate its own interest to the requirements of trade liberalization. The challenge is made even greater when calls for lower tariffs, market access, and less protection continue to be heard. The best solution may lie in improved productivity, reduced costs of production, and an enhanced competitive edge in the market. Along with this approach, some trade management measures should be developed during the very process of integrated adjustment for the agricultural sector, for which Taiwan formally initiated a six-year program in July 1991.

While the momentum toward trade liberalization for farm products is sure and irreversible, its pace has to be measured and carefully planned, because agriculture, besides being a biological process, involves nature conservation and the livelihood of the producers. The government of the ROC, of course, subscribes to the principle of reducing protection for agriculture. Along with many other countries, however, Taiwan also advocates a more flexible schedule with regard to both timing and particular products, an approach that will in fact accelerate the pace of liberalization on the one hand and minimize impact and damage on the other.

# Authors' Note

1. The units of area and quantity are metric. Some important conversions to units used in the United States are:

1 kilogram = 2.2046 pounds
1 metric ton = 2,204.6 pounds or 1.1023 short tons
1 hectare = 2.471 acres
1 liter = 1.1 quarts

2. Unless indicated otherwise, the monetary unit used is the U.S. dollar. When the Taiwanese dollar is used, it is indicated as NT$. The rates of exchange between the NT$ and the U.S.$ have been as follows:

| (NT$ per one U.S.$) | |
| --- | --- |
| 1985 | 39.85 |
| 1986 | 37.84 |
| 1987 | 31.85 |
| 1988 | 28.59 |
| 1989 | 26.40 |
| 1990 | 26.89 |
| 1991 | 26.82 |
| 1992 | 25.30 |

William M. Landes
Clifton R. Musser Professor of
Economics
University of Chicago Law School

Glenn C. Loury
Department of Economics
Boston University

Sam Peltzman
Sears Roebuck Professor of Economics
and Financial Services
University of Chicago
Graduate School of Business

Nelson W. Polsby
Professor of Political Science
University of California at Berkeley

Murray L. Weidenbaum
Mallinckrodt Distinguished
University Professor
Washington University

## Research Staff

Leon Aron
Resident Scholar

Claude E. Barfield
Resident Scholar; Director, Science
and Technology Policy Studies

Walter Berns
Adjunct Scholar

Douglas J. Besharov
Resident Scholar

Jagdish Bhagwati
Visiting Scholar

Robert H. Bork
John M. Olin Scholar in Legal Studies

Michael Boskin
Visiting Scholar

Karlyn Bowman
Resident Fellow; Editor,
*The American Enterprise*

David Bradford
Visiting Scholar

Dick B. Cheney
Senior Fellow

Lynne V. Cheney
W.H. Brady, Jr., Distinguished Fellow

Dinesh D'Souza
John M. Olin Research Fellow

Nicholas N. Eberstadt
Visiting Scholar

Mark Falcoff
Resident Scholar

Gerald R. Ford
Distinguished Fellow

Murray F. Foss
Visiting Scholar

Suzanne Garment
Resident Scholar

Patrick Glynn
Resident Scholar

Robert A. Goldwin
Resident Scholar

Gottfried Haberler
Resident Scholar

Robert W. Hahn
Resident Scholar

Robert B. Helms
Resident Scholar

Jeane J. Kirkpatrick
Senior Fellow; Director, Foreign and
Defense Policy Studies

Marvin H. Kosters
Resident Scholar; Director,
Economic Policy Studies

Irving Kristol
John M. Olin Distinguished Fellow

Michael A. Ledeen
Resident Scholar

Susan Lee
DeWitt Wallace–Reader's Digest
Fellow in Communications
in a Free Society

Robert A. Licht
Resident Scholar; Director,
Constitution Project

Chong-Pin Lin
Resident Scholar; Associate Director,
China Studies Program

John H. Makin
Resident Scholar; Director, Fiscal
Policy Studies

Allan H. Meltzer
Visiting Scholar

Joshua Muravchik
Resident Scholar

Charles Murray
Bradley Fellow

Michael Novak
George F. Jewett Scholar in Religion,
Philosophy, and Public Policy;
Director, Social and
Political Studies

Norman J. Ornstein
Resident Scholar

Richard N. Perle
Resident Fellow

Thomas W. Robinson
Resident Scholar; Director, China
Studies Program

William Schneider
Resident Fellow

Bill Shew
Visiting Scholar

J. Gregory Sidak
Resident Scholar

Herbert Stein
Senior Fellow

Irwin M. Stelzer
Resident Scholar; Director, Regulatory
Policy Studies

Edward Styles
Director of Publications

W. Allen Wallis
Resident Scholar

Ben J. Wattenberg
Senior Fellow

Carolyn L. Weaver
Resident Scholar; Director, Social
Security and Pension Studies

A NOTE ON THE BOOK

*This book was edited by Dana Lane and*
*Cheryl Weissman*
*of the staff of the AEI Press.*
*The text was set in Palatino, a typeface designed by*
*the twentieth-century Swiss designer Hermann Zapf.*
*Coghill Composition, of Richmond, Virginia,*
*set the type, and Data Reproductions Corporation,*
*of Rochester Hills, Michigan, printed and bound the book,*
*using permanent acid-free paper.*

The AEI PRESS is the publisher for the American Enterprise Institute for
Public Policy Research, 1150 17th Street, N.W., Washington, D.C. 20036;
*Christopher C. DeMuth,* publisher; *Edward Styles,* director; *Dana Lane,* assistant
director; *Ann Petty,* editor; *Cheryl Weissman,* editor; *Mary Cristina Delaney,*
editorial assistant (rights and permissions). Books published by the AEI
PRESS are distributed by arrangement with the University Press of America,
4720 Boston Way, Lanham, Md. 20706.